SB
Shojo Beat

BABY & Me
Vol. 13

This story is about Mama and Papa.
Marimo.95

Story & Art by Marimo Ragawa

BABY & ME, Vol. 13
The Shojo Beat Manga Edition

STORY & ART BY
MARIMO RAGAWA

English Adaptation/Lance Caselman
Translation/JN Productions
Touch-up Art & Lettering/Hudson Yards
Design/Yuki Ameda
Editor/Shaenon K. Garrity

Editor in Chief, Books/Alvin Lu
Editor in Chief, Magazines/Marc Weidenbaum
VP, Publishing Licensing/Rika Inouye
VP, Sales & Product Marketing/Gonzalo Ferreyra
VP, Creative/Linda Espinosa
Publisher/Hyoe Narita

Printed in Canada

Published by VIZ Media, LLC
P.O. Box 77010
San Francisco, CA 94107

Shojo Beat Manga Edition
10 9 8 7 6 5 4 3 2 1
First printing, April 2009

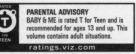

PARENTAL ADVISORY
BABY & ME is rated T for Teen and is
recommended for ages 13 and up. This
volume contains adult situations.
ratings.viz.com

3 2872 50021 3966

Creator: Marimo Ragawa

SBM Title: *Baby & Me*

Date of Birth: September 21

Blood Type: B

Major Works: *Time Limit,*
Baby & Me, N.Y. N.Y., and
Shanimuni-Go (Desperately—Go)

● ●

Marimo Ragawa first started submitting manga to a comic magazine when she was 12 years old. She kept up her submissions
for four years, but to no avail. She decided to submit her work
to the magazine *Hana to Yume*, where she received Top Prize in
the Monthly Manga Contest as well as an honorable mention (Kasaku) in the
magazine's Big Challenge contest. Her first manga was titled *Time Limit. Baby
& Me* was honored with a Shogakukan Manga Award in 1995 and was spun
off into an anime.

Ragawa's work showcases some very cute and expressive line work along with
an incredible ability to depict complex emotions and relationships. Some of
her other works include *N.Y. N.Y.* and the tennis manga *Shanimuni-Go*.

Ragawa has two brothers and two sisters.

Table of Contents

Chapter 69   5

Chapter 70   35

Chapter 71   65

Chapter 72   98

Chapter 73   141

Chapter 74   172

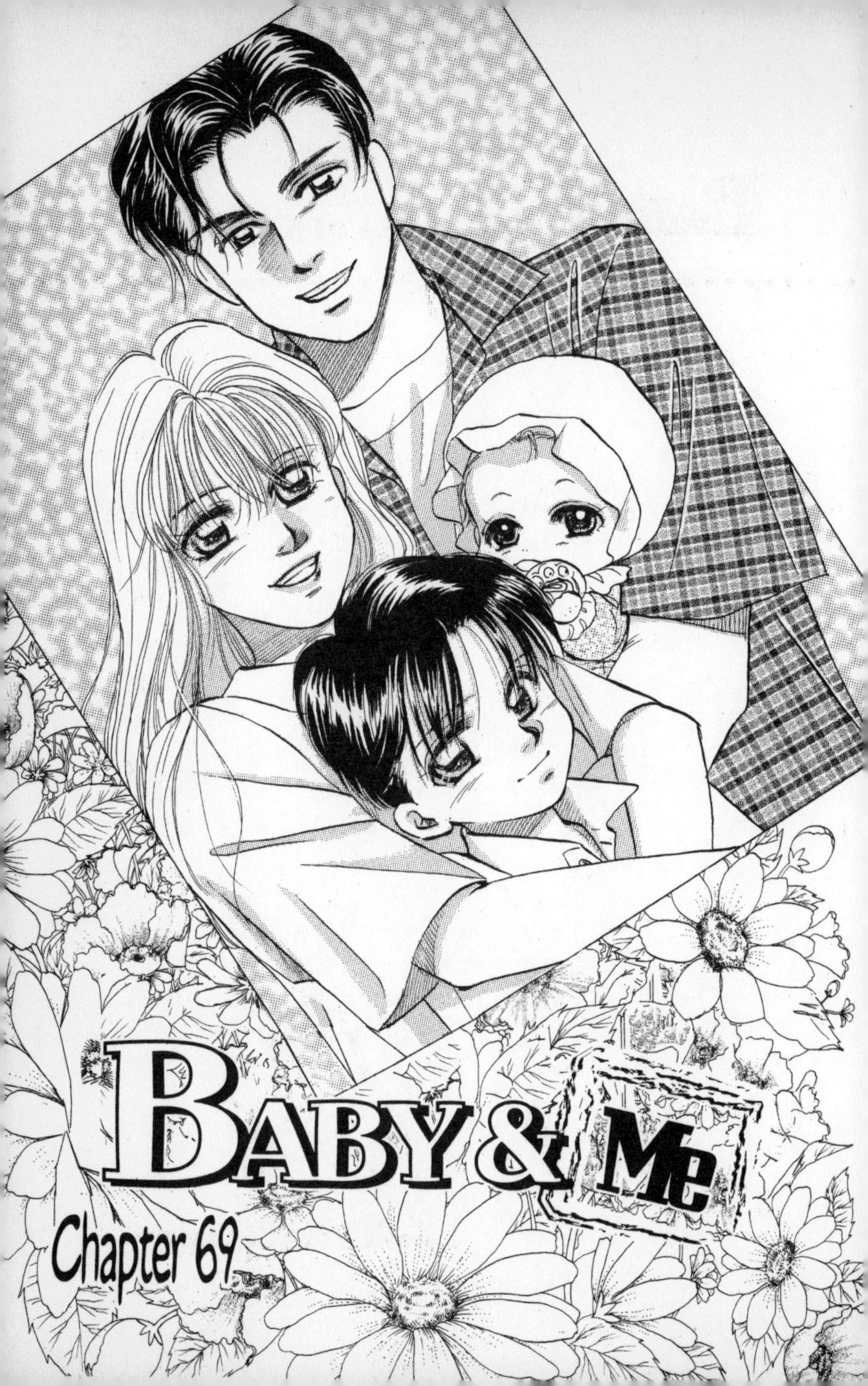
BABY & Me
Chapter 69

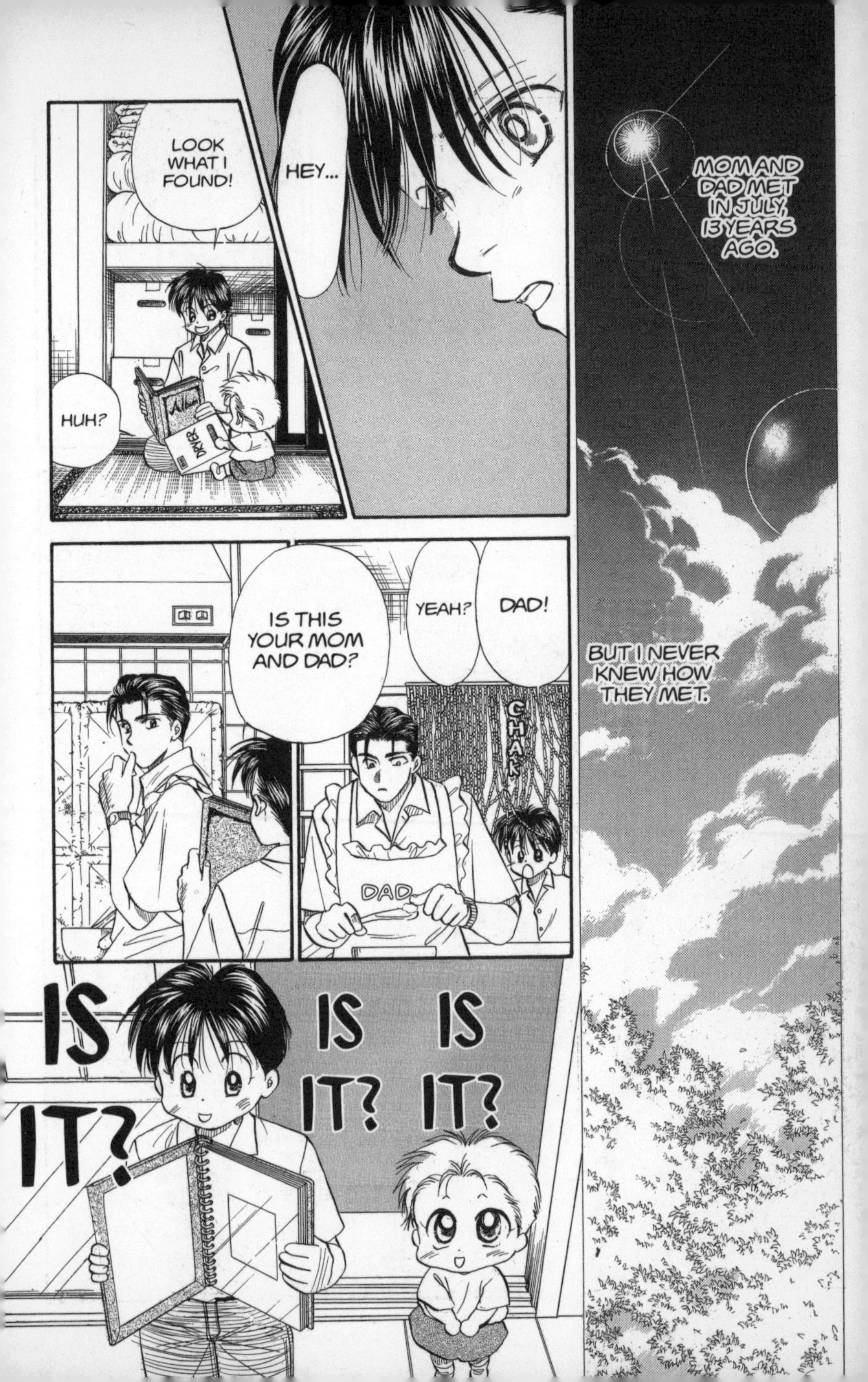
MOM AND DAD MET IN JULY, 13 YEARS AGO.
BUT I NEVER KNEW HOW THEY MET.
HEY...
LOOK WHAT I FOUND!
HUH?
DRYER
DAD!
YEAH?
GHAK
DAD
IS THIS YOUR MOM AND DAD?
IS IT?
IS IT?
IS IT?

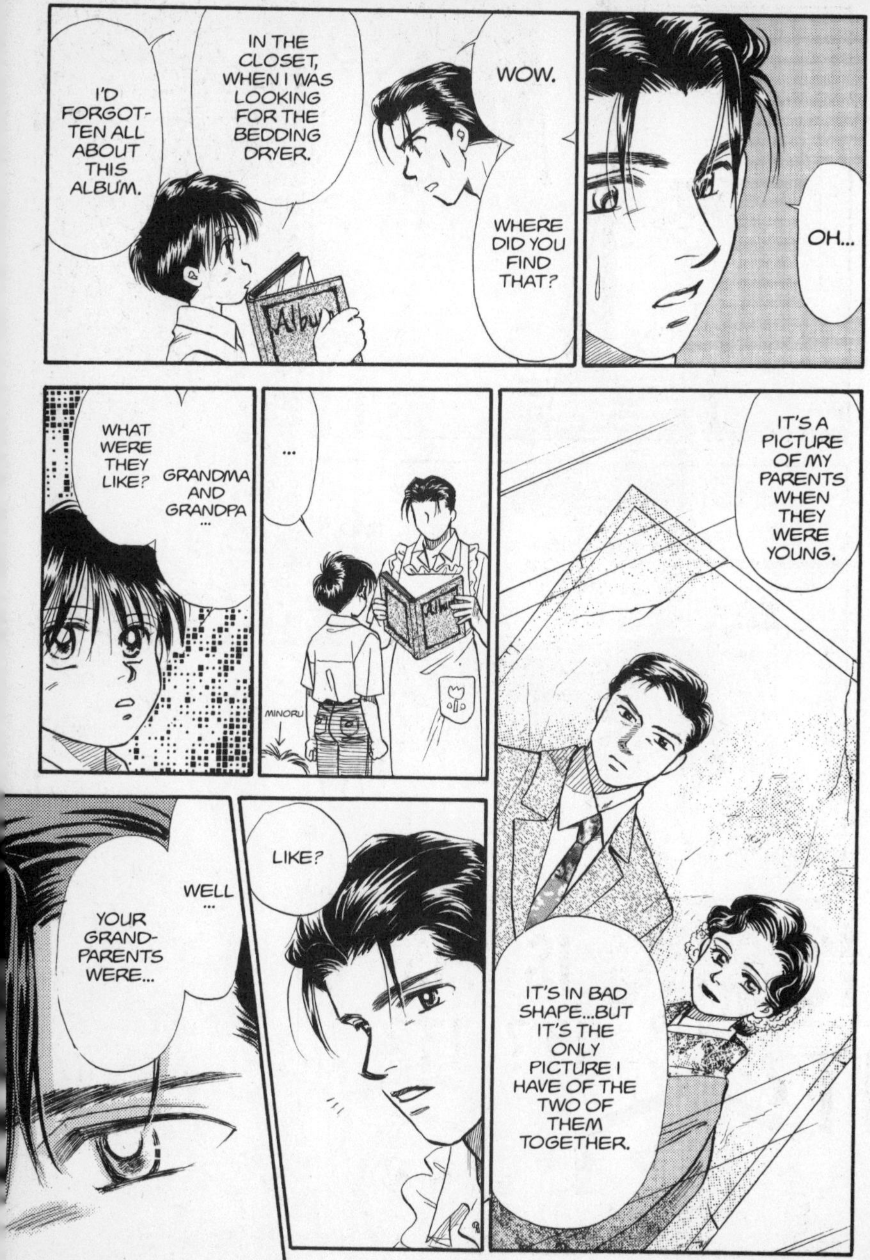
OH...
WOW.
WHERE DID YOU FIND THAT?
IN THE CLOSET, WHEN I WAS LOOKING FOR THE BEDDING DRYER.
I'D FORGOT-TEN ALL ABOUT THIS ALBUM.
Album
IT'S A PICTURE OF MY PARENTS WHEN THEY WERE YOUNG.
IT'S IN BAD SHAPE...BUT IT'S THE ONLY PICTURE I HAVE OF THE TWO OF THEM TOGETHER.
...
MINORU
GRANDMA AND GRANDPA ...
WHAT WERE THEY LIKE?
LIKE?
WELL ...
YOUR GRAND-PARENTS WERE...

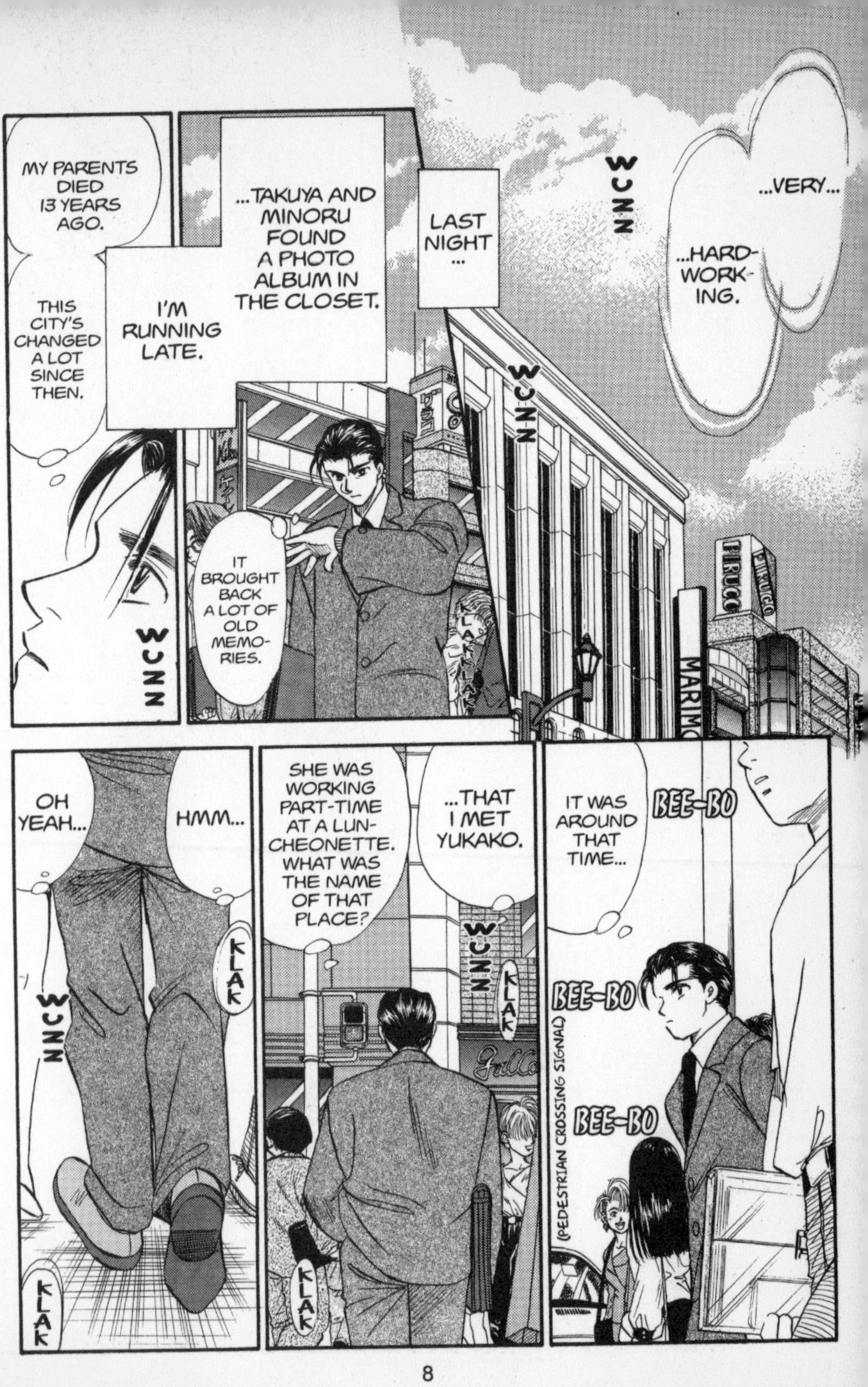
...VERY...
...HARD-WORKING.
LAST NIGHT...
WUNN
...TAKUYA AND MINORU FOUND A PHOTO ALBUM IN THE CLOSET.
I'M RUNNING LATE.
WUNN
IT BROUGHT BACK A LOT OF OLD MEMORIES.
KLAK KLAK KLAK
MY PARENTS DIED 13 YEARS AGO.
THIS CITY'S CHANGED A LOT SINCE THEN.
WUNN
IT WAS AROUND THAT TIME...
BEE-BO
BEE-BO
BEE-BO
(PEDESTRIAN CROSSING SIGNAL)
...THAT I MET YUKAKO.
SHE WAS WORKING PART-TIME AT A LUNCHEONETTE. WHAT WAS THE NAME OF THAT PLACE?
WUNN
KLAK
KLAK
HMM...
OH YEAH...
KLAK
WUNN
KLAK

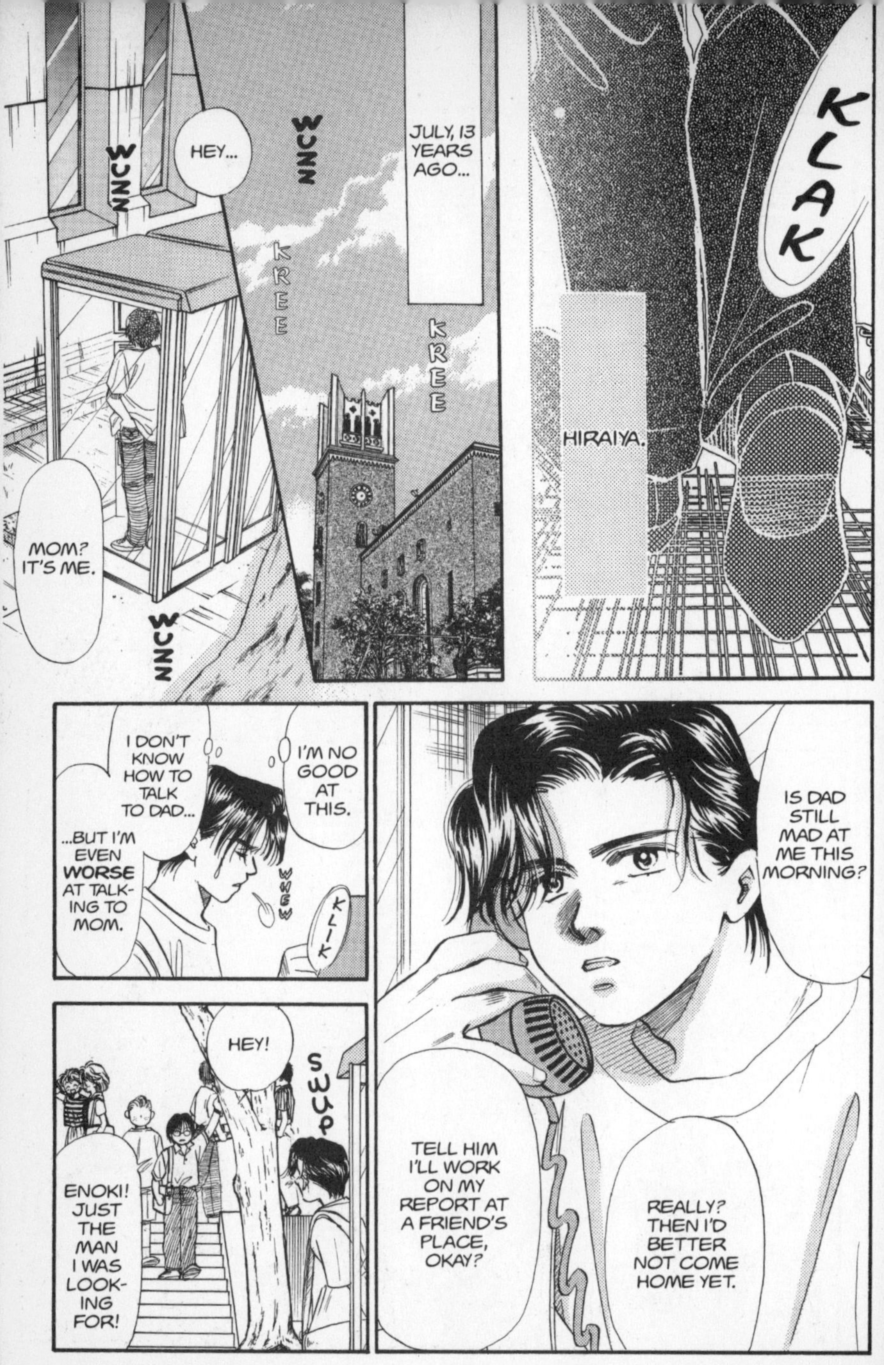
KLAK
HIRAIYA.
JULY, 13 YEARS AGO...
WUNN
KREE
KREE
HEY...
WUNN
MOM? IT'S ME.
WUNN
IS DAD STILL MAD AT ME THIS MORNING?
REALLY? THEN I'D BETTER NOT COME HOME YET.
TELL HIM I'LL WORK ON MY REPORT AT A FRIEND'S PLACE, OKAY?
I'M NO GOOD AT THIS.
KLIK
WHEW
I DON'T KNOW HOW TO TALK TO DAD...
...BUT I'M EVEN **WORSE** AT TALKING TO MOM.
SWUP
HEY!
ENOKI! JUST THE MAN I WAS LOOKING FOR!

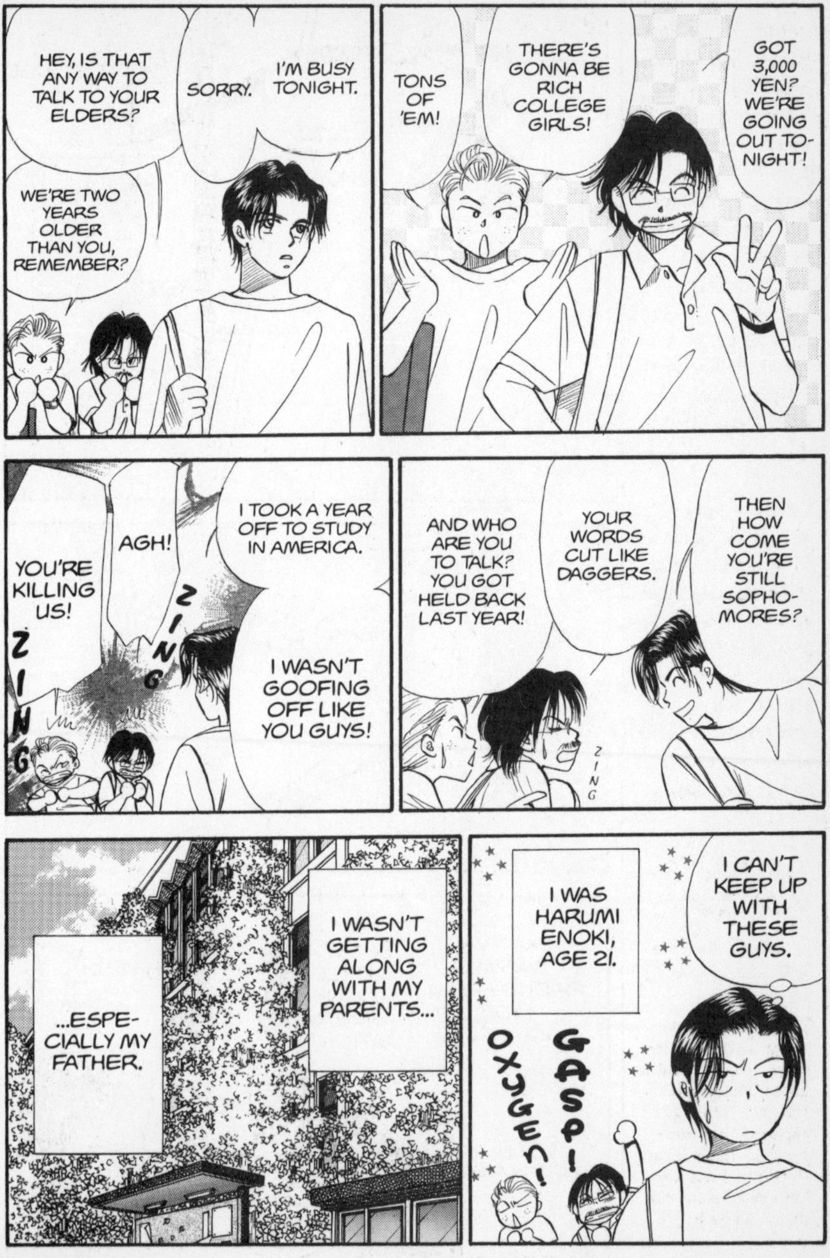
GOT 3,000 YEN? WE'RE GOING OUT TO-NIGHT!
THERE'S GONNA BE RICH COLLEGE GIRLS!
TONS OF 'EM!
I'M BUSY TONIGHT.
SORRY.
HEY, IS THAT ANY WAY TO TALK TO YOUR ELDERS?
WE'RE TWO YEARS OLDER THAN YOU, REMEMBER?
THEN HOW COME YOU'RE STILL SOPHO-MORES?
YOUR WORDS CUT LIKE DAGGERS.
AND WHO ARE YOU TO TALK? YOU GOT HELD BACK LAST YEAR!
ZING
I TOOK A YEAR OFF TO STUDY IN AMERICA.
I WASN'T GOOFING OFF LIKE YOU GUYS!
ZING
AGH!
YOU'RE KILLING US!
ZING
I CAN'T KEEP UP WITH THESE GUYS.
I WAS HARUMI ENOKI, AGE 21.
GASP!
OXYGEN!
I WASN'T GETTING ALONG WITH MY PARENTS...
...ESPE-CIALLY MY FATHER.

Author's Note Part 1

Hi, Marimo Ragawa here. ***Baby & Me*** Volume 13 is all about Mom and Dad. That's why Takuya and Minoru aren't on the cover. I've been thinking a lot about these stories, so I'm glad I finally got to draw them. It always feels great to finish a story I've wanted to draw.

I think of Yuki Asahi as a quiet character. Even his face is kind of nondescript. But he was surprisingly popular with older women. Harumi was popular with students, and Yuki with working women and housewives.

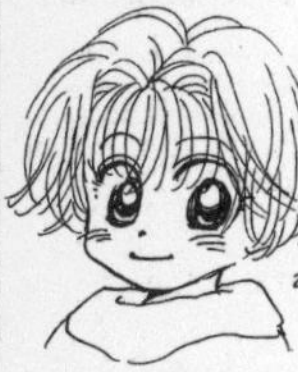

Yukako looks a lot like Takuya.

I don't know what Tokyo looked like ten years ago, so I had to guess. But people told me, "You really captured the atmosphere." That's when I realized I was about ten years behind the times. Ha ha ha...

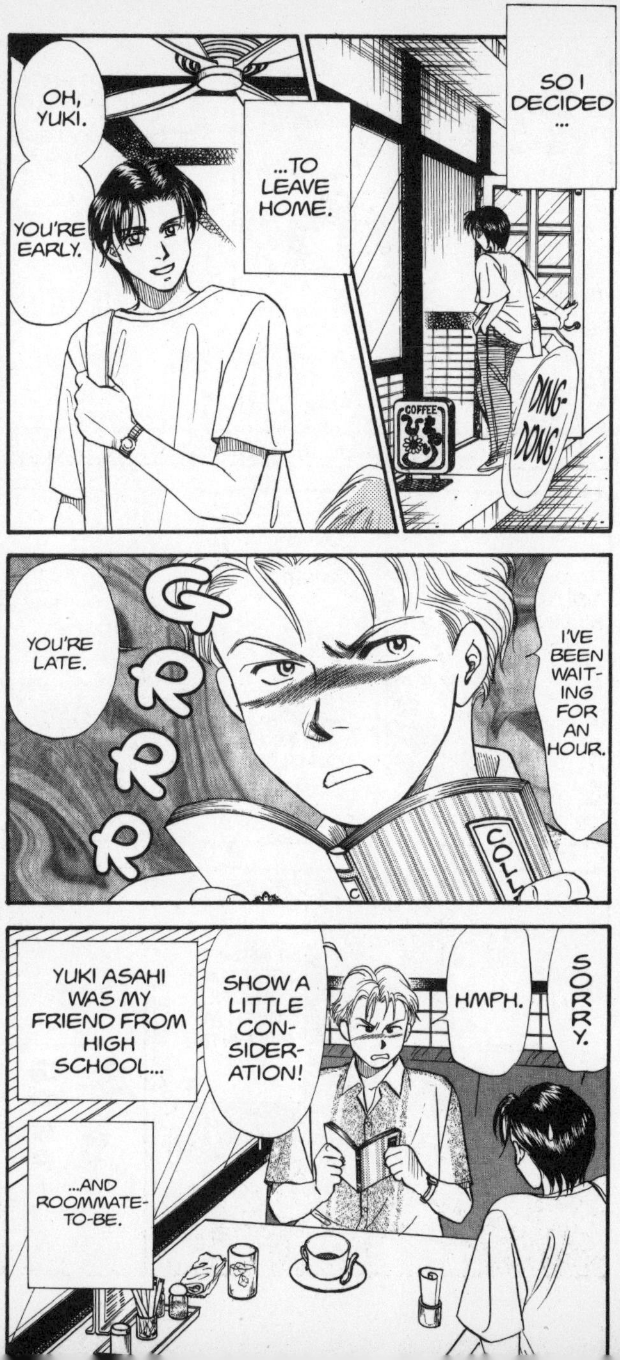
SO I DECIDED...
...TO LEAVE HOME.
COFFEE
DING-DONG
OH, YUKI.
YOU'RE EARLY.
I'VE BEEN WAITING FOR AN HOUR.
GRRR
YOU'RE LATE.
SORRY.
HMPH.
SHOW A LITTLE CONSIDERATION!
YUKI ASAHI WAS MY FRIEND FROM HIGH SCHOOL...
...AND ROOMMATE-TO-BE.

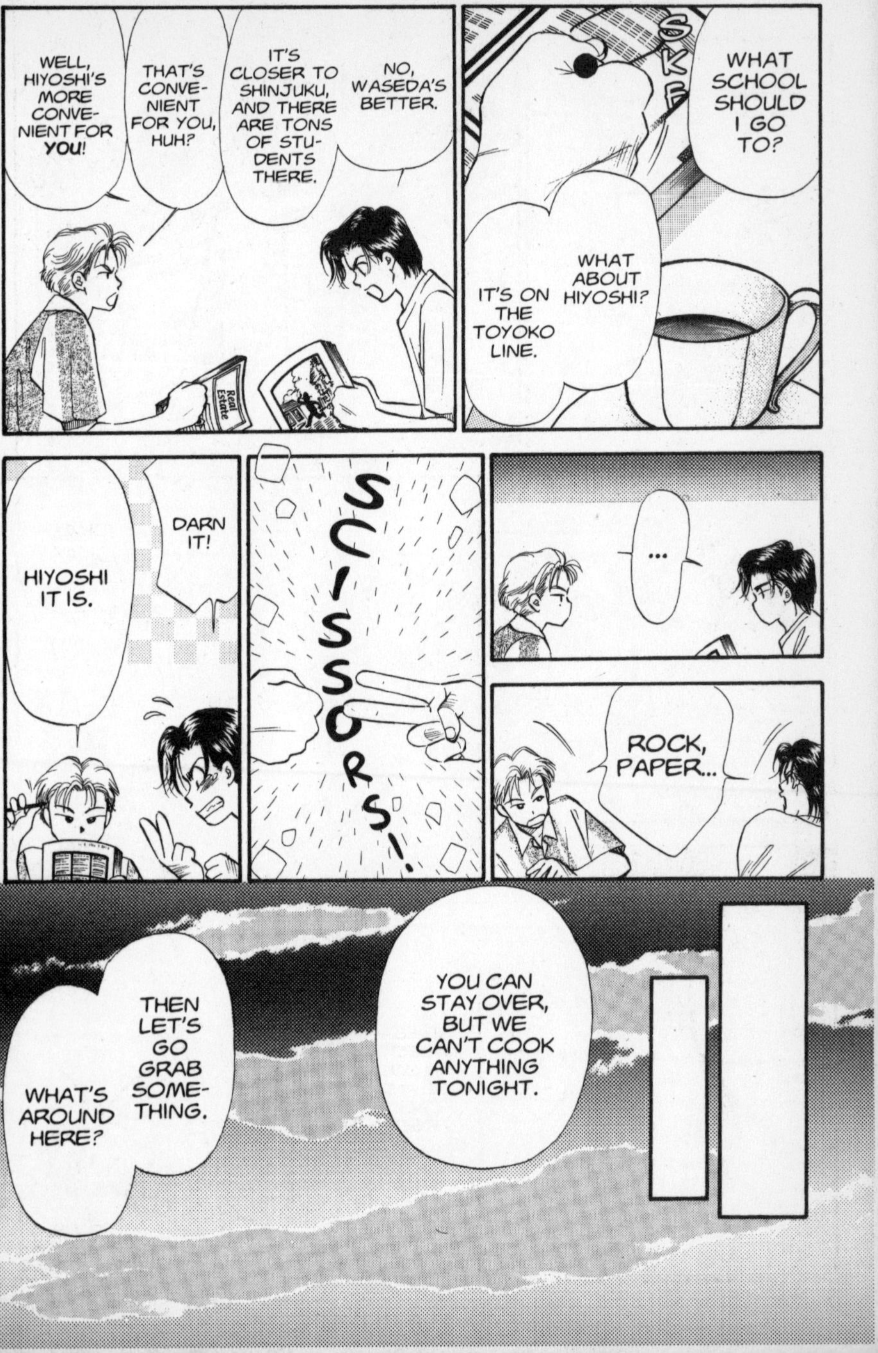
WHAT SCHOOL SHOULD I GO TO?
WHAT ABOUT HIYOSHI?
IT'S ON THE TOYOKO LINE.
NO, WASEDA'S BETTER.
IT'S CLOSER TO SHINJUKU, AND THERE ARE TONS OF STUDENTS THERE.
THAT'S CONVENIENT FOR YOU, HUH?
WELL, HIYOSHI'S MORE CONVENIENT FOR **YOU**!
Real Estate
...
ROCK, PAPER...
SCISSORS!
DARN IT!
HIYOSHI IT IS.
YOU CAN STAY OVER, BUT WE CAN'T COOK ANYTHING TONIGHT.
THEN LET'S GO GRAB SOMETHING.
WHAT'S AROUND HERE?

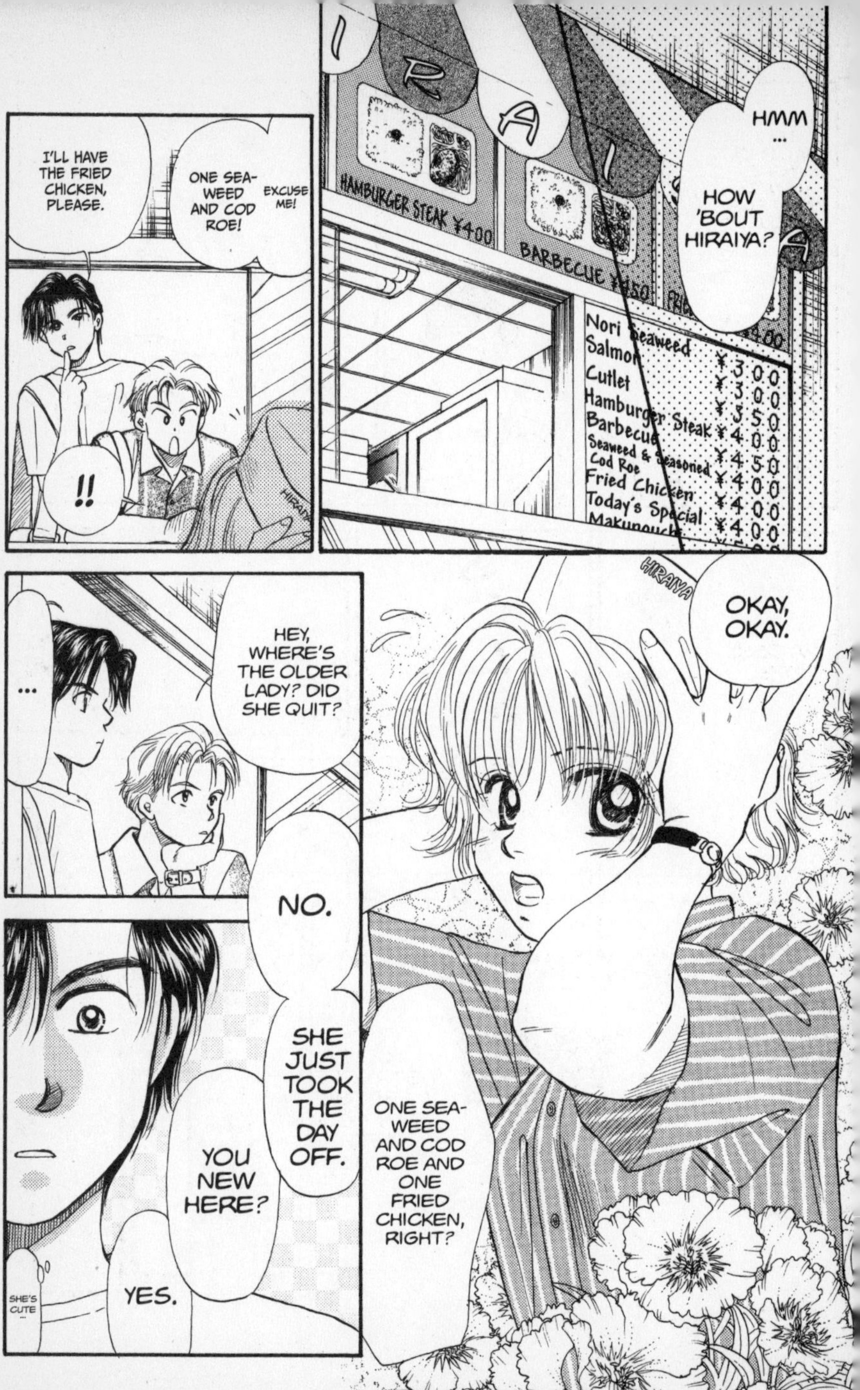
HMM ...
HOW 'BOUT HIRAIYA?
HAMBURGER STEAK ¥400
BARBECUE ¥450
Nori Seaweed
Salmon
Cutlet
Hamburger Steak
Barbecue
Seaweed & Seasoned Cod Roe
Fried Chicken
Today's Special
¥300
¥300
¥350
¥400
¥450
¥400
¥400
¥400
EXCUSE ME!
ONE SEA-WEED AND COD ROE!
I'LL HAVE THE FRIED CHICKEN, PLEASE.
!!
HIRAIYA
OKAY, OKAY.
ONE SEA-WEED AND COD ROE AND ONE FRIED CHICKEN, RIGHT?
HEY, WHERE'S THE OLDER LADY? DID SHE QUIT?
...
NO.
SHE JUST TOOK THE DAY OFF.
YOU NEW HERE?
YES.
SHE'S CUTE ...

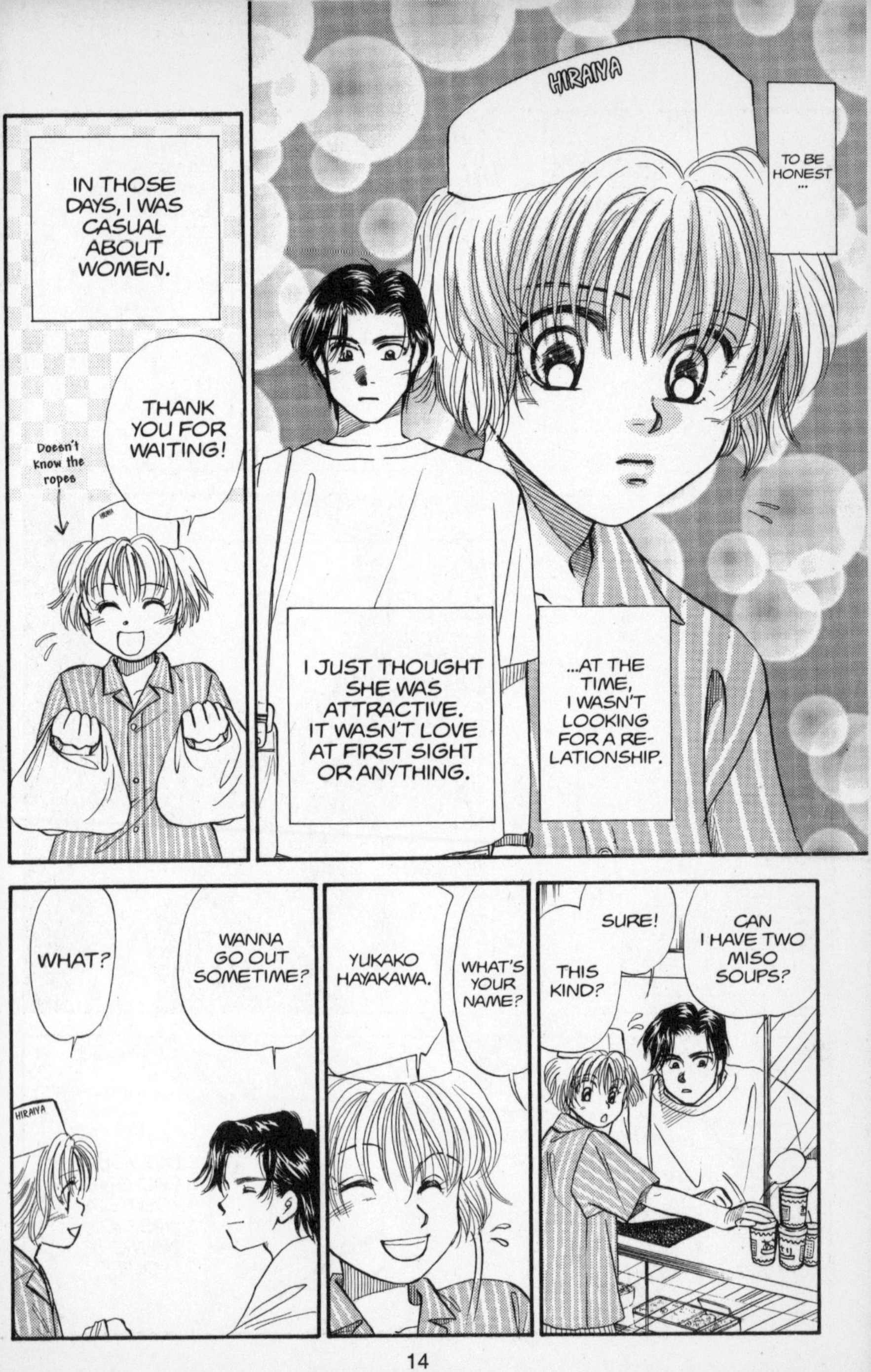
HIRAIYA
TO BE HONEST ...
...AT THE TIME, I WASN'T LOOKING FOR A RE-LATIONSHIP.
I JUST THOUGHT SHE WAS ATTRACTIVE. IT WASN'T LOVE AT FIRST SIGHT OR ANYTHING.
IN THOSE DAYS, I WAS CASUAL ABOUT WOMEN.
THANK YOU FOR WAITING!
Doesn't know the ropes
CAN I HAVE TWO MISO SOUPS?
SURE!
THIS KIND?
WHAT'S YOUR NAME?
YUKAKO HAYAKAWA.
WANNA GO OUT SOMETIME?
WHAT?
HIRAIYA

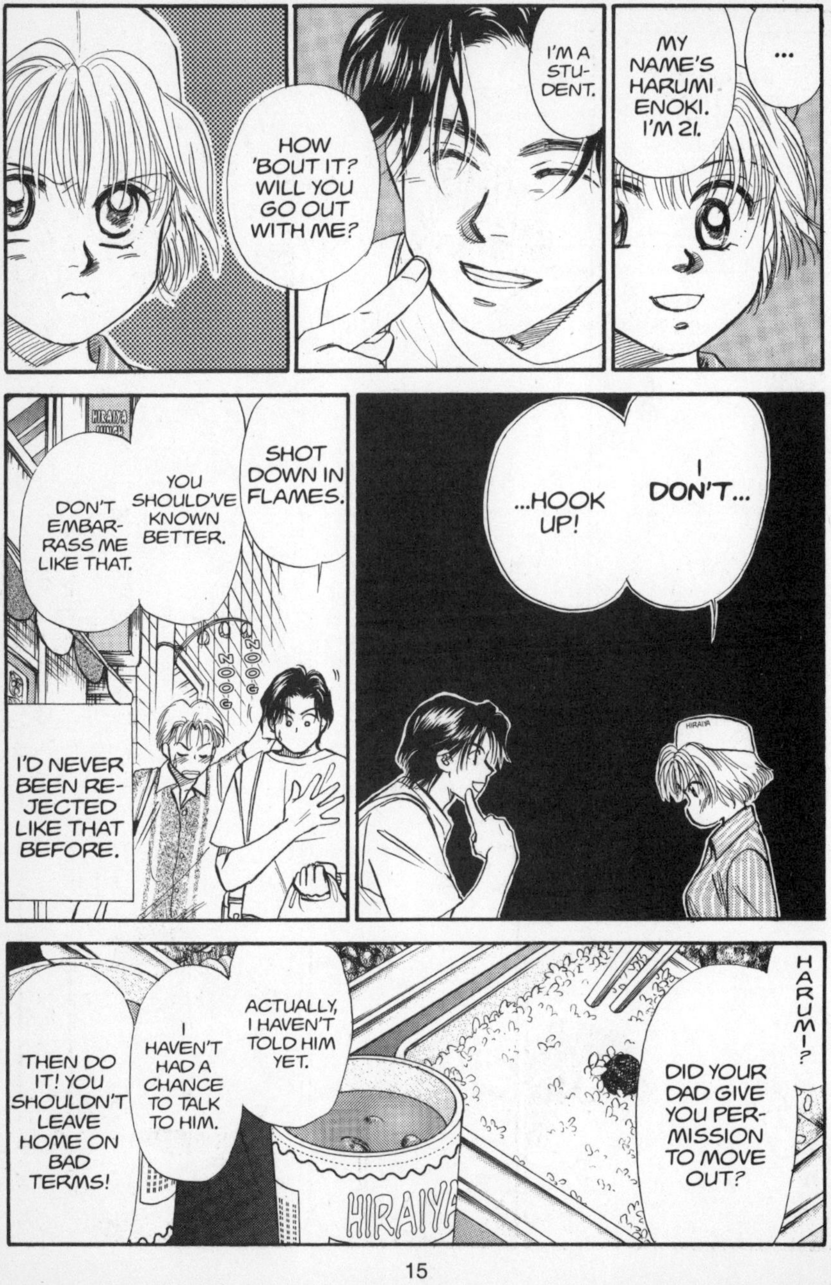
...
MY NAME'S HARUMI ENOKI. I'M 21.
I'M A STUDENT.
HOW 'BOUT IT? WILL YOU GO OUT WITH ME?
I DON'T...
...HOOK UP!
SHOT DOWN IN FLAMES.
YOU SHOULD'VE KNOWN BETTER.
DON'T EMBARRASS ME LIKE THAT.
I'D NEVER BEEN REJECTED LIKE THAT BEFORE.
HARUMI?
DID YOUR DAD GIVE YOU PERMISSION TO MOVE OUT?
ACTUALLY, I HAVEN'T TOLD HIM YET.
I HAVEN'T HAD A CHANCE TO TALK TO HIM.
THEN DO IT! YOU SHOULDN'T LEAVE HOME ON BAD TERMS!
HIRAIYA

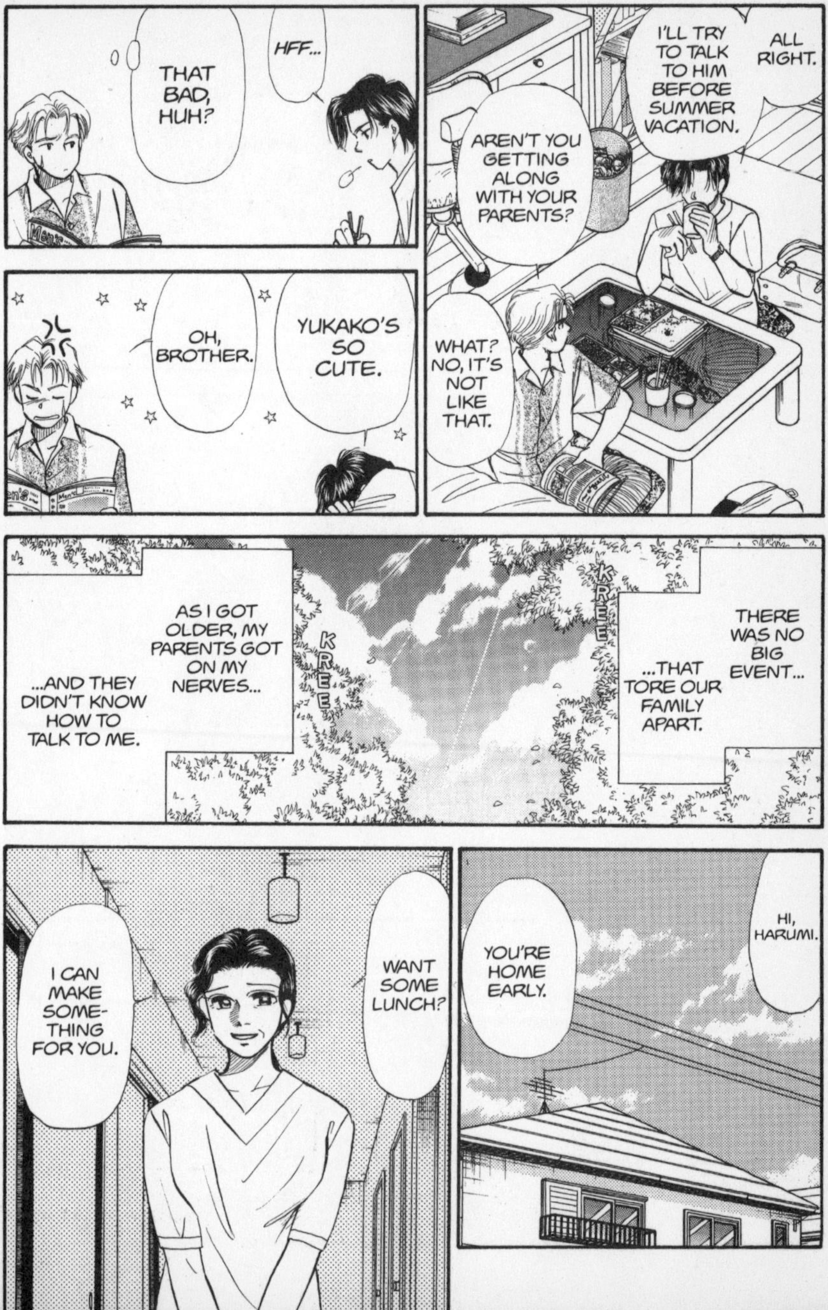
ALL RIGHT.
I'LL TRY TO TALK TO HIM BEFORE SUMMER VACATION.
AREN'T YOU GETTING ALONG WITH YOUR PARENTS?
WHAT? NO, IT'S NOT LIKE THAT.
HFF...
THAT BAD, HUH?
YUKAKO'S SO CUTE.
OH, BROTHER.
THERE WAS NO BIG EVENT...
...THAT TORE OUR FAMILY APART.
KREE
AS I GOT OLDER, MY PARENTS GOT ON MY NERVES...
KREE
...AND THEY DIDN'T KNOW HOW TO TALK TO ME.
HI, HARUMI.
YOU'RE HOME EARLY.
WANT SOME LUNCH?
I CAN MAKE SOME-THING FOR YOU.

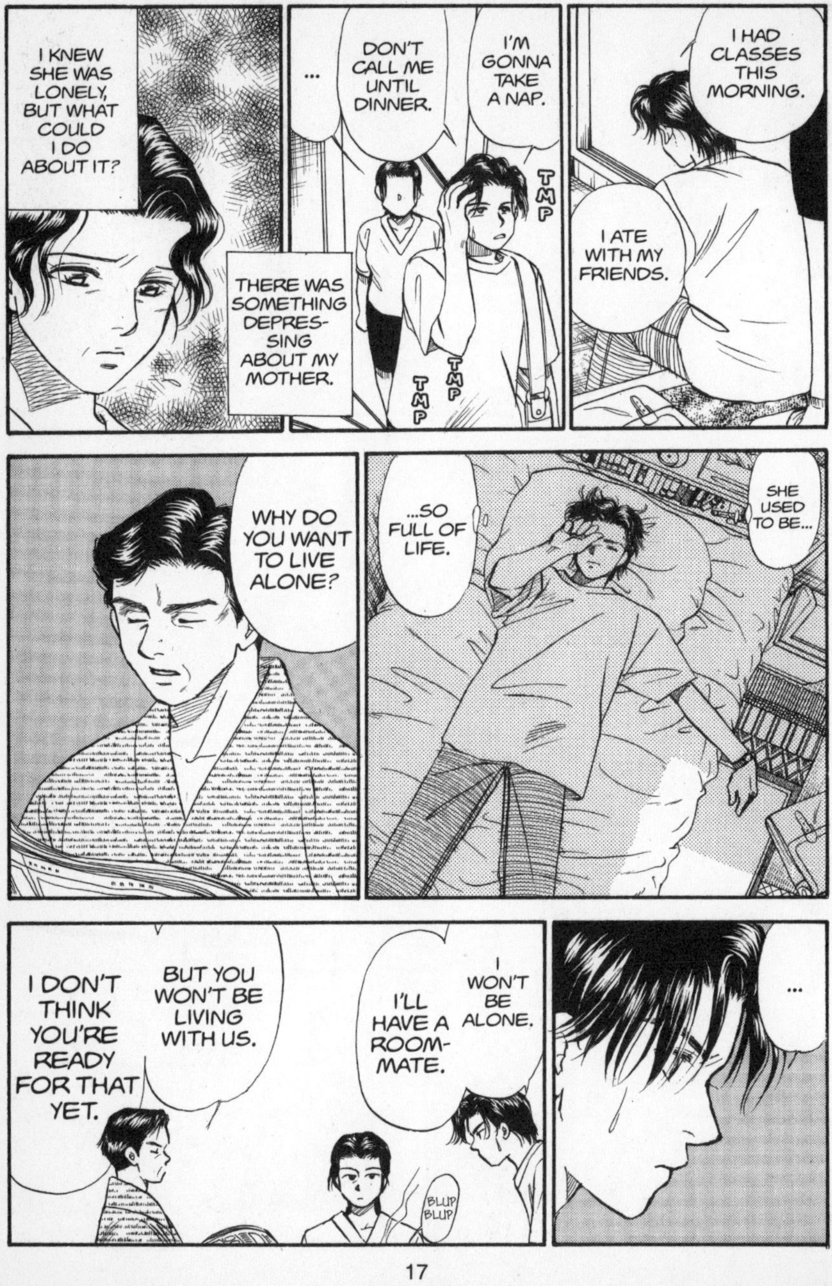
I HAD CLASSES THIS MORNING.
I ATE WITH MY FRIENDS.
I'M GONNA TAKE A NAP.
TMP
DON'T CALL ME UNTIL DINNER.
...
THERE WAS SOMETHING DEPRES- SING ABOUT MY MOTHER.
TMP
TMP
I KNEW SHE WAS LONELY, BUT WHAT COULD I DO ABOUT IT?
SHE USED TO BE...
...SO FULL OF LIFE.
WHY DO YOU WANT TO LIVE ALONE?
...
I WON'T BE ALONE.
I'LL HAVE A ROOM- MATE.
BLUP BLUP
BUT YOU WON'T BE LIVING WITH US.
I DON'T THINK YOU'RE READY FOR THAT YET.

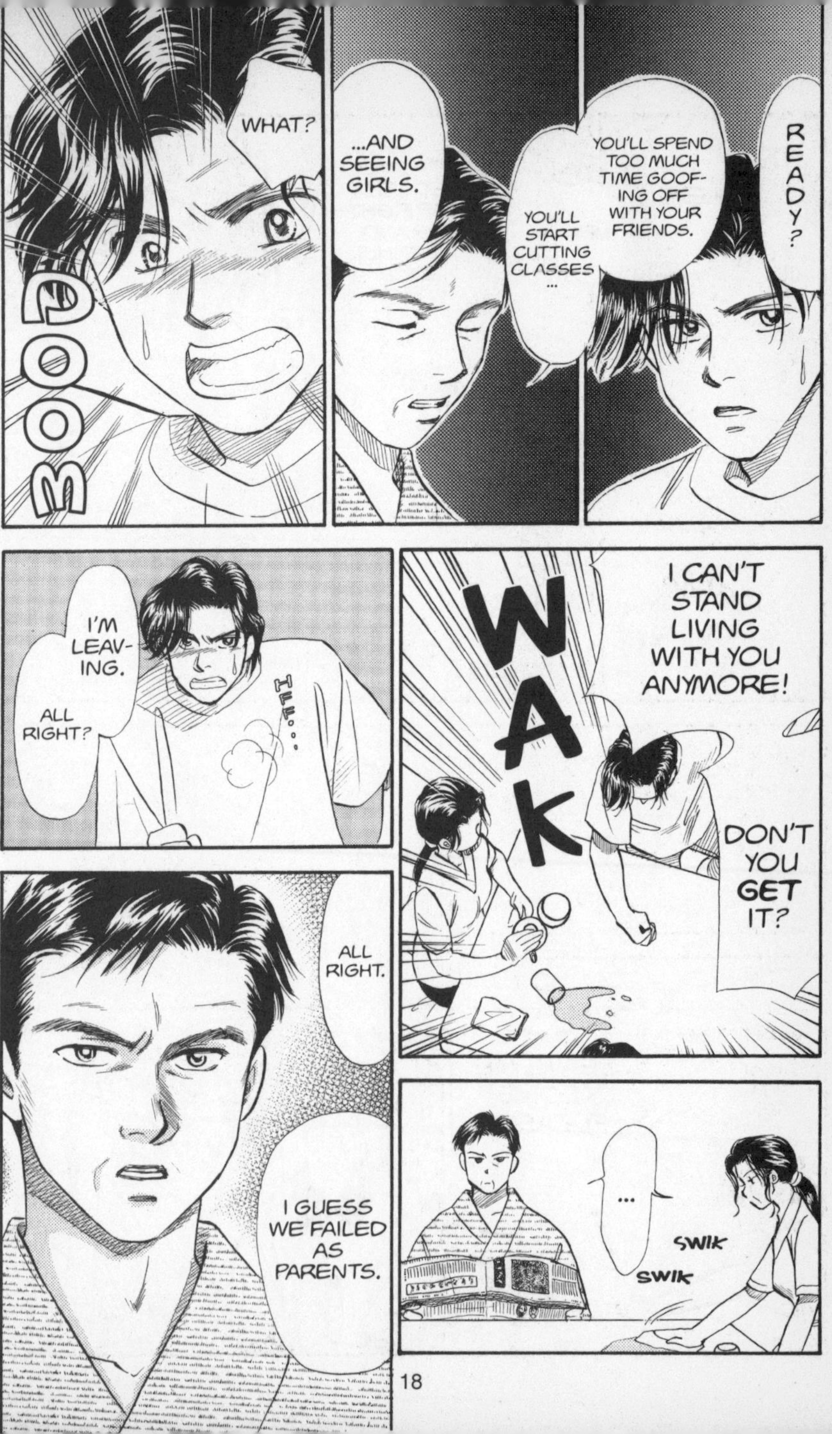
READY?
YOU'LL SPEND TOO MUCH TIME GOOF-ING OFF WITH YOUR FRIENDS.
YOU'LL START CUTTING CLASSES ...
...AND SEEING GIRLS.
WHAT?
I CAN'T STAND LIVING WITH YOU ANYMORE!
WAK
DON'T YOU GET IT?
I'M LEAV-ING.
ALL RIGHT?
HFF...
ALL RIGHT.
I GUESS WE FAILED AS PARENTS.
...
SWIK
SWIK

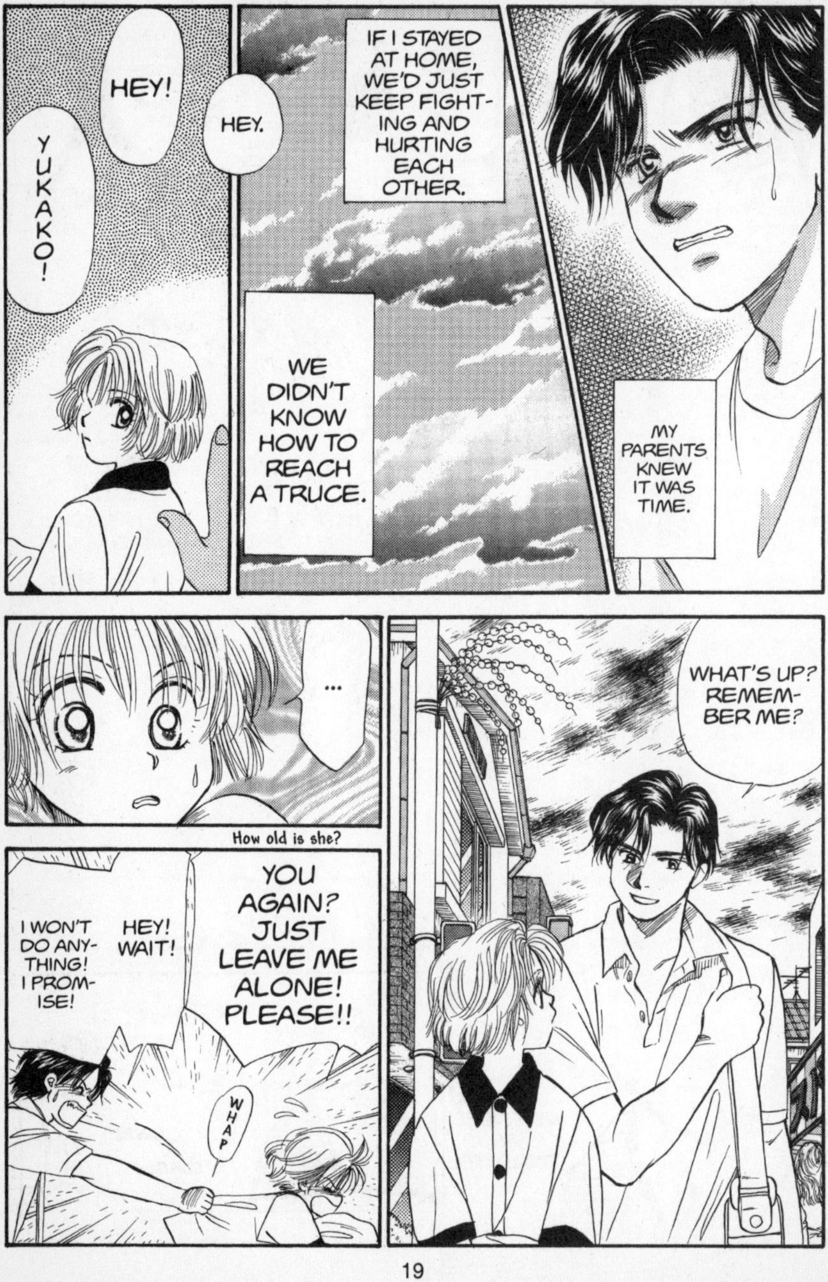
MY PARENTS KNEW IT WAS TIME.
IF I STAYED AT HOME, WE'D JUST KEEP FIGHTING AND HURTING EACH OTHER.
WE DIDN'T KNOW HOW TO REACH A TRUCE.
HEY.
HEY!
YUKAKO!
WHAT'S UP? REMEMBER ME?
...
How old is she?
YOU AGAIN? JUST LEAVE ME ALONE! PLEASE!!
HEY! WAIT!
I WON'T DO ANYTHING! I PROMISE!
WHAP

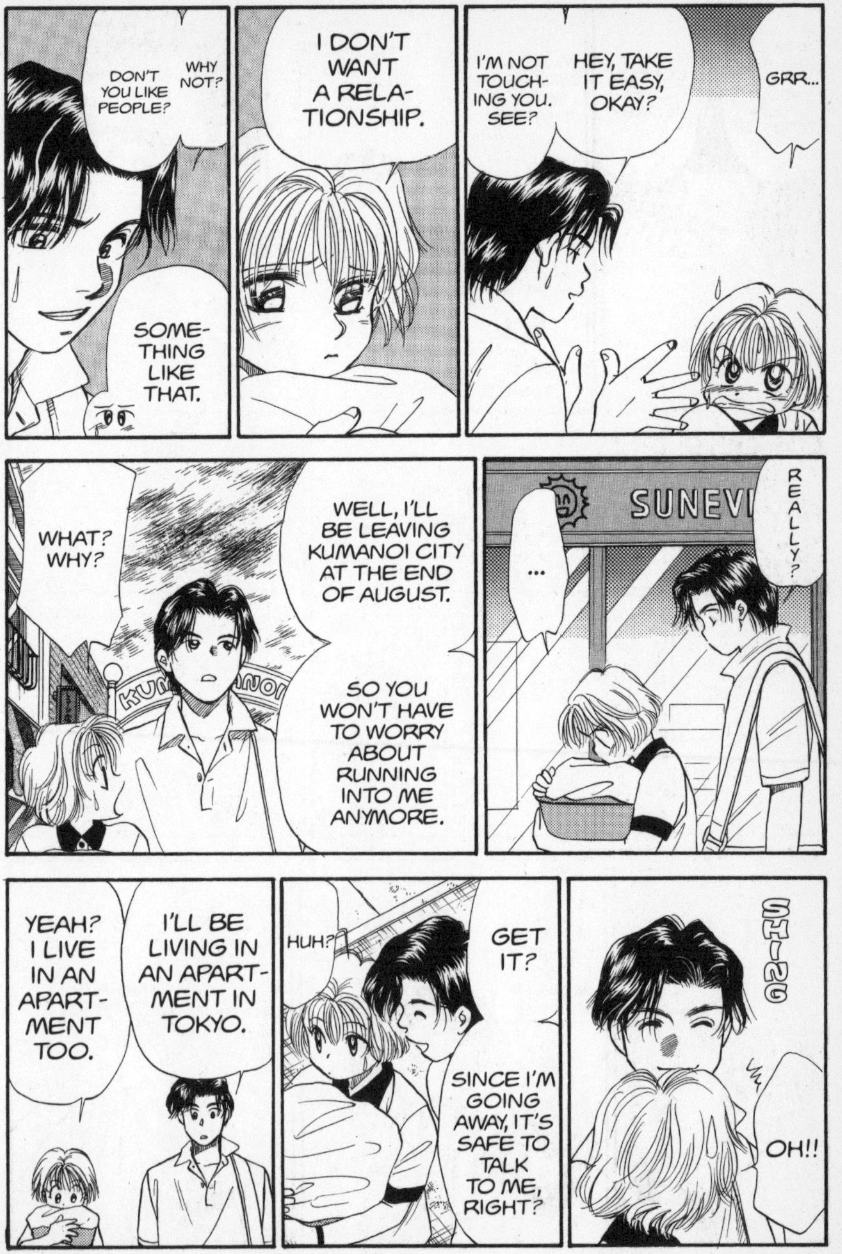
GRR...
HEY, TAKE IT EASY, OKAY?
I'M NOT TOUCHING YOU. SEE?
I DON'T WANT A RELATIONSHIP.
WHY NOT?
DON'T YOU LIKE PEOPLE?
SOMETHING LIKE THAT.
REALLY?
SUNEVI
...
WELL, I'LL BE LEAVING KUMANOI CITY AT THE END OF AUGUST.
SO YOU WON'T HAVE TO WORRY ABOUT RUNNING INTO ME ANYMORE.
WHAT? WHY?
KUMANOI
SHING
OH!!
GET IT?
SINCE I'M GOING AWAY, IT'S SAFE TO TALK TO ME, RIGHT?
HUH?
I'LL BE LIVING IN AN APARTMENT IN TOKYO.
YEAH? I LIVE IN AN APARTMENT TOO.

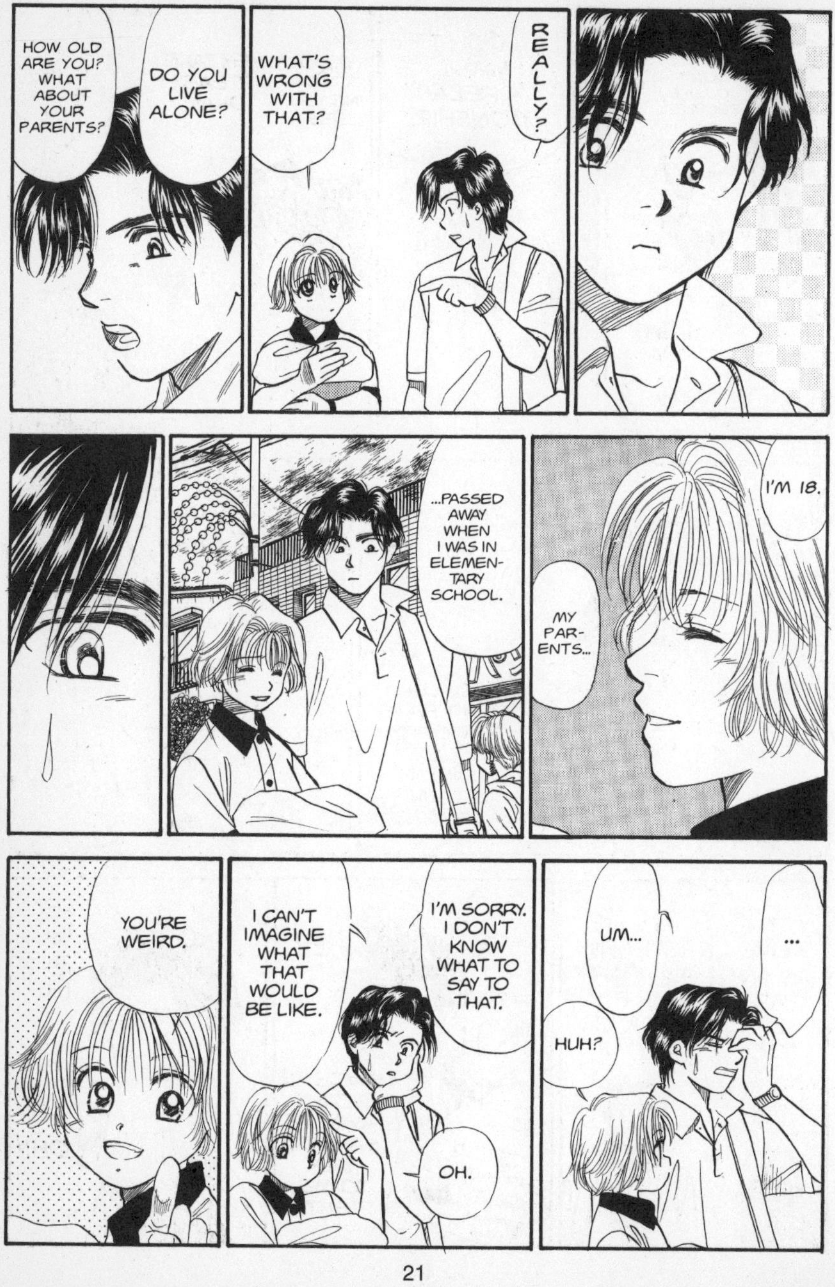

REALLY?
WHAT'S WRONG WITH THAT?
DO YOU LIVE ALONE?
HOW OLD ARE YOU? WHAT ABOUT YOUR PARENTS?
I'M 18.
MY PARENTS...
...PASSED AWAY WHEN I WAS IN ELEMENTARY SCHOOL.
...
UM...
HUH?
I'M SORRY. I DON'T KNOW WHAT TO SAY TO THAT.
I CAN'T IMAGINE WHAT THAT WOULD BE LIKE.
OH.
YOU'RE WEIRD.

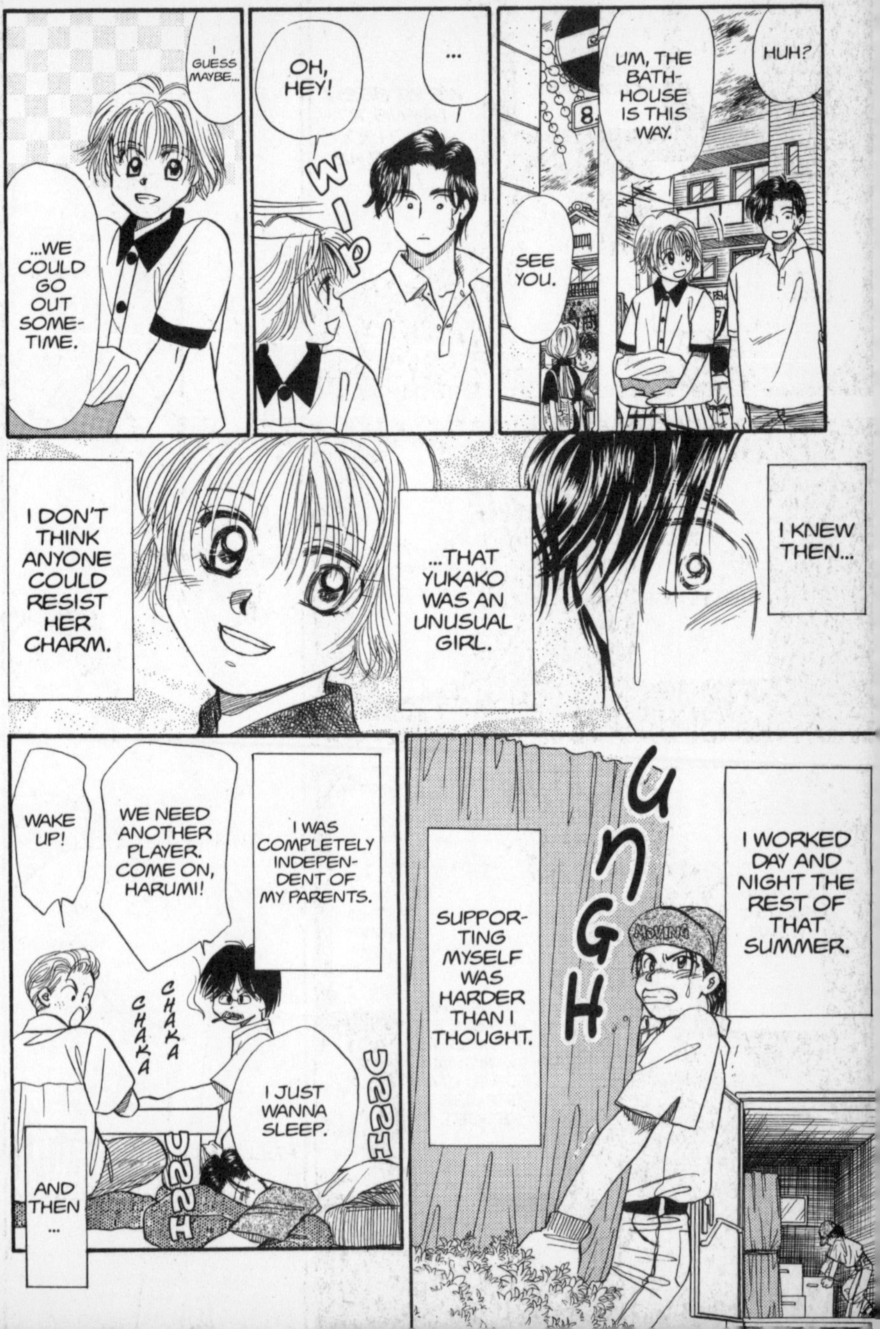
HUH?
UM, THE BATH-HOUSE IS THIS WAY.
SEE YOU.
...
OH, HEY!
WHIP
I GUESS MAYBE...
...WE COULD GO OUT SOME-TIME.
I KNEW THEN...
...THAT YUKAKO WAS AN UNUSUAL GIRL.
I DON'T THINK ANYONE COULD RESIST HER CHARM.
I WORKED DAY AND NIGHT THE REST OF THAT SUMMER.
UNGH
SUPPORTING MYSELF WAS HARDER THAN I THOUGHT.
I WAS COMPLETELY INDEPEN-DENT OF MY PARENTS.
WE NEED ANOTHER PLAYER. COME ON, HARUMI!
WAKE UP!
CHAKA CHAKA
UNNH
I JUST WANNA SLEEP.
UNNH
AND THEN ...

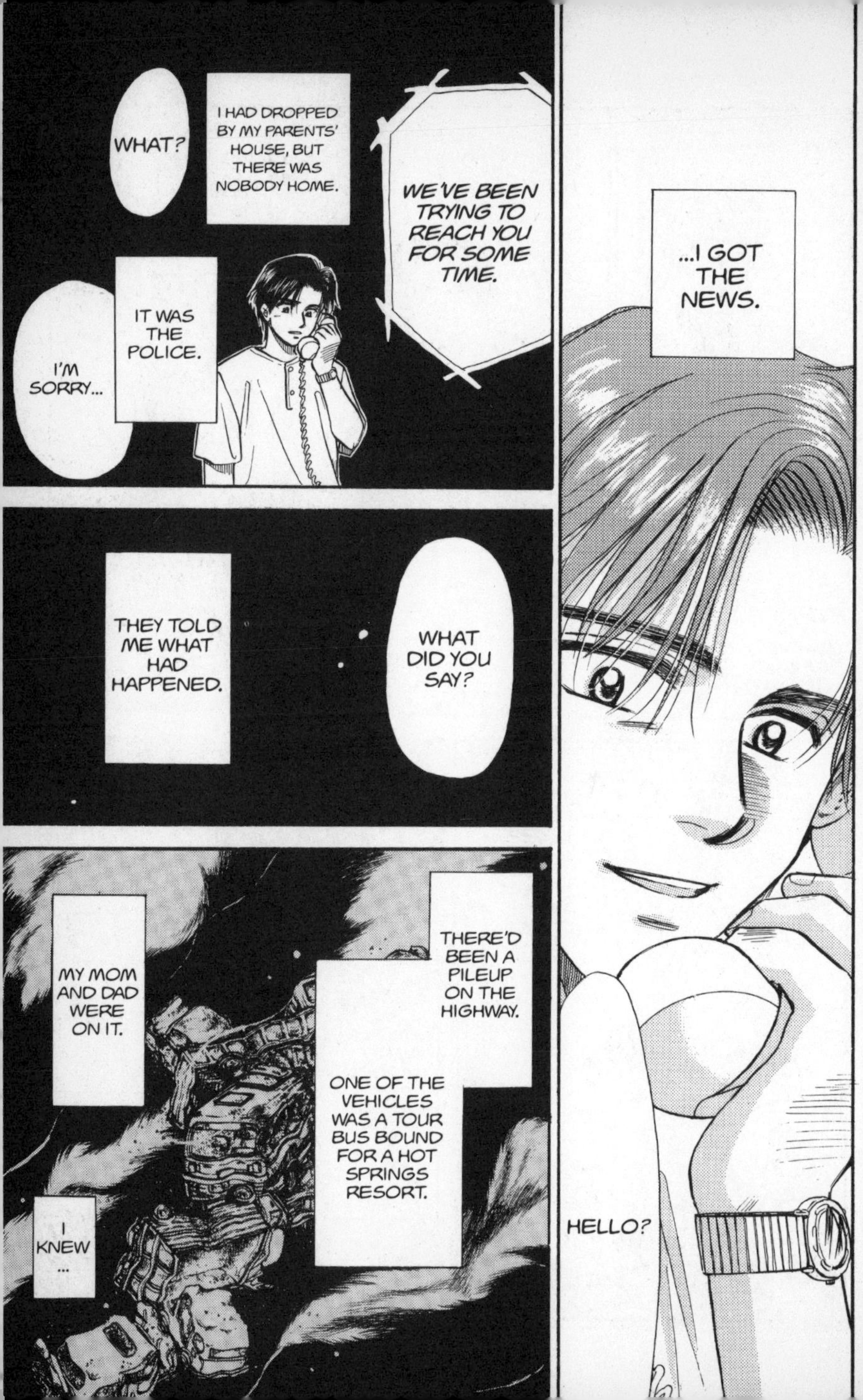
...I GOT THE NEWS.
HELLO?
WE'VE BEEN TRYING TO REACH YOU FOR SOME TIME.
I HAD DROPPED BY MY PARENTS' HOUSE, BUT THERE WAS NOBODY HOME.
WHAT?
IT WAS THE POLICE.
I'M SORRY...
WHAT DID YOU SAY?
THEY TOLD ME WHAT HAD HAPPENED.
THERE'D BEEN A PILEUP ON THE HIGHWAY.
ONE OF THE VEHICLES WAS A TOUR BUS BOUND FOR A HOT SPRINGS RESORT.
MY MOM AND DAD WERE ON IT.
I KNEW ...

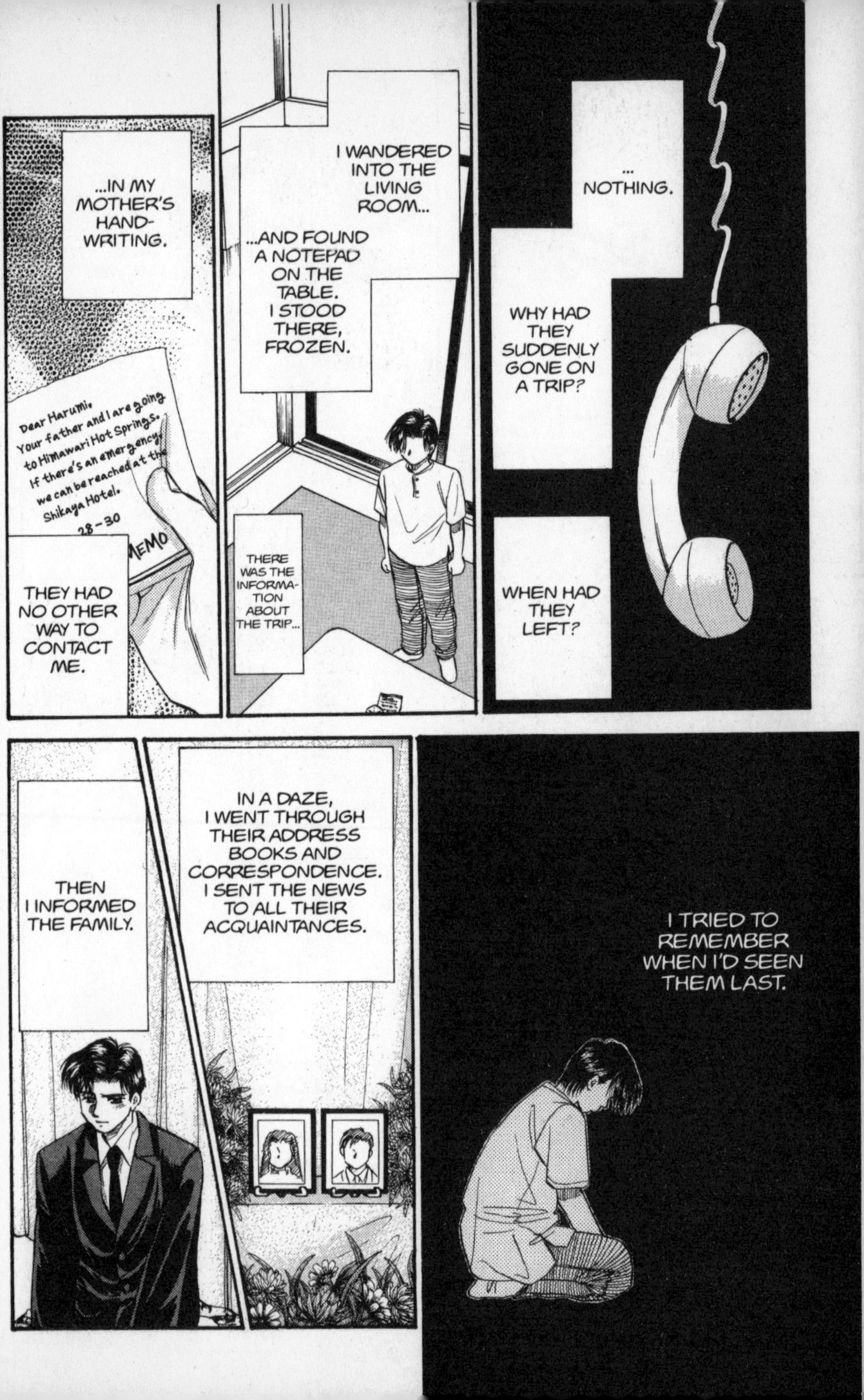
... NOTHING.
WHY HAD THEY SUDDENLY GONE ON A TRIP?
WHEN HAD THEY LEFT?
I WANDERED INTO THE LIVING ROOM...
...AND FOUND A NOTEPAD ON THE TABLE. I STOOD THERE, FROZEN.
THERE WAS THE INFORMATION ABOUT THE TRIP...
...IN MY MOTHER'S HAND-WRITING.
Dear Harumi,
Your father and I are going to Himawari Hot Springs.
If there's an emergency, we can be reached at the Shikaya Hotel.
28 - 30
MEMO
THEY HAD NO OTHER WAY TO CONTACT ME.
I TRIED TO REMEMBER WHEN I'D SEEN THEM LAST.
IN A DAZE, I WENT THROUGH THEIR ADDRESS BOOKS AND CORRESPONDENCE. I SENT THE NEWS TO ALL THEIR ACQUAINTANCES.
THEN I INFORMED THE FAMILY.

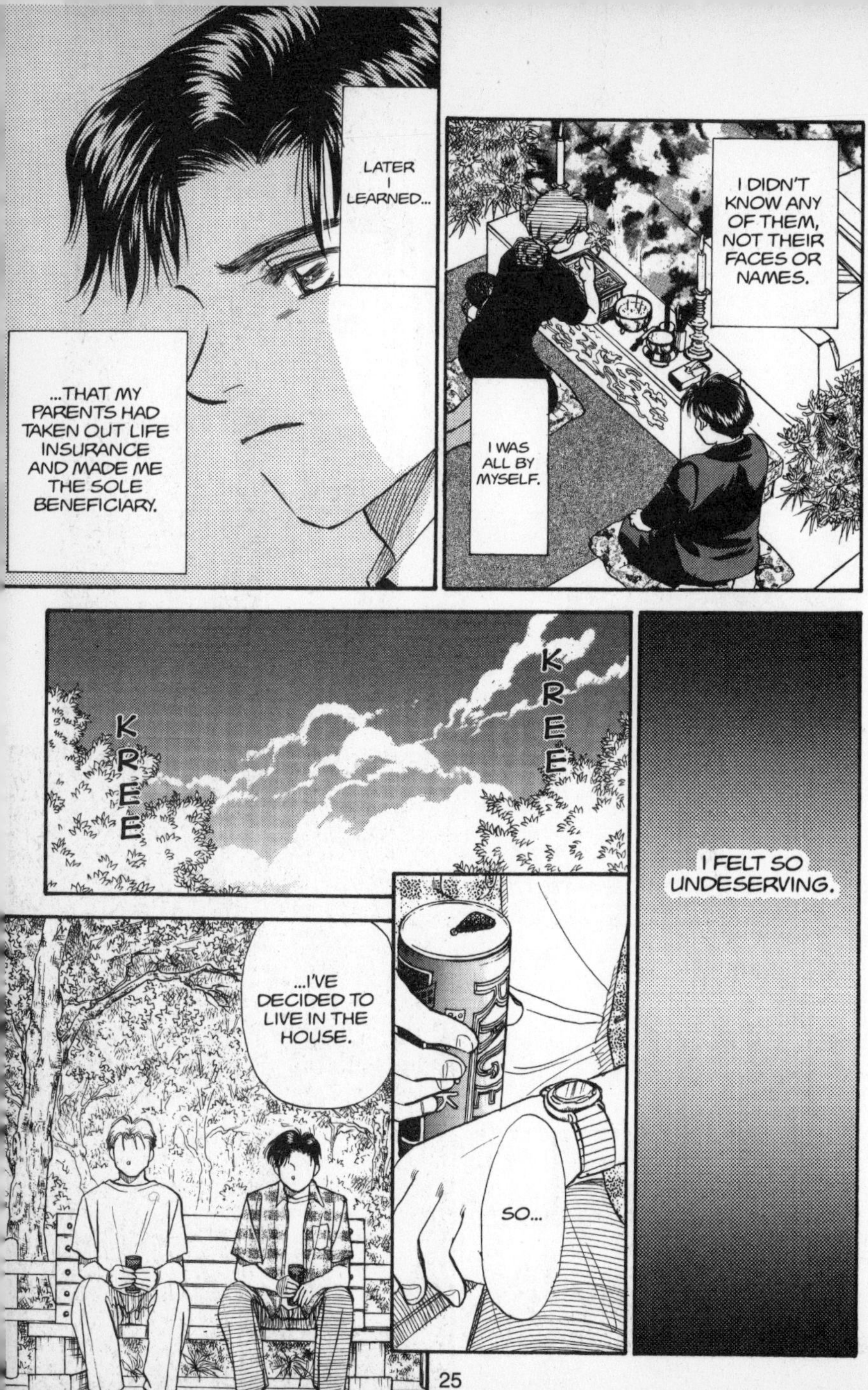
I DIDN'T KNOW ANY OF THEM, NOT THEIR FACES OR NAMES.
I WAS ALL BY MYSELF.
LATER I LEARNED...
...THAT MY PARENTS HAD TAKEN OUT LIFE INSURANCE AND MADE ME THE SOLE BENEFICIARY.
I FELT SO UNDESERVING.
KREE
KREE
SO...
...I'VE DECIDED TO LIVE IN THE HOUSE.

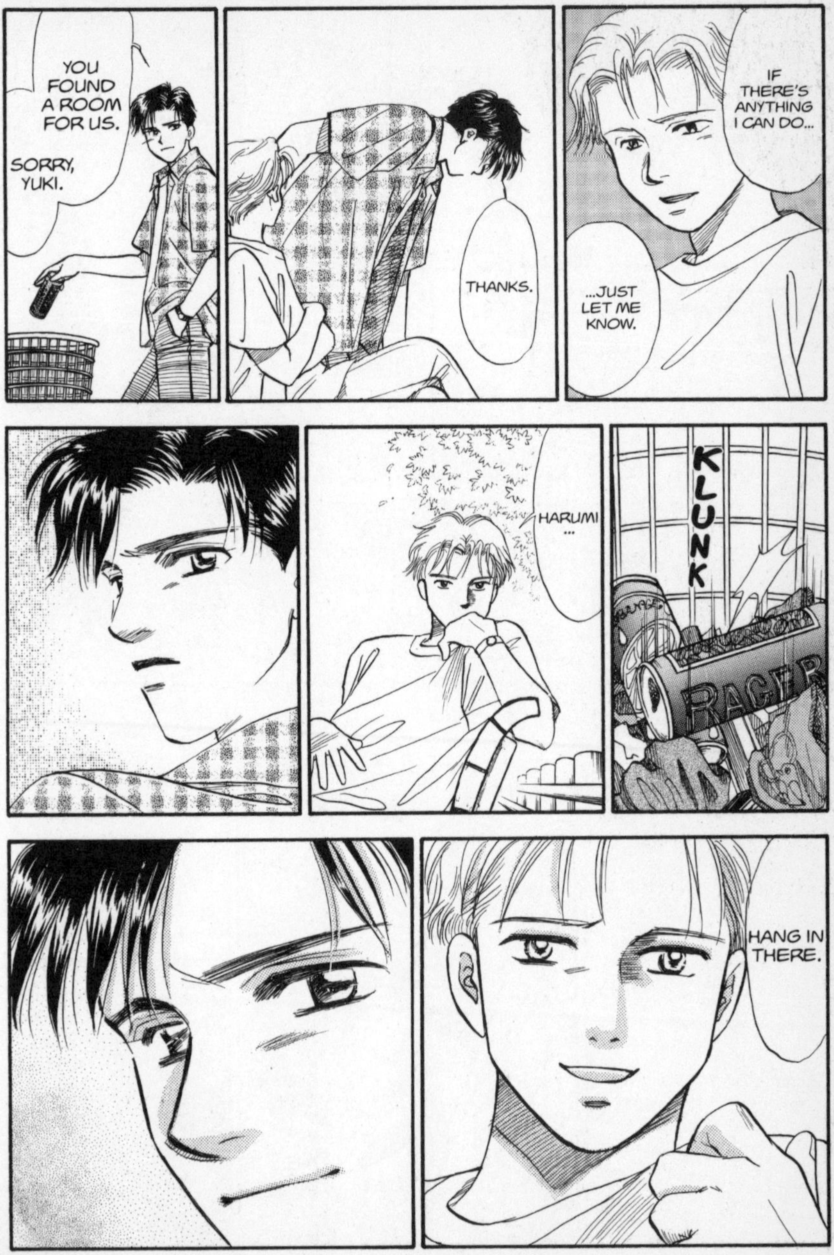
IF THERE'S ANYTHING I CAN DO...
...JUST LET ME KNOW.
THANKS.
YOU FOUND A ROOM FOR US.
SORRY, YUKI.
KLUNK
RAGER
HARUMI ...
HANG IN THERE.

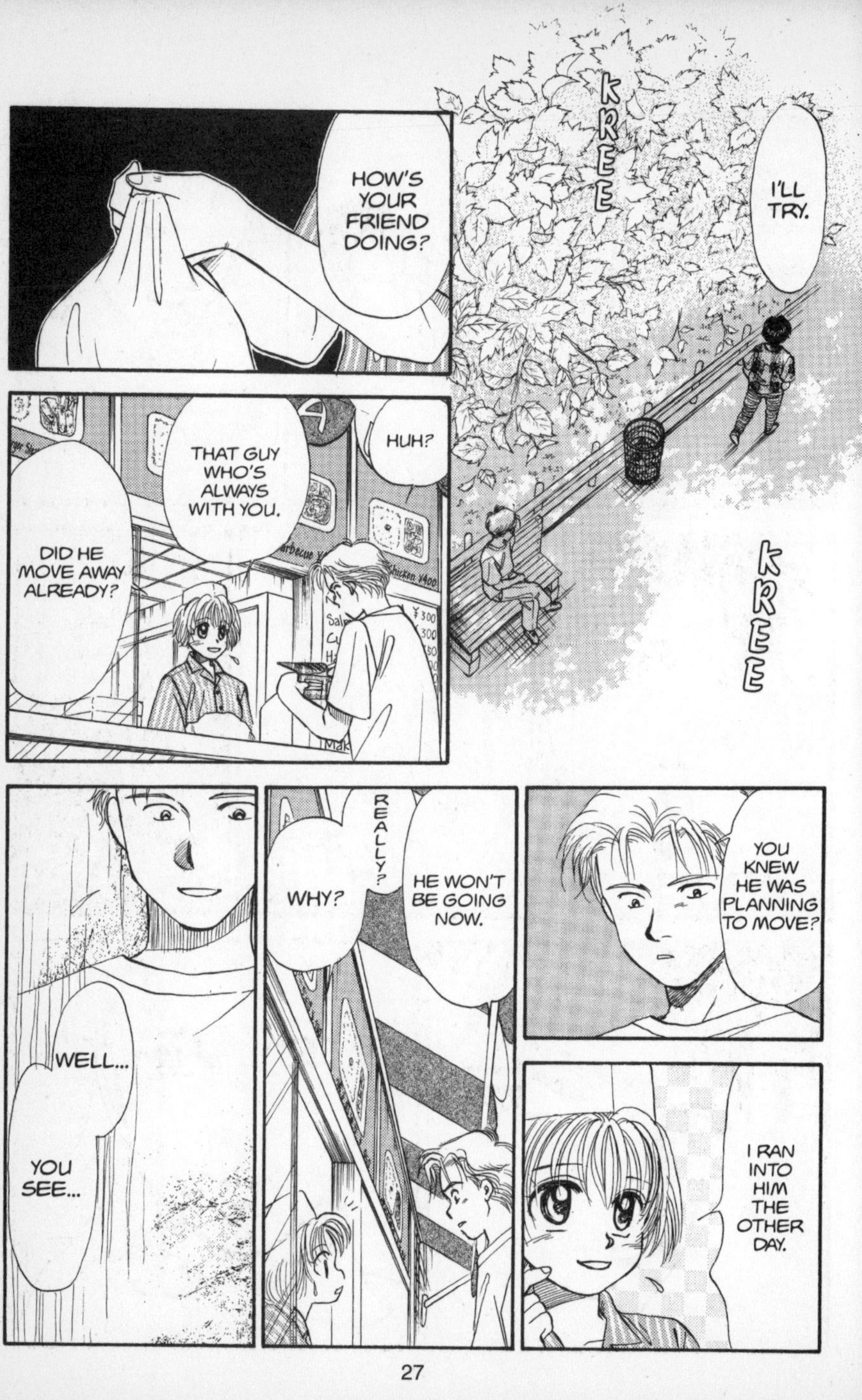
I'LL TRY.
KREE
KREE
HOW'S YOUR FRIEND DOING?
HUH?
THAT GUY WHO'S ALWAYS WITH YOU.
DID HE MOVE AWAY ALREADY?
YOU KNEW HE WAS PLANNING TO MOVE?
I RAN INTO HIM THE OTHER DAY.
HE WON'T BE GOING NOW.
REALLY?
WHY?
WELL...
YOU SEE...

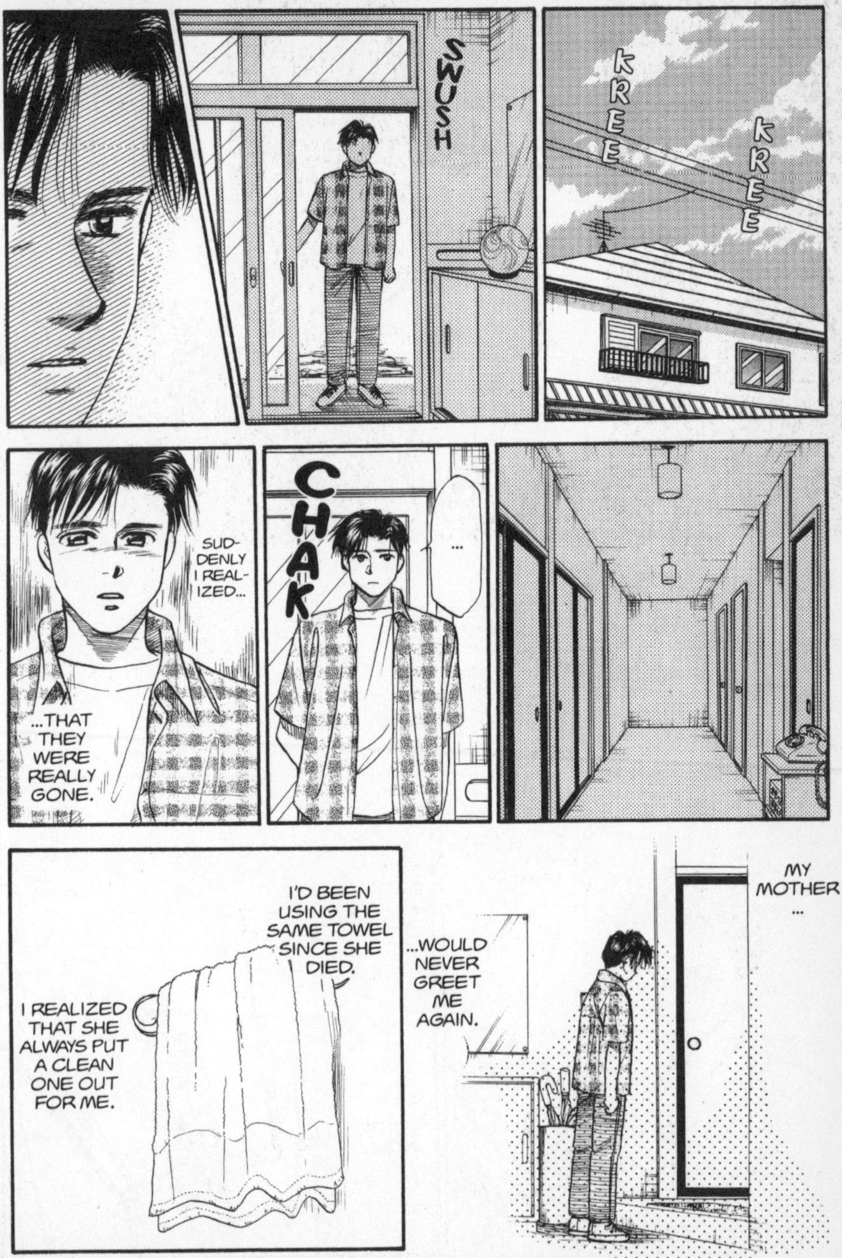
KREE
KREE
SWUSH
CHAK
...
SUDDENLY I REALIZED...
...THAT THEY WERE REALLY GONE.
MY MOTHER ...
...WOULD NEVER GREET ME AGAIN.
I'D BEEN USING THE SAME TOWEL SINCE SHE DIED.
I REALIZED THAT SHE ALWAYS PUT A CLEAN ONE OUT FOR ME.

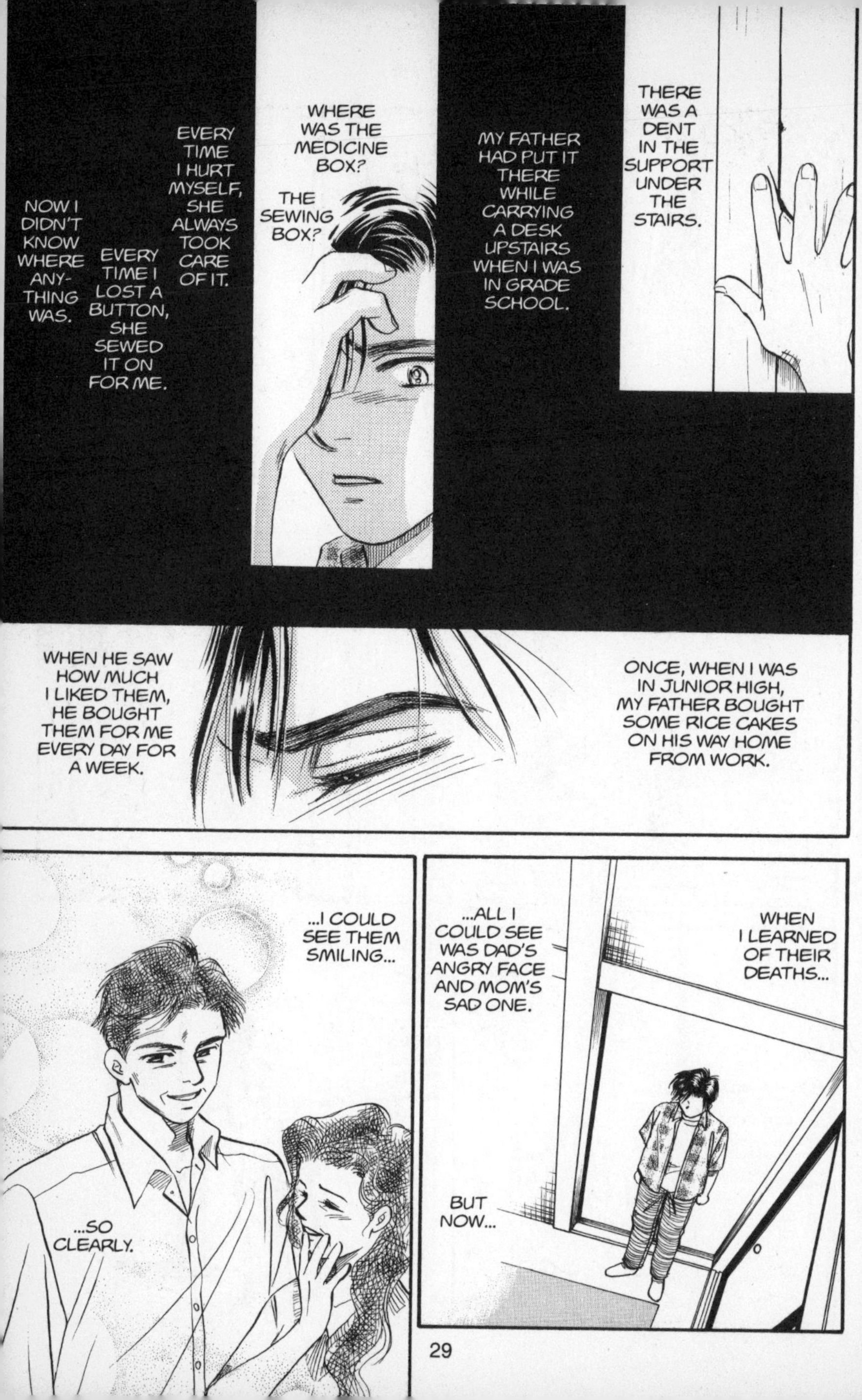
THERE WAS A DENT IN THE SUPPORT UNDER THE STAIRS.
MY FATHER HAD PUT IT THERE WHILE CARRYING A DESK UPSTAIRS WHEN I WAS IN GRADE SCHOOL.
WHERE WAS THE MEDICINE BOX?
THE SEWING BOX?
EVERY TIME I HURT MYSELF, SHE ALWAYS TOOK CARE OF IT.
EVERY TIME I LOST A BUTTON, SHE SEWED IT ON FOR ME.
NOW I DIDN'T KNOW WHERE ANY-THING WAS.
ONCE, WHEN I WAS IN JUNIOR HIGH, MY FATHER BOUGHT SOME RICE CAKES ON HIS WAY HOME FROM WORK.
WHEN HE SAW HOW MUCH I LIKED THEM, HE BOUGHT THEM FOR ME EVERY DAY FOR A WEEK.
WHEN I LEARNED OF THEIR DEATHS...
...ALL I COULD SEE WAS DAD'S ANGRY FACE AND MOM'S SAD ONE.
BUT NOW...
...I COULD SEE THEM SMILING...
...SO CLEARLY.

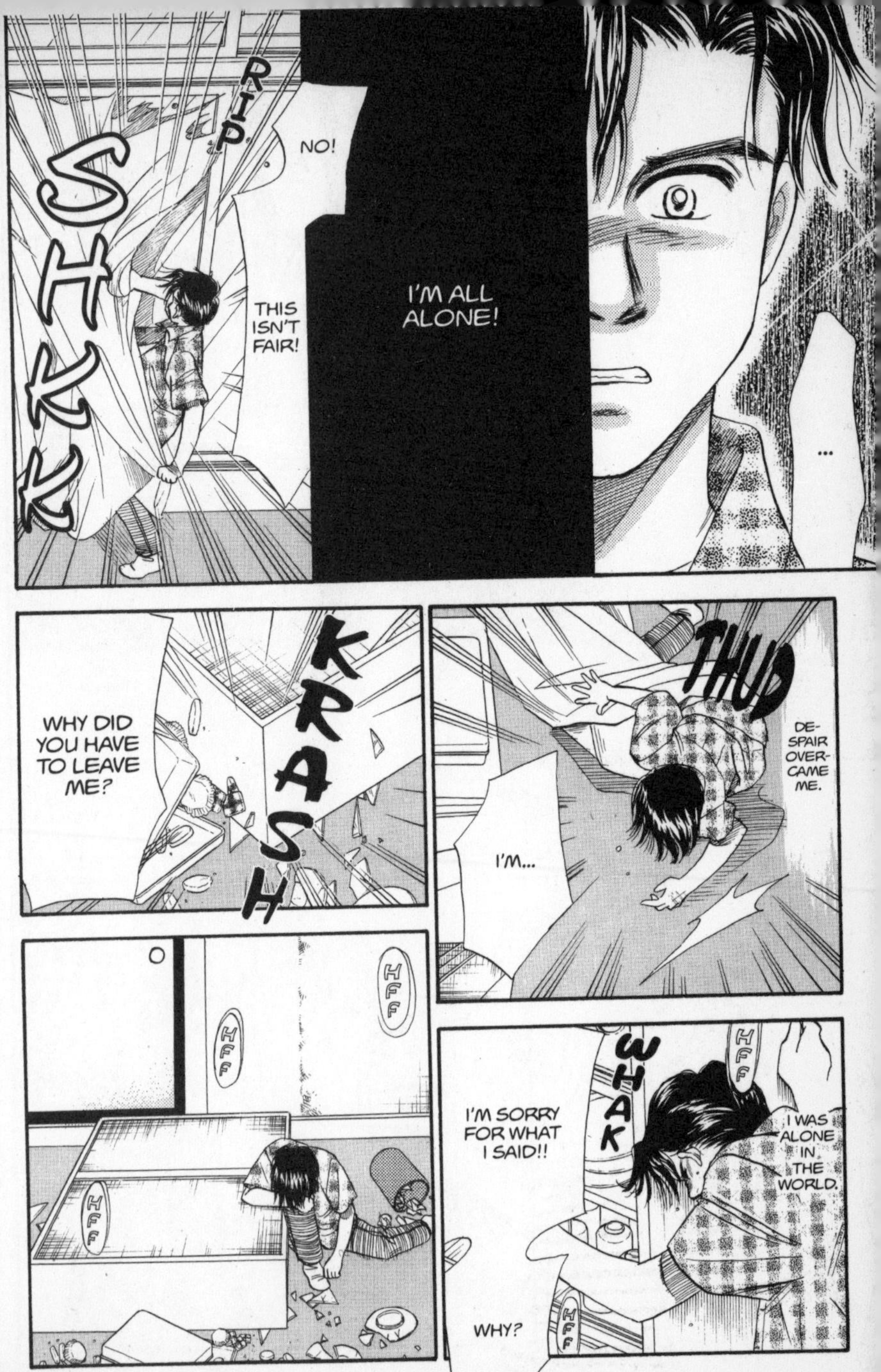
...
I'M ALL ALONE!
RIP
NO!
THIS ISN'T FAIR!
SHKKK
THUD
DE-SPAIR OVER-CAME ME.
I'M...
KRASH
WHY DID YOU HAVE TO LEAVE ME?
WHAK
HFF
I WAS ALONE IN THE WORLD.
I'M SORRY FOR WHAT I SAID!!
HFF
WHY?
HFF
HFF
HFF

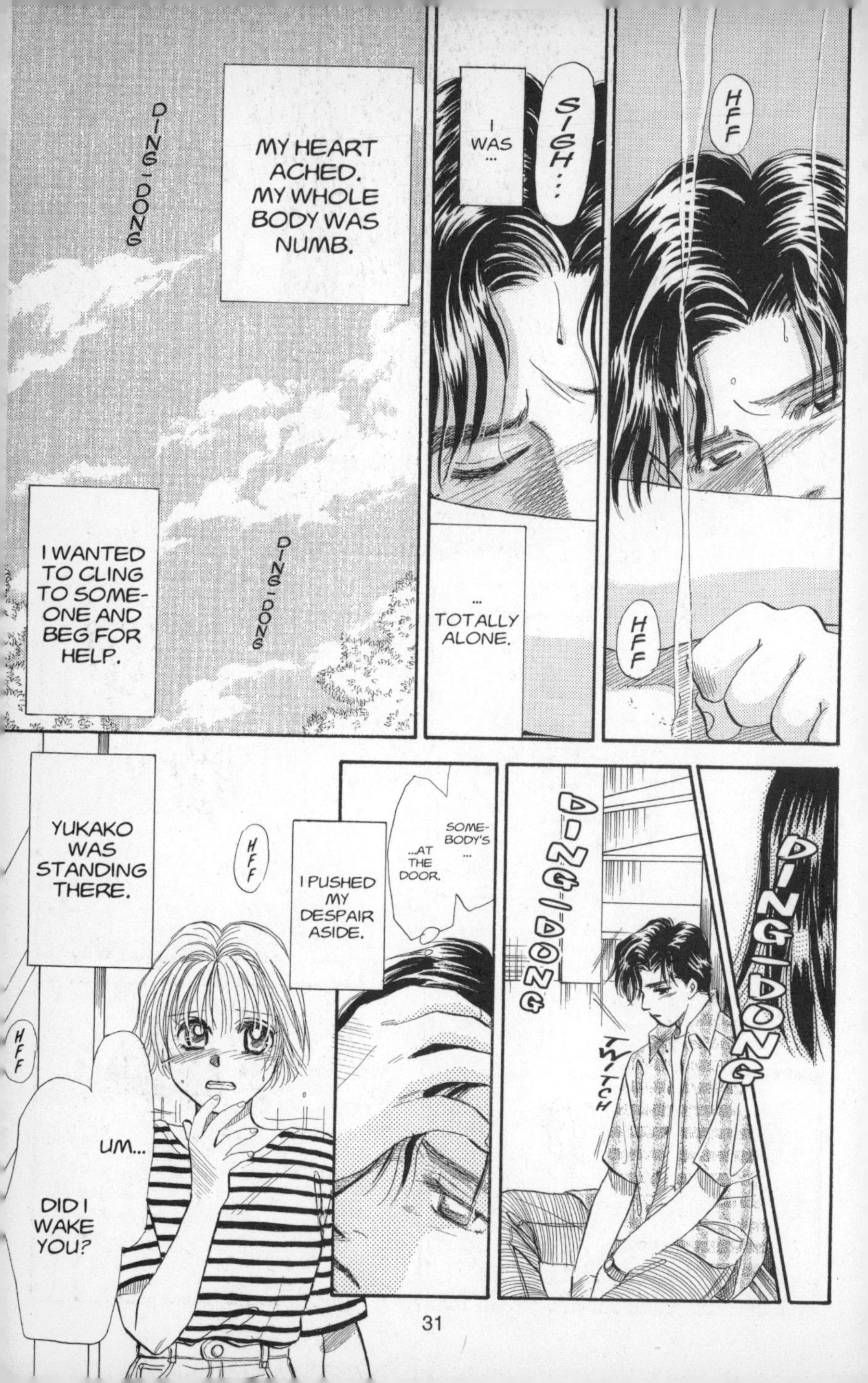
HFF
HFF
SIGH...
I WAS...
... TOTALLY ALONE.
MY HEART ACHED. MY WHOLE BODY WAS NUMB.
DING-DONG
I WANTED TO CLING TO SOME-ONE AND BEG FOR HELP.
DING-DONG
DING-DONG
DING-DONG
TWITCH
SOME-BODY'S...
...AT THE DOOR.
I PUSHED MY DESPAIR ASIDE.
YUKAKO WAS STANDING THERE.
HFF
HFF
UM...
DID I WAKE YOU?

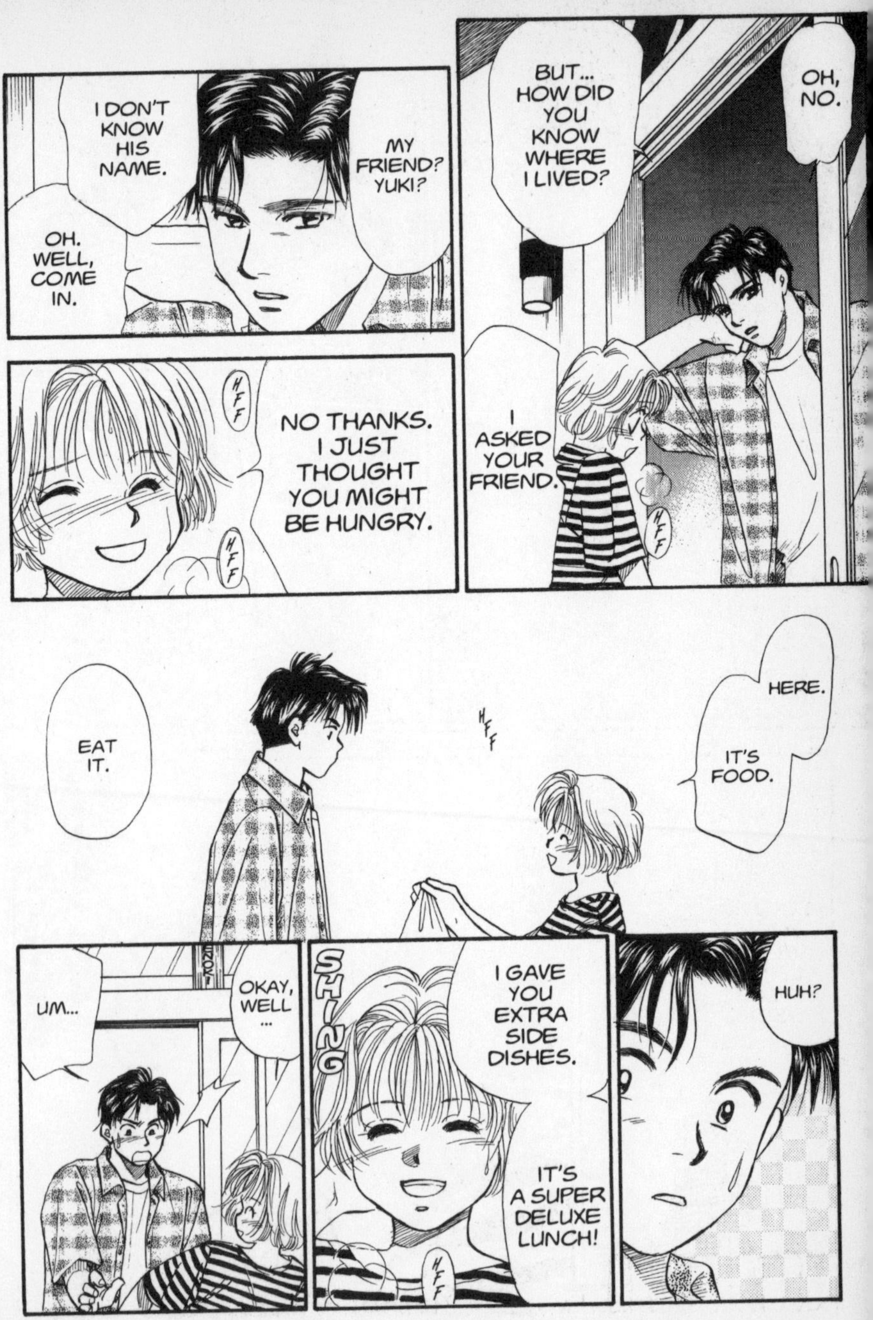
OH, NO.
BUT... HOW DID YOU KNOW WHERE I LIVED?
I ASKED YOUR FRIEND.
HFF
MY FRIEND? YUKI?
I DON'T KNOW HIS NAME.
OH. WELL, COME IN.
HFF
NO THANKS. I JUST THOUGHT YOU MIGHT BE HUNGRY.
HFF
HERE.
IT'S FOOD.
HFF
EAT IT.
HUH?
I GAVE YOU EXTRA SIDE DISHES.
SHING
IT'S A SUPER DELUXE LUNCH!
HFF
OKAY, WELL ...
UM...

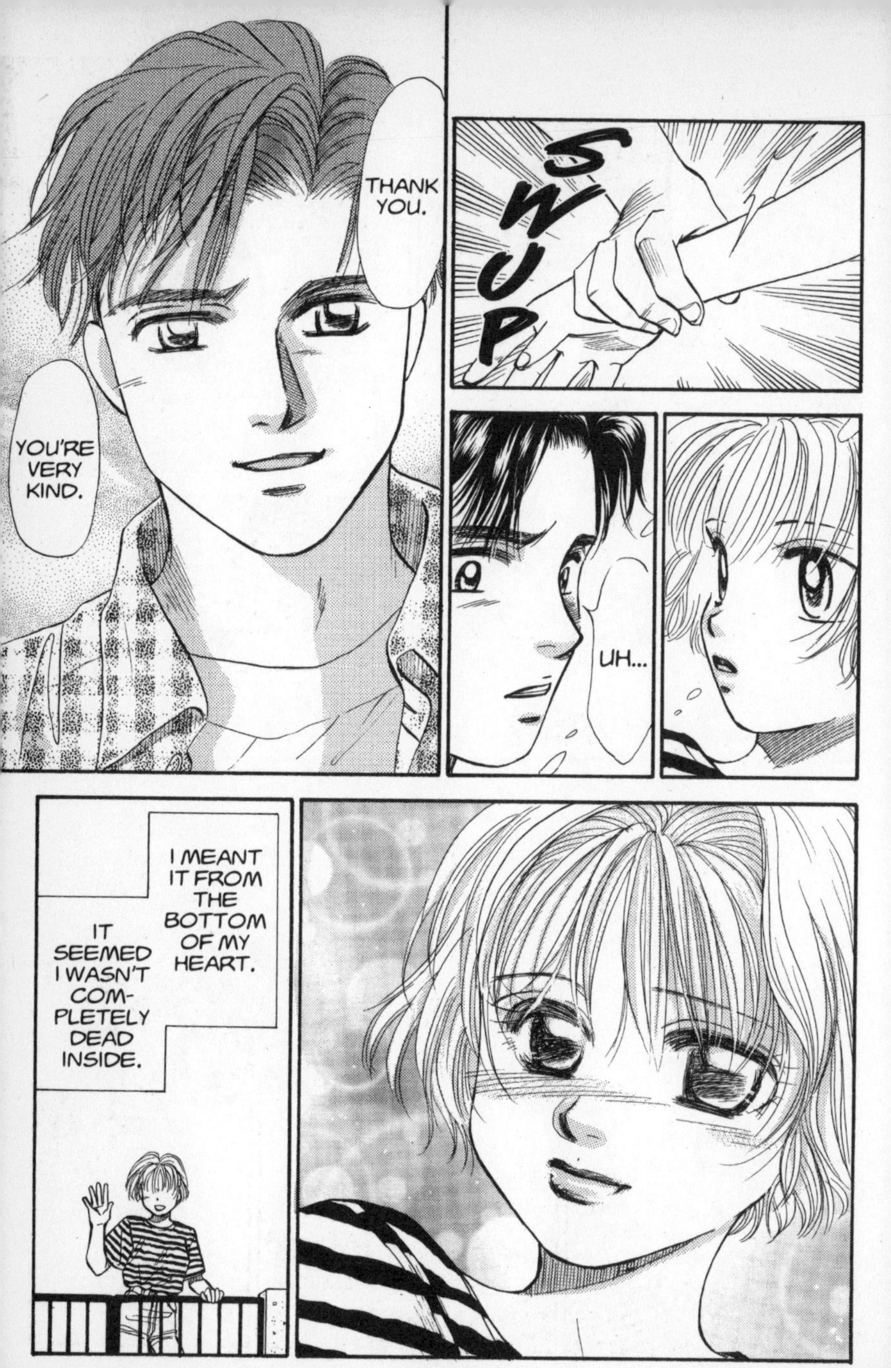
SWUP
UH...
THANK YOU.
YOU'RE VERY KIND.
I MEANT IT FROM THE BOTTOM OF MY HEART.
IT SEEMED I WASN'T COMPLETELY DEAD INSIDE.

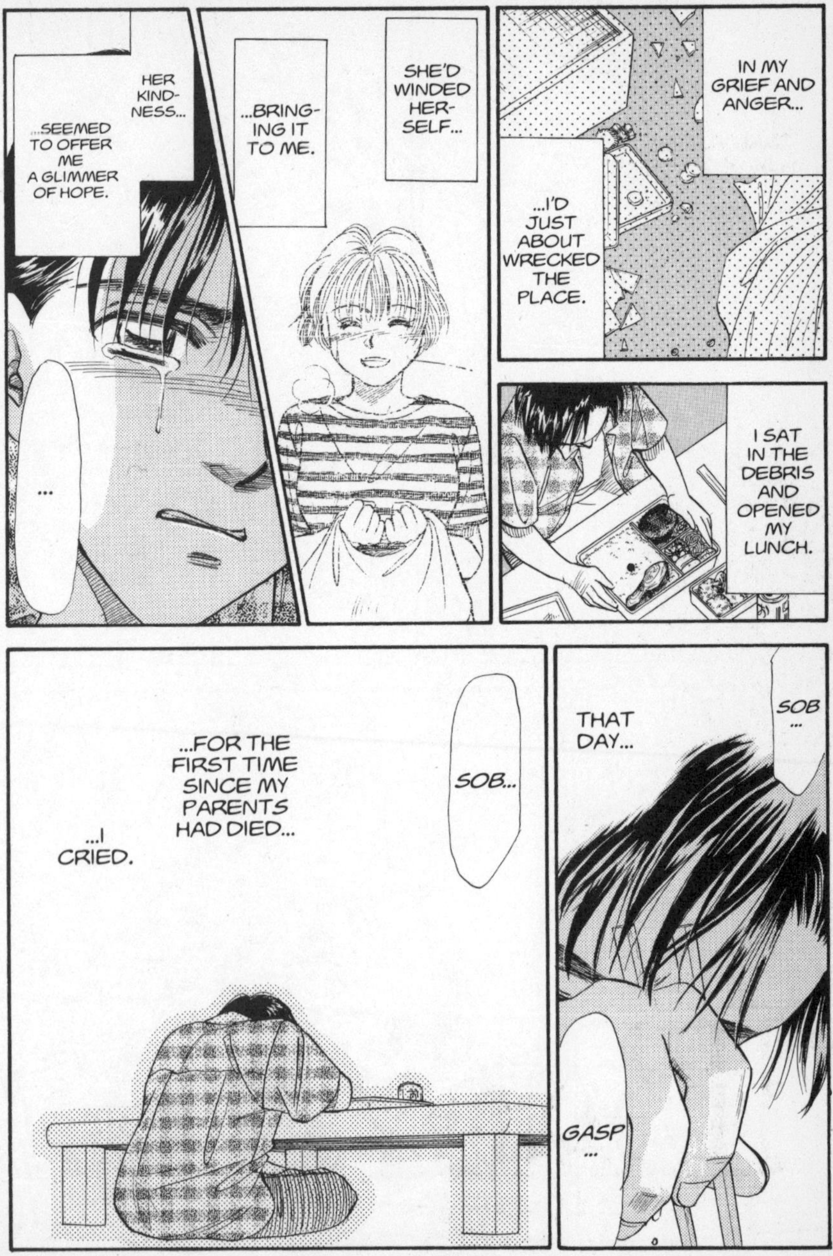
IN MY GRIEF AND ANGER...
...I'D JUST ABOUT WRECKED THE PLACE.
I SAT IN THE DEBRIS AND OPENED MY LUNCH.
SHE'D WINDED HERSELF...
...BRINGING IT TO ME.
HER KINDNESS...
...SEEMED TO OFFER ME A GLIMMER OF HOPE.
...
SOB...
THAT DAY...
GASP...
SOB...
...FOR THE FIRST TIME SINCE MY PARENTS HAD DIED...
...I CRIED.

Chapter 69 / The End

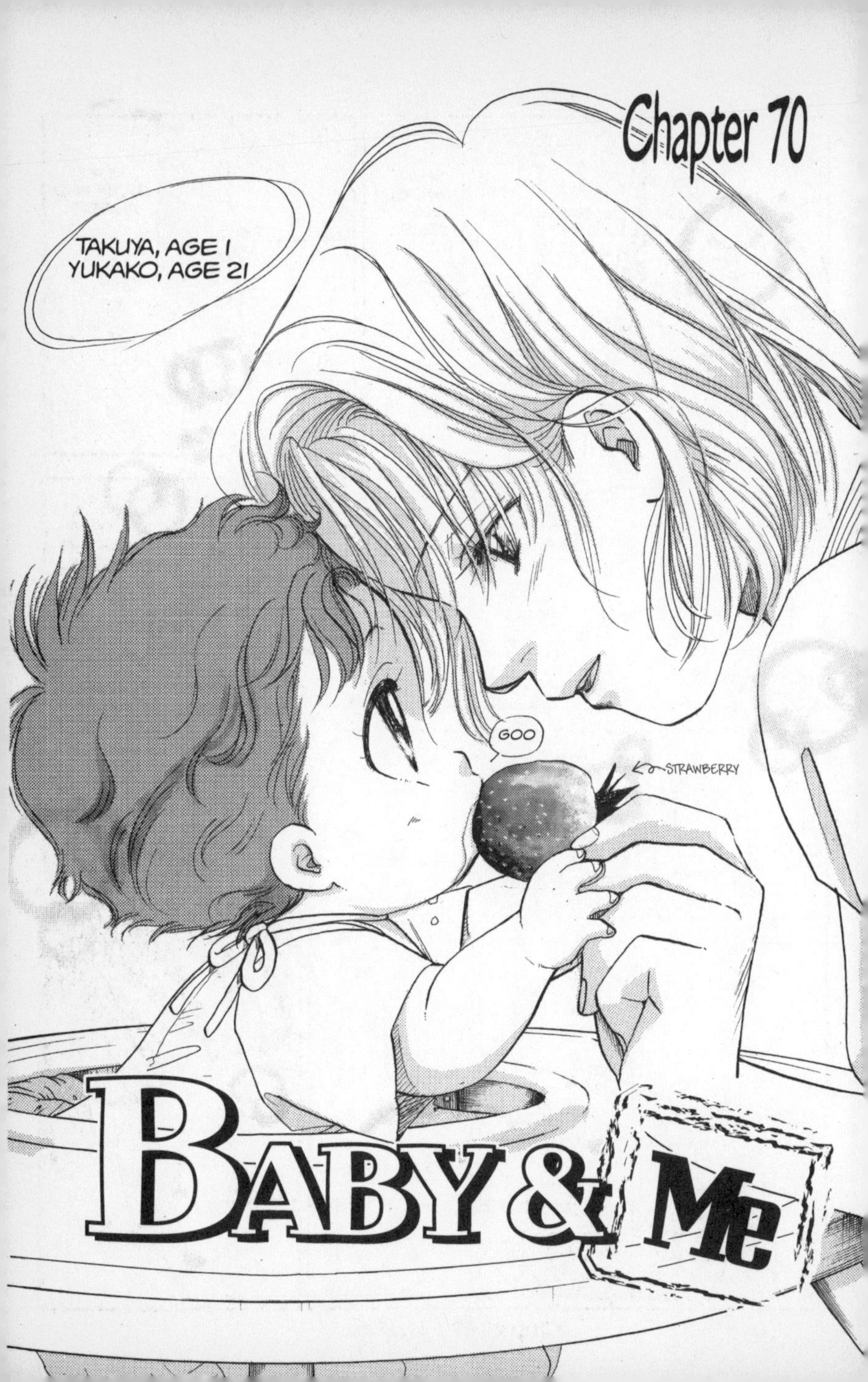
Chapter 70
TAKUYA, AGE 1
YUKAKO, AGE 21
GOO
STRAWBERRY
BABY & Me

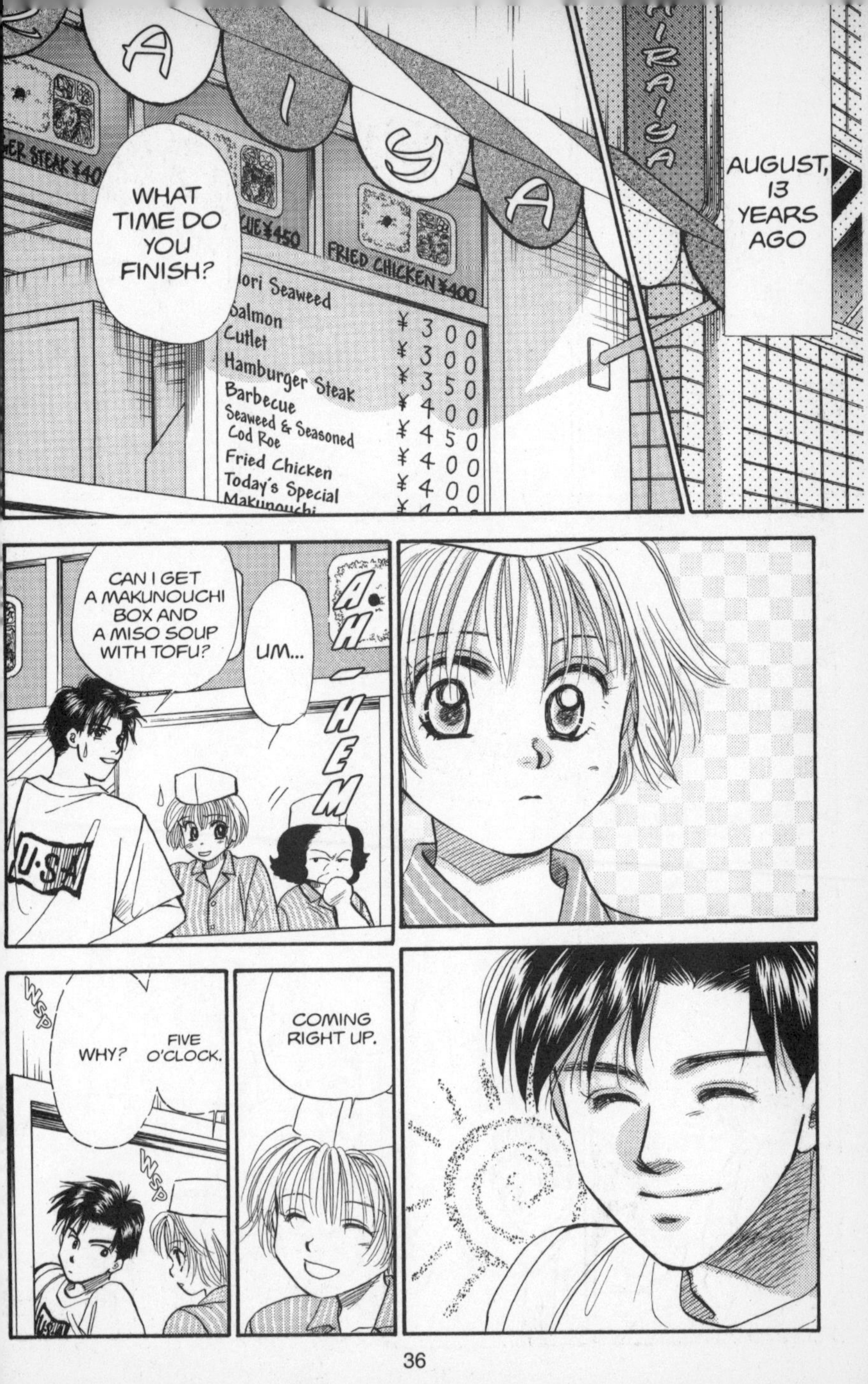
AUGUST, 13 YEARS AGO
A I Y A
FRIED CHICKEN ¥400
WHAT TIME DO YOU FINISH?
Salmon ¥300
Cutlet ¥300
Hamburger Steak ¥350
Barbecue ¥400
Seaweed & Seasoned Cod Roe ¥450
Fried Chicken ¥400
Today's Special ¥400
UM...
AH-HEM
CAN I GET A MAKUNOUCHI BOX AND A MISO SOUP WITH TOFU?
COMING RIGHT UP.
FIVE O'CLOCK.
WHY?
WSP
WSP

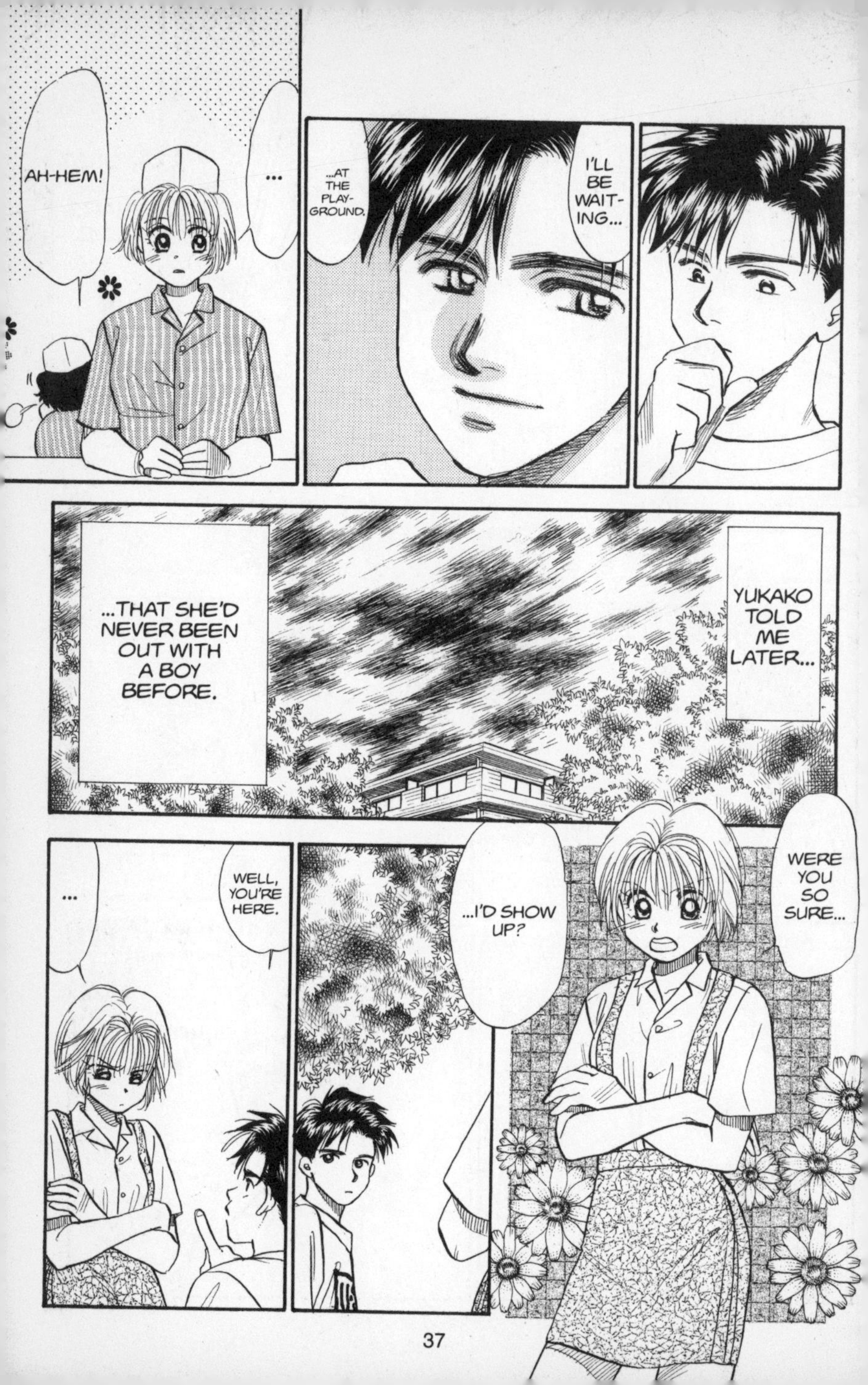
I'LL BE WAITING...
...AT THE PLAYGROUND.
...
AH-HEM!
YUKAKO TOLD ME LATER...
...THAT SHE'D NEVER BEEN OUT WITH A BOY BEFORE.
WERE YOU SO SURE...
...I'D SHOW UP?
WELL, YOU'RE HERE.
...

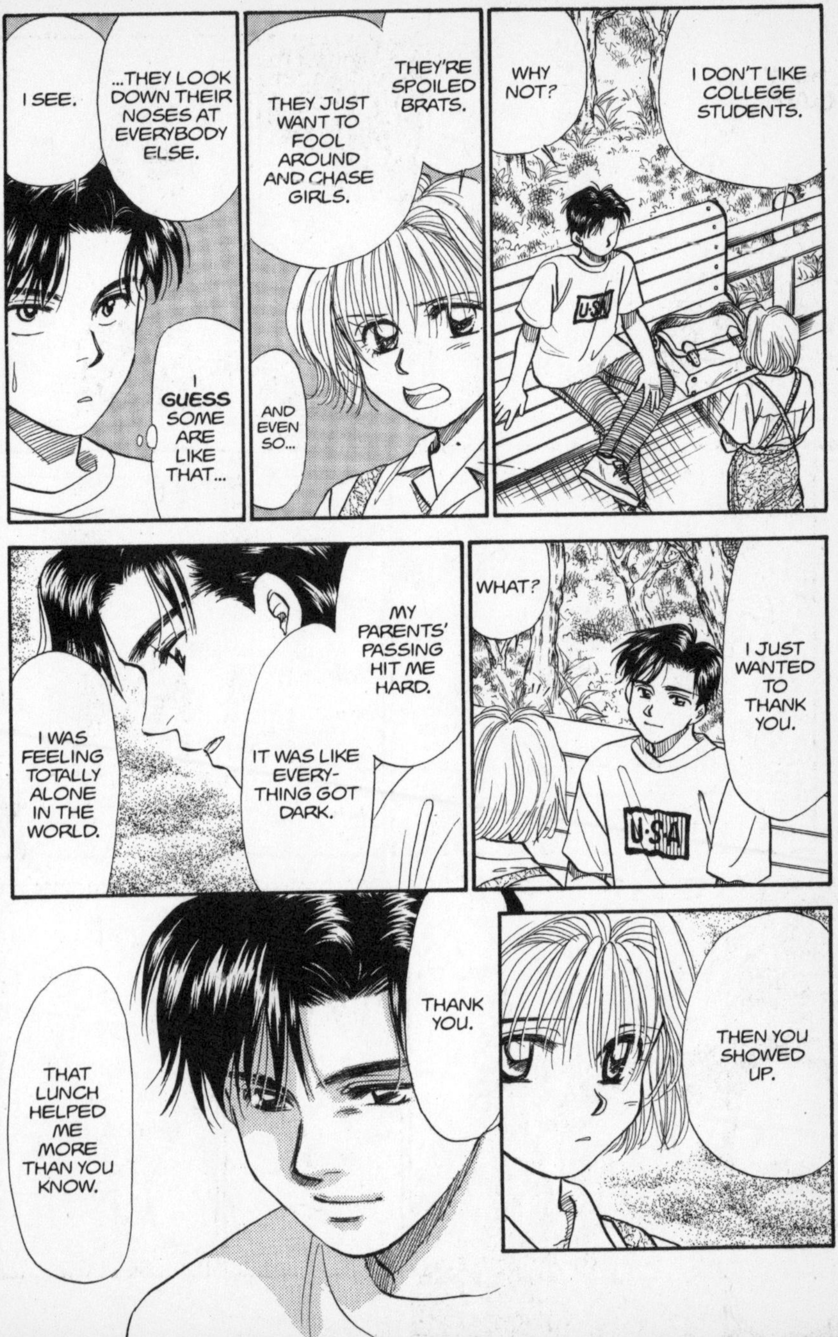
I DON'T LIKE COLLEGE STUDENTS.
WHY NOT?
THEY'RE SPOILED BRATS.
THEY JUST WANT TO FOOL AROUND AND CHASE GIRLS.
AND EVEN SO...
...THEY LOOK DOWN THEIR NOSES AT EVERYBODY ELSE.
I SEE.
I GUESS SOME ARE LIKE THAT...
I JUST WANTED TO THANK YOU.
WHAT?
MY PARENTS' PASSING HIT ME HARD.
IT WAS LIKE EVERY-THING GOT DARK.
I WAS FEELING TOTALLY ALONE IN THE WORLD.
THEN YOU SHOWED UP.
THANK YOU.
THAT LUNCH HELPED ME MORE THAN YOU KNOW.

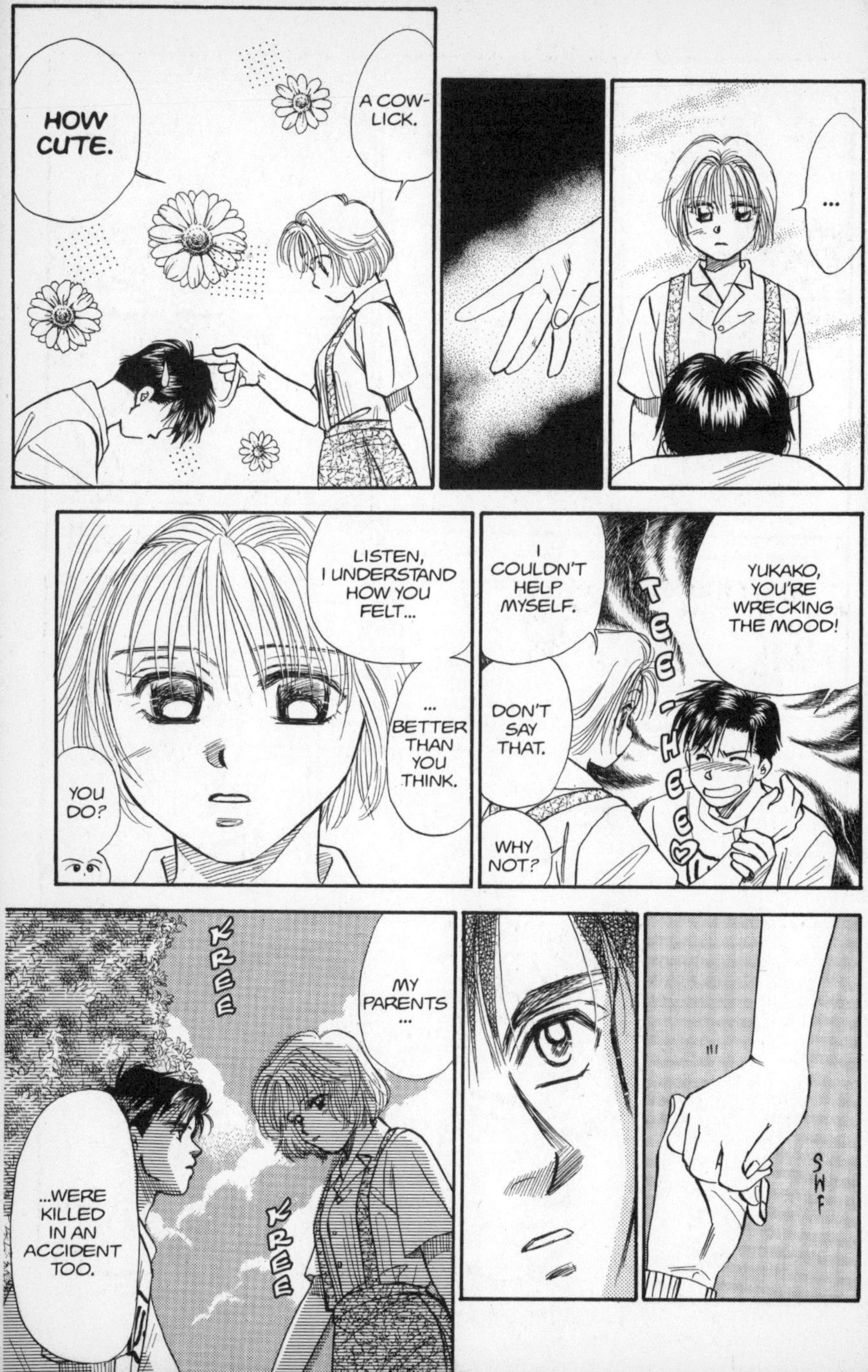
...
A COW-LICK.
HOW CUTE.
YUKAKO, YOU'RE WRECKING THE MOOD!
TEE-HEE-HEE♡
I COULDN'T HELP MYSELF.
DON'T SAY THAT.
WHY NOT?
LISTEN, I UNDERSTAND HOW YOU FELT...
...BETTER THAN YOU THINK.
YOU DO?
!!!
SWF
MY PARENTS...
KREE
KREE
...WERE KILLED IN AN ACCIDENT TOO.

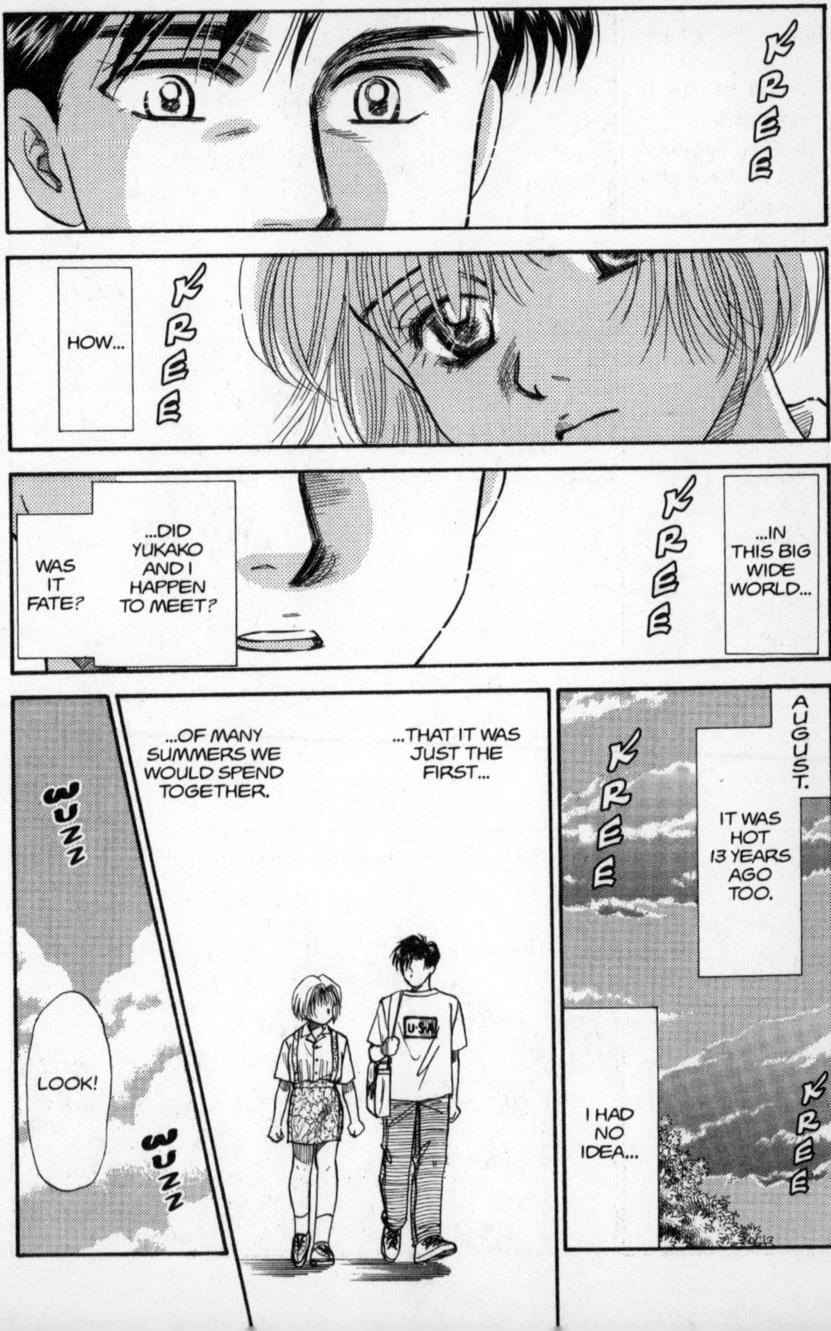
KREE
KREE
HOW...
...IN THIS BIG WIDE WORLD...
KREE
...DID YUKAKO AND I HAPPEN TO MEET?
WAS IT FATE?
AUGUST.
IT WAS HOT 13 YEARS AGO TOO.
KREE
KREE
I HAD NO IDEA...
...THAT IT WAS JUST THE FIRST...
...OF MANY SUMMERS WE WOULD SPEND TOGETHER.
WUZZ
LOOK!
WUZZ

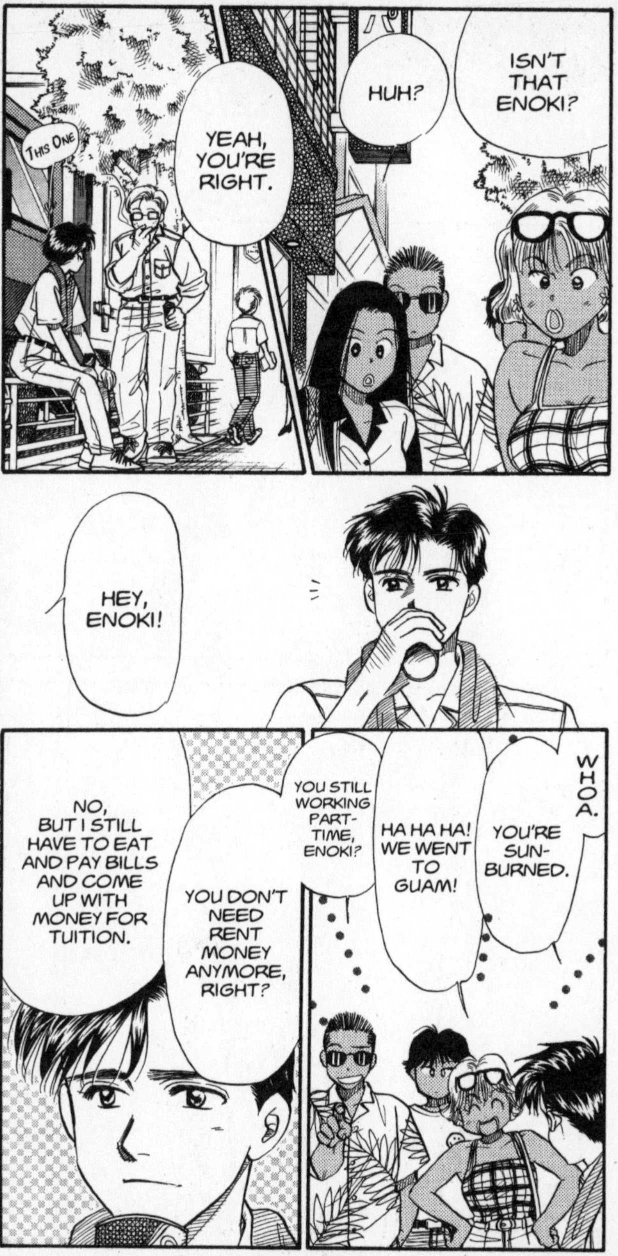
ISN'T THAT ENOKI?
HUH?
YEAH, YOU'RE RIGHT.
THIS ONE
HEY, ENOKI!
WHOA.
YOU'RE SUN-BURNED.
HA HA HA! WE WENT TO GUAM!
YOU STILL WORKING PART-TIME, ENOKI?
YOU DON'T NEED RENT MONEY ANYMORE, RIGHT?
NO, BUT I STILL HAVE TO EAT AND PAY BILLS AND COME UP WITH MONEY FOR TUITION.

Author's Note Part 2

Out of the blue, right here... Marimo Ragawa's Let Me Draw What I Want! By Request

Can you tell I can't think of anything to write about?

Attack of the Girl Clothes! Disguise #1: Takuya Enoki in a Pink House outfit

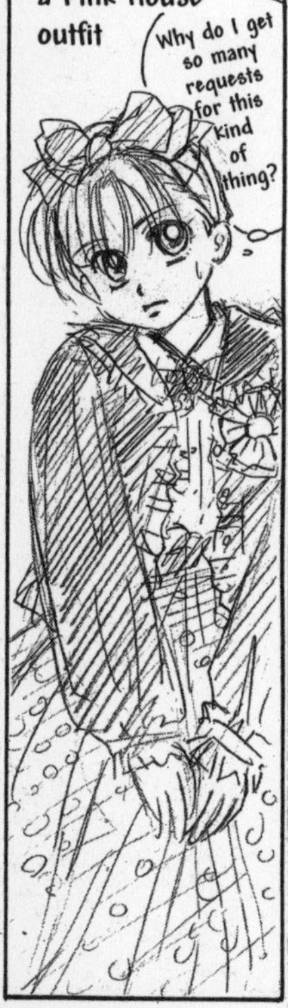
Why do I get so many requests for this kind of thing?

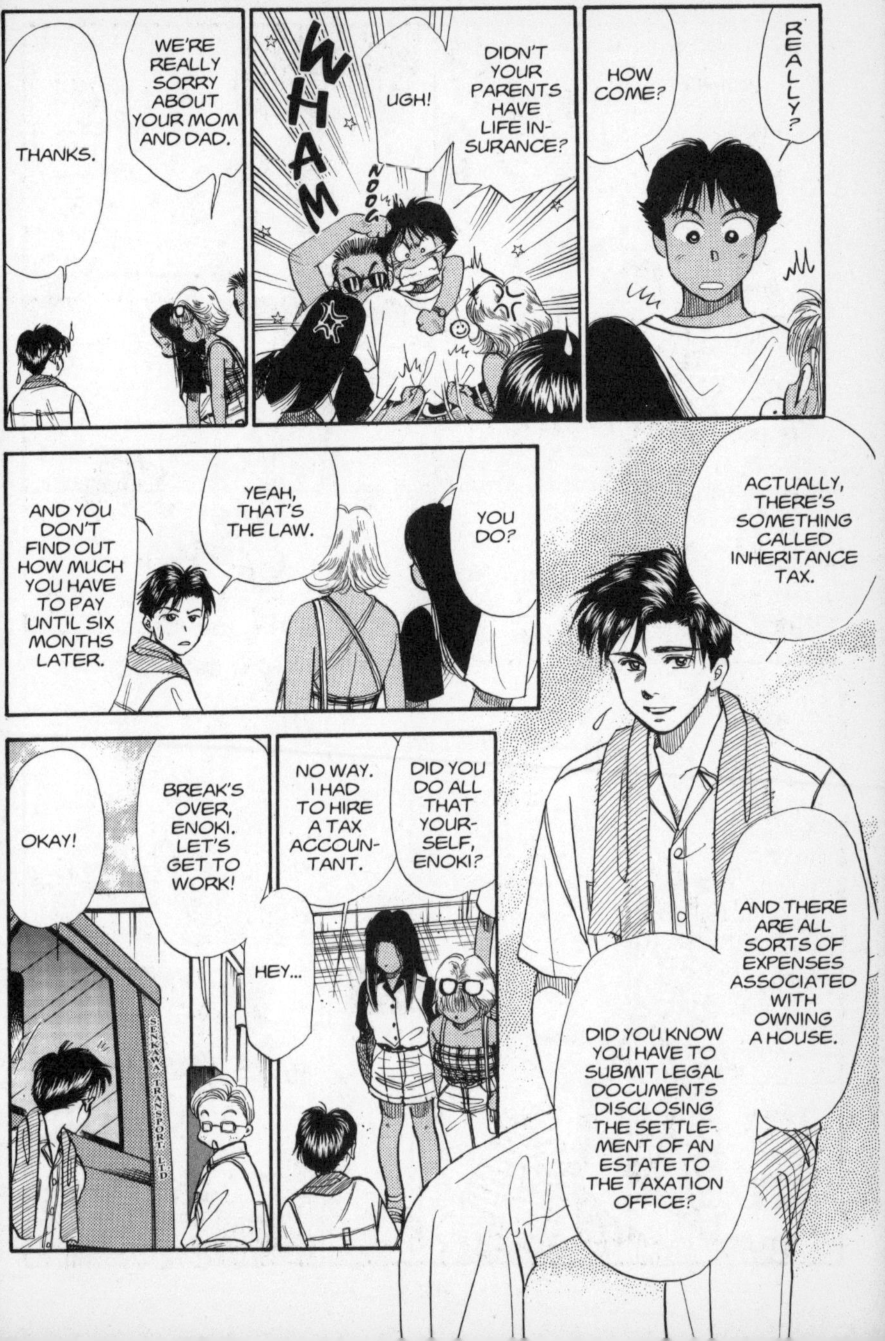
REALLY?
HOW COME?
DIDN'T YOUR PARENTS HAVE LIFE INSURANCE?
UGH!
WHAM
NOOG
WE'RE REALLY SORRY ABOUT YOUR MOM AND DAD.
THANKS.
ACTUALLY, THERE'S SOMETHING CALLED INHERITANCE TAX.
AND THERE ARE ALL SORTS OF EXPENSES ASSOCIATED WITH OWNING A HOUSE.
DID YOU KNOW YOU HAVE TO SUBMIT LEGAL DOCUMENTS DISCLOSING THE SETTLEMENT OF AN ESTATE TO THE TAXATION OFFICE?
YOU DO?
YEAH, THAT'S THE LAW.
AND YOU DON'T FIND OUT HOW MUCH YOU HAVE TO PAY UNTIL SIX MONTHS LATER.
DID YOU DO ALL THAT YOURSELF, ENOKI?
NO WAY. I HAD TO HIRE A TAX ACCOUNTANT.
HEY...
BREAK'S OVER, ENOKI. LET'S GET TO WORK!
OKAY!
SENKAWA TRANSPORT, LTD

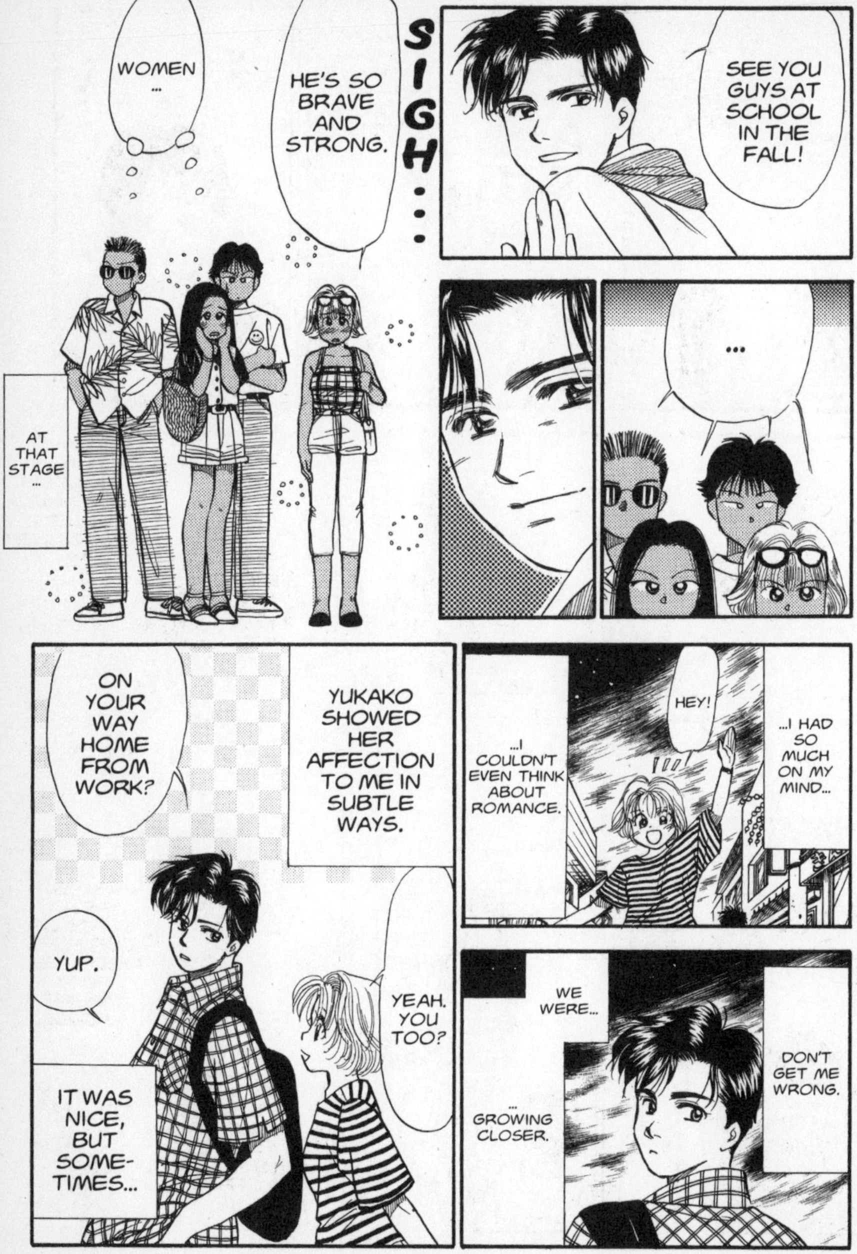
SEE YOU GUYS AT SCHOOL IN THE FALL!
...
SIGH...
HE'S SO BRAVE AND STRONG.
WOMEN...
AT THAT STAGE...
...I HAD SO MUCH ON MY MIND...
HEY!
...I COULDN'T EVEN THINK ABOUT ROMANCE.
WE WERE...
DON'T GET ME WRONG.
...GROWING CLOSER.
YUKAKO SHOWED HER AFFECTION TO ME IN SUBTLE WAYS.
ON YOUR WAY HOME FROM WORK?
YEAH. YOU TOO?
YUP.
IT WAS NICE, BUT SOMETIMES...

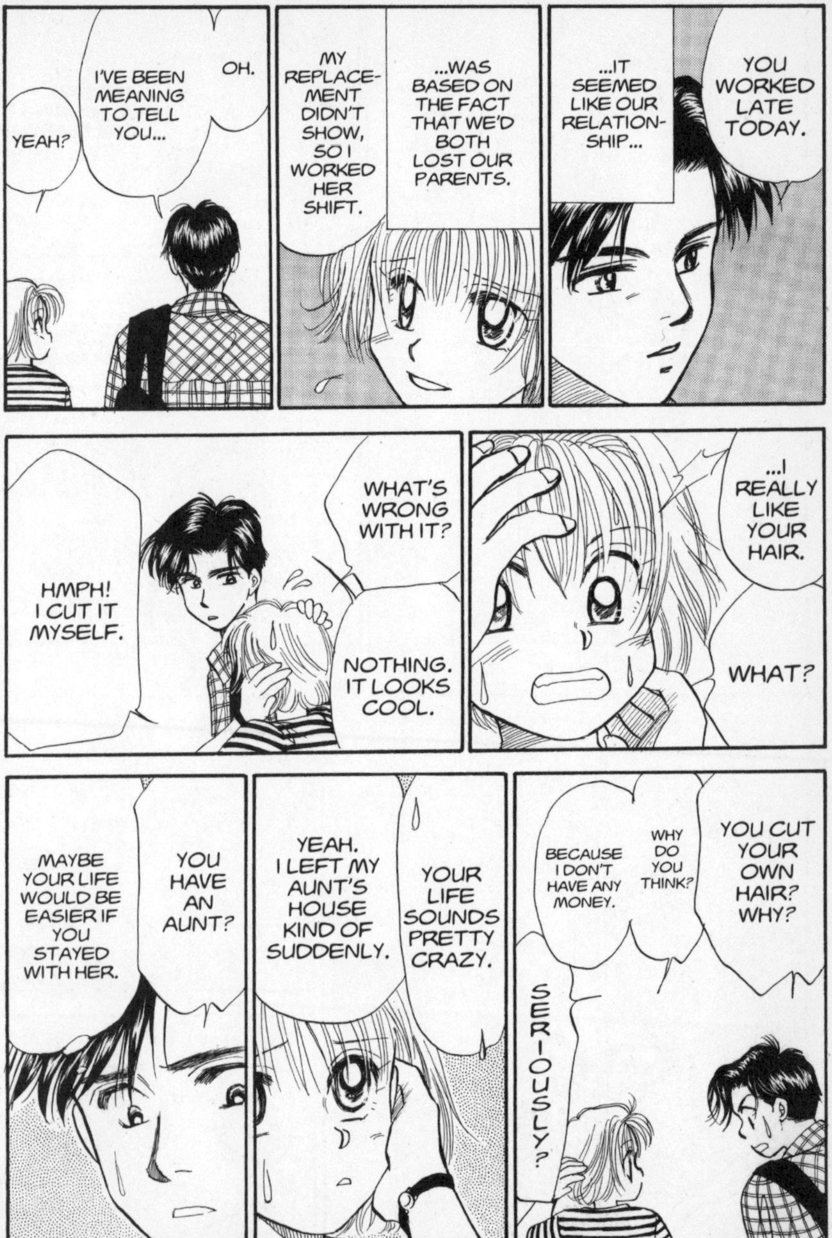
YOU WORKED LATE TODAY.
...IT SEEMED LIKE OUR RELATIONSHIP...
...WAS BASED ON THE FACT THAT WE'D BOTH LOST OUR PARENTS.
MY REPLACEMENT DIDN'T SHOW, SO I WORKED HER SHIFT.
OH.
I'VE BEEN MEANING TO TELL YOU...
YEAH?
...I REALLY LIKE YOUR HAIR.
WHAT?
WHAT'S WRONG WITH IT?
NOTHING. IT LOOKS COOL.
HMPH! I CUT IT MYSELF.
YOU CUT YOUR OWN HAIR? WHY?
WHY DO YOU THINK?
BECAUSE I DON'T HAVE ANY MONEY.
SERIOUSLY?
YOUR LIFE SOUNDS PRETTY CRAZY.
YEAH. I LEFT MY AUNT'S HOUSE KIND OF SUDDENLY.
YOU HAVE AN AUNT?
MAYBE YOUR LIFE WOULD BE EASIER IF YOU STAYED WITH HER.

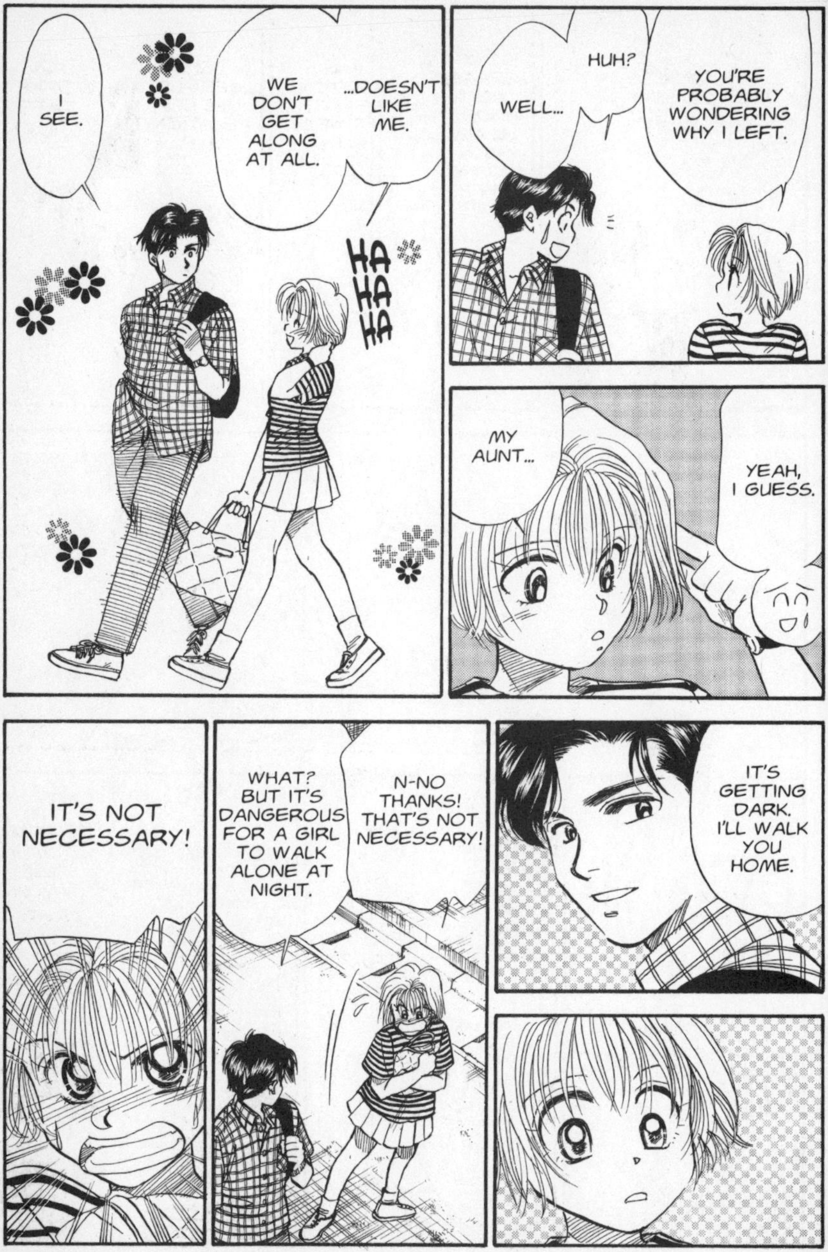
YOU'RE PROBABLY WONDERING WHY I LEFT.
HUH?
WELL...
YEAH, I GUESS.
MY AUNT...
...DOESN'T LIKE ME.
WE DON'T GET ALONG AT ALL.
HA HA HA
I SEE.
IT'S GETTING DARK. I'LL WALK YOU HOME.
N-NO THANKS! THAT'S NOT NECESSARY!
WHAT? BUT IT'S DANGEROUS FOR A GIRL TO WALK ALONE AT NIGHT.
IT'S NOT NECESSARY!

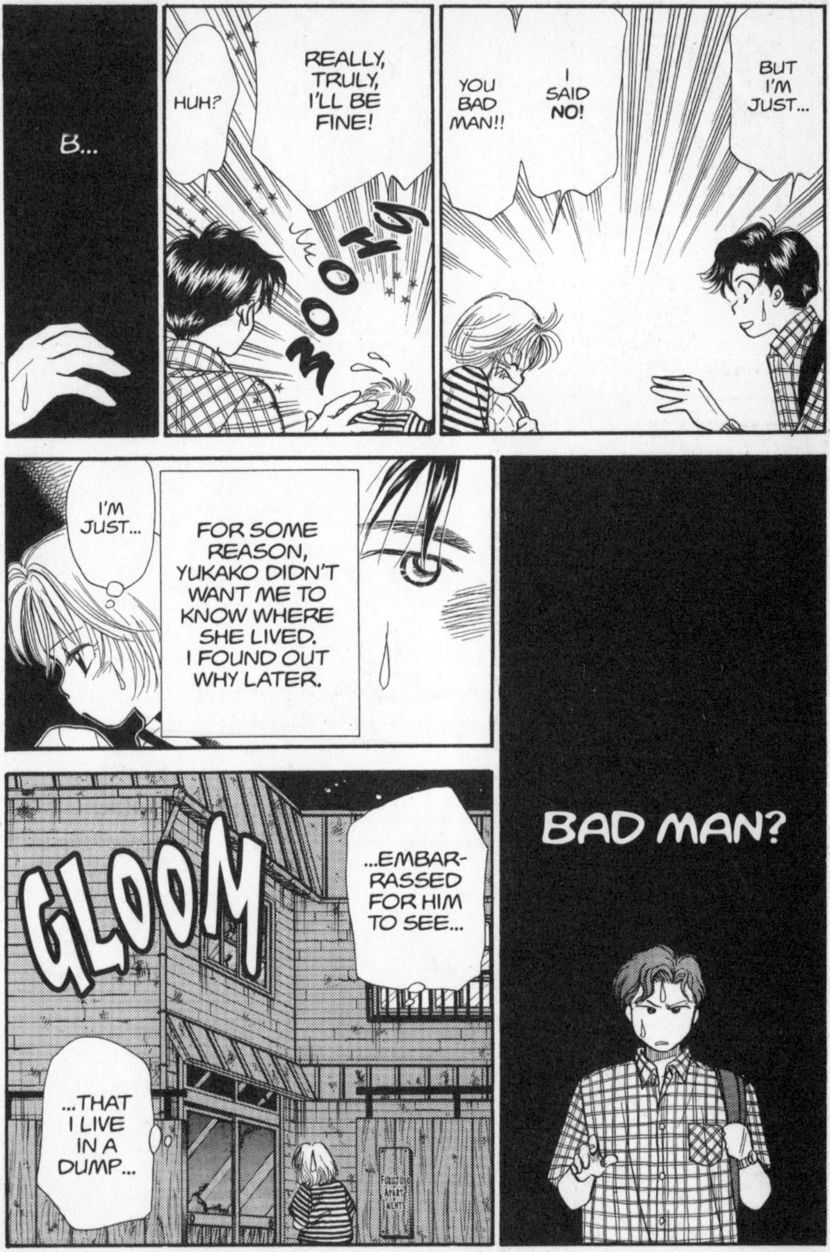
BUT I'M JUST...
I SAID NO!
YOU BAD MAN!!
REALLY, TRULY, I'LL BE FINE!
HUH?
SHOOM
B...
BAD MAN?
FOR SOME REASON, YUKAKO DIDN'T WANT ME TO KNOW WHERE SHE LIVED. I FOUND OUT WHY LATER.
I'M JUST...
...EMBAR-RASSED FOR HIM TO SEE...
GLOOM
...THAT I LIVE IN A DUMP...

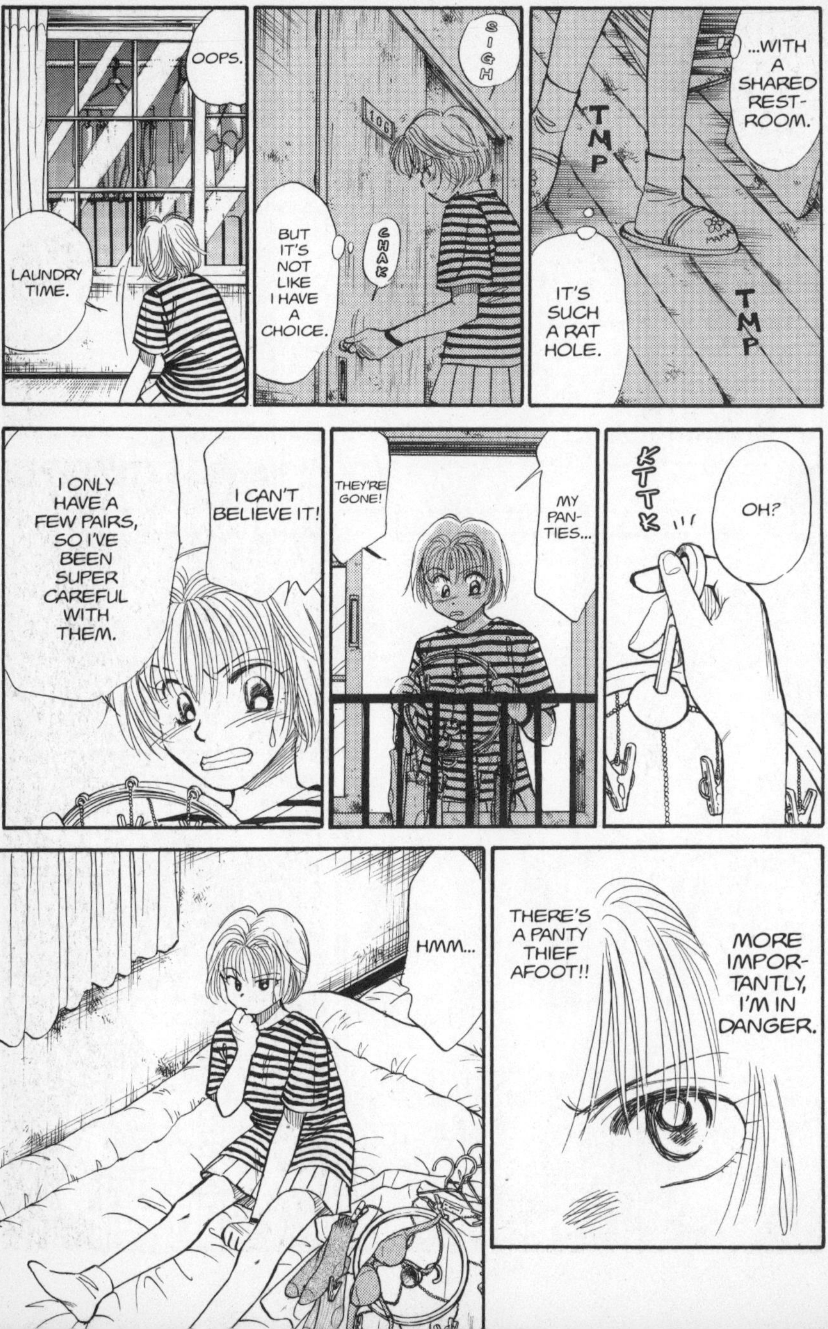
...WITH A SHARED REST-ROOM.
TMP
TMP
IT'S SUCH A RAT HOLE.
SIGH
CHAK
BUT IT'S NOT LIKE I HAVE A CHOICE.
OOPS.
LAUNDRY TIME.
KTTK
OH?
MY PAN-TIES...
THEY'RE GONE!
I CAN'T BELIEVE IT!
I ONLY HAVE A FEW PAIRS, SO I'VE BEEN SUPER CAREFUL WITH THEM.
MORE IMPOR-TANTLY, I'M IN DANGER.
THERE'S A PANTY THIEF AFOOT!!
HMM...

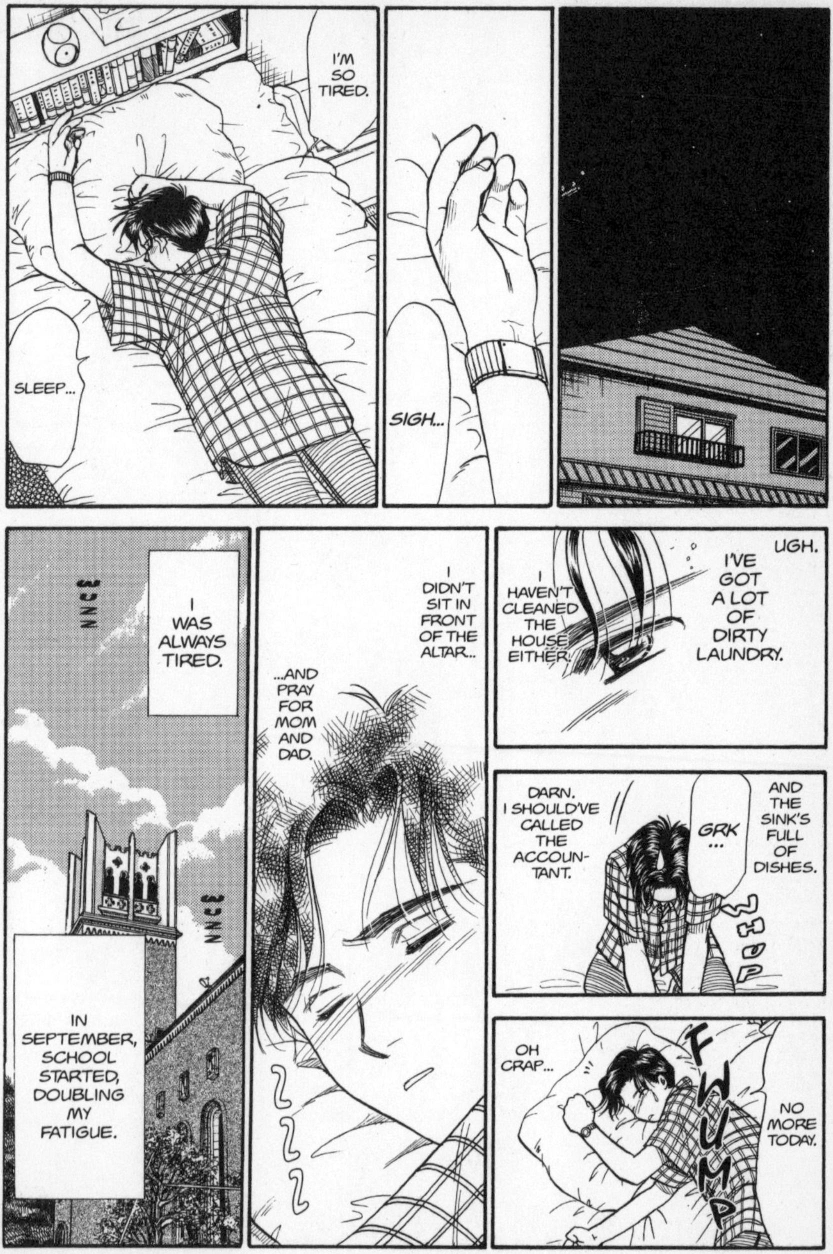
SIGH...
I'M SO TIRED.
SLEEP...
UGH.
I'VE GOT A LOT OF DIRTY LAUNDRY.
I HAVEN'T CLEANED THE HOUSE EITHER.
AND THE SINK'S FULL OF DISHES.
GRK...
DARN. I SHOULD'VE CALLED THE ACCOUNTANT.
WHUP
FWUMP
NO MORE TODAY.
OH CRAP...
I DIDN'T SIT IN FRONT OF THE ALTAR...
...AND PRAY FOR MOM AND DAD.
Z Z Z
I WAS ALWAYS TIRED.
IN SEPTEMBER, SCHOOL STARTED, DOUBLING MY FATIGUE.

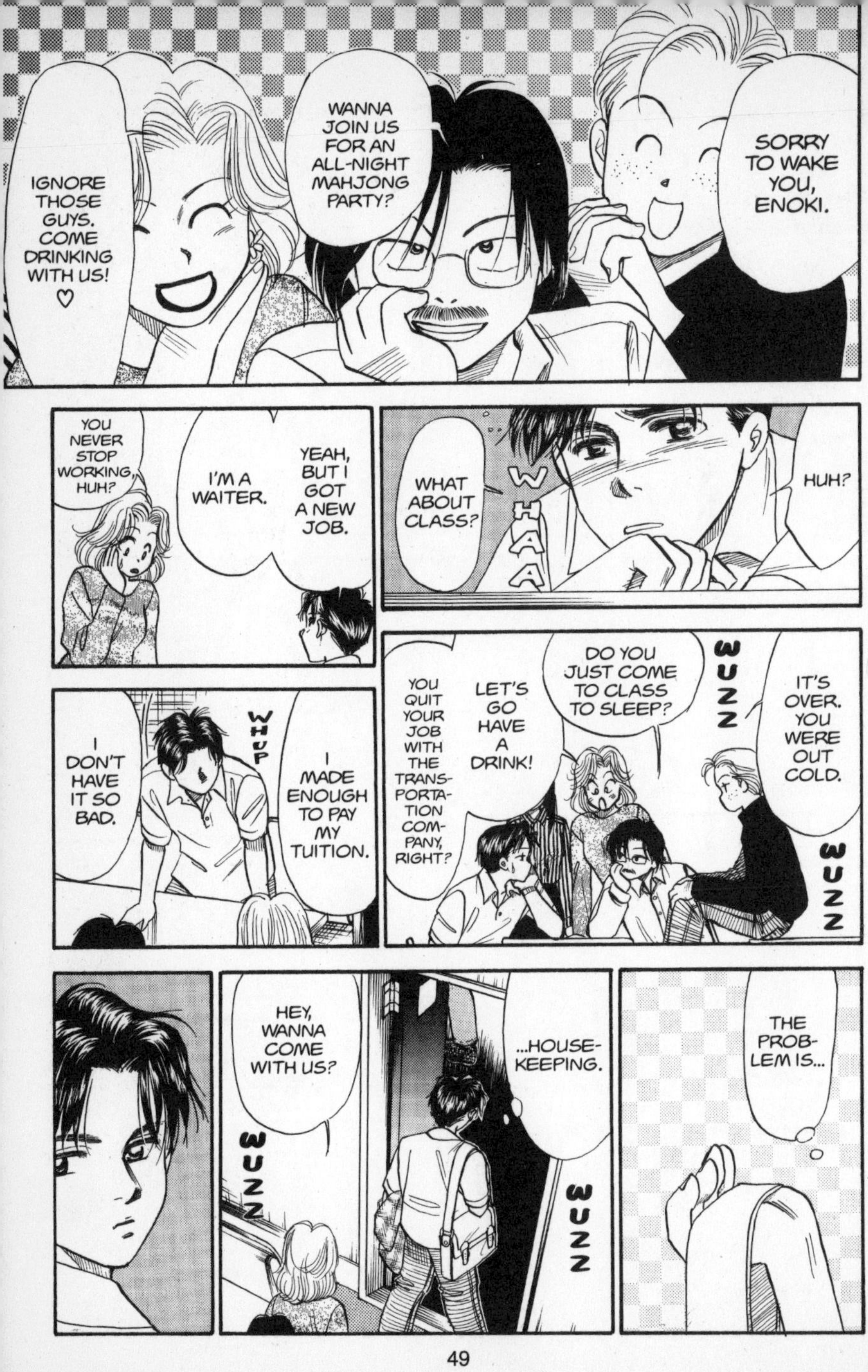
SORRY TO WAKE YOU, ENOKI.
WANNA JOIN US FOR AN ALL-NIGHT MAHJONG PARTY?
IGNORE THOSE GUYS. COME DRINKING WITH US! ♡
HUH?
WHAAA
WHAT ABOUT CLASS?
YEAH, BUT I GOT A NEW JOB.
I'M A WAITER.
YOU NEVER STOP WORKING, HUH?
WUZZ
IT'S OVER. YOU WERE OUT COLD.
DO YOU JUST COME TO CLASS TO SLEEP?
WUZZ
LET'S GO HAVE A DRINK!
YOU QUIT YOUR JOB WITH THE TRANSPORTATION COMPANY, RIGHT?
WHUP
I MADE ENOUGH TO PAY MY TUITION.
I DON'T HAVE IT SO BAD.
THE PROBLEM IS...
...HOUSEKEEPING.
WUZZ
HEY, WANNA COME WITH US?
WUZZ

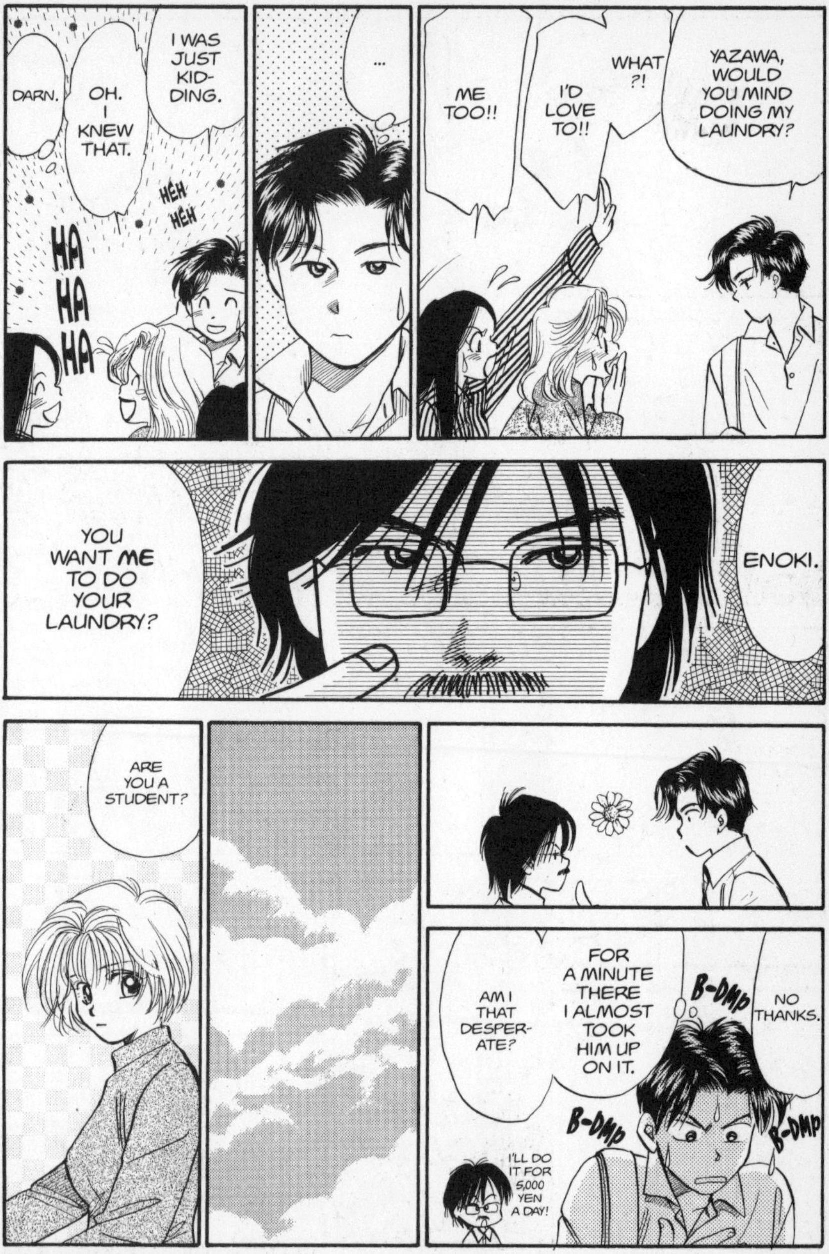
YAZAWA, WOULD YOU MIND DOING MY LAUNDRY?
WHAT?!
I'D LOVE TO!!
ME TOO!!
...
I WAS JUST KID-DING.
OH. I KNEW THAT.
DARN.
HEH HEH
HA HA HA
ENOKI.
YOU WANT ME TO DO YOUR LAUNDRY?
NO THANKS.
B-DMP
FOR A MINUTE THERE I ALMOST TOOK HIM UP ON IT.
AM I THAT DESPER-ATE?
B-DMP
B-DMP
I'LL DO IT FOR 5,000 YEN A DAY!
ARE YOU A STUDENT?

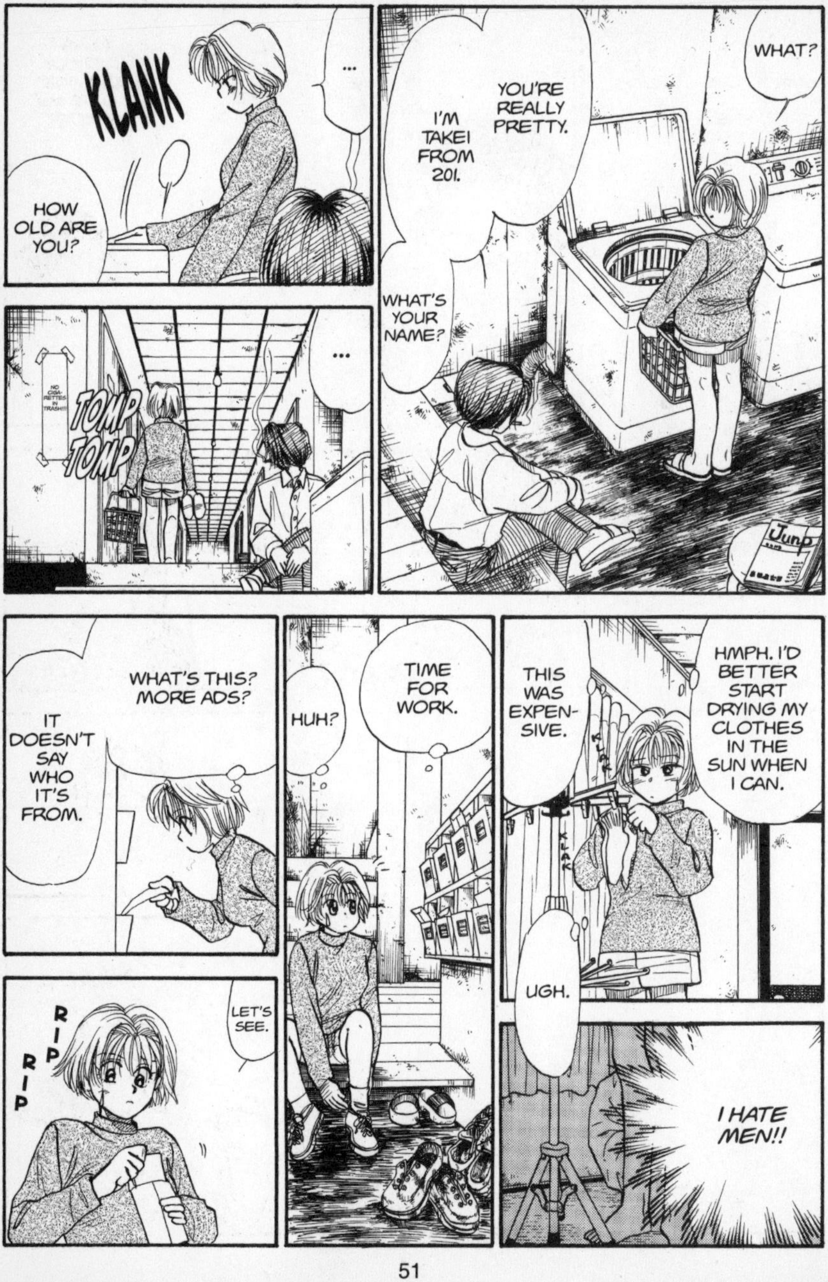
WHAT?
YOU'RE REALLY PRETTY.
I'M TAKEI FROM 201.
WHAT'S YOUR NAME?
...
KLANK
HOW OLD ARE YOU?
...
TOMP TOMP
NO CIGA-RETTES IN TRASH!!!
HMPH. I'D BETTER START DRYING MY CLOTHES IN THE SUN WHEN I CAN.
THIS WAS EXPEN-SIVE.
KLAK
KLAK
UGH.
I HATE MEN!!
TIME FOR WORK.
HUH?
WHAT'S THIS? MORE ADS?
IT DOESN'T SAY WHO IT'S FROM.
LET'S SEE.
RIP RIP
RIP

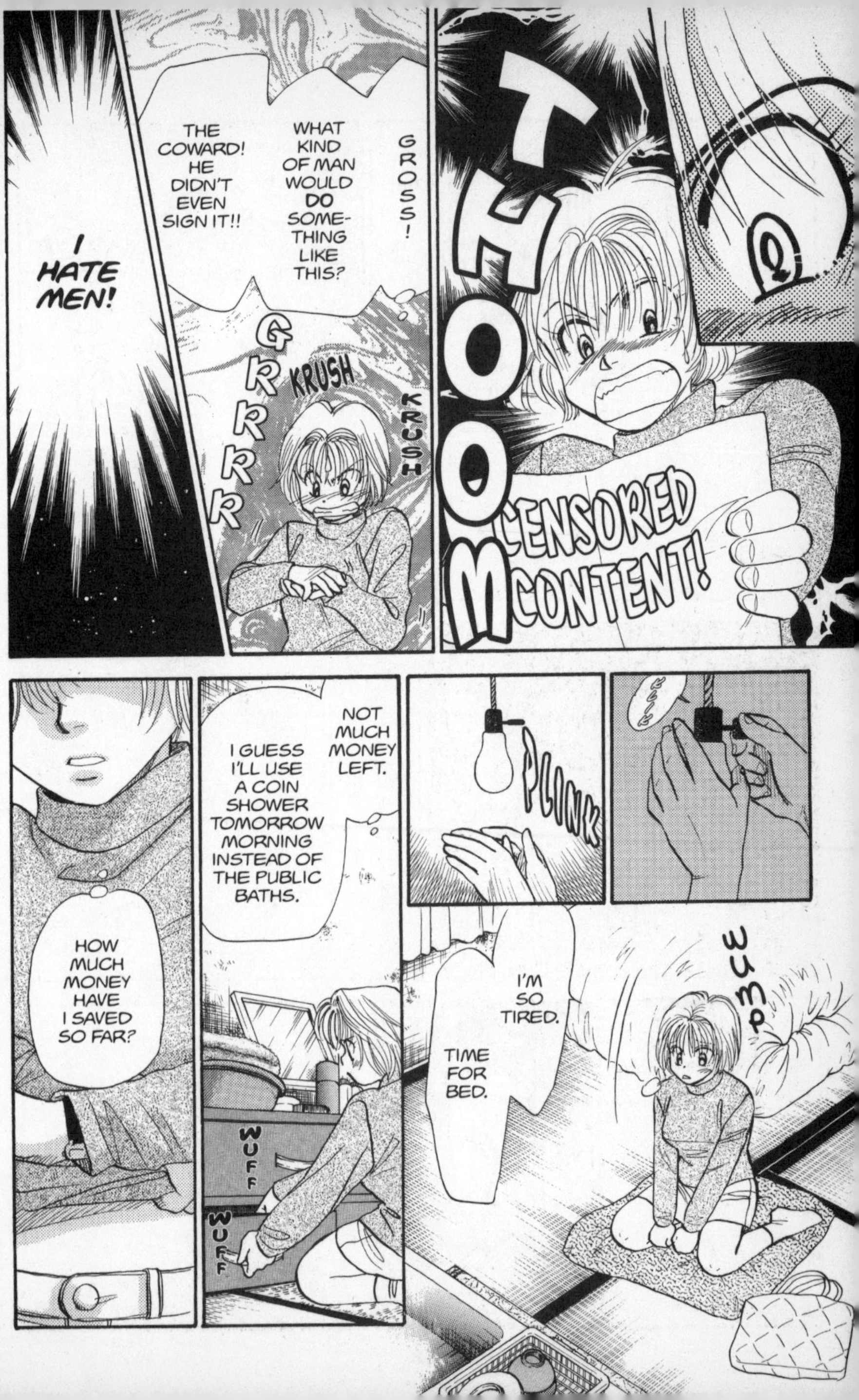
THOOM
CENSORED CONTENT!
GROSS!
WHAT KIND OF MAN WOULD DO SOMETHING LIKE THIS?
THE COWARD! HE DIDN'T EVEN SIGN IT!!
KRUSH
KRUSH
GRRRRR
I HATE MEN!
PLINK
WUMP
I'M SO TIRED.
TIME FOR BED.
NOT MUCH MONEY LEFT.
I GUESS I'LL USE A COIN SHOWER TOMORROW MORNING INSTEAD OF THE PUBLIC BATHS.
WUFF
WUFF
HOW MUCH MONEY HAVE I SAVED SO FAR?

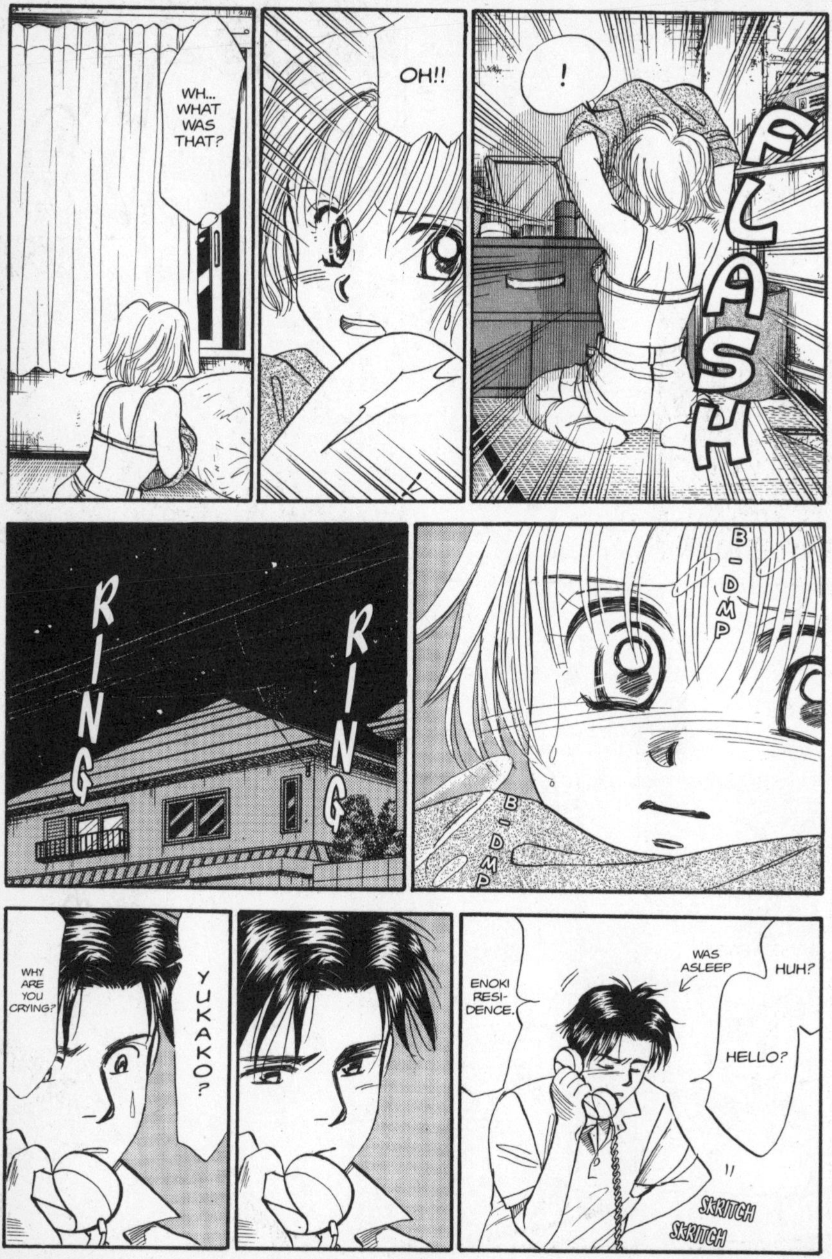
!
FLASH
OH!!
WH... WHAT WAS THAT?
B-DMP
B-DMP
RING
RING
HUH?
WAS ASLEEP
ENOKI RESI-DENCE.
HELLO?
SKRITCH
SKRITCH
YUKAKO?
WHY ARE YOU CRYING?

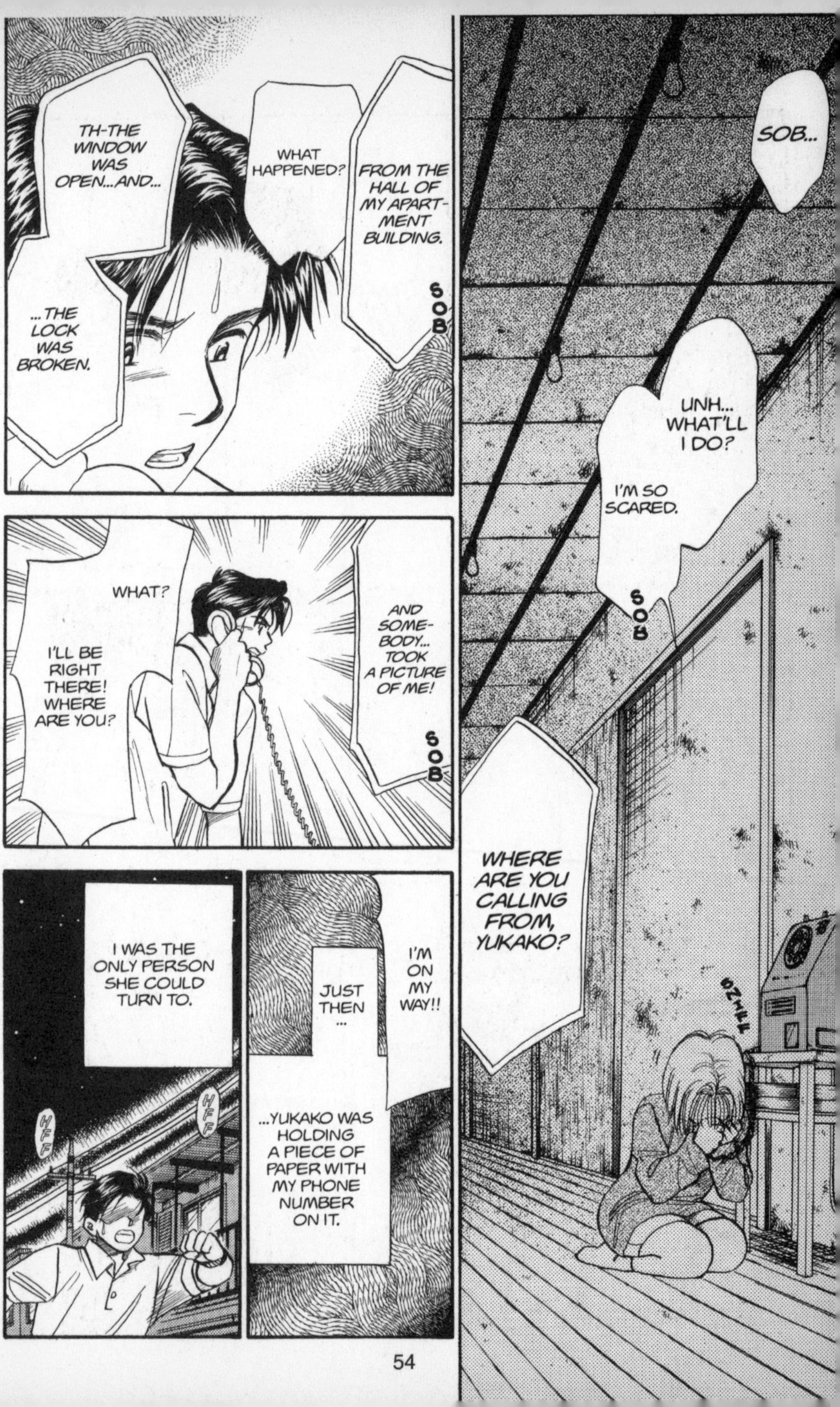
SOB...
UNH... WHAT'LL I DO?
I'M SO SCARED.
SOB
WHERE ARE YOU CALLING FROM, YUKAKO?
FROM THE HALL OF MY APARTMENT BUILDING.
SOB
WHAT HAPPENED?
TH-THE WINDOW WAS OPEN...AND...
...THE LOCK WAS BROKEN.
AND SOMEBODY... TOOK A PICTURE OF ME!
SOB
WHAT?
I'LL BE RIGHT THERE! WHERE ARE YOU?
I'M ON MY WAY!!
JUST THEN...
...YUKAKO WAS HOLDING A PIECE OF PAPER WITH MY PHONE NUMBER ON IT.
I WAS THE ONLY PERSON SHE COULD TURN TO.
HFF
HFF

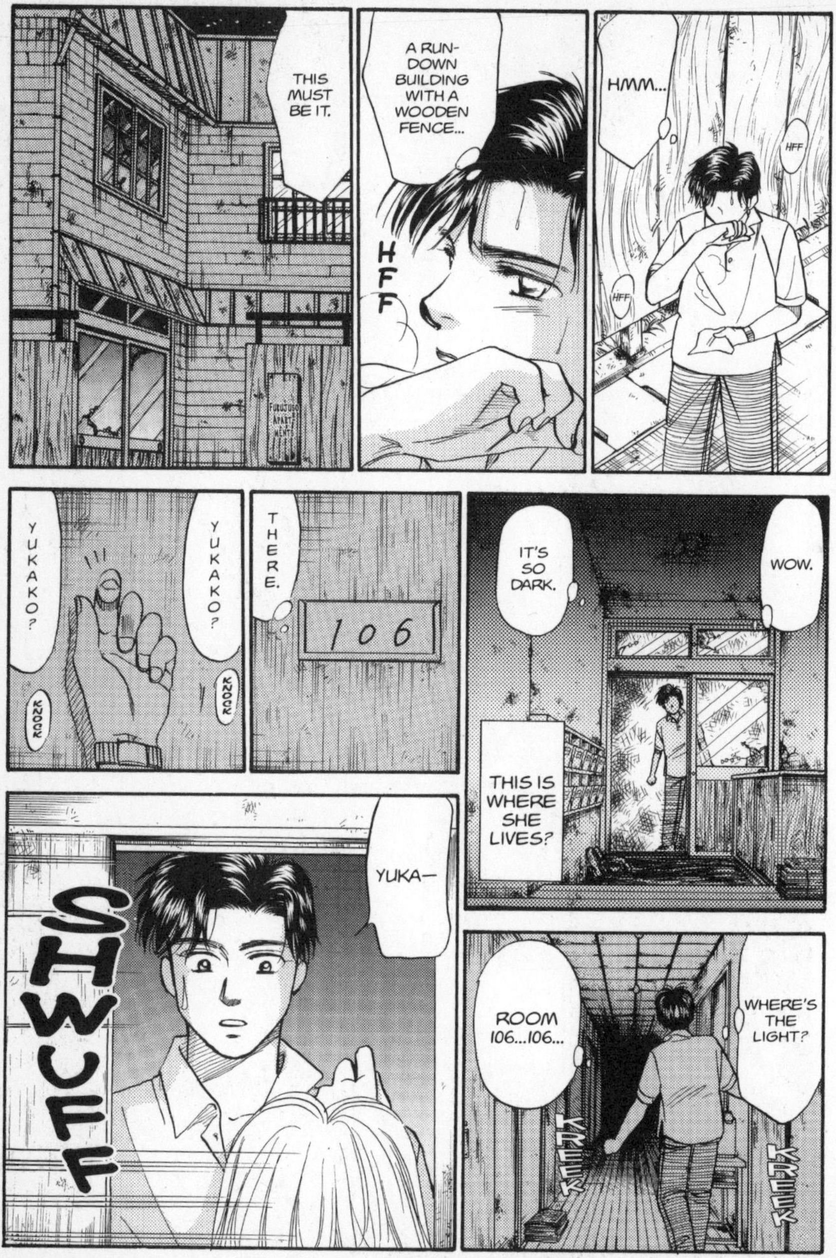
HMM...
HFF
HFF
A RUN-DOWN BUILDING WITH A WOODEN FENCE...
HFF
THIS MUST BE IT.
FURUJUGO APARTMENT
WOW.
IT'S SO DARK.
THIS IS WHERE SHE LIVES?
WHERE'S THE LIGHT?
ROOM 106...106...
KREEK
KREEK
THERE.
106
YUKAKO?
KNOCK
YUKAKO?
KNOCK
YUKA—
SHWUFF

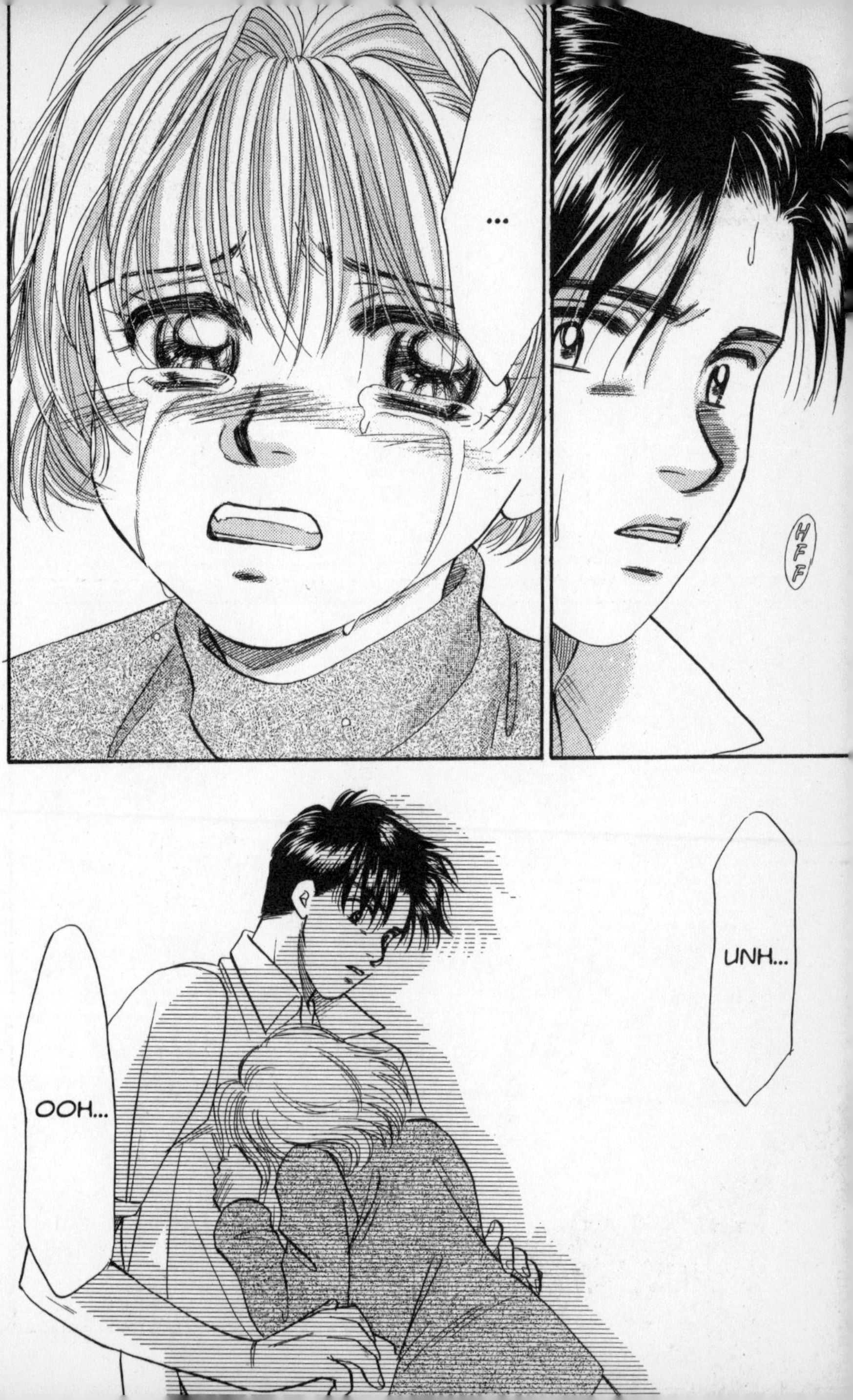
HFF
...
UNH...
OOH...

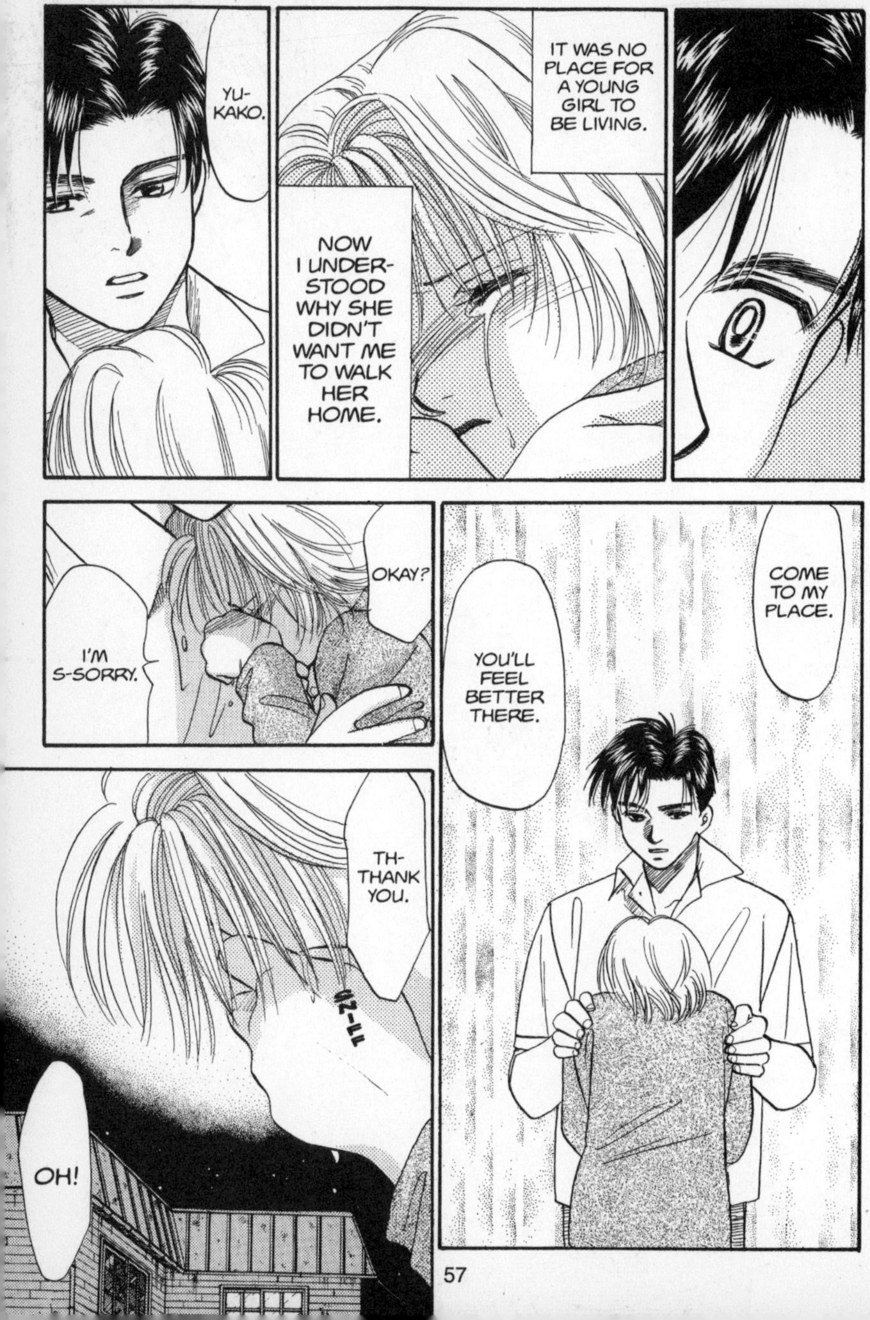
IT WAS NO PLACE FOR A YOUNG GIRL TO BE LIVING.
NOW I UNDERSTOOD WHY SHE DIDN'T WANT ME TO WALK HER HOME.
YU-KAKO.
COME TO MY PLACE.
YOU'LL FEEL BETTER THERE.
OKAY?
I'M S-SORRY.
TH-THANK YOU.
SNIFF
OH!

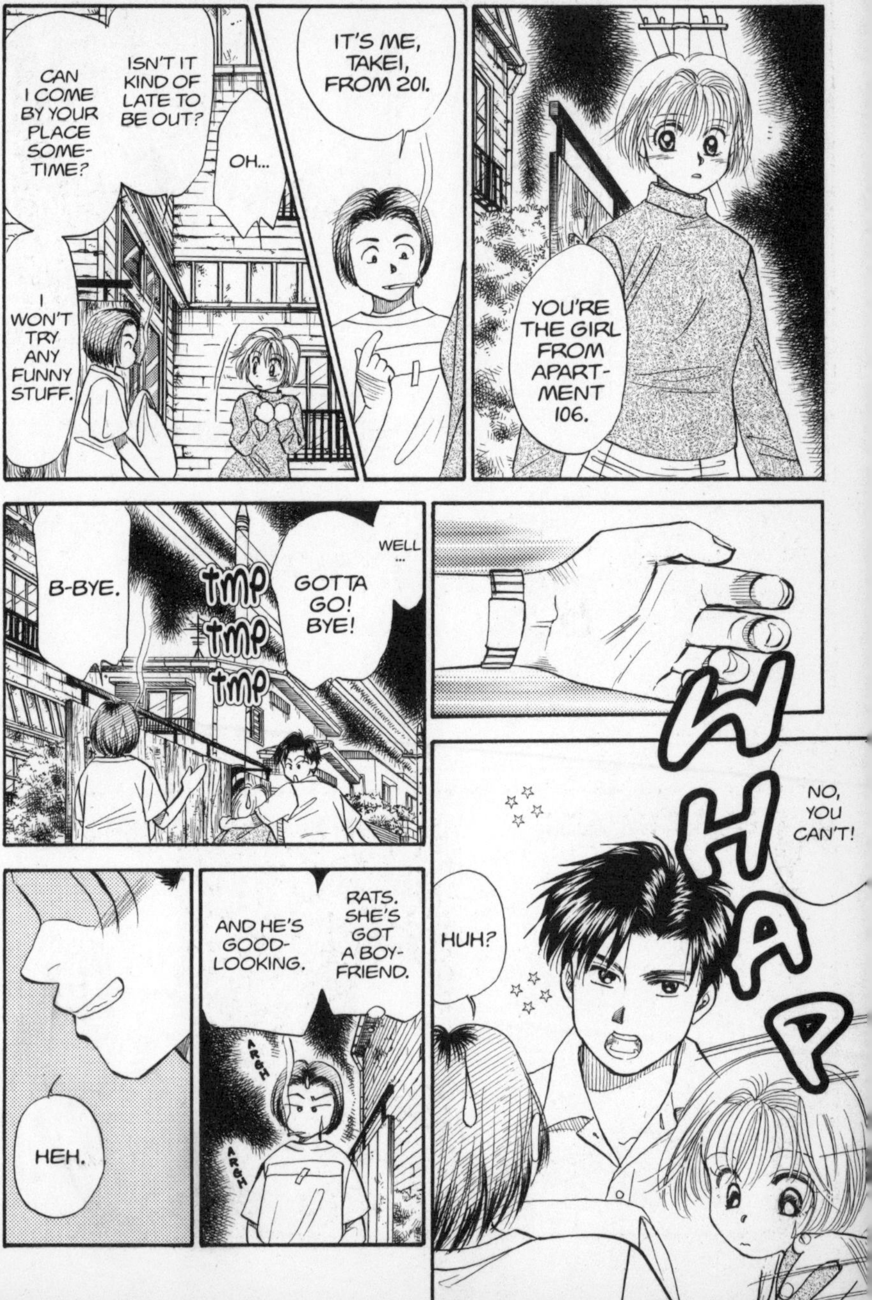
YOU'RE THE GIRL FROM APARTMENT 106.
IT'S ME, TAKEI, FROM 201.
OH...
ISN'T IT KIND OF LATE TO BE OUT?
CAN I COME BY YOUR PLACE SOMETIME?
I WON'T TRY ANY FUNNY STUFF.
WHAP
NO, YOU CAN'T!
HUH?
WELL...
GOTTA GO! BYE!
tmp tmp tmp
B-BYE.
RATS. SHE'S GOT A BOY-FRIEND.
AND HE'S GOOD-LOOKING.
ARGH
ARGH
HEH.

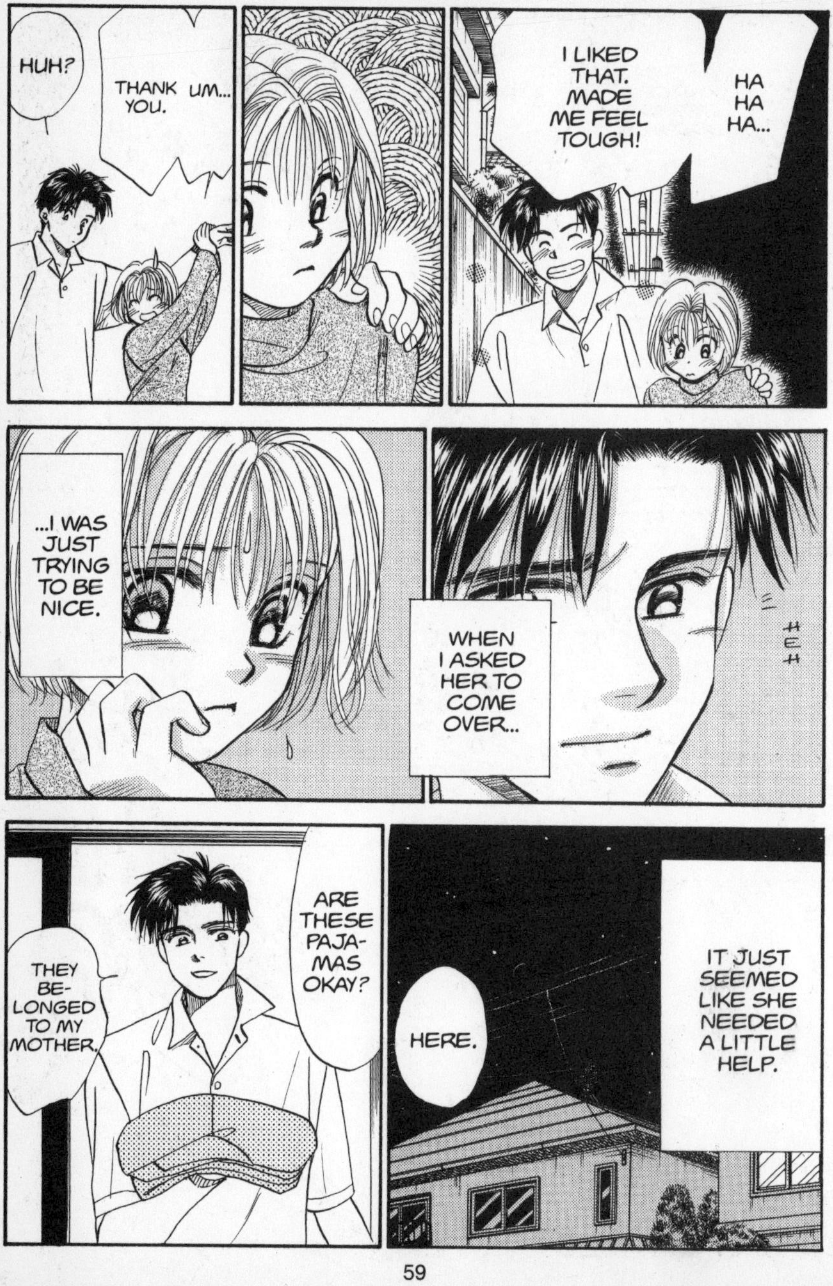
I LIKED THAT. MADE ME FEEL TOUGH!
HA HA HA...
UM... THANK YOU.
HUH?
WHEN I ASKED HER TO COME OVER...
HEH
...I WAS JUST TRYING TO BE NICE.
IT JUST SEEMED LIKE SHE NEEDED A LITTLE HELP.
HERE.
ARE THESE PAJAMAS OKAY?
THEY BELONGED TO MY MOTHER.

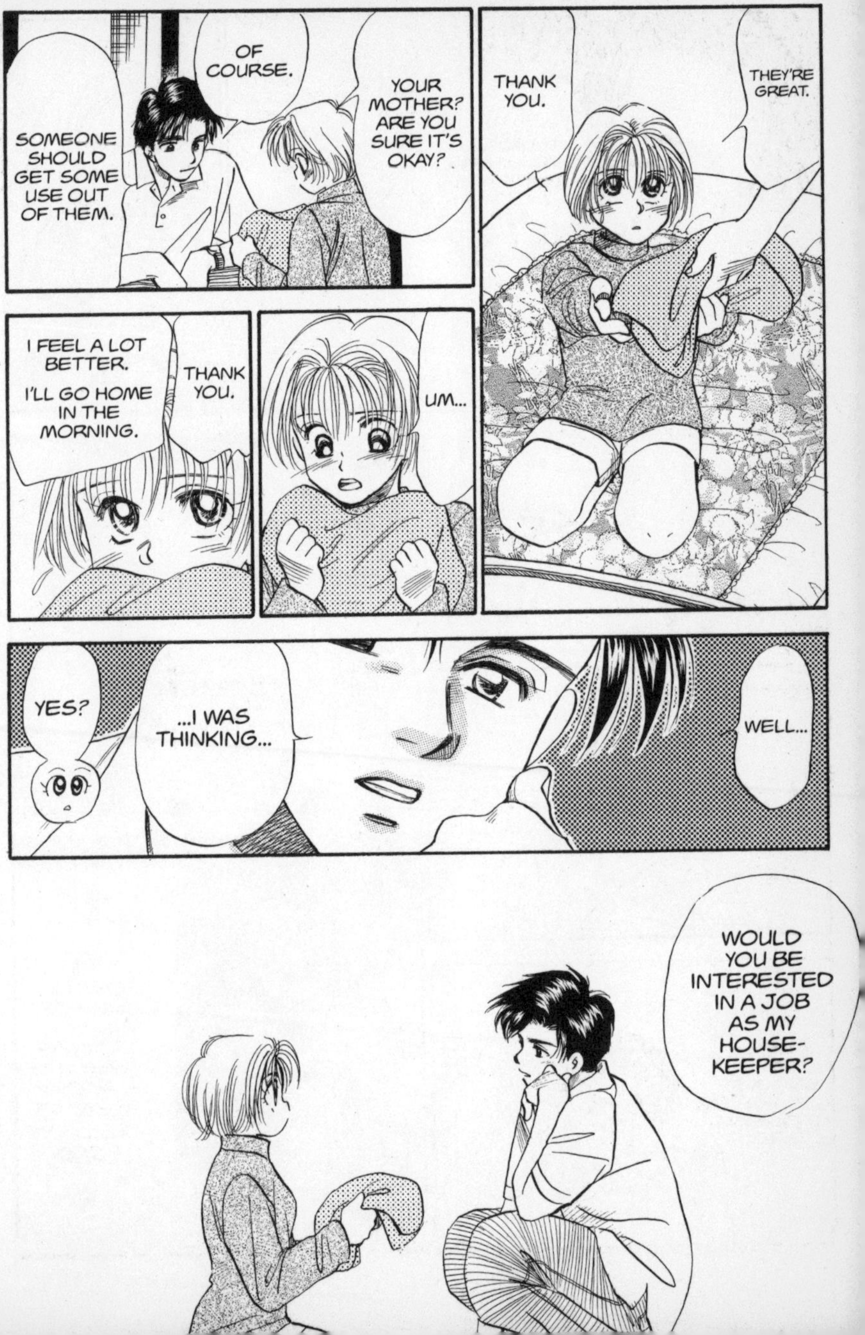
THEY'RE GREAT.
THANK YOU.
YOUR MOTHER? ARE YOU SURE IT'S OKAY?
OF COURSE.
SOMEONE SHOULD GET SOME USE OUT OF THEM.
UM...
THANK YOU.
I FEEL A LOT BETTER.
I'LL GO HOME IN THE MORNING.
WELL...
...I WAS THINKING...
YES?
WOULD YOU BE INTERESTED IN A JOB AS MY HOUSE-KEEPER?

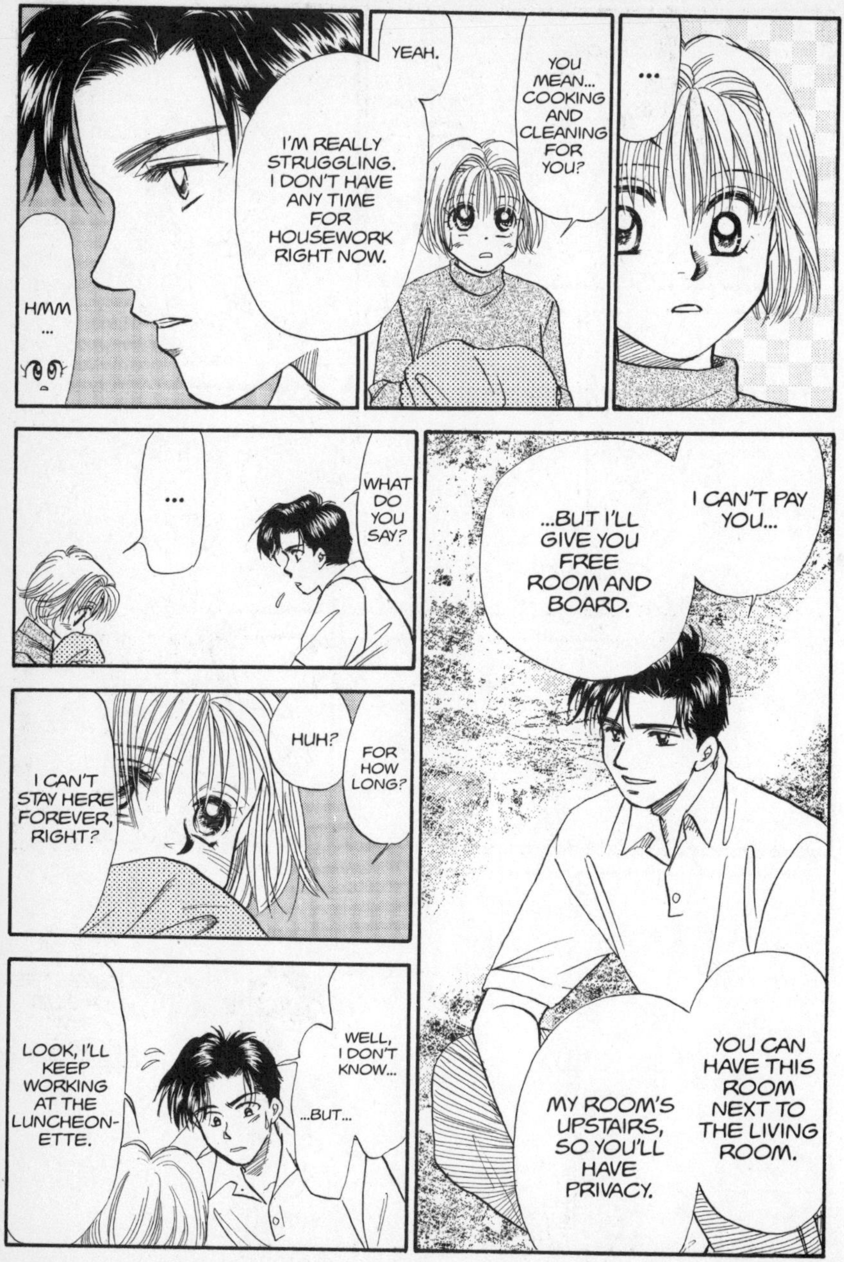
...
YOU MEAN... COOKING AND CLEANING FOR YOU?
YEAH.
I'M REALLY STRUGGLING. I DON'T HAVE ANY TIME FOR HOUSEWORK RIGHT NOW.
HMM ...
I CAN'T PAY YOU...
...BUT I'LL GIVE YOU FREE ROOM AND BOARD.
YOU CAN HAVE THIS ROOM NEXT TO THE LIVING ROOM.
MY ROOM'S UPSTAIRS, SO YOU'LL HAVE PRIVACY.
WHAT DO YOU SAY?
...
FOR HOW LONG?
HUH?
I CAN'T STAY HERE FOREVER, RIGHT?
WELL, I DON'T KNOW...
...BUT...
LOOK, I'LL KEEP WORKING AT THE LUNCHEON-ETTE.

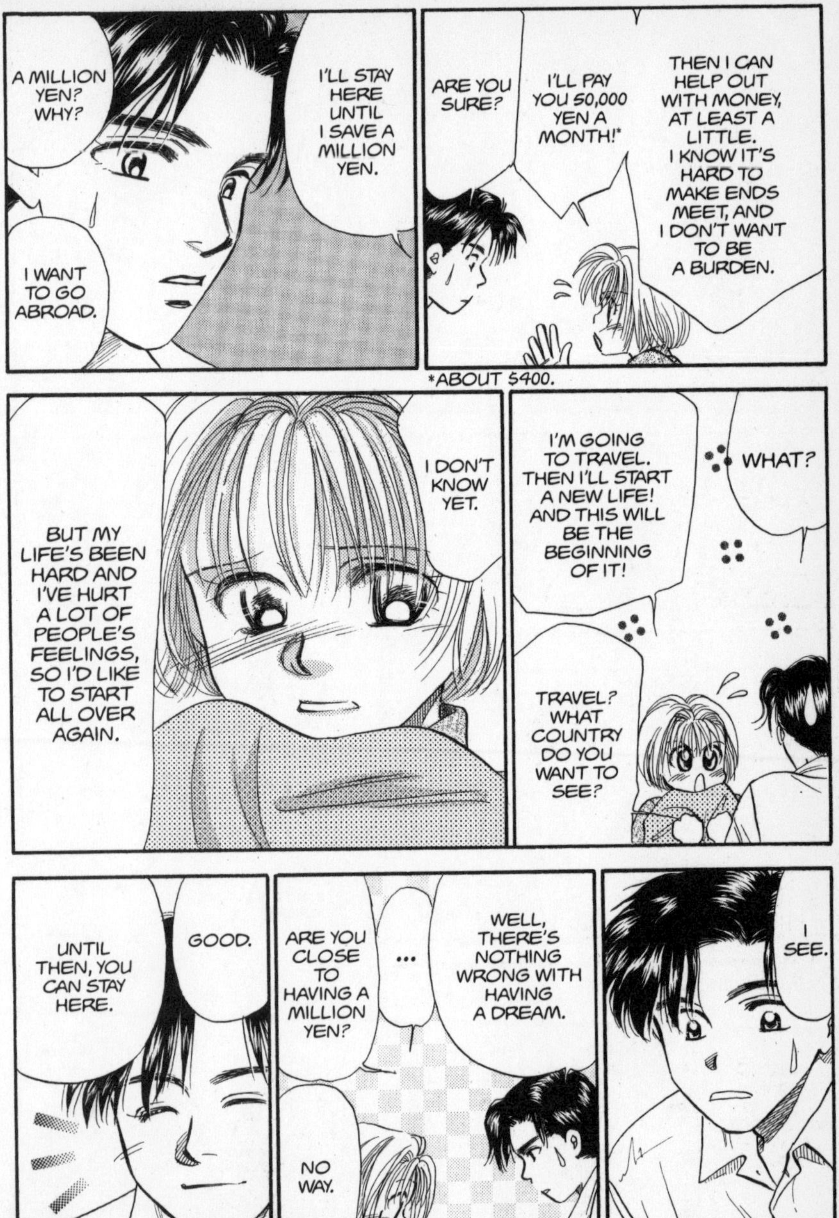
THEN I CAN HELP OUT WITH MONEY, AT LEAST A LITTLE. I KNOW IT'S HARD TO MAKE ENDS MEET, AND I DON'T WANT TO BE A BURDEN.
I'LL PAY YOU 50,000 YEN A MONTH!*
ARE YOU SURE?
I'LL STAY HERE UNTIL I SAVE A MILLION YEN.
A MILLION YEN? WHY?
I WANT TO GO ABROAD.
*ABOUT $400.
WHAT?
I'M GOING TO TRAVEL. THEN I'LL START A NEW LIFE! AND THIS WILL BE THE BEGINNING OF IT!
TRAVEL? WHAT COUNTRY DO YOU WANT TO SEE?
I DON'T KNOW YET.
BUT MY LIFE'S BEEN HARD AND I'VE HURT A LOT OF PEOPLE'S FEELINGS, SO I'D LIKE TO START ALL OVER AGAIN.
I SEE.
WELL, THERE'S NOTHING WRONG WITH HAVING A DREAM.
...
ARE YOU CLOSE TO HAVING A MILLION YEN?
NO WAY.
GOOD.
UNTIL THEN, YOU CAN STAY HERE.

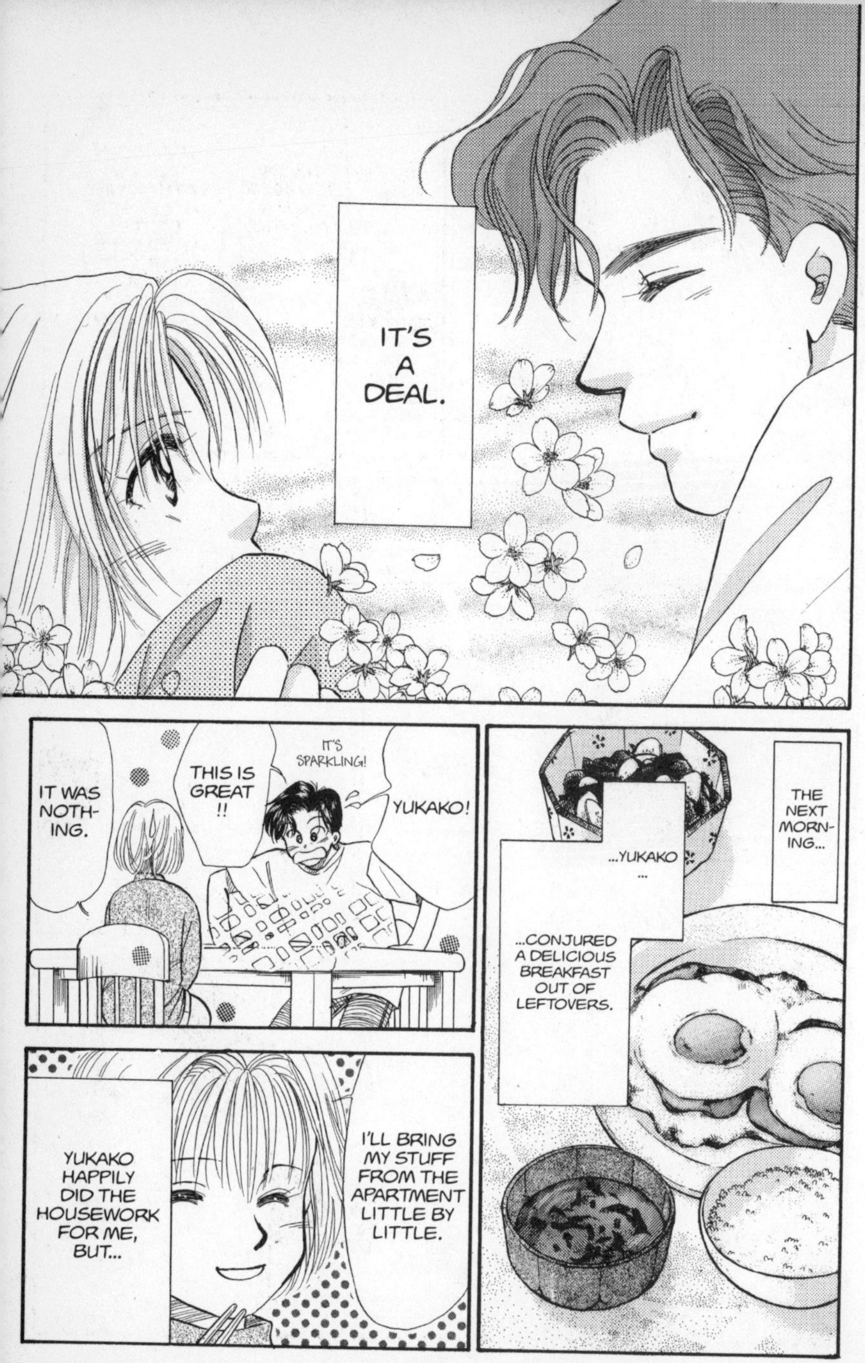
IT'S A DEAL.
THE NEXT MORNING...
...YUKAKO ...
...CONJURED A DELICIOUS BREAKFAST OUT OF LEFTOVERS.
YUKAKO!
IT'S SPARKLING!
THIS IS GREAT !!
IT WAS NOTHING.
I'LL BRING MY STUFF FROM THE APARTMENT LITTLE BY LITTLE.
YUKAKO HAPPILY DID THE HOUSEWORK FOR ME, BUT...

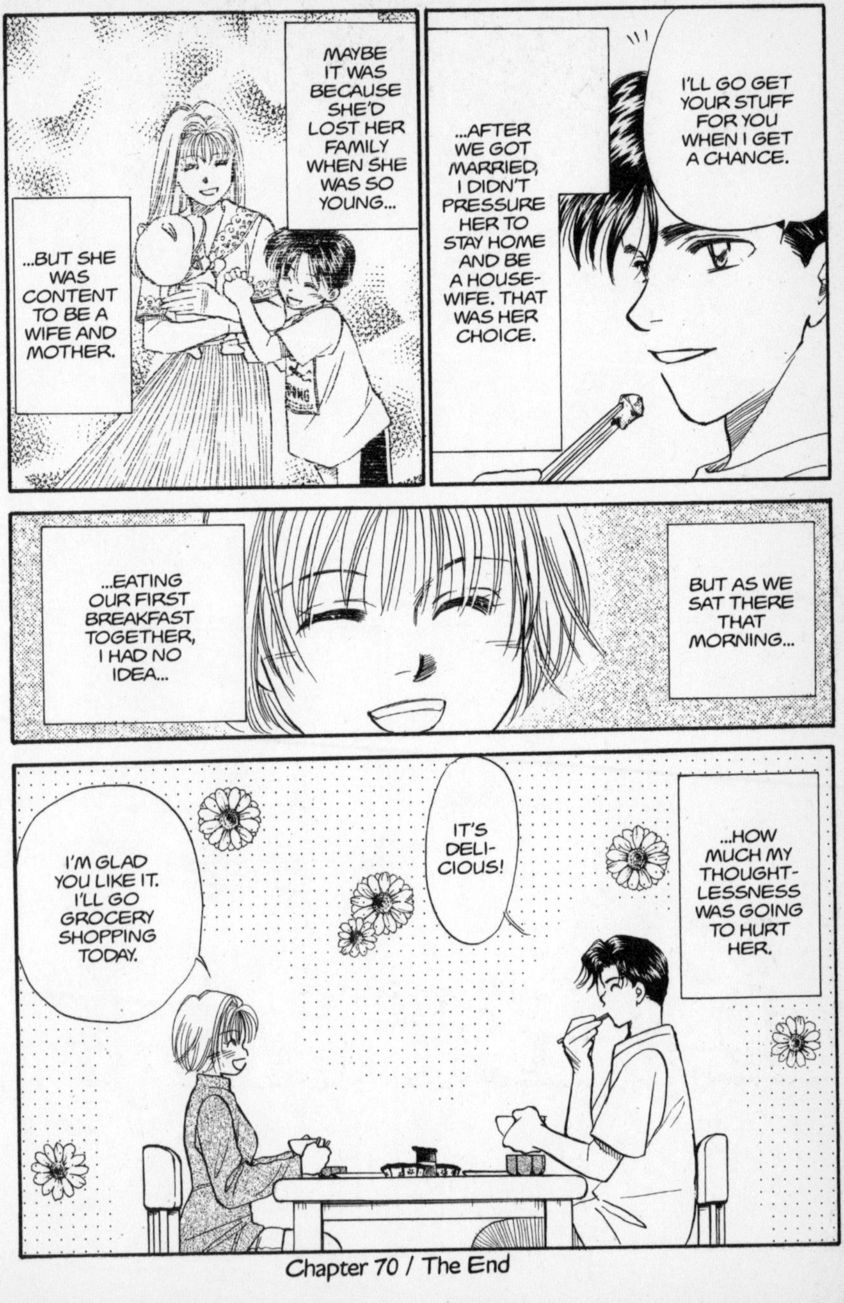
I'LL GO GET YOUR STUFF FOR YOU WHEN I GET A CHANCE.
...AFTER WE GOT MARRIED, I DIDN'T PRESSURE HER TO STAY HOME AND BE A HOUSE-WIFE. THAT WAS HER CHOICE.
MAYBE IT WAS BECAUSE SHE'D LOST HER FAMILY WHEN SHE WAS SO YOUNG...
...BUT SHE WAS CONTENT TO BE A WIFE AND MOTHER.
BUT AS WE SAT THERE THAT MORNING...
...EATING OUR FIRST BREAKFAST TOGETHER, I HAD NO IDEA...
...HOW MUCH MY THOUGHT-LESSNESS WAS GOING TO HURT HER.
IT'S DELI-CIOUS!
I'M GLAD YOU LIKE IT. I'LL GO GROCERY SHOPPING TODAY.

Chapter 70 / The End

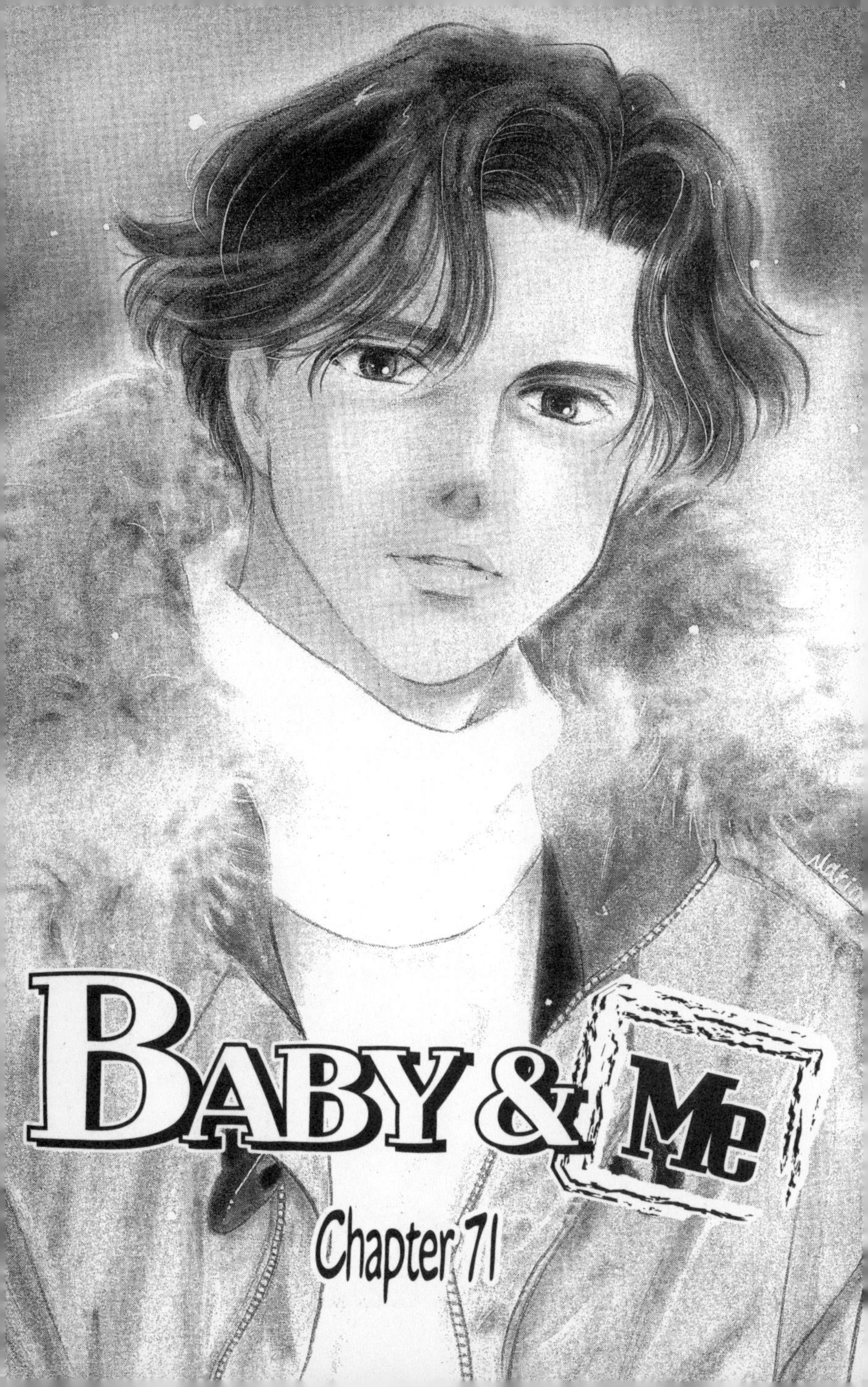
BABY & Me
Chapter 71

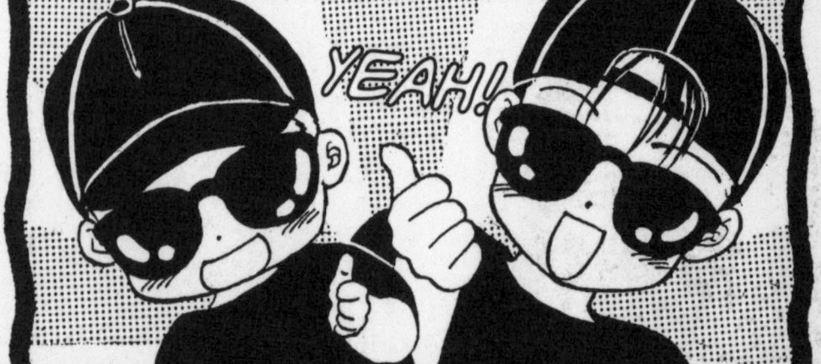
YEAH!

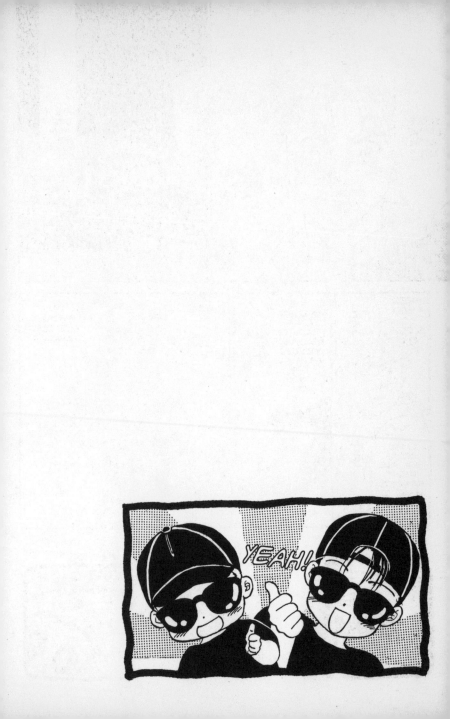

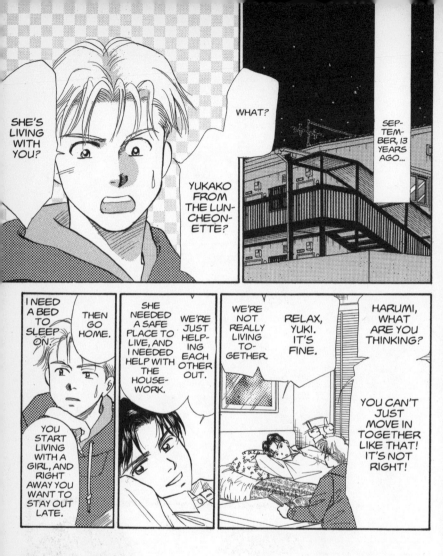

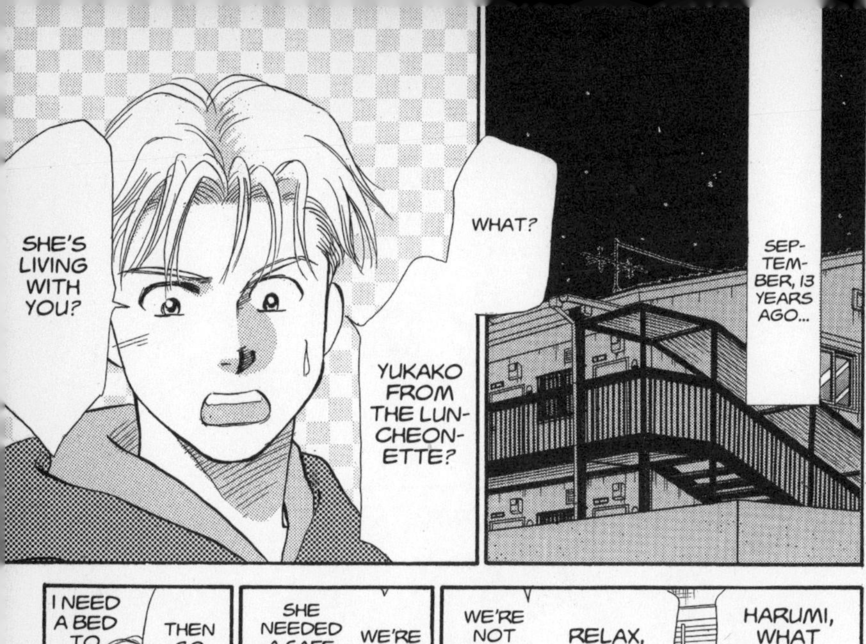
SEP-TEM-BER, 13 YEARS AGO...
WHAT?
YUKAKO FROM THE LUN-CHEON-ETTE?
SHE'S LIVING WITH YOU?
HARUMI, WHAT ARE YOU THINKING?
RELAX, YUKI. IT'S FINE.
WE'RE NOT REALLY LIVING TO-GETHER.
YOU CAN'T JUST MOVE IN TOGETHER LIKE THAT! IT'S NOT RIGHT!
WE'RE JUST HELP-ING EACH OTHER OUT.
SHE NEEDED A SAFE PLACE TO LIVE, AND I NEEDED HELP WITH THE HOUSE-WORK.
THEN GO HOME.
I NEED A BED TO SLEEP ON.
YOU START LIVING WITH A GIRL, AND RIGHT AWAY YOU WANT TO STAY OUT LATE.
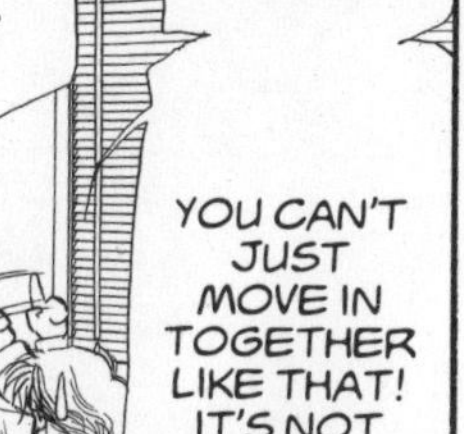
DAT'S GWEAT!
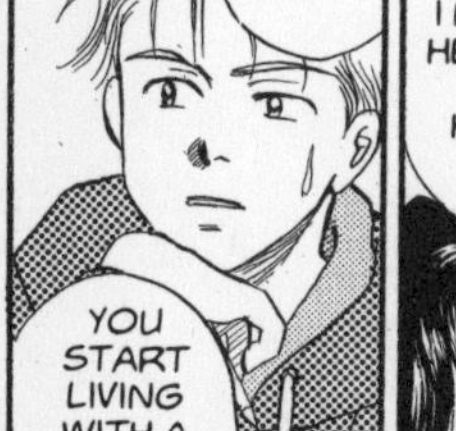
PEACE♥

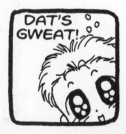

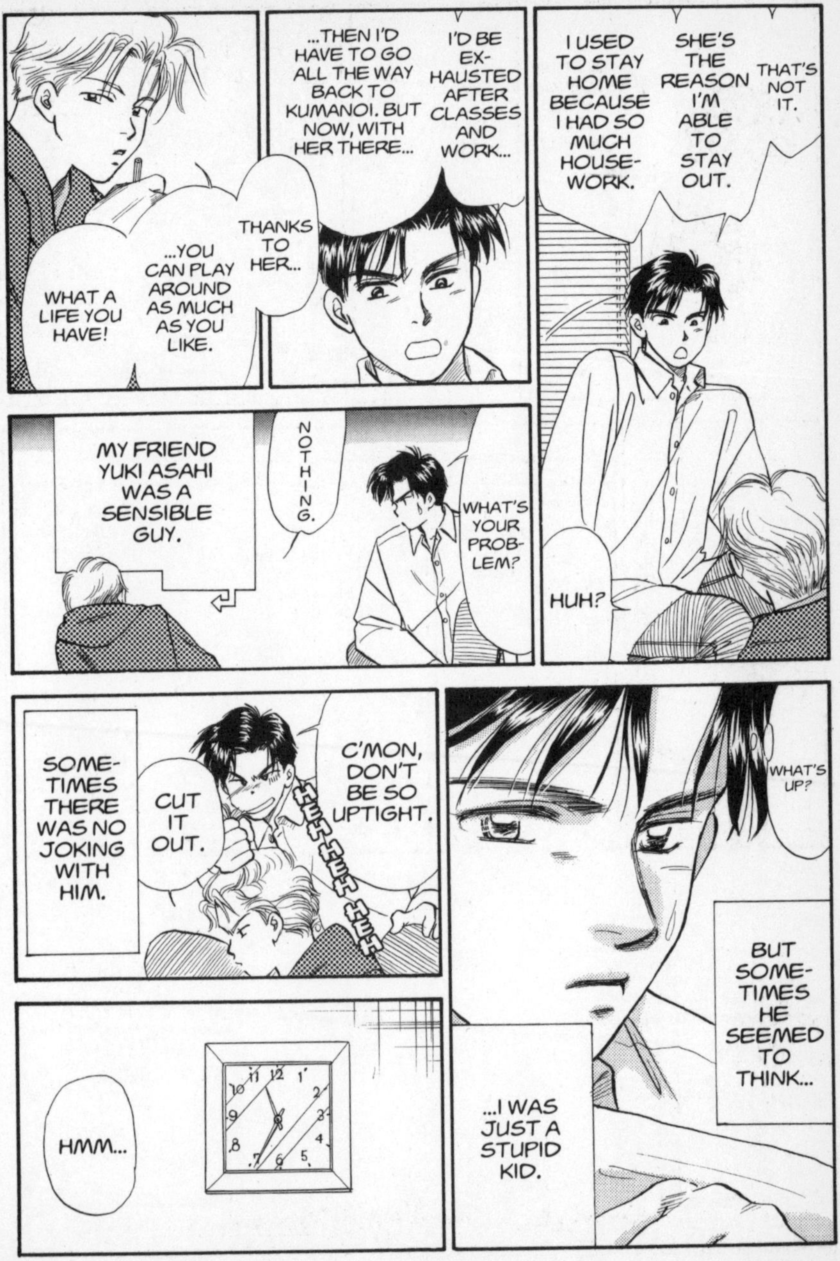
THAT'S NOT IT.
SHE'S THE REASON I'M ABLE TO STAY OUT.
I USED TO STAY HOME BECAUSE I HAD SO MUCH HOUSE-WORK.
HUH?
I'D BE EX-HAUSTED AFTER CLASSES AND WORK...
...THEN I'D HAVE TO GO ALL THE WAY BACK TO KUMANOI. BUT NOW, WITH HER THERE...
THANKS TO HER...
...YOU CAN PLAY AROUND AS MUCH AS YOU LIKE.
WHAT A LIFE YOU HAVE!
WHAT'S YOUR PROB-LEM?
NOTHING.
MY FRIEND YUKI ASAHI WAS A SENSIBLE GUY.
WHAT'S UP?
BUT SOME-TIMES HE SEEMED TO THINK...
...I WAS JUST A STUPID KID.
C'MON, DON'T BE SO UPTIGHT.
HEH HEH HEH
CUT IT OUT.
SOME-TIMES THERE WAS NO JOKING WITH HIM.
HMM...

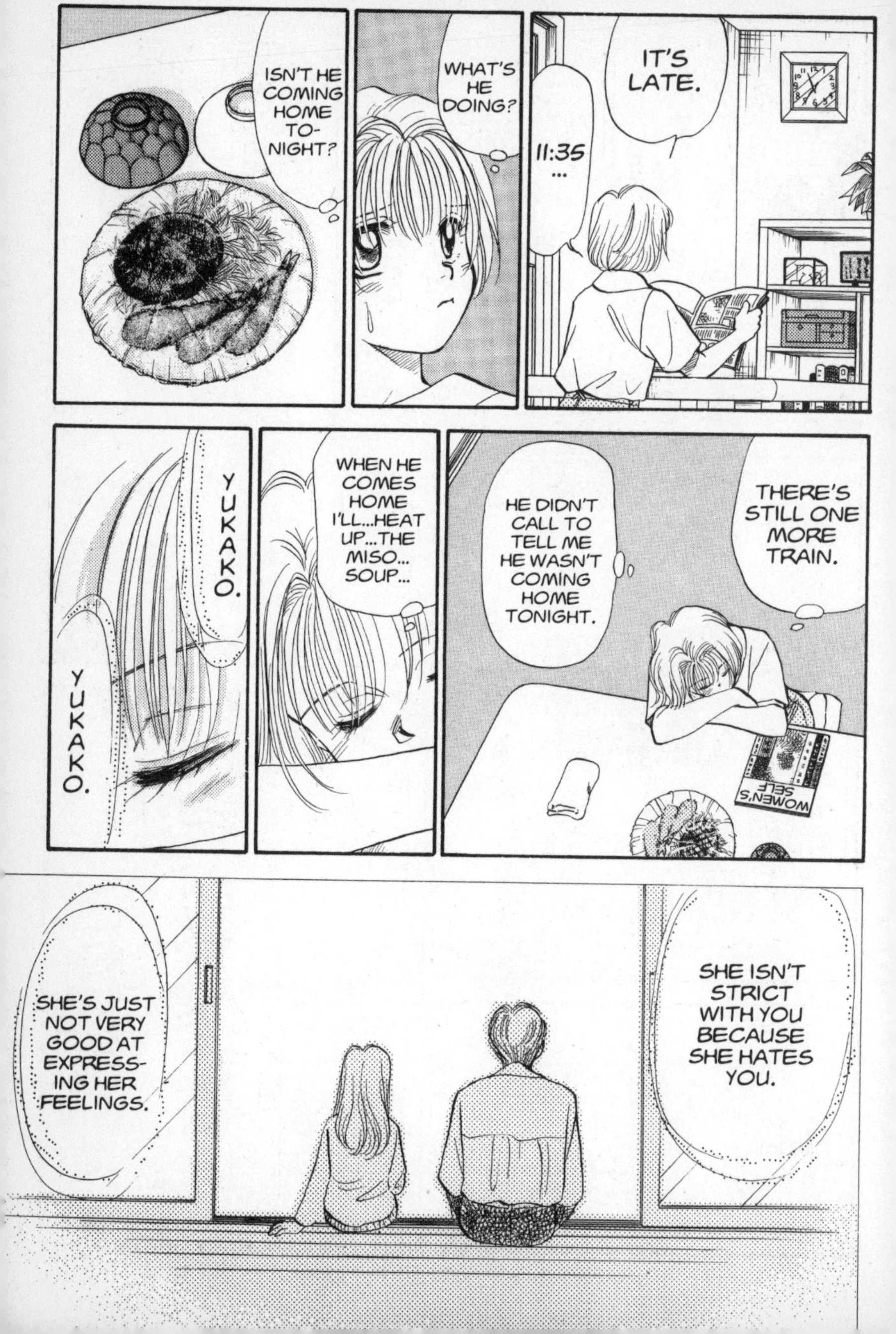
IT'S LATE.
11:35 ...
WHAT'S HE DOING?
ISN'T HE COMING HOME TO-NIGHT?
THERE'S STILL ONE MORE TRAIN.
HE DIDN'T CALL TO TELL ME HE WASN'T COMING HOME TONIGHT.
WOMEN'S SELF
WHEN HE COMES HOME I'LL...HEAT UP...THE MISO... SOUP...
YUKAKO.
YUKAKO.
SHE ISN'T STRICT WITH YOU BECAUSE SHE HATES YOU.
SHE'S JUST NOT VERY GOOD AT EXPRESS-ING HER FEELINGS.

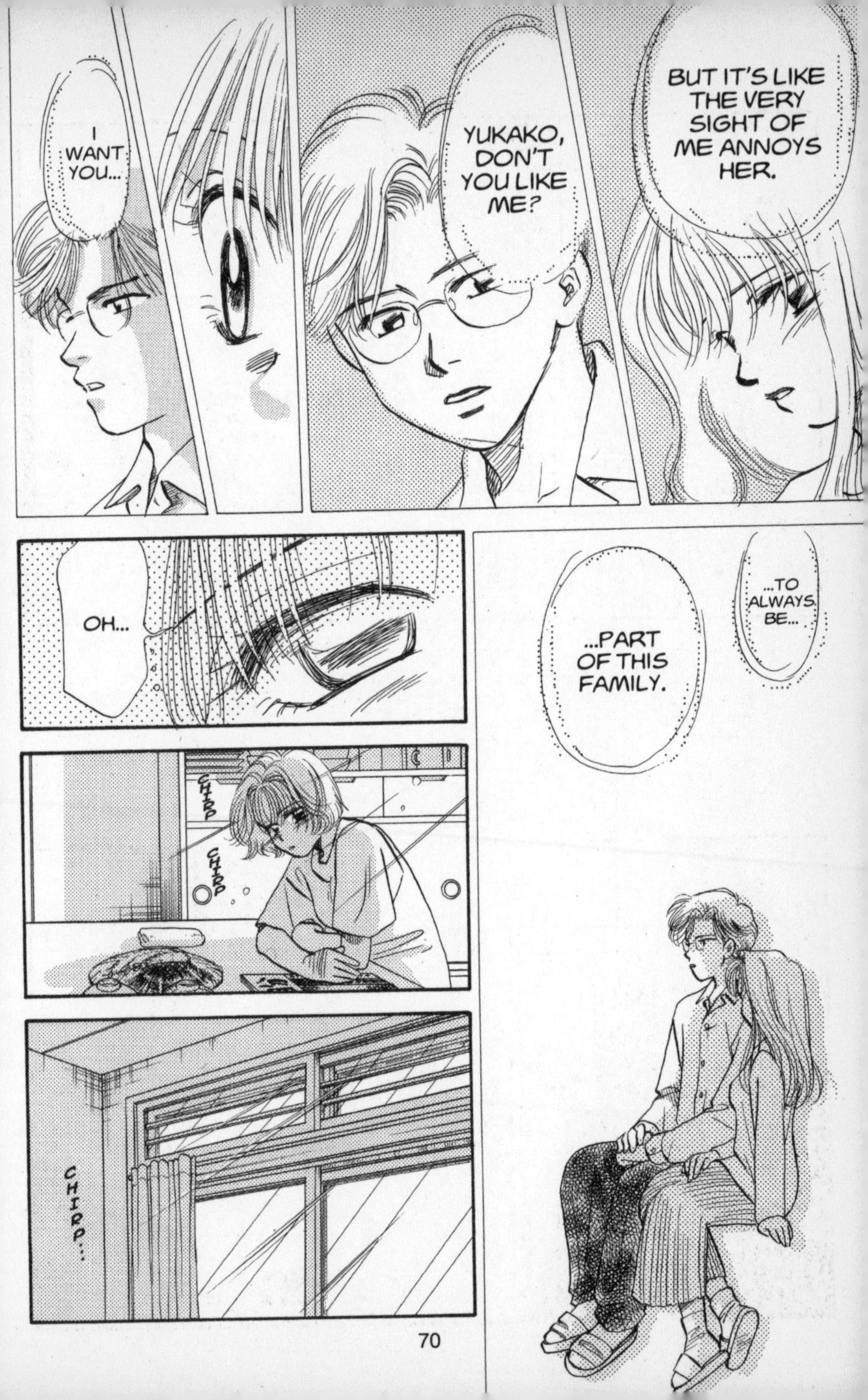
BUT IT'S LIKE THE VERY SIGHT OF ME ANNOYS HER.
YUKAKO, DON'T YOU LIKE ME?
I WANT YOU...
...TO ALWAYS BE...
...PART OF THIS FAMILY.
OH...
CHIRP
CHIRP
CHIRP...

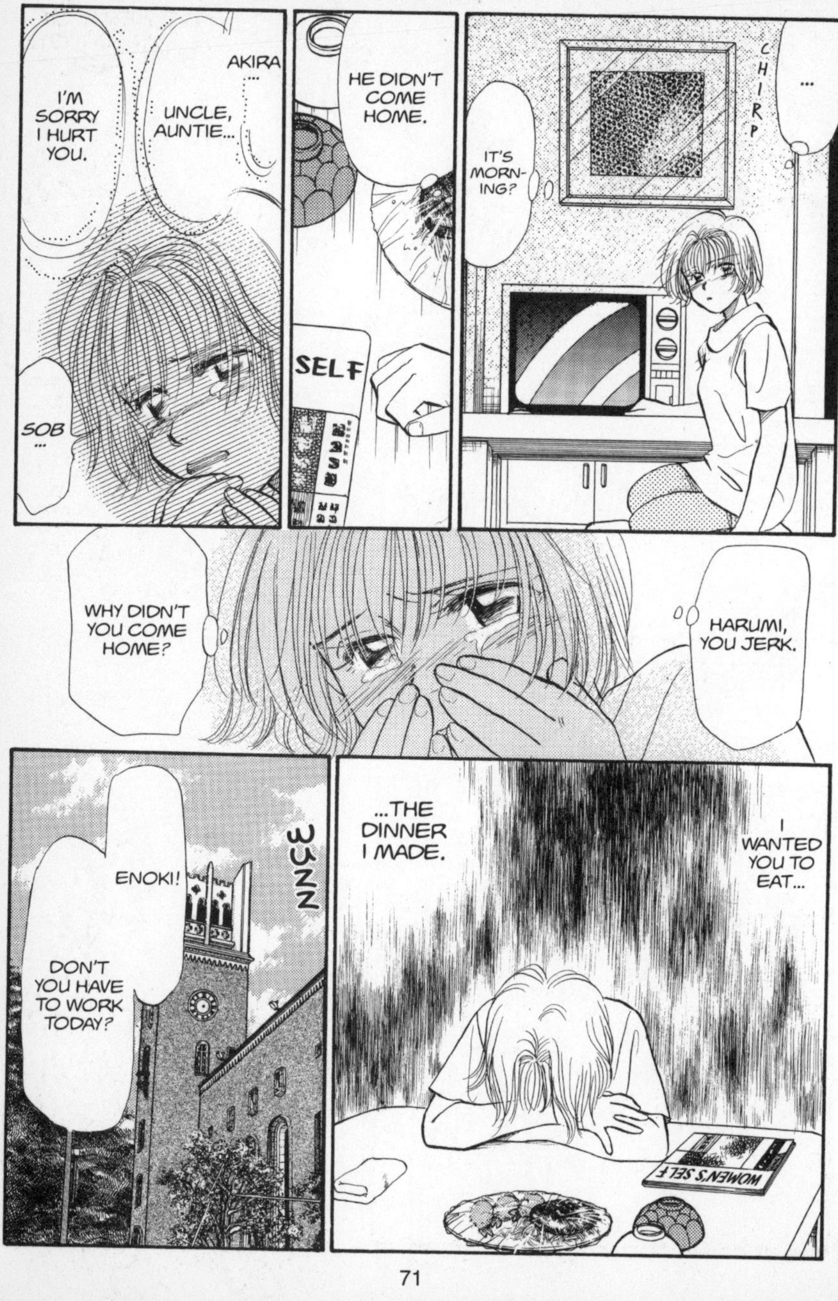
CHIRP
...
IT'S MORNING?
HE DIDN'T COME HOME.
SELF
AKIRA...
UNCLE, AUNTIE...
I'M SORRY I HURT YOU.
SOB...
HARUMI, YOU JERK.
WHY DIDN'T YOU COME HOME?
I WANTED YOU TO EAT...
...THE DINNER I MADE.
WOMEN'S SELF
ENOKI!
DON'T YOU HAVE TO WORK TODAY?

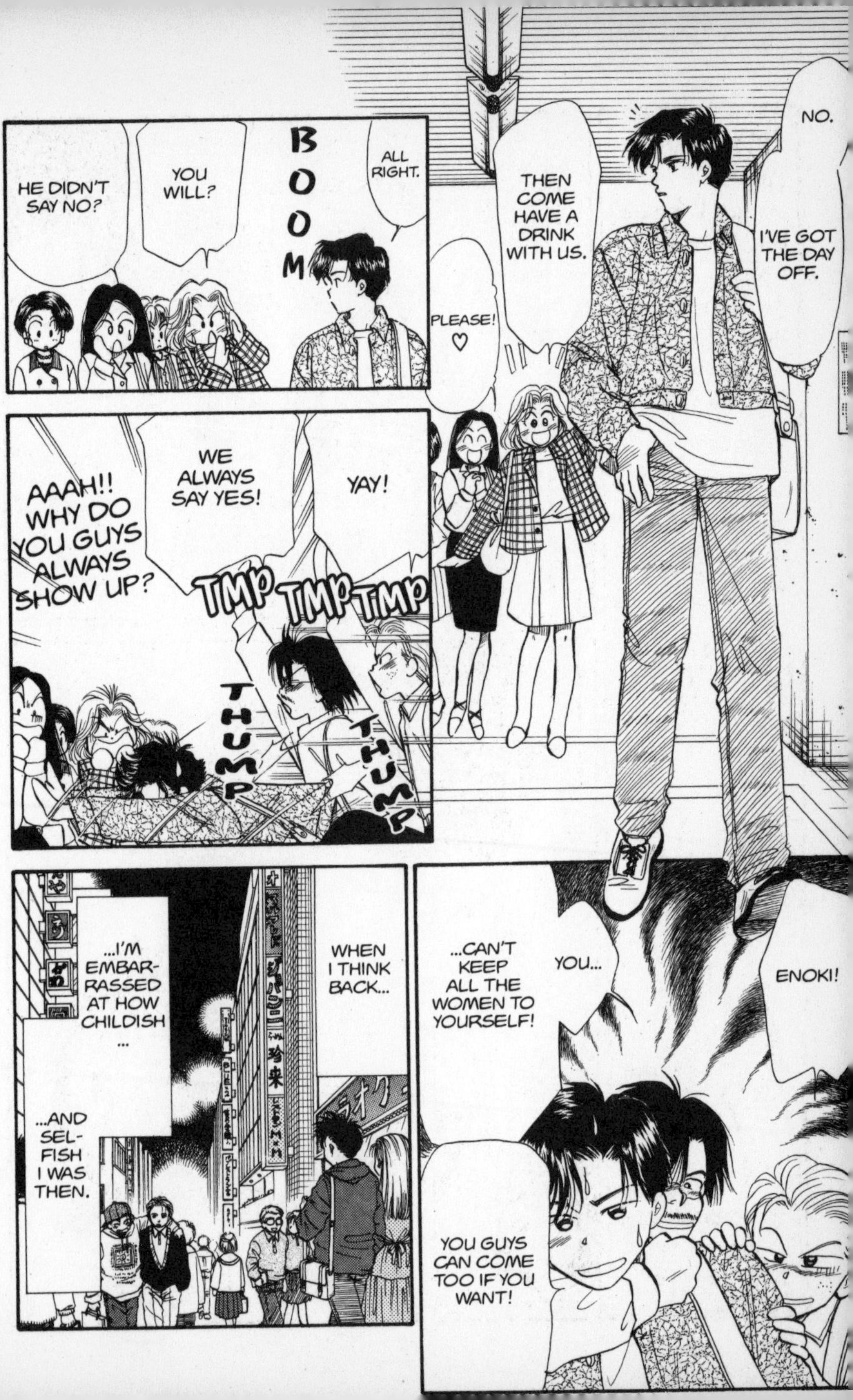
NO.
I'VE GOT THE DAY OFF.
THEN COME HAVE A DRINK WITH US.
PLEASE! ♡
ALL RIGHT.
BOOM
YOU WILL?
HE DIDN'T SAY NO?
YAY!
WE ALWAYS SAY YES!
AAAH!! WHY DO YOU GUYS ALWAYS SHOW UP?
TMP TMP TMP
THUMP
THUMP
ENOKI!
YOU...
...CAN'T KEEP ALL THE WOMEN TO YOURSELF!
YOU GUYS CAN COME TOO IF YOU WANT!
WHEN I THINK BACK...
...I'M EMBAR-RASSED AT HOW CHILDISH ...
...AND SEL-FISH I WAS THEN.

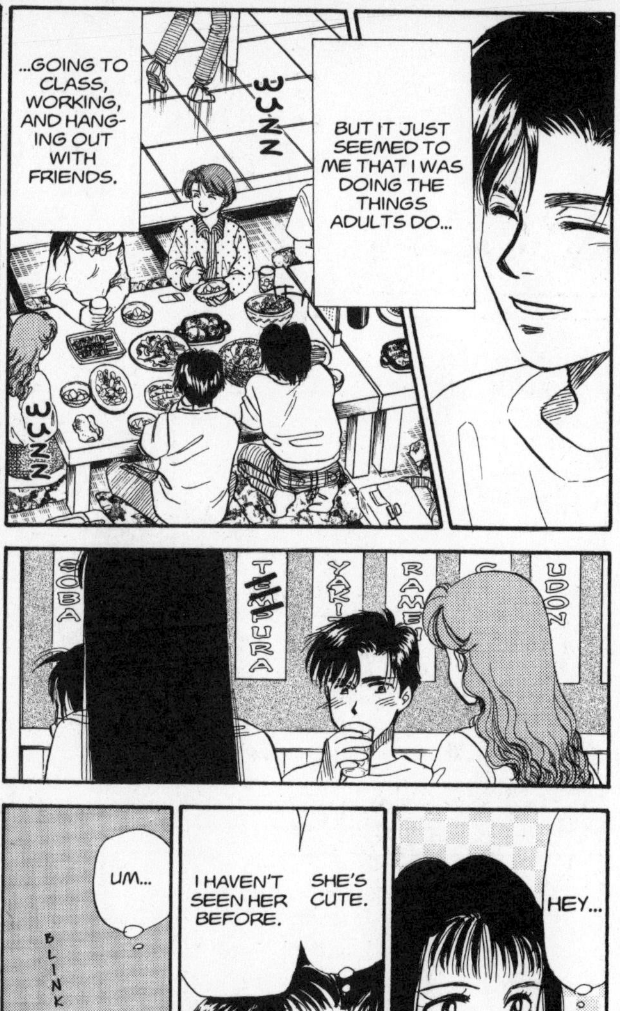

BUT IT JUST SEEMED TO ME THAT I WAS DOING THE THINGS ADULTS DO...
...GOING TO CLASS, WORKING, AND HANG-ING OUT WITH FRIENDS.
WUZZ
WUZZ
SOBA
TEMPURA
UDON
HEY...
SHE'S CUTE.
I HAVEN'T SEEN HER BEFORE.
UM...
BLINK

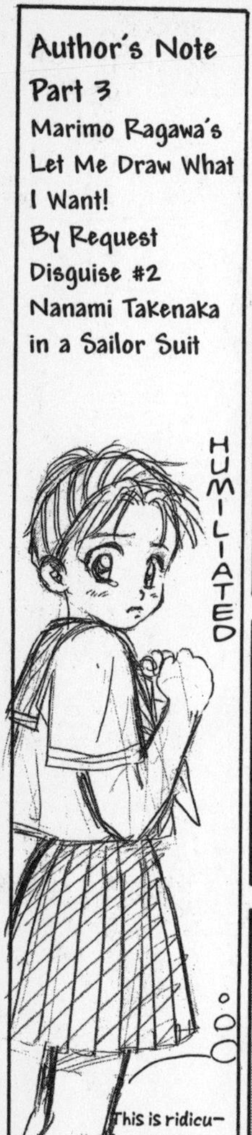

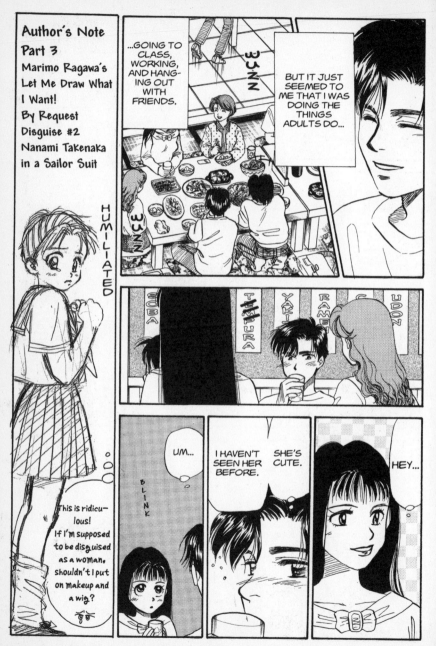

Author's Note
Part 3
Marimo Ragawa's Let Me Draw What I Want!
By Request
Disguise #2
Nanami Takenaka in a Sailor Suit
HUMILIATED
This is ridicu-lous! If I'm supposed to be disguised as a woman, shouldn't I put on makeup and a wig?

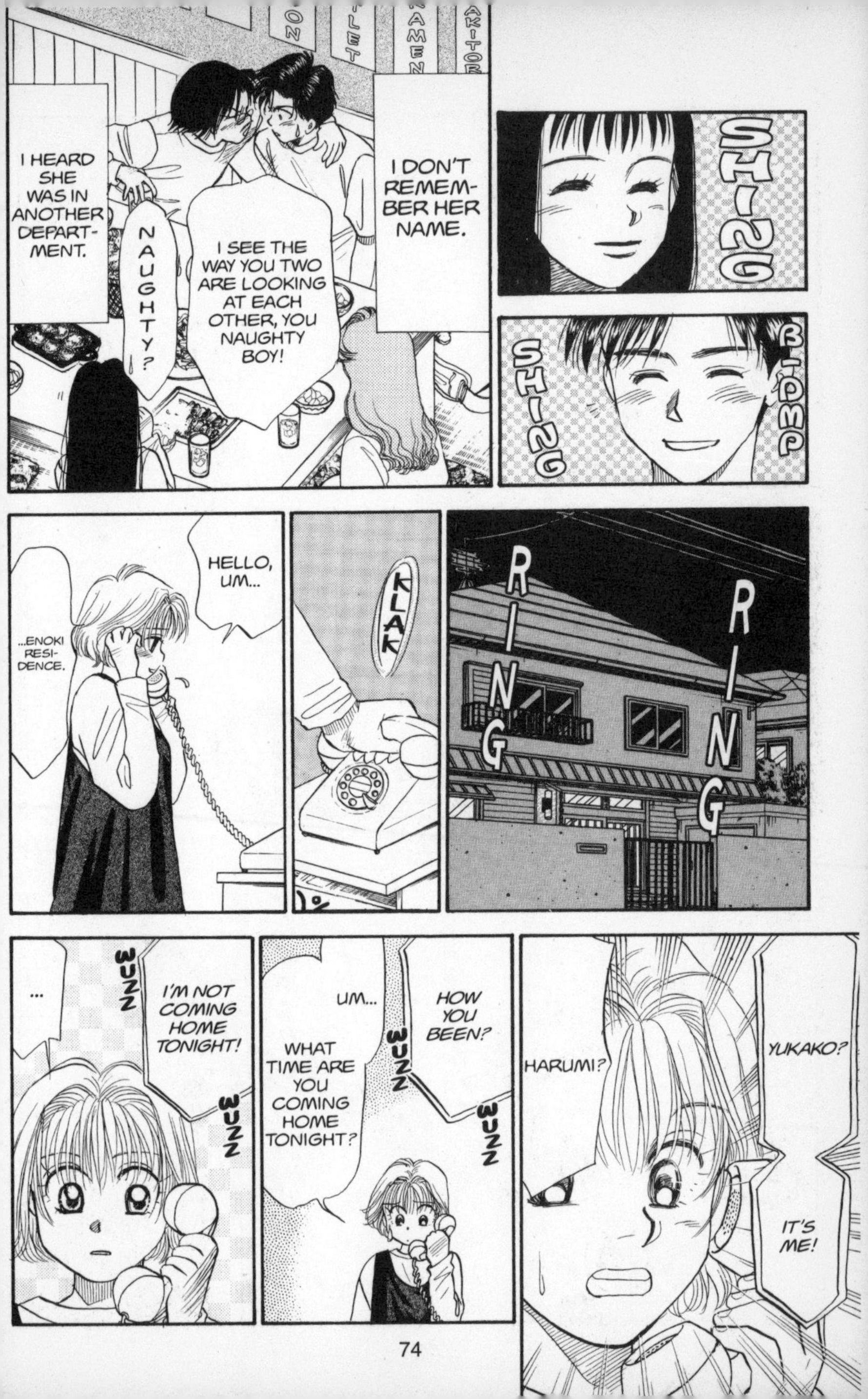
SHING
B-DMP
SHING
I DON'T REMEMBER HER NAME.
I SEE THE WAY YOU TWO ARE LOOKING AT EACH OTHER, YOU NAUGHTY BOY!
NAUGHTY?
I HEARD SHE WAS IN ANOTHER DEPARTMENT.
RING
RING
KLAK
HELLO, UM...
...ENOKI RESIDENCE.
YUKAKO?
IT'S ME!
HARUMI?
HOW YOU BEEN?
WUZZ
UM...
WHAT TIME ARE YOU COMING HOME TONIGHT?
WUZZ
I'M NOT COMING HOME TONIGHT!
WUZZ
...
WUZZ

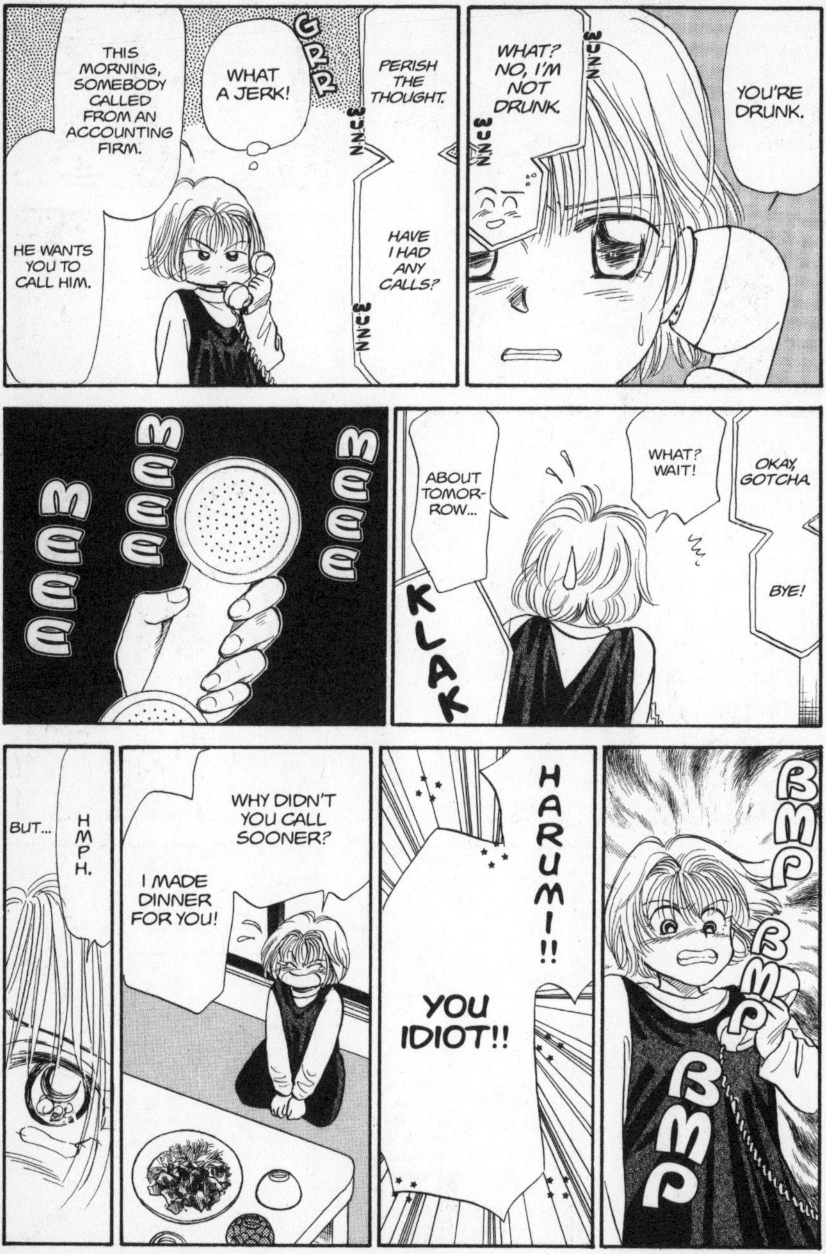
YOU'RE DRUNK.
WHAT? NO, I'M NOT DRUNK.
PERISH THE THOUGHT.
HAVE I HAD ANY CALLS?
GRR
WHAT A JERK!
THIS MORNING, SOMEBODY CALLED FROM AN ACCOUNTING FIRM.
HE WANTS YOU TO CALL HIM.
OKAY, GOTCHA.
BYE!
WHAT? WAIT!
ABOUT TOMORROW...
KLAK
MEEE
MEEE
MEEE
BMP
BMP
BMP
HARUMI!!
YOU IDIOT!!
WHY DIDN'T YOU CALL SOONER?
I MADE DINNER FOR YOU!
HMPH.
BUT...

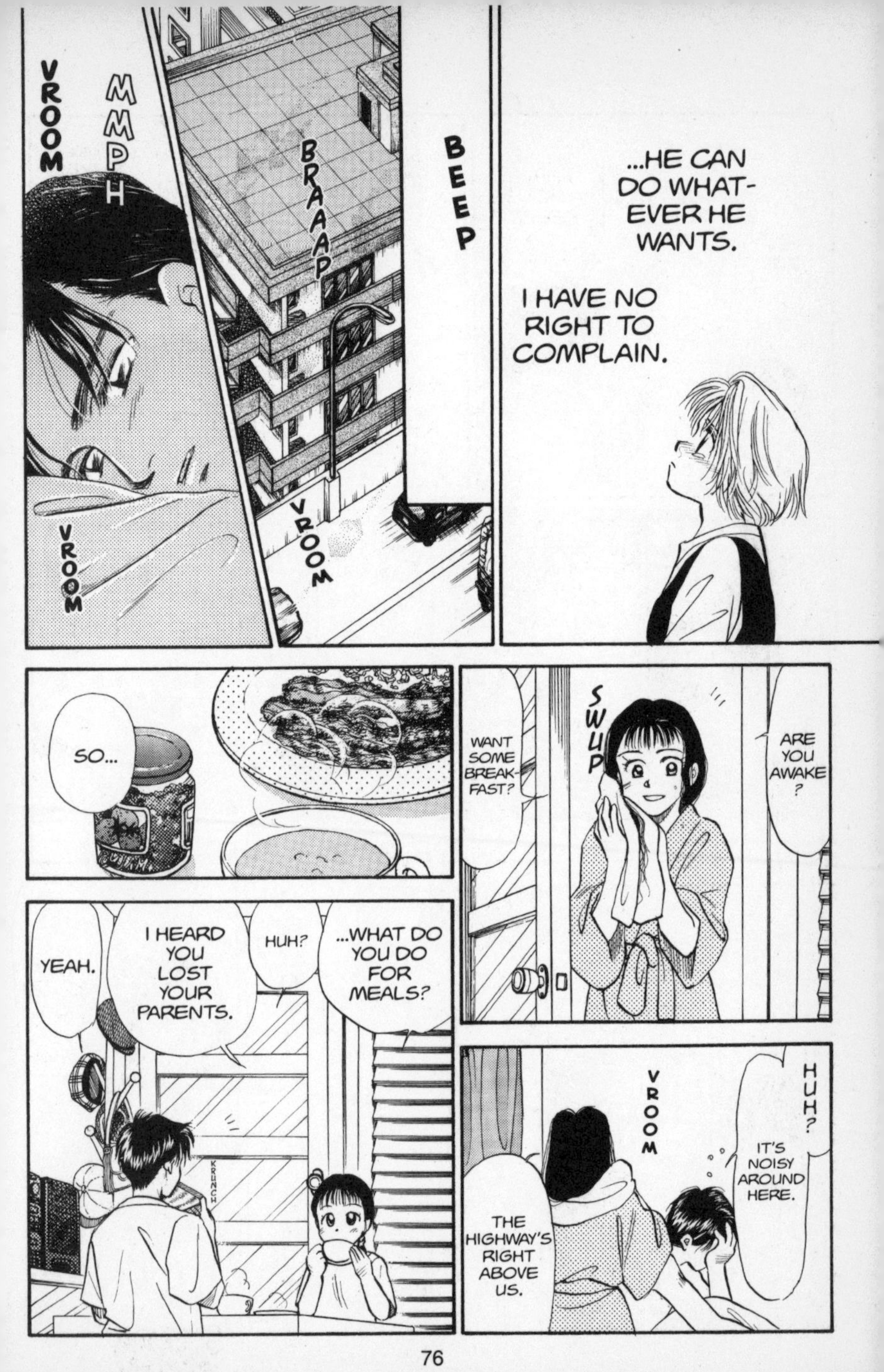
...HE CAN DO WHAT-EVER HE WANTS.
I HAVE NO RIGHT TO COMPLAIN.
BEEP
BRAAAAP
VROOM
VROOM
MMPH
VROOM
ARE YOU AWAKE?
SWUP
WANT SOME BREAK-FAST?
HUH?
IT'S NOISY AROUND HERE.
VROOM
THE HIGHWAY'S RIGHT ABOVE US.
SO...
...WHAT DO YOU DO FOR MEALS?
HUH?
I HEARD YOU LOST YOUR PARENTS.
YEAH.
KRUNCH

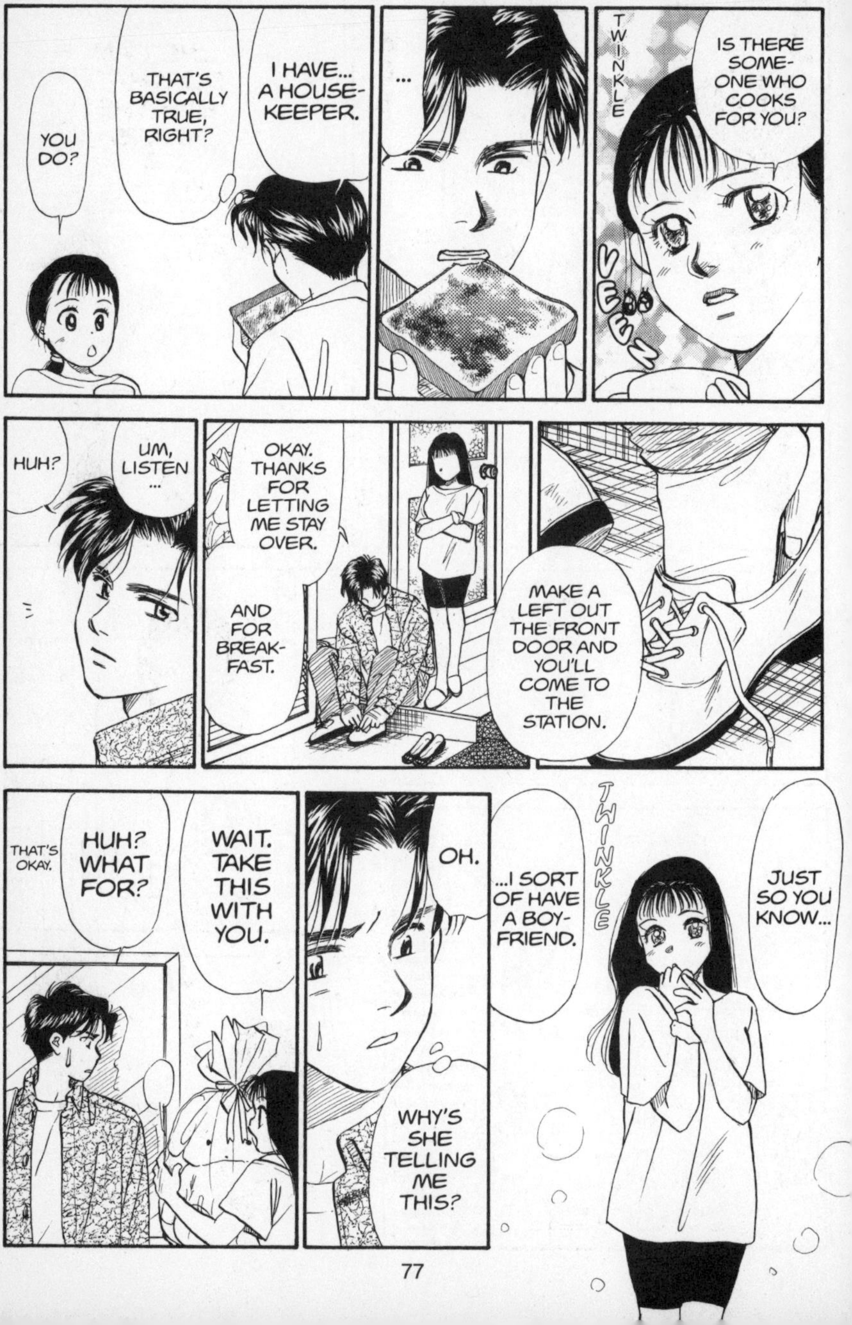
TWINKLE
IS THERE SOME-ONE WHO COOKS FOR YOU?
...
I HAVE... A HOUSE-KEEPER.
THAT'S BASICALLY TRUE, RIGHT?
YOU DO?
MAKE A LEFT OUT THE FRONT DOOR AND YOU'LL COME TO THE STATION.
OKAY. THANKS FOR LETTING ME STAY OVER.
AND FOR BREAK-FAST.
UM, LISTEN ...
HUH?
JUST SO YOU KNOW...
TWINKLE
...I SORT OF HAVE A BOY-FRIEND.
OH.
WHY'S SHE TELLING ME THIS?
WAIT. TAKE THIS WITH YOU.
HUH? WHAT FOR?
THAT'S OKAY.

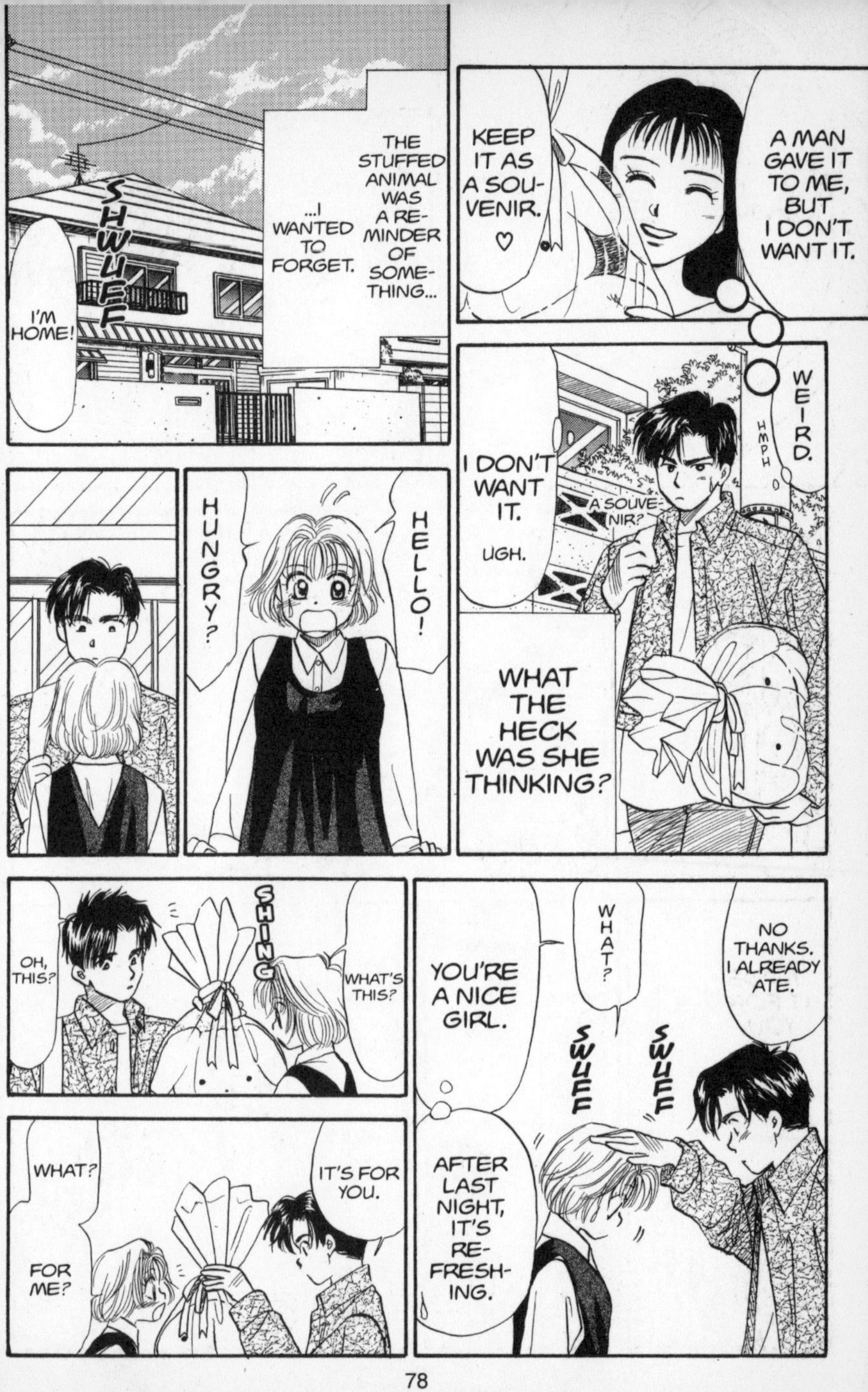
A MAN GAVE IT TO ME, BUT I DON'T WANT IT.
KEEP IT AS A SOUVENIR. ♡
THE STUFFED ANIMAL WAS A REMINDER OF SOMETHING...
...I WANTED TO FORGET.
SHWUFF
I'M HOME!
WEIRD.
HMPH
A SOUVENIR?
I DON'T WANT IT.
UGH.
WHAT THE HECK WAS SHE THINKING?
HELLO!
HUNGRY?
NO THANKS. I ALREADY ATE.
WHAT?
YOU'RE A NICE GIRL.
SWUFF
SWUFF
AFTER LAST NIGHT, IT'S REFRESHING.
WHAT'S THIS?
SHING
OH, THIS?
IT'S FOR YOU.
WHAT?
FOR ME?

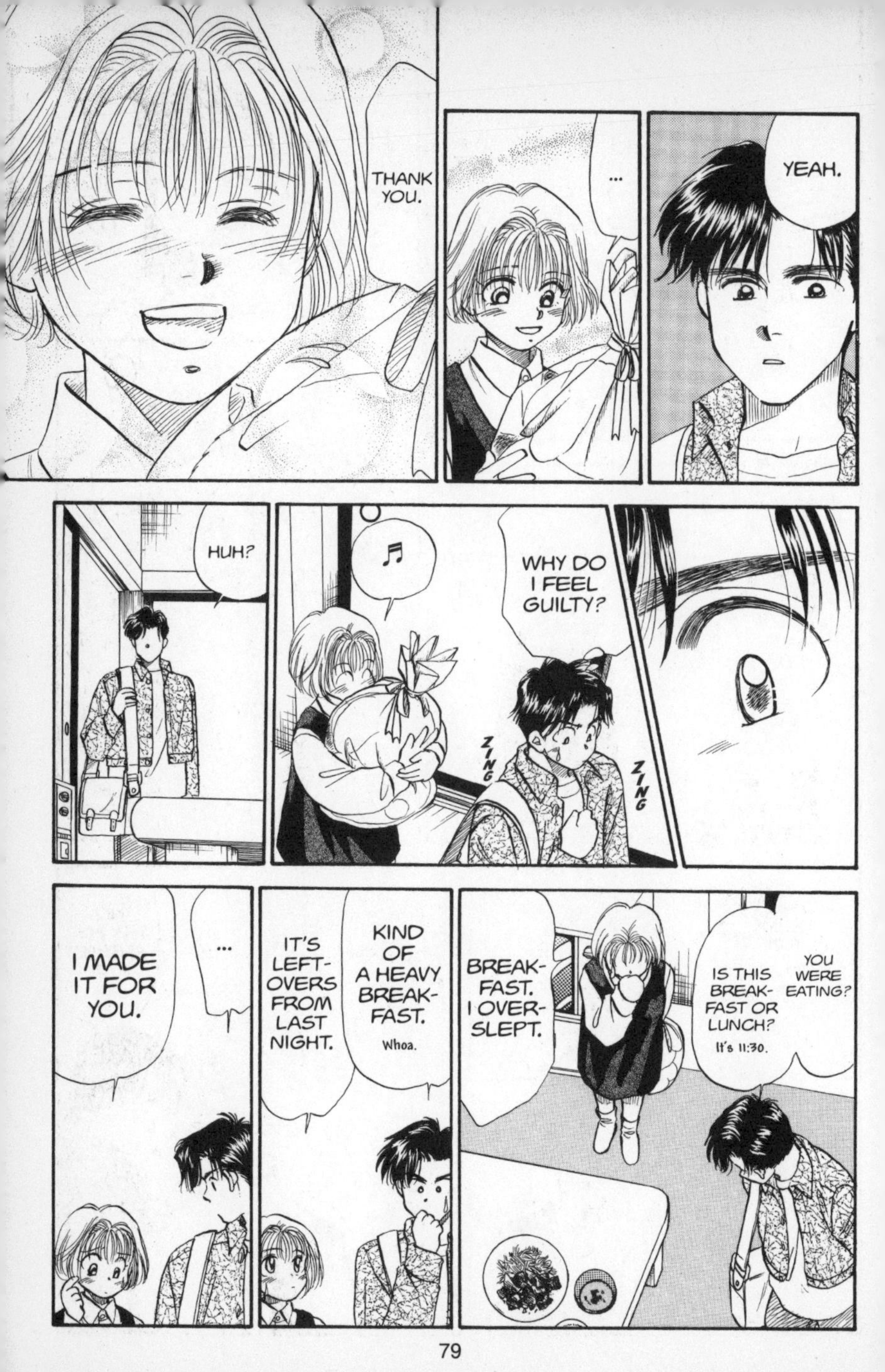
YEAH.
...
THANK YOU.
WHY DO I FEEL GUILTY?
♬
ZING
ZING
HUH?
YOU WERE EATING?
IS THIS BREAKFAST OR LUNCH?
It's 11:30.
BREAKFAST. I OVERSLEPT.
KIND OF A HEAVY BREAKFAST.
Whoa.
IT'S LEFTOVERS FROM LAST NIGHT.
...
I MADE IT FOR YOU.

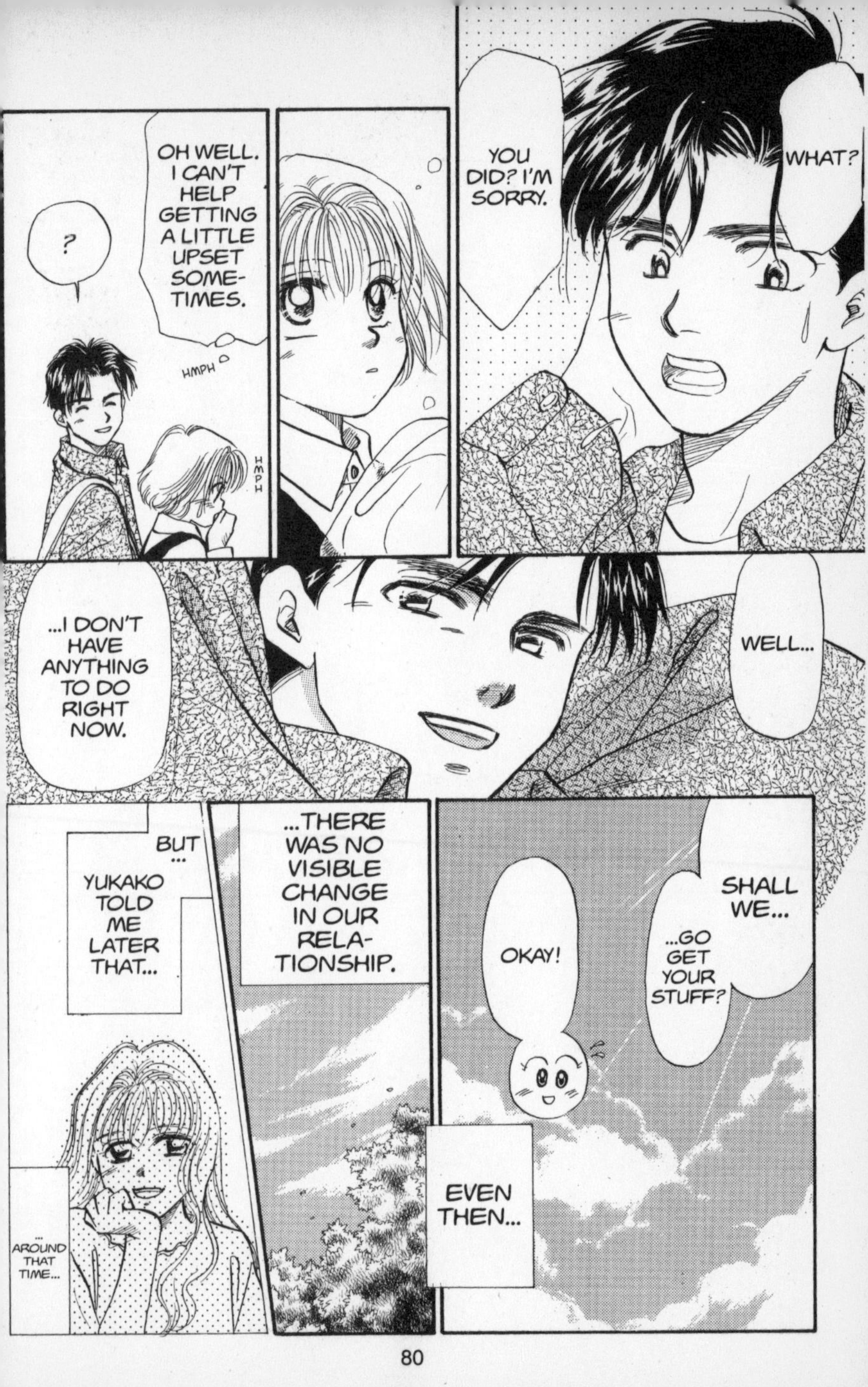
WHAT?
YOU DID? I'M SORRY.
OH WELL. I CAN'T HELP GETTING A LITTLE UPSET SOME-TIMES.
?
HMPH
HMPH
WELL...
...I DON'T HAVE ANYTHING TO DO RIGHT NOW.
SHALL WE...
...GO GET YOUR STUFF?
OKAY!
EVEN THEN...
...THERE WAS NO VISIBLE CHANGE IN OUR RELA-TIONSHIP.
BUT...
YUKAKO TOLD ME LATER THAT...
...AROUND THAT TIME...

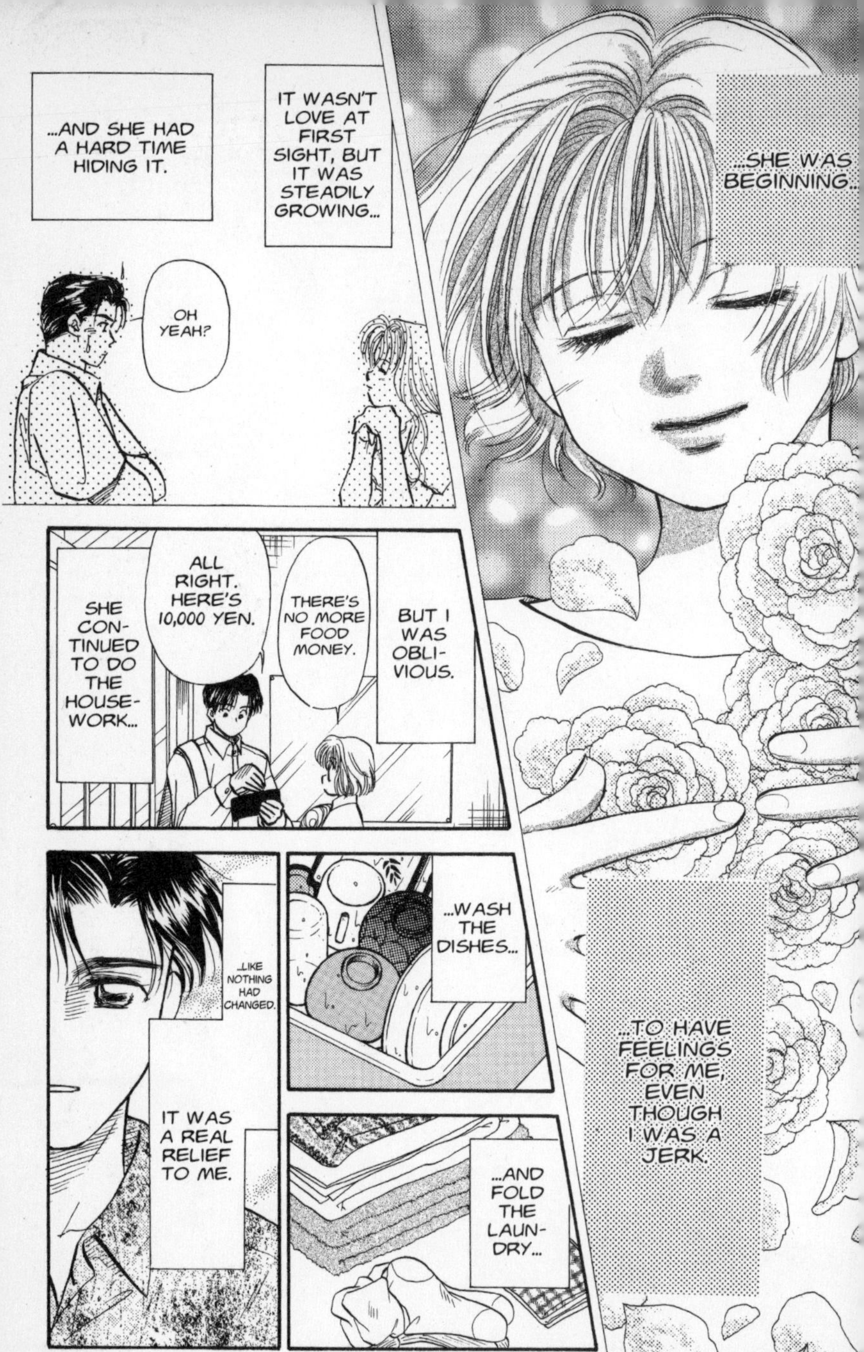

...SHE WAS BEGINNING...
...TO HAVE FEELINGS FOR ME, EVEN THOUGH I WAS A JERK.
IT WASN'T LOVE AT FIRST SIGHT, BUT IT WAS STEADILY GROWING...
...AND SHE HAD A HARD TIME HIDING IT.
OH YEAH?
BUT I WAS OBLIVIOUS.
THERE'S NO MORE FOOD MONEY.
ALL RIGHT. HERE'S 10,000 YEN.
SHE CONTINUED TO DO THE HOUSE-WORK...
...WASH THE DISHES...
...AND FOLD THE LAUNDRY...
...LIKE NOTHING HAD CHANGED.
IT WAS A REAL RELIEF TO ME.

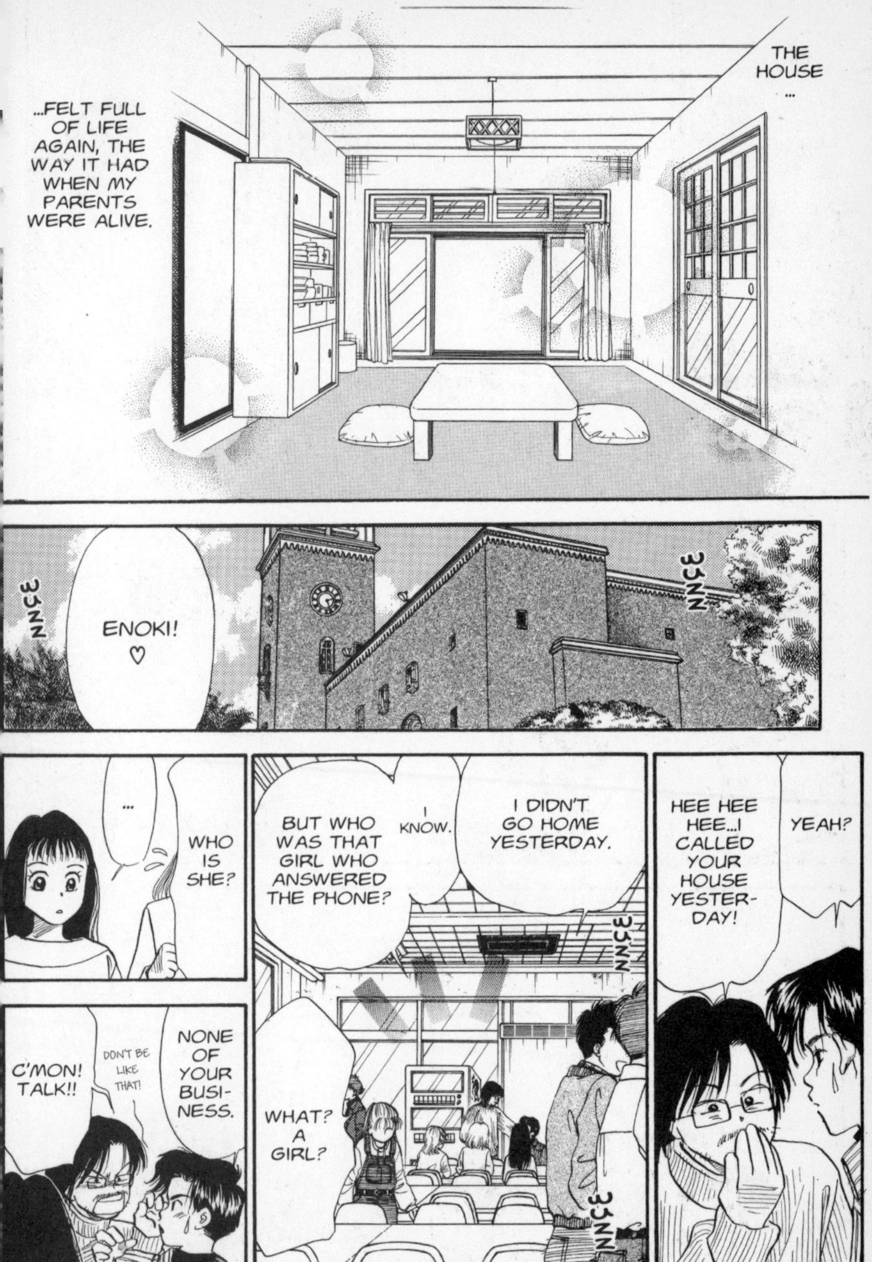
THE HOUSE ...
...FELT FULL OF LIFE AGAIN, THE WAY IT HAD WHEN MY PARENTS WERE ALIVE.
ENOKI! ♡
YEAH?
HEE HEE HEE...I CALLED YOUR HOUSE YESTERDAY!
I DIDN'T GO HOME YESTERDAY.
I KNOW.
BUT WHO WAS THAT GIRL WHO ANSWERED THE PHONE?
WHAT? A GIRL?
WHO IS SHE?
...
NONE OF YOUR BUSINESS.
DON'T BE LIKE THAT!
C'MON! TALK!!

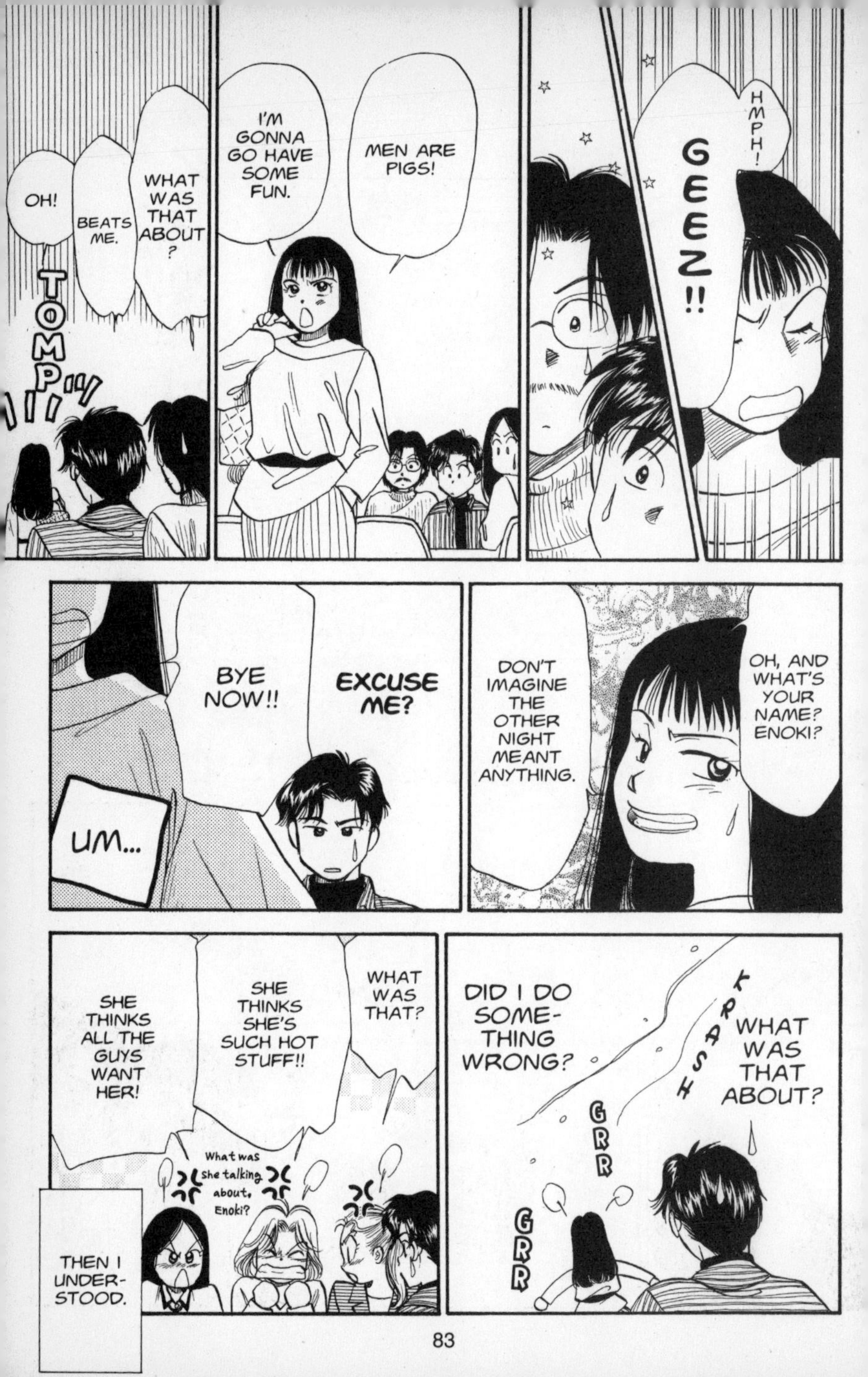

HMPH!
GEEZ!!
MEN ARE PIGS!
I'M GONNA GO HAVE SOME FUN.
WHAT WAS THAT ABOUT?
BEATS ME.
OH!
TOMP!
OH, AND WHAT'S YOUR NAME? ENOKI?
DON'T IMAGINE THE OTHER NIGHT MEANT ANYTHING.
EXCUSE ME?
BYE NOW!!
UM...
WHAT WAS THAT ABOUT?
KRASH
DID I DO SOME-THING WRONG?
GRR
GRR
WHAT WAS THAT?
SHE THINKS SHE'S SUCH HOT STUFF!!
SHE THINKS ALL THE GUYS WANT HER!
What was she talking about, Enoki?
THEN I UNDER-STOOD.

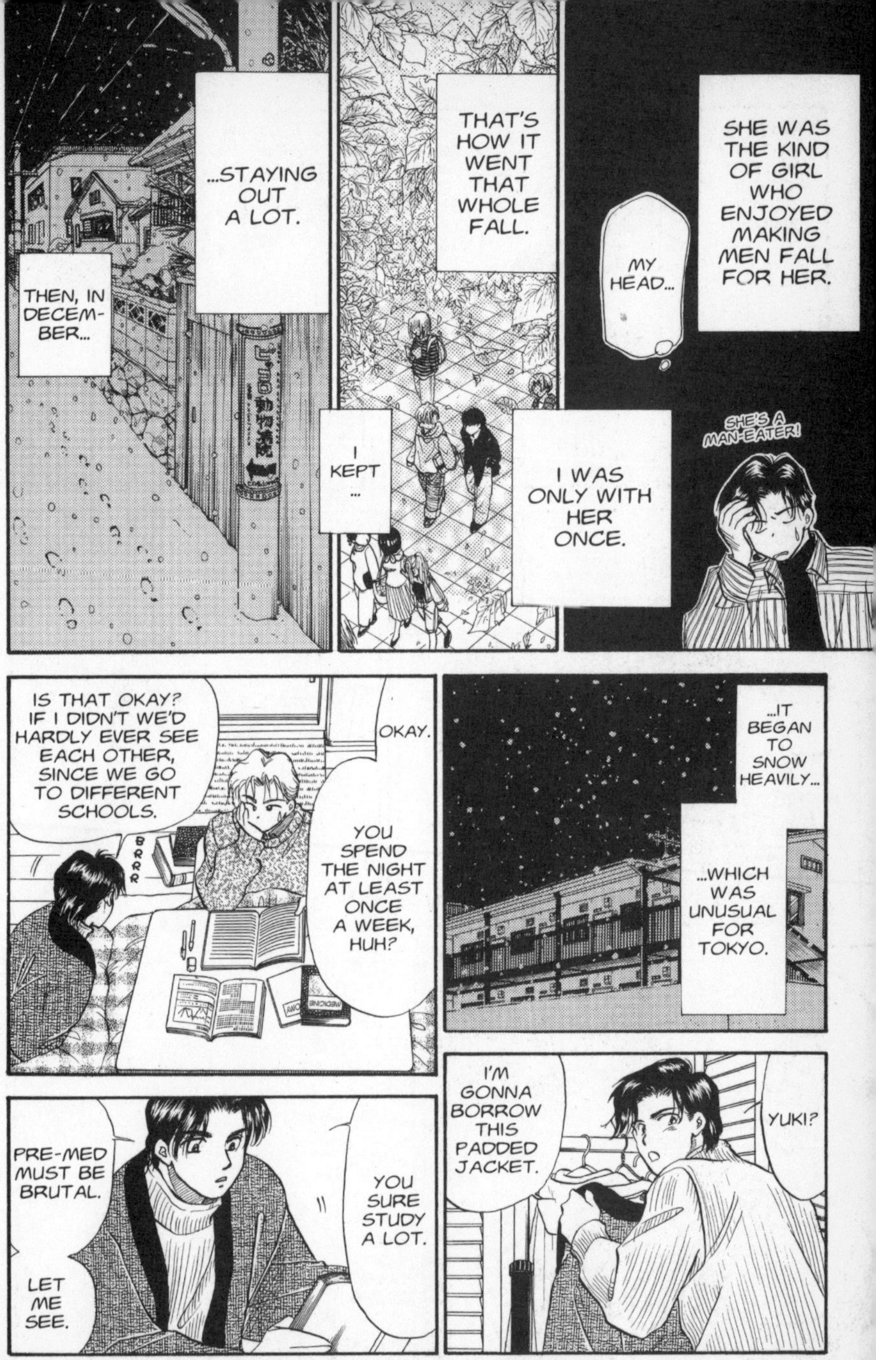
SHE WAS THE KIND OF GIRL WHO ENJOYED MAKING MEN FALL FOR HER.
MY HEAD...
SHE'S A MAN-EATER!
I WAS ONLY WITH HER ONCE.
THAT'S HOW IT WENT THAT WHOLE FALL.
I KEPT ...
...STAYING OUT A LOT.
THEN, IN DECEMBER...
...IT BEGAN TO SNOW HEAVILY...
...WHICH WAS UNUSUAL FOR TOKYO.
OKAY.
YOU SPEND THE NIGHT AT LEAST ONCE A WEEK, HUH?
IS THAT OKAY? IF I DIDN'T WE'D HARDLY EVER SEE EACH OTHER, SINCE WE GO TO DIFFERENT SCHOOLS.
BRRR
YUKI?
I'M GONNA BORROW THIS PADDED JACKET.
YOU SURE STUDY A LOT.
PRE-MED MUST BE BRUTAL.
LET ME SEE.

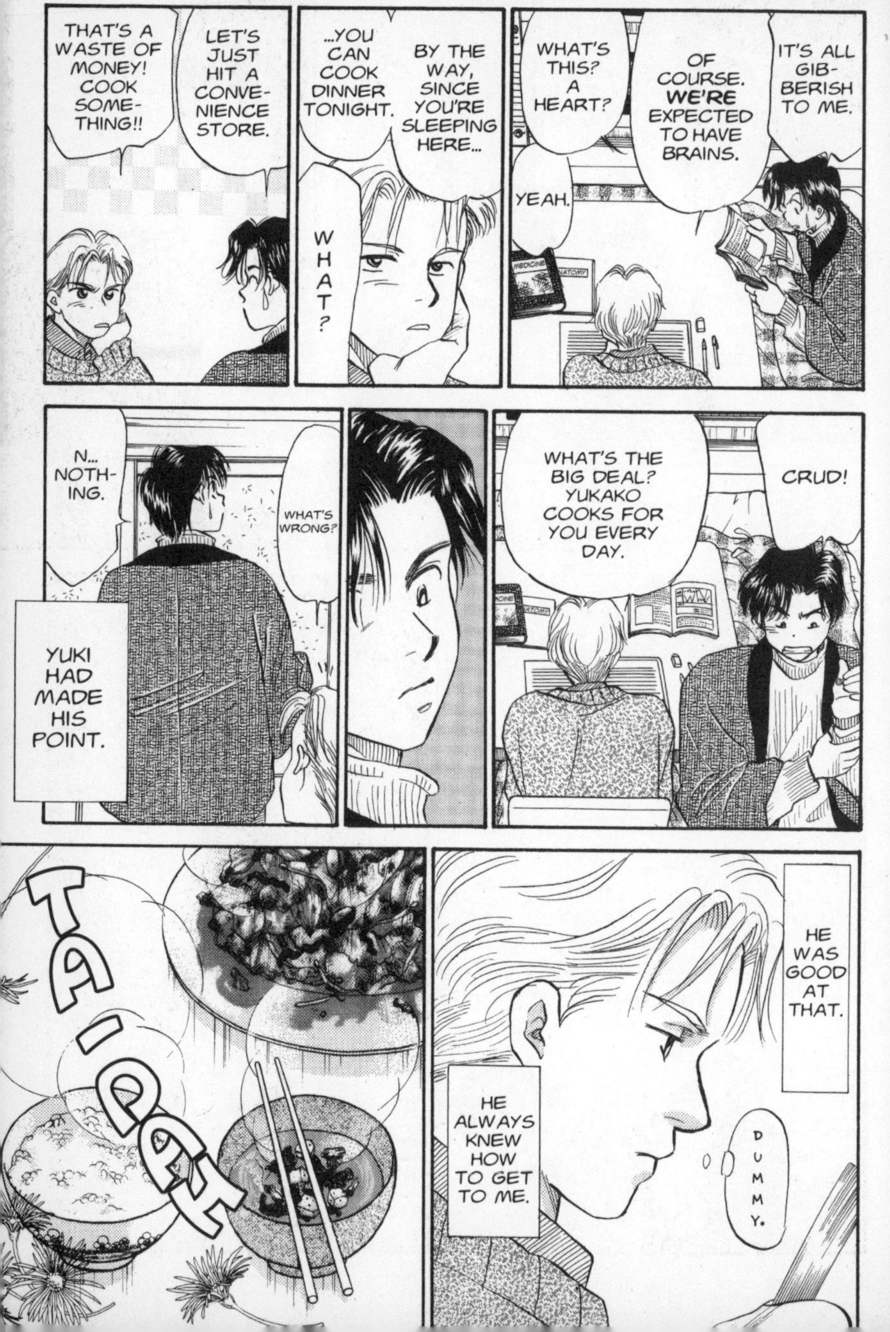
IT'S ALL GIBBERISH TO ME.
OF COURSE. WE'RE EXPECTED TO HAVE BRAINS.
WHAT'S THIS? A HEART?
YEAH.
MEDICINE
ANATOMY
BY THE WAY, SINCE YOU'RE SLEEPING HERE...
...YOU CAN COOK DINNER TONIGHT.
WHAT?
LET'S JUST HIT A CONVENIENCE STORE.
THAT'S A WASTE OF MONEY! COOK SOMETHING!!
CRUD!
WHAT'S THE BIG DEAL? YUKAKO COOKS FOR YOU EVERY DAY.
WHAT'S WRONG?
N... NOTHING.
YUKI HAD MADE HIS POINT.
HE WAS GOOD AT THAT.
DUMMY.
HE ALWAYS KNEW HOW TO GET TO ME.
TA-DAH

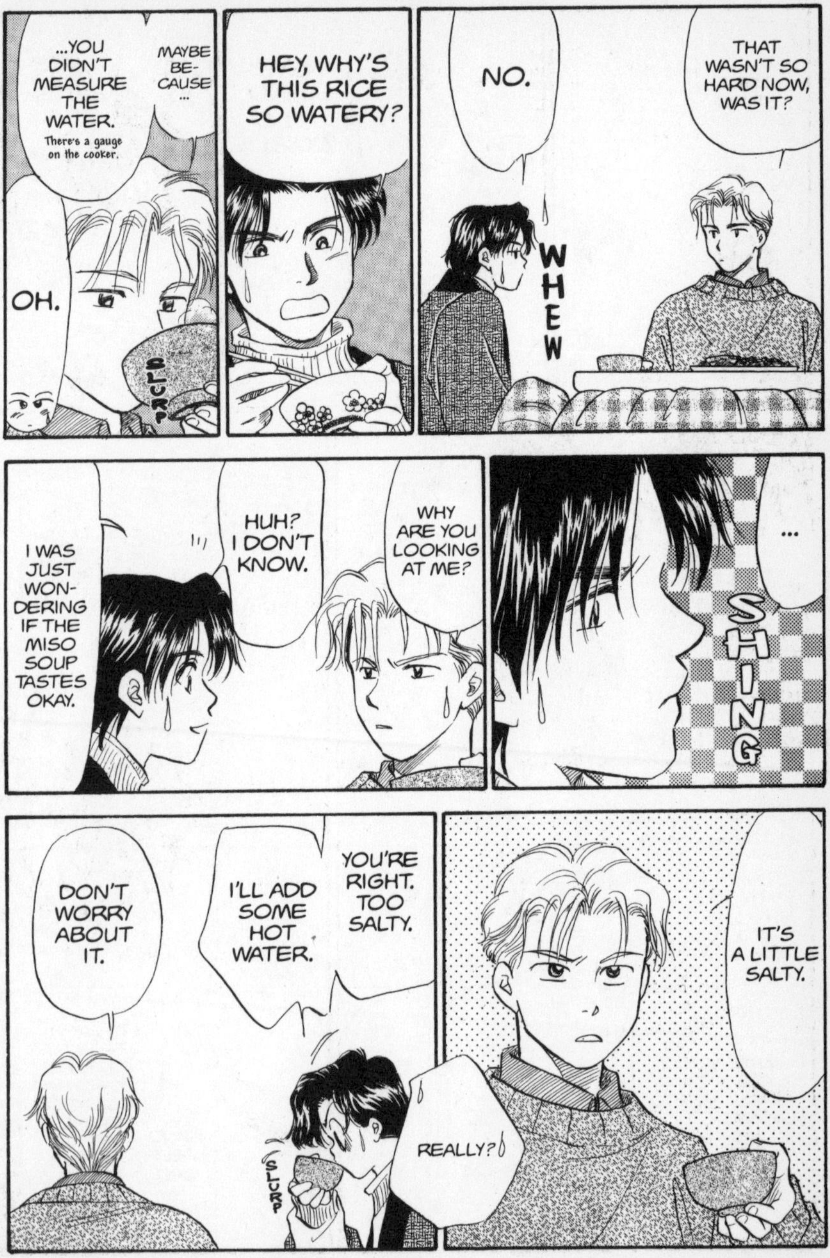
THAT WASN'T SO HARD NOW, WAS IT?
NO.
WHEW
HEY, WHY'S THIS RICE SO WATERY?
MAYBE BE-CAUSE ...
...YOU DIDN'T MEASURE THE WATER.
There's a gauge on the cooker.
SLURP
OH.
...
SHING
WHY ARE YOU LOOKING AT ME?
HUH? I DON'T KNOW.
I WAS JUST WONDERING IF THE MISO SOUP TASTES OKAY.
IT'S A LITTLE SALTY.
REALLY?
YOU'RE RIGHT. TOO SALTY.
I'LL ADD SOME HOT WATER.
SLURP
DON'T WORRY ABOUT IT.

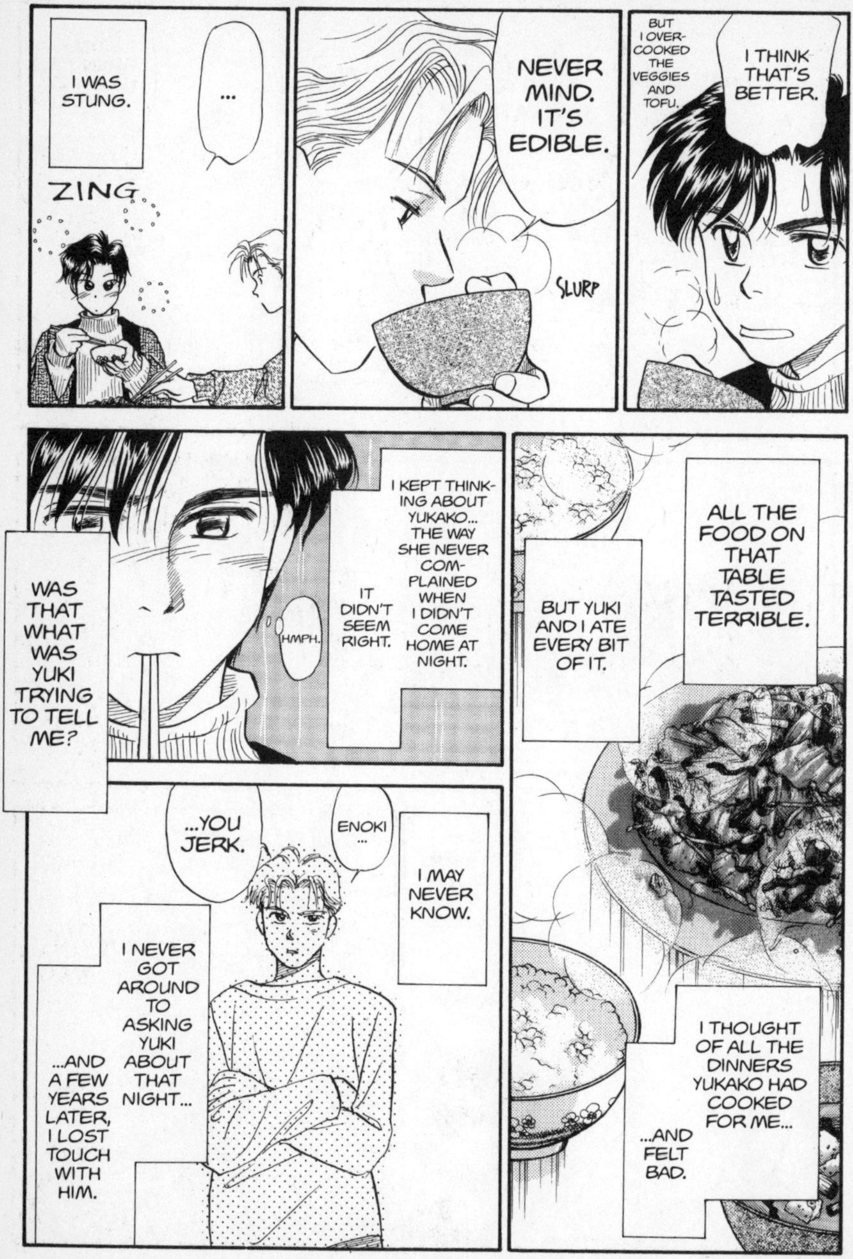
I THINK THAT'S BETTER.
BUT I OVER-COOKED THE VEGGIES AND TOFU.
NEVER MIND. IT'S EDIBLE.
SLURP
...
I WAS STUNG.
ZING
ALL THE FOOD ON THAT TABLE TASTED TERRIBLE.
BUT YUKI AND I ATE EVERY BIT OF IT.
I THOUGHT OF ALL THE DINNERS YUKAKO HAD COOKED FOR ME...
...AND FELT BAD.
I KEPT THINKING ABOUT YUKAKO... THE WAY SHE NEVER COMPLAINED WHEN I DIDN'T COME HOME AT NIGHT.
IT DIDN'T SEEM RIGHT.
HMPH.
WAS THAT WHAT WAS YUKI TRYING TO TELL ME?
I MAY NEVER KNOW.
ENOKI...
...YOU JERK.
I NEVER GOT AROUND TO ASKING YUKI ABOUT THAT NIGHT...
...AND A FEW YEARS LATER, I LOST TOUCH WITH HIM.

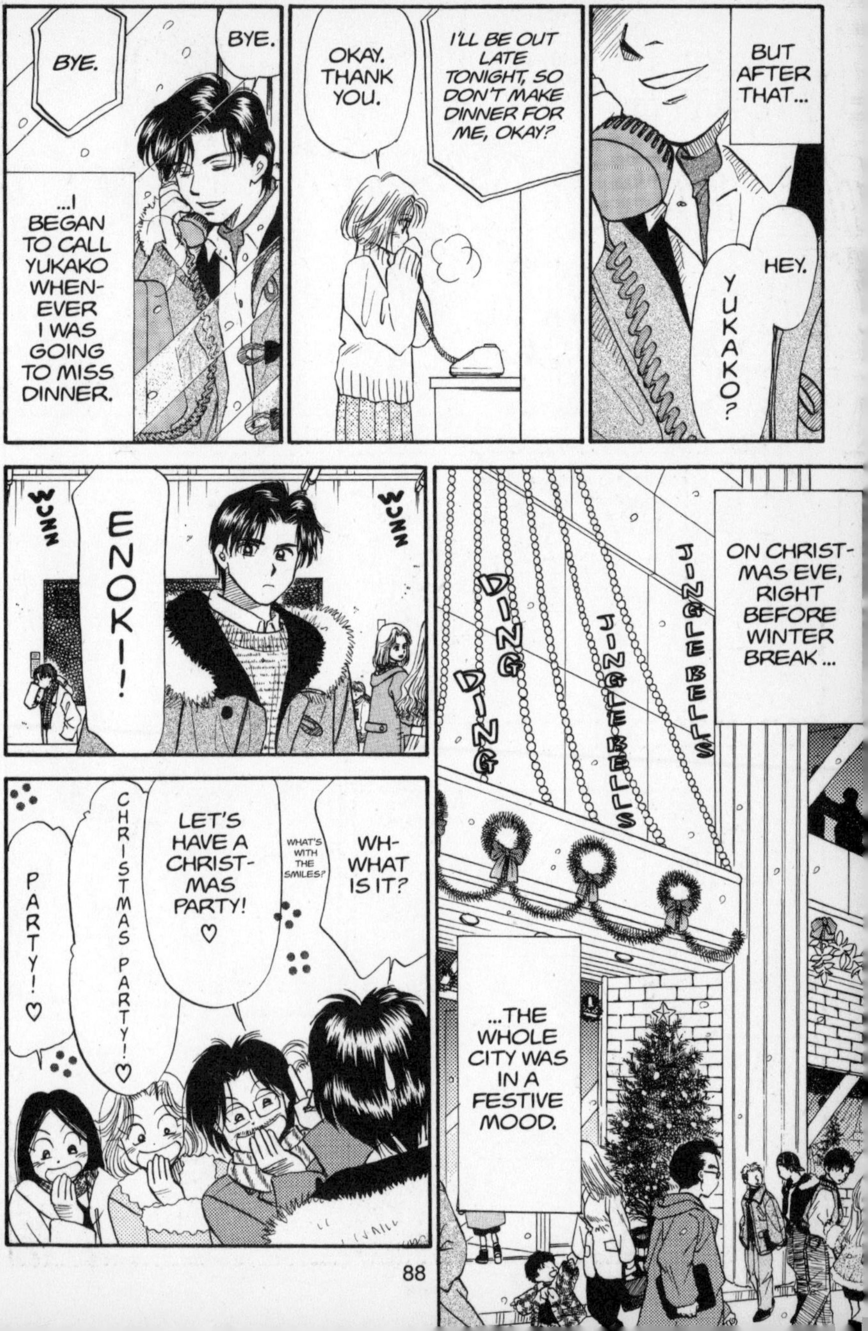
BUT AFTER THAT...
HEY.
YUKAKO?
I'LL BE OUT LATE TONIGHT, SO DON'T MAKE DINNER FOR ME, OKAY?
OKAY. THANK YOU.
BYE.
BYE.
...I BEGAN TO CALL YUKAKO WHENEVER I WAS GOING TO MISS DINNER.
ON CHRISTMAS EVE, RIGHT BEFORE WINTER BREAK...
JINGLE BELLS
JINGLE BELLS
DING
DING
...THE WHOLE CITY WAS IN A FESTIVE MOOD.
WUNN
ENOKI!
WUNN
WH-WHAT IS IT?
WHAT'S WITH THE SMILES?
LET'S HAVE A CHRISTMAS PARTY! ♡
CHRISTMAS PARTY! ♡
PARTY! ♡

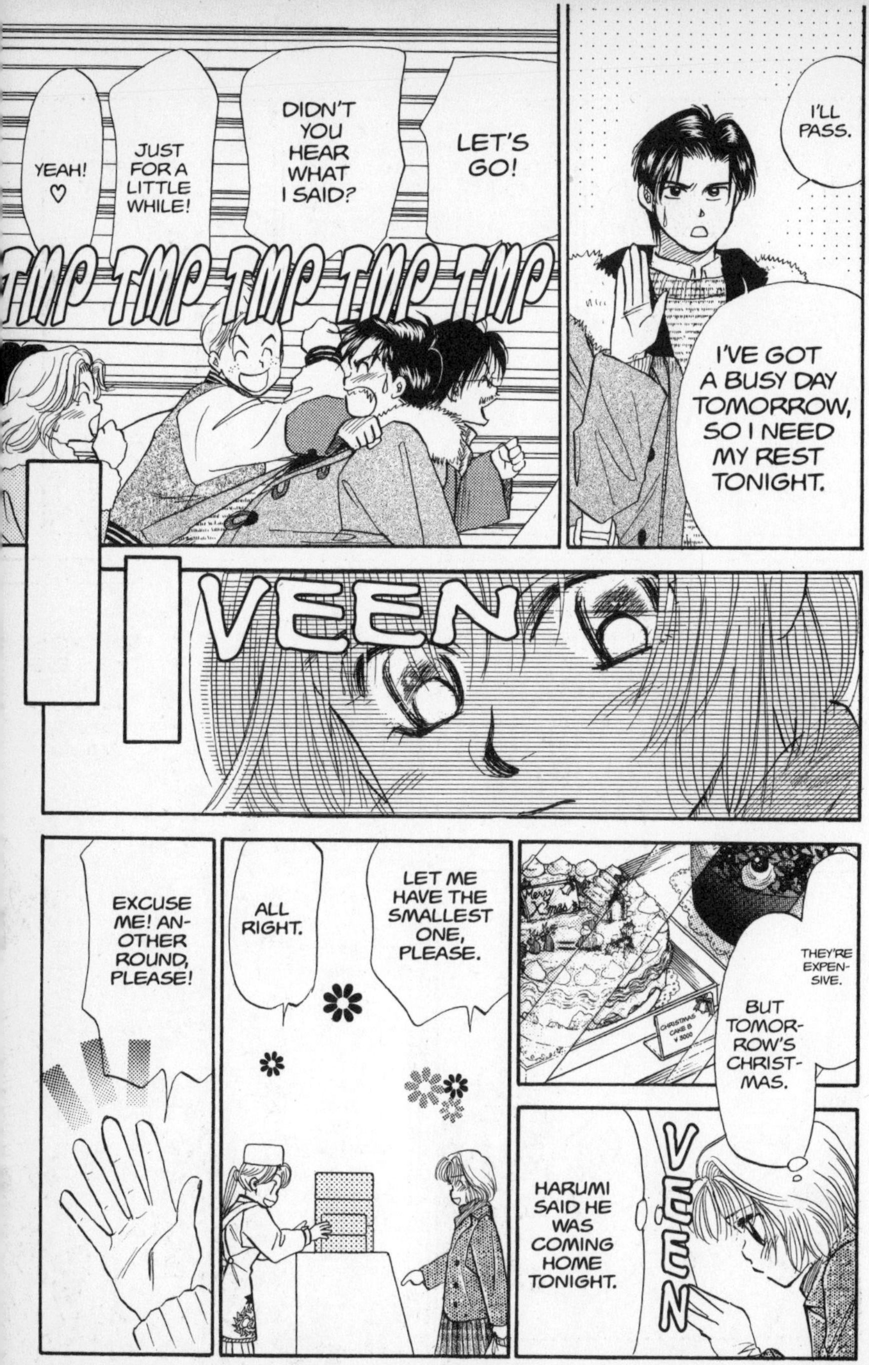
I'LL PASS.
I'VE GOT A BUSY DAY TOMORROW, SO I NEED MY REST TONIGHT.
LET'S GO!
DIDN'T YOU HEAR WHAT I SAID?
JUST FOR A LITTLE WHILE!
YEAH! ♡
TMP TMP TMP TMP TMP
VEEN
Merry X'mas
CHRISTMAS CAKE B ¥3000
THEY'RE EXPEN-SIVE.
BUT TOMOR-ROW'S CHRIST-MAS.
VEEN
HARUMI SAID HE WAS COMING HOME TONIGHT.
LET ME HAVE THE SMALLEST ONE, PLEASE.
ALL RIGHT.
EXCUSE ME! AN-OTHER ROUND, PLEASE!

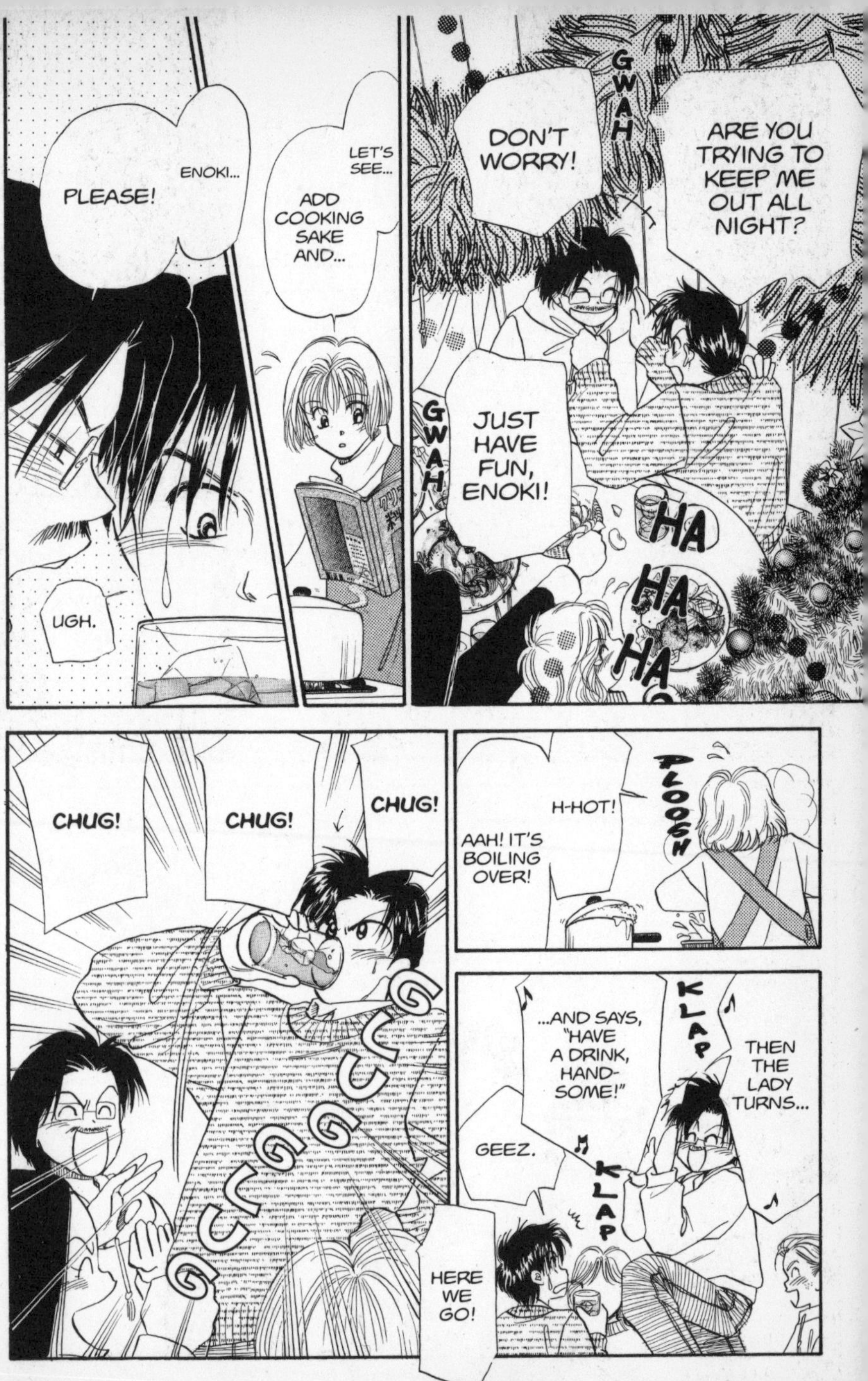
ARE YOU TRYING TO KEEP ME OUT ALL NIGHT?
GWAH
DON'T WORRY!
JUST HAVE FUN, ENOKI!
GWAH
HA HA HA
LET'S SEE...
ADD COOKING SAKE AND...
ENOKI...
PLEASE!
UGH.
PLOOSH
H-HOT!
AAH! IT'S BOILING OVER!
THEN THE LADY TURNS...
KLAP
...AND SAYS, "HAVE A DRINK, HANDSOME!"
KLAP
GEEZ.
CHUG!
CHUG!
CHUG!
HERE WE GO!

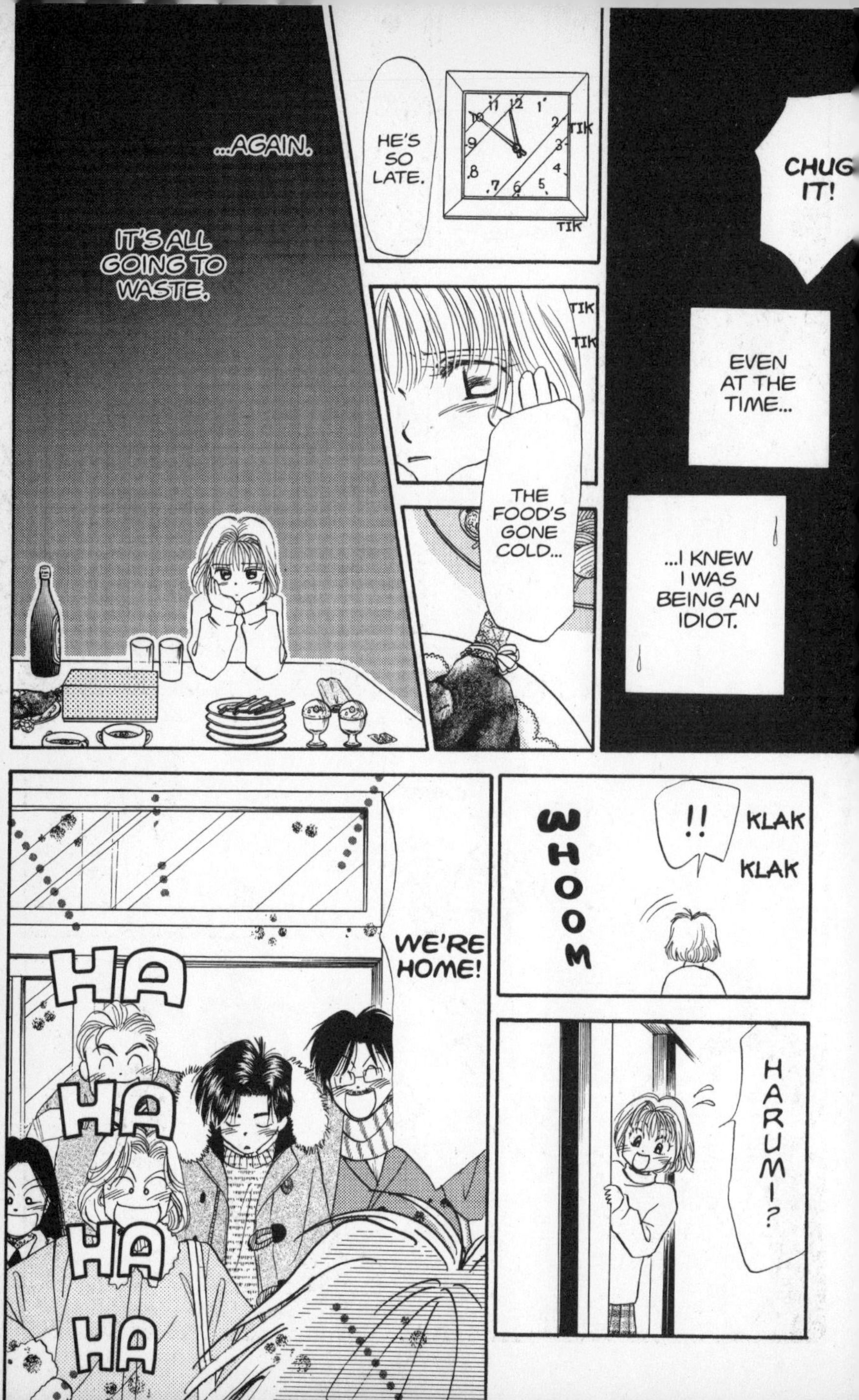

CHUG IT!
EVEN AT THE TIME...
...I KNEW I WAS BEING AN IDIOT.
HE'S SO LATE.
TIK
TIK
TIK
TIK
THE FOOD'S GONE COLD...
...AGAIN.
IT'S ALL GOING TO WASTE.
!!
KLAK
KLAK
WHOOM
HARUMI?
WE'RE HOME!
HA HA HA HA

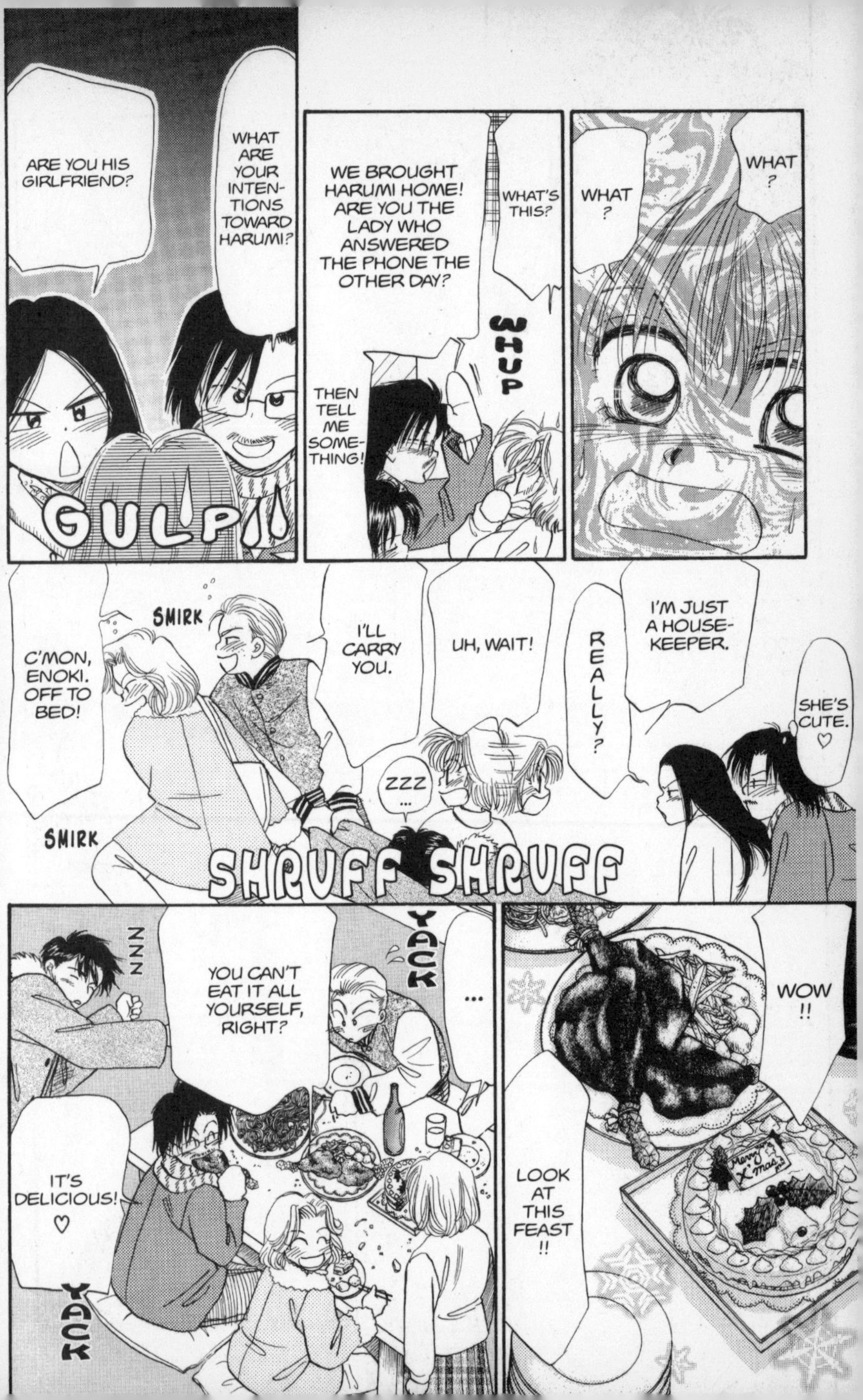
WHAT ?
WHAT ?
WHAT'S THIS?
WE BROUGHT HARUMI HOME! ARE YOU THE LADY WHO ANSWERED THE PHONE THE OTHER DAY?
WHUP
THEN TELL ME SOME-THING!
WHAT ARE YOUR INTEN-TIONS TOWARD HARUMI?
ARE YOU HIS GIRLFRIEND?
GULP
SHE'S CUTE. ♡
I'M JUST A HOUSE-KEEPER.
REALLY?
UH, WAIT!
I'LL CARRY YOU.
ZZZ ...
SMIRK
C'MON, ENOKI. OFF TO BED!
SMIRK
SHRUFF SHRUFF
WOW !!
LOOK AT THIS FEAST !!
YACK
...
YOU CAN'T EAT IT ALL YOURSELF, RIGHT?
ZZZ
IT'S DELICIOUS! ♡
YACK

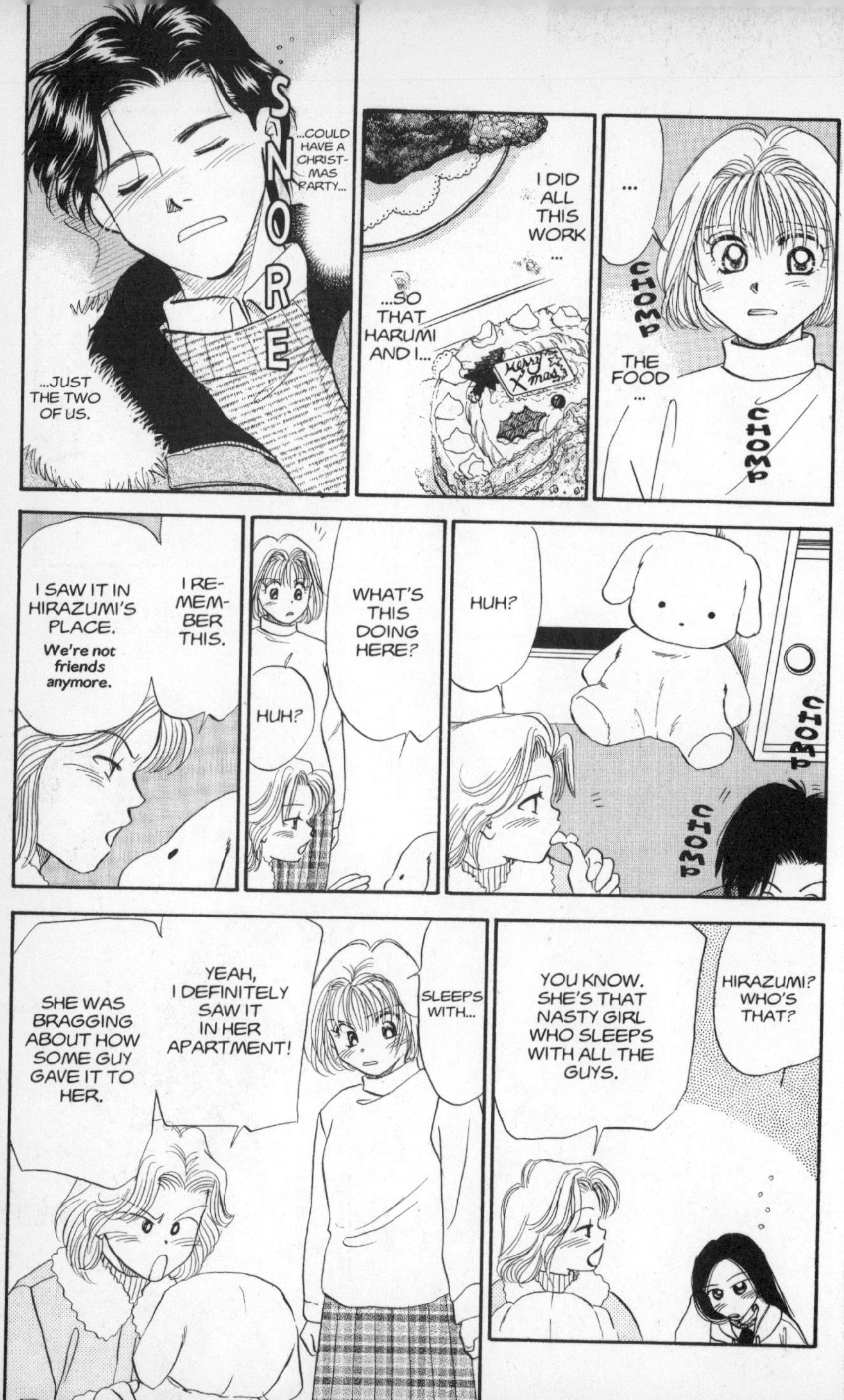
...
THE FOOD ...
CHOMP
CHOMP
I DID ALL THIS WORK ...
...SO THAT HARUMI AND I...
Merry X'mas
...COULD HAVE A CHRISTMAS PARTY...
SNORE
...JUST THE TWO OF US.
HUH?
CHOMP
CHOMP
WHAT'S THIS DOING HERE?
HUH?
I REMEMBER THIS.
I SAW IT IN HIRAZUMI'S PLACE.
We're not friends anymore.
HIRAZUMI? WHO'S THAT?
YOU KNOW. SHE'S THAT NASTY GIRL WHO SLEEPS WITH ALL THE GUYS.
SLEEPS WITH...
YEAH, I DEFINITELY SAW IT IN HER APARTMENT!
SHE WAS BRAGGING ABOUT HOW SOME GUY GAVE IT TO HER.

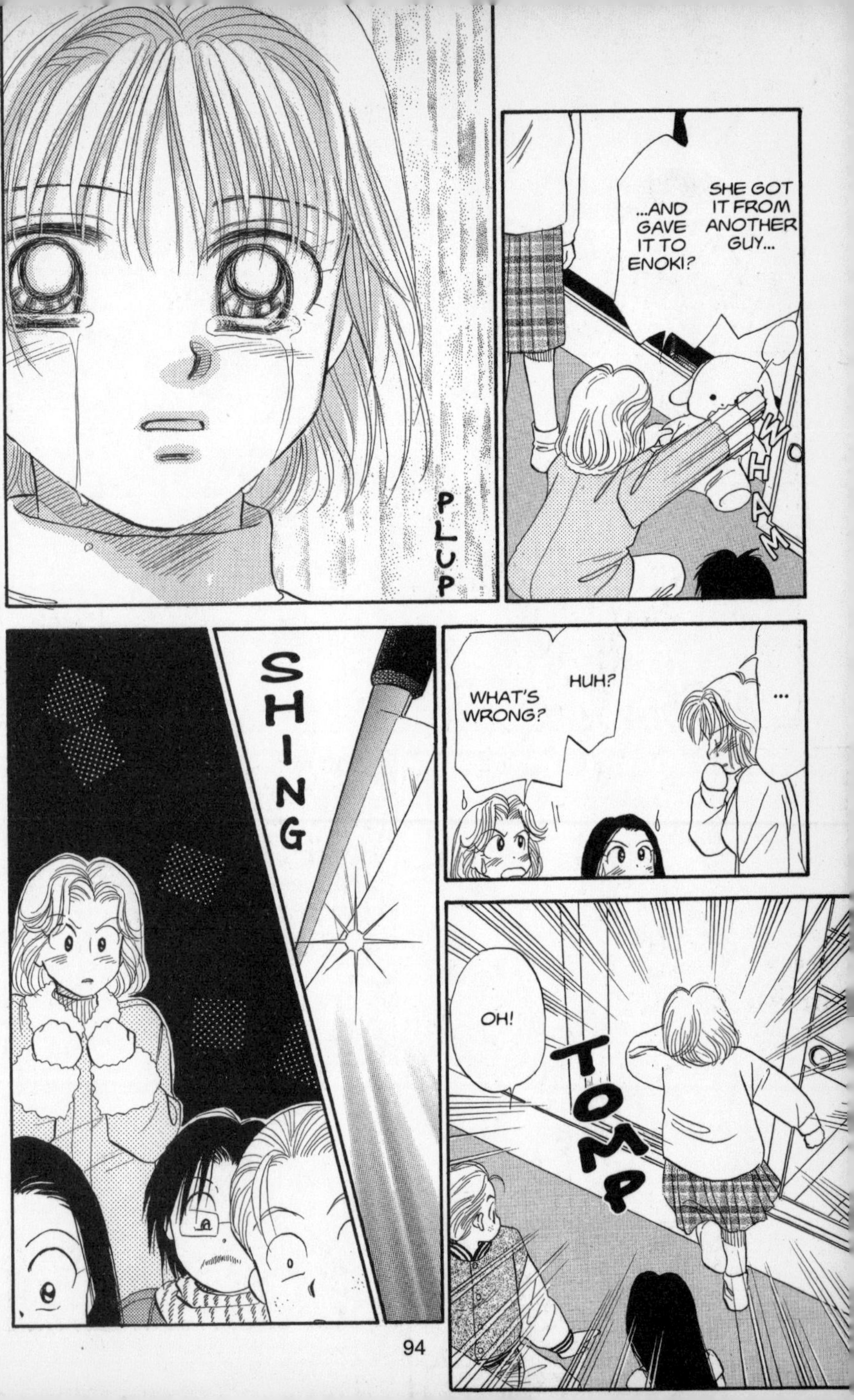
SHE GOT IT FROM ANOTHER GUY...
...AND GAVE IT TO ENOKI?
WHAM
PLUP
...
HUH?
WHAT'S WRONG?
OH!
TOMP
SHING

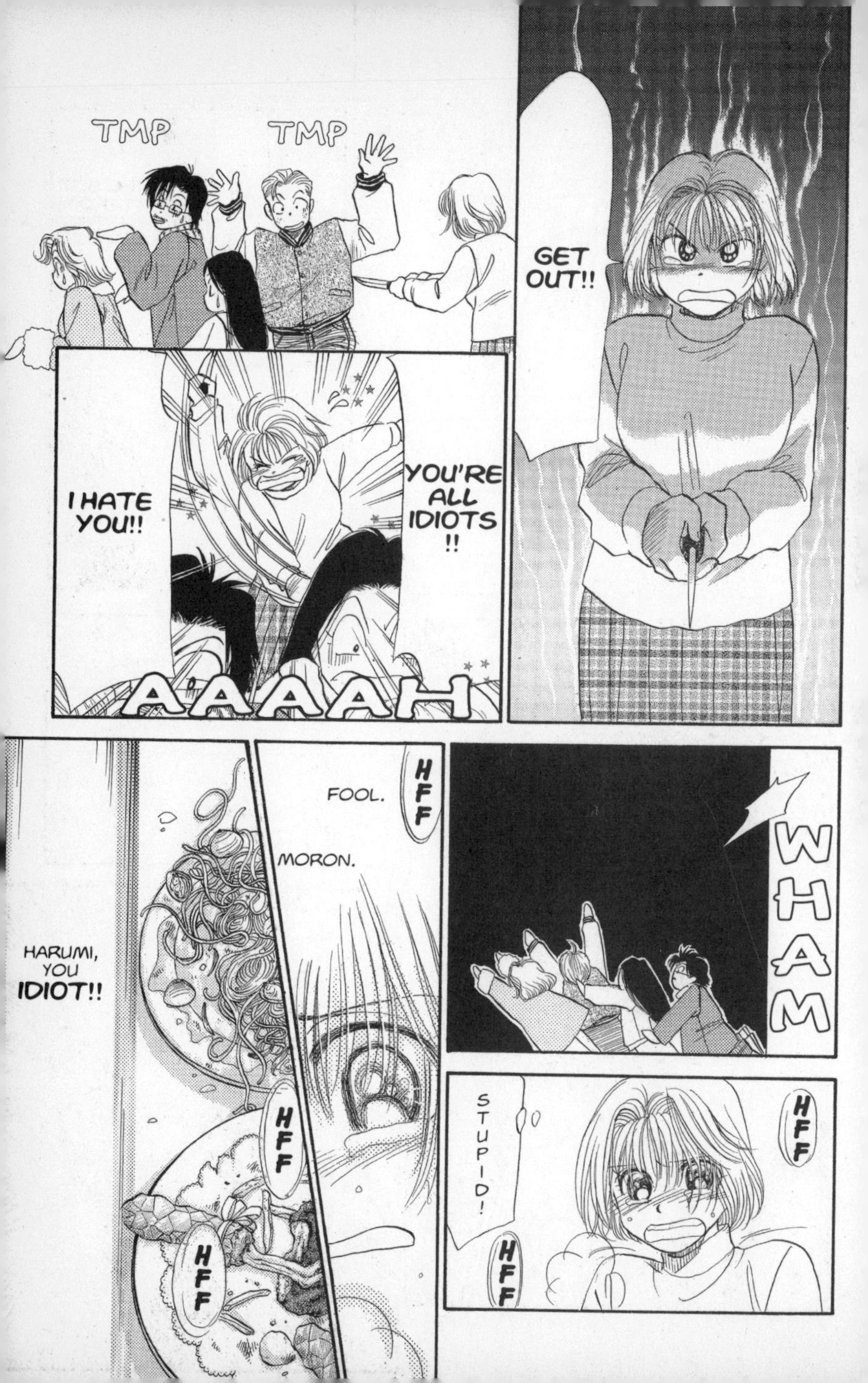
GET OUT!!
TMP
TMP
YOU'RE ALL IDIOTS!!
I HATE YOU!!
AAAAH
WHAM
HFF
STUPID!
HFF
HFF
FOOL.
MORON.
HARUMI, YOU IDIOT!!
HFF
HFF

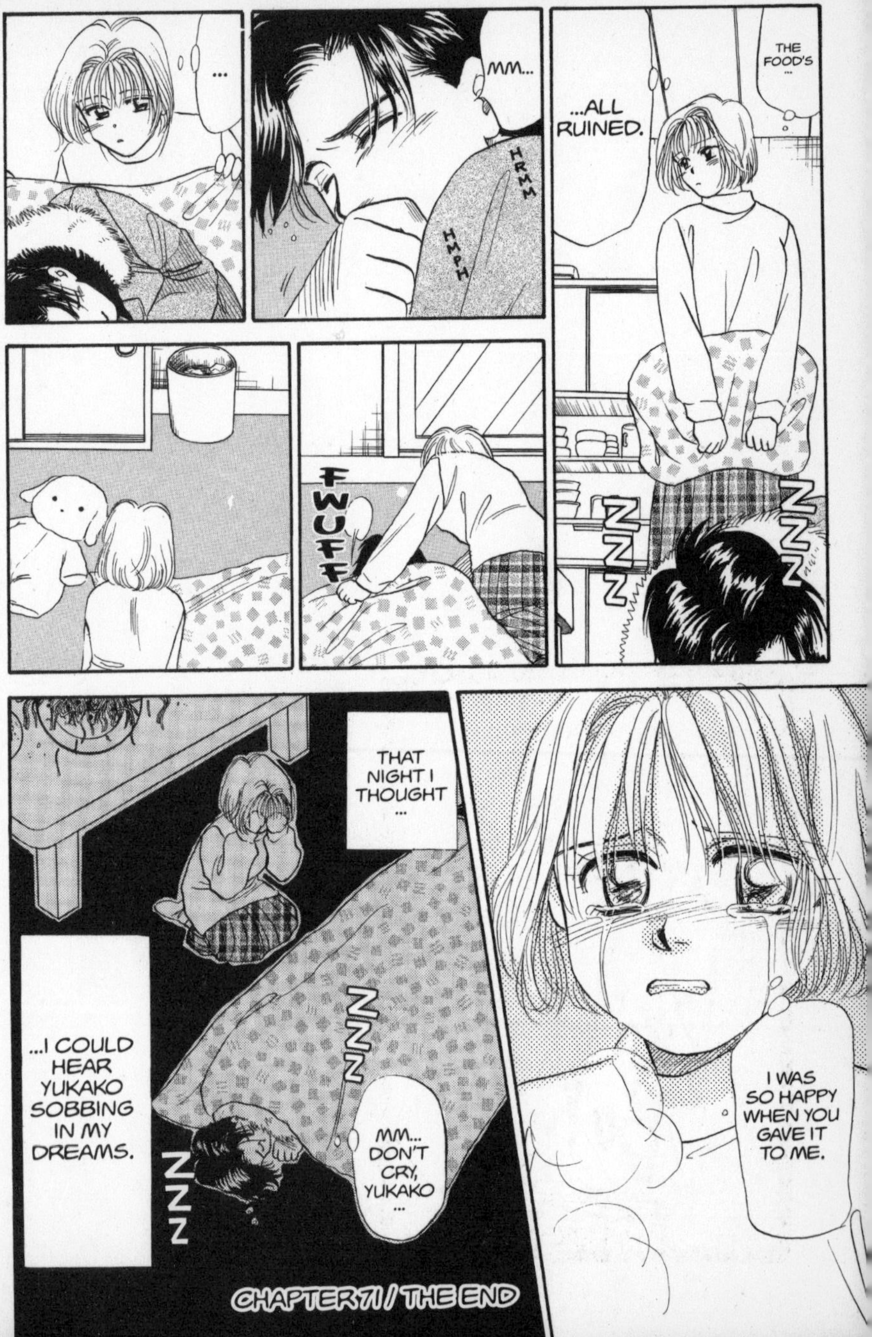
THE FOOD'S ...
...ALL RUINED.
MM...
HRMM
HMPH
...
ZZZ
ZZZ
FWUFF
I WAS SO HAPPY WHEN YOU GAVE IT TO ME.
THAT NIGHT I THOUGHT ...
ZZZ
MM... DON'T CRY, YUKAKO ...
...I COULD HEAR YUKAKO SOBBING IN MY DREAMS.
ZZZ
CHAPTER 71 / THE END

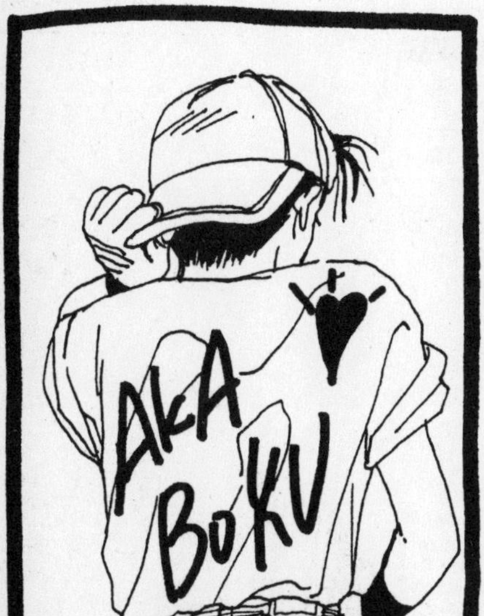
AkA
BoKU

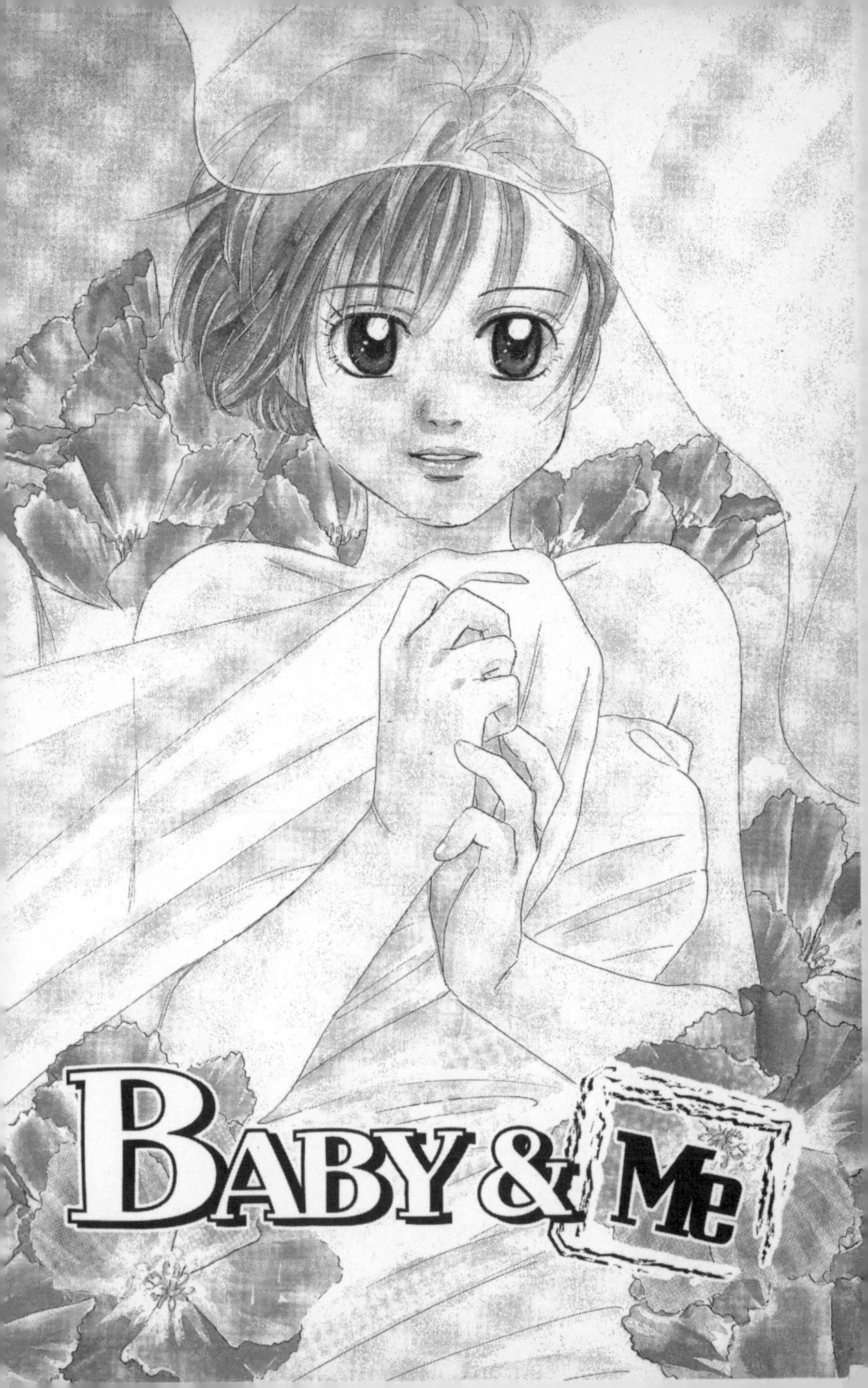
BABY & Me

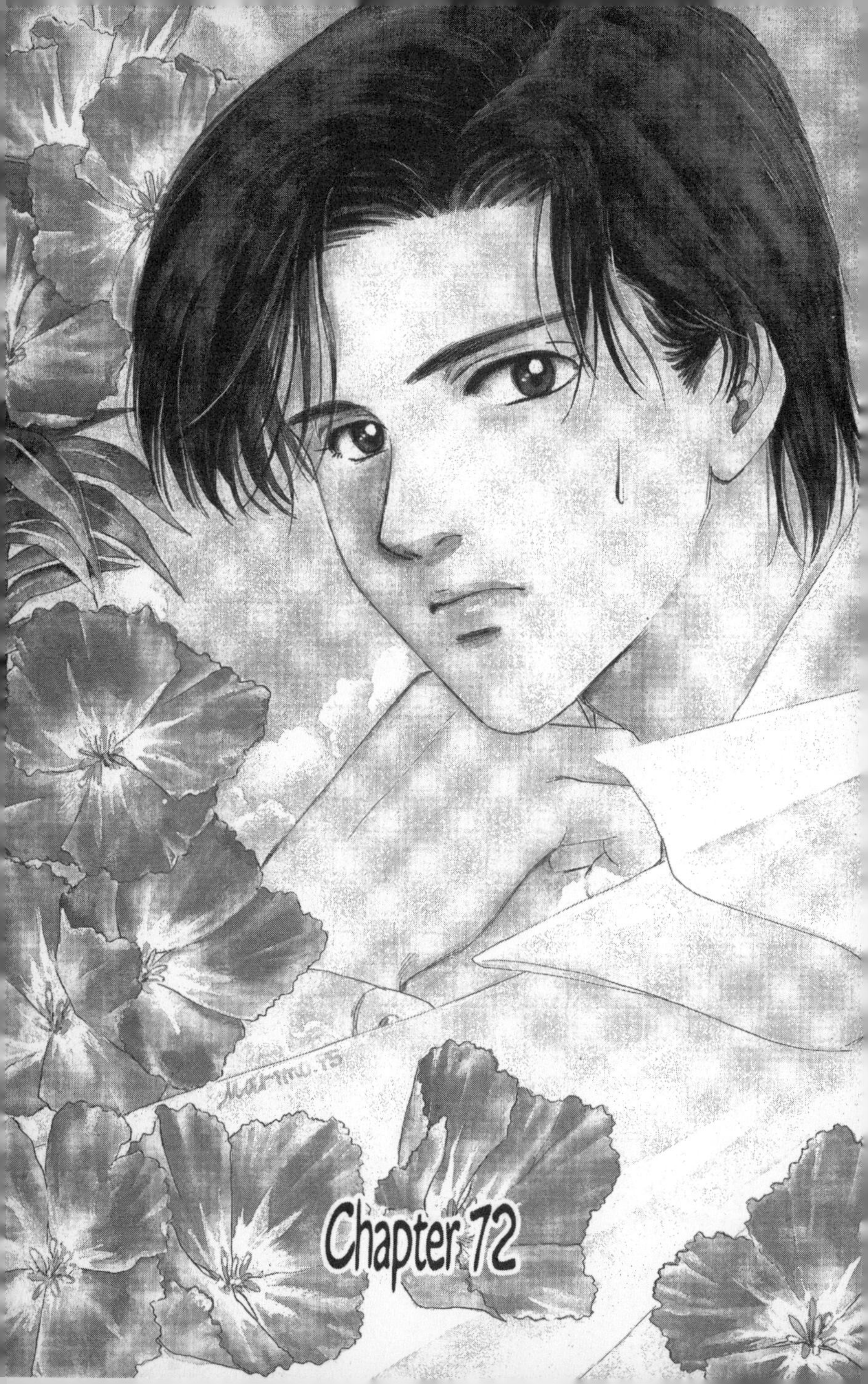
Chapter 72

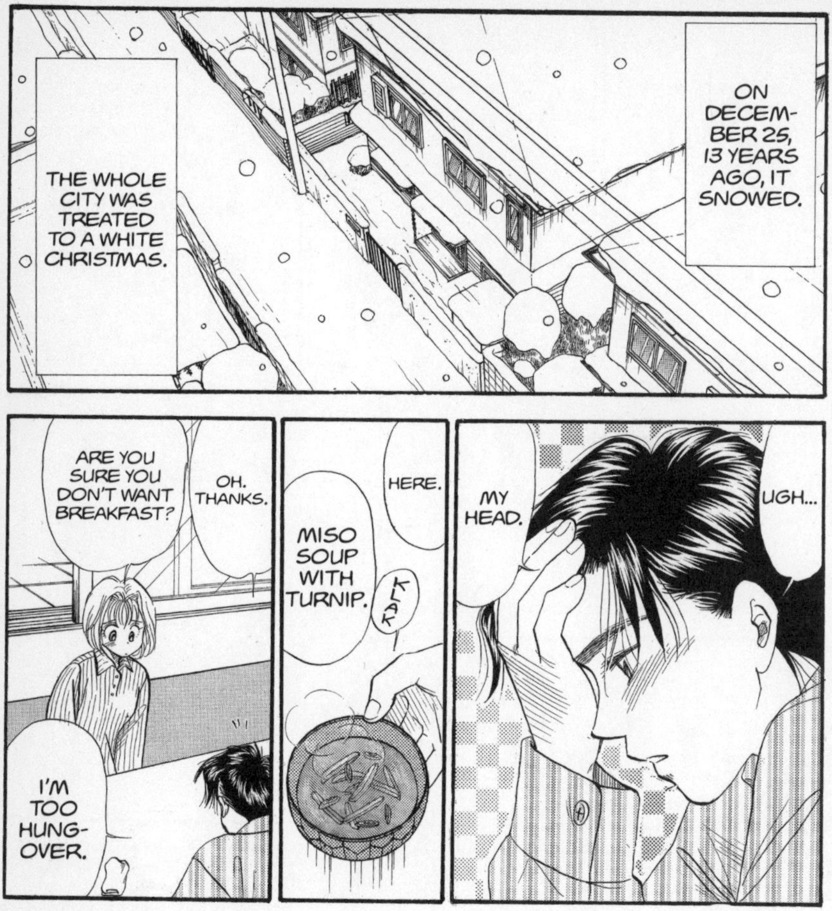
ON DECEMBER 25, 13 YEARS AGO, IT SNOWED.
THE WHOLE CITY WAS TREATED TO A WHITE CHRISTMAS.
UGH...
MY HEAD.
HERE.
MISO SOUP WITH TURNIP.
KLAK
OH. THANKS.
ARE YOU SURE YOU DON'T WANT BREAKFAST?
I'M TOO HUNG-OVER.

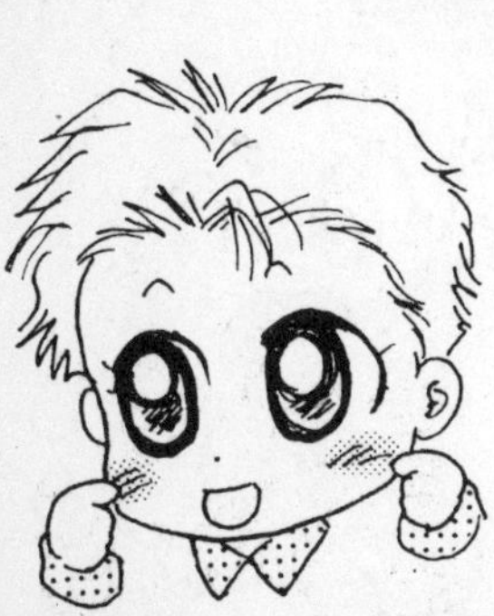

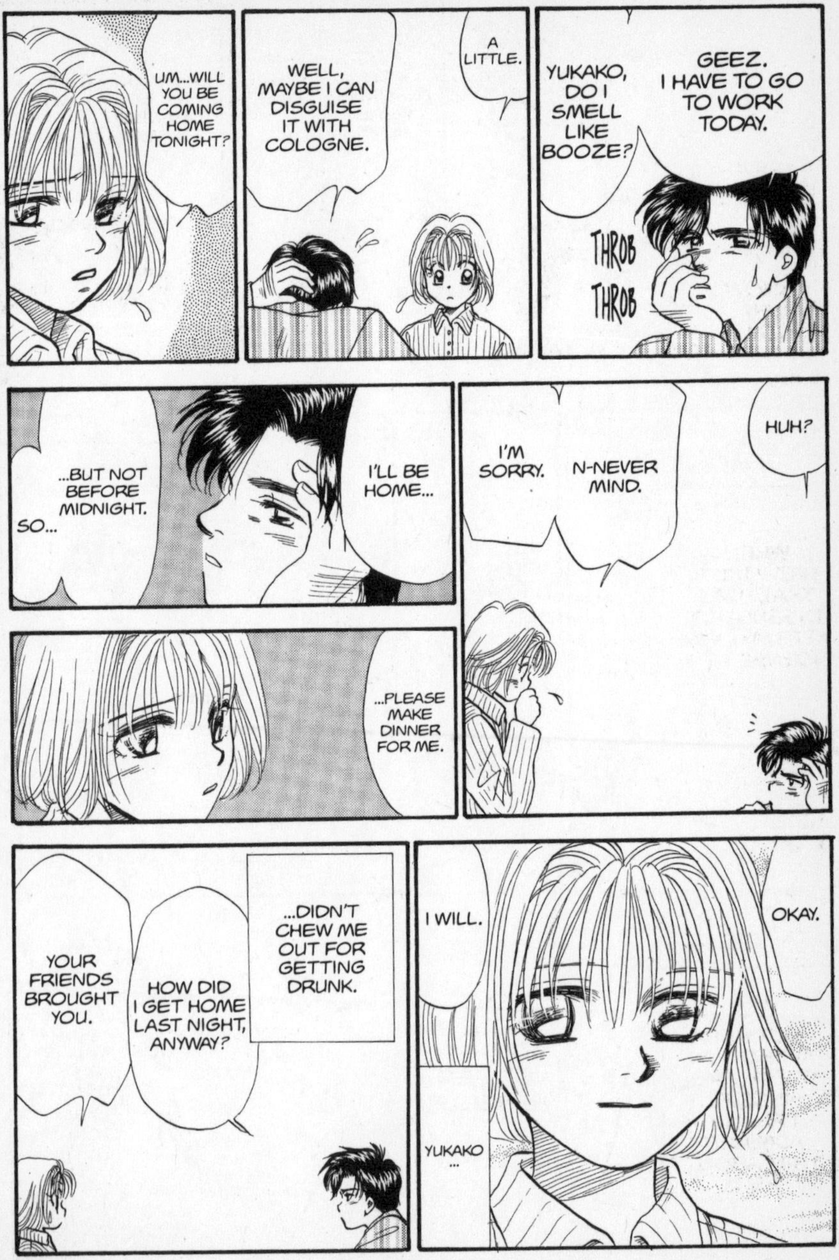
GEEZ. I HAVE TO GO TO WORK TODAY.
YUKAKO, DO I SMELL LIKE BOOZE?
THROB THROB
A LITTLE.
WELL, MAYBE I CAN DISGUISE IT WITH COLOGNE.
UM...WILL YOU BE COMING HOME TONIGHT?
HUH?
N-NEVER MIND.
I'M SORRY.
I'LL BE HOME...
...BUT NOT BEFORE MIDNIGHT. SO...
...PLEASE MAKE DINNER FOR ME.
OKAY.
I WILL.
YUKAKO ...
...DIDN'T CHEW ME OUT FOR GETTING DRUNK.
HOW DID I GET HOME LAST NIGHT, ANYWAY?
YOUR FRIENDS BROUGHT YOU.

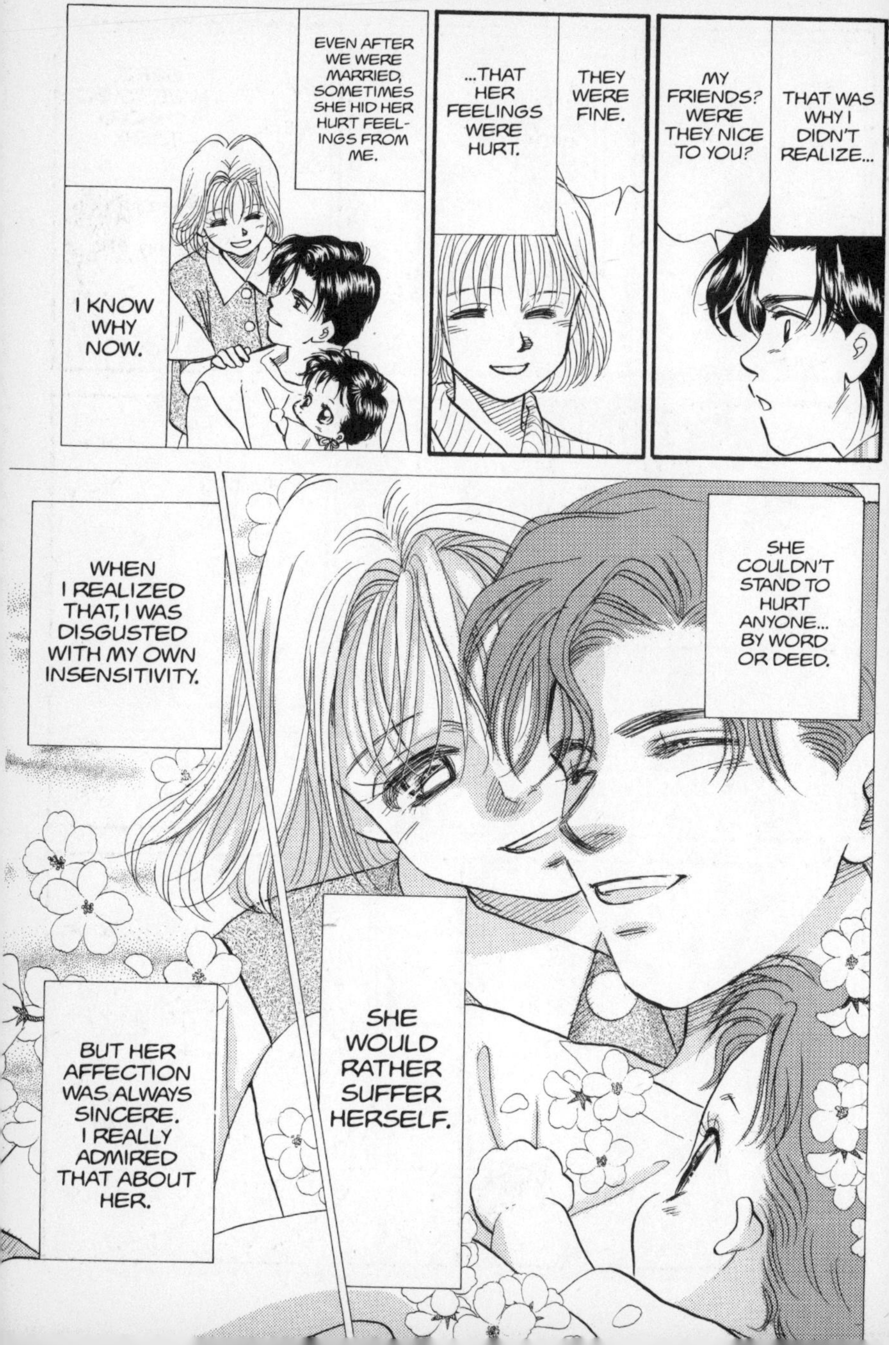
THAT WAS WHY I DIDN'T REALIZE...
MY FRIENDS? WERE THEY NICE TO YOU?
THEY WERE FINE.
...THAT HER FEELINGS WERE HURT.
EVEN AFTER WE WERE MARRIED, SOMETIMES SHE HID HER HURT FEEL- INGS FROM ME.
I KNOW WHY NOW.
SHE COULDN'T STAND TO HURT ANYONE... BY WORD OR DEED.
SHE WOULD RATHER SUFFER HERSELF.
WHEN I REALIZED THAT, I WAS DISGUSTED WITH MY OWN INSENSITIVITY.
BUT HER AFFECTION WAS ALWAYS SINCERE. I REALLY ADMIRED THAT ABOUT HER.

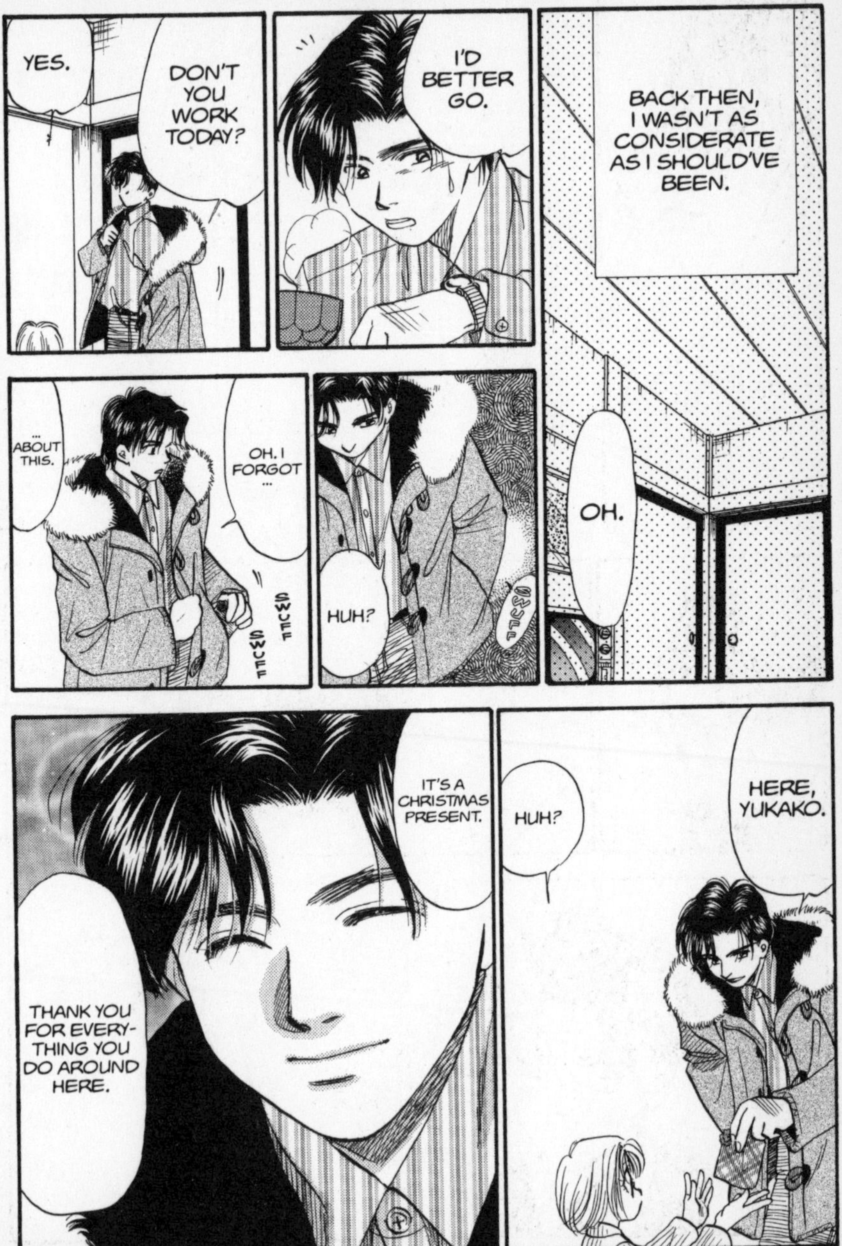
BACK THEN, I WASN'T AS CONSIDERATE AS I SHOULD'VE BEEN.
OH.
I'D BETTER GO.
DON'T YOU WORK TODAY?
YES.
SWUFF
HUH?
OH. I FORGOT ...
... ABOUT THIS.
SWUFF
SWUFF
HERE, YUKAKO.
HUH?
IT'S A CHRISTMAS PRESENT.
THANK YOU FOR EVERY-THING YOU DO AROUND HERE.

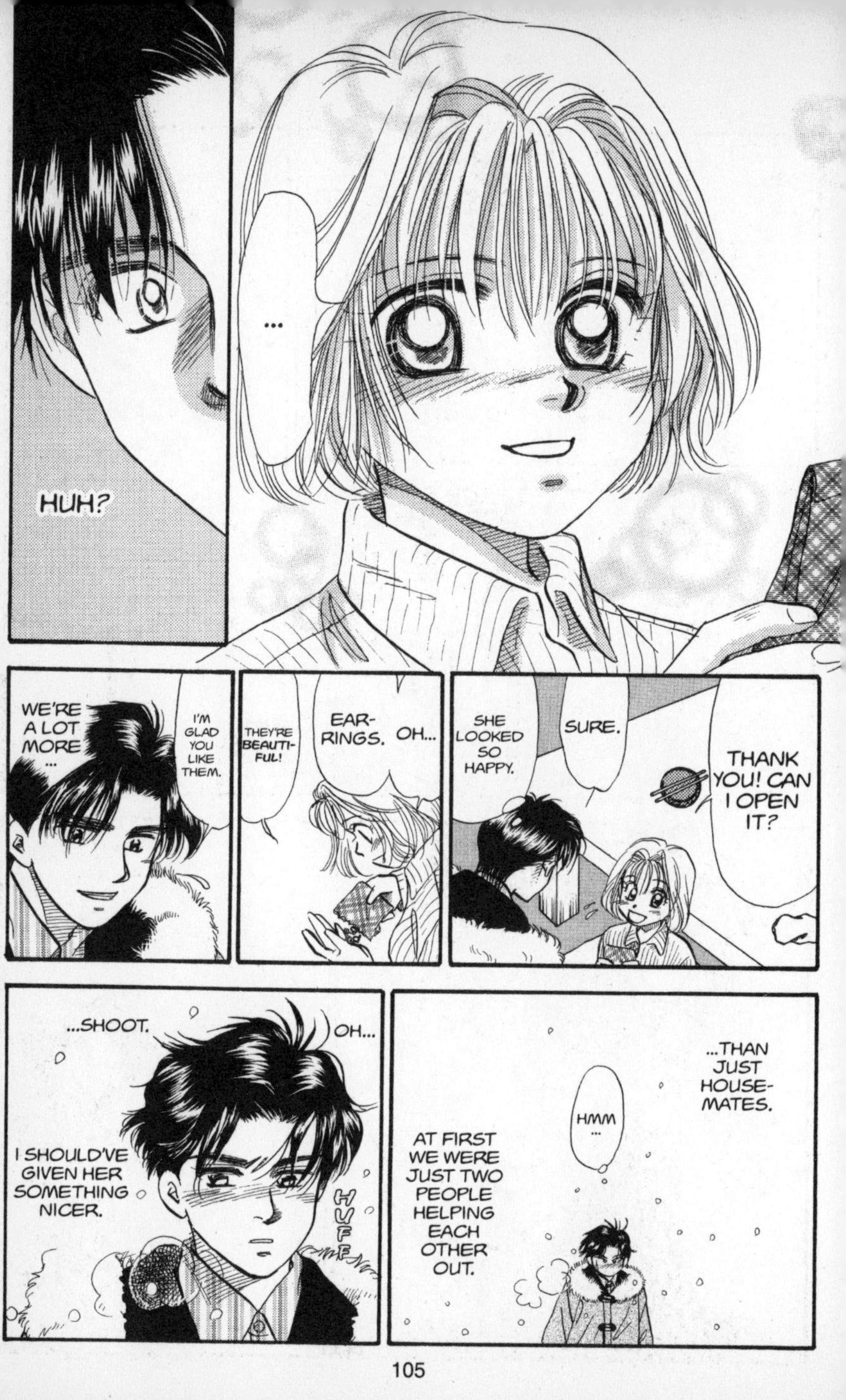
...
HUH?
THANK YOU! CAN I OPEN IT?
SURE.
SHE LOOKED SO HAPPY.
OH...
EAR-RINGS.
THEY'RE BEAUTI-FUL!
I'M GLAD YOU LIKE THEM.
WE'RE A LOT MORE ...
...THAN JUST HOUSE-MATES.
HMM ...
AT FIRST WE WERE JUST TWO PEOPLE HELPING EACH OTHER OUT.
OH...
...SHOOT.
HUFF
I SHOULD'VE GIVEN HER SOMETHING NICER.

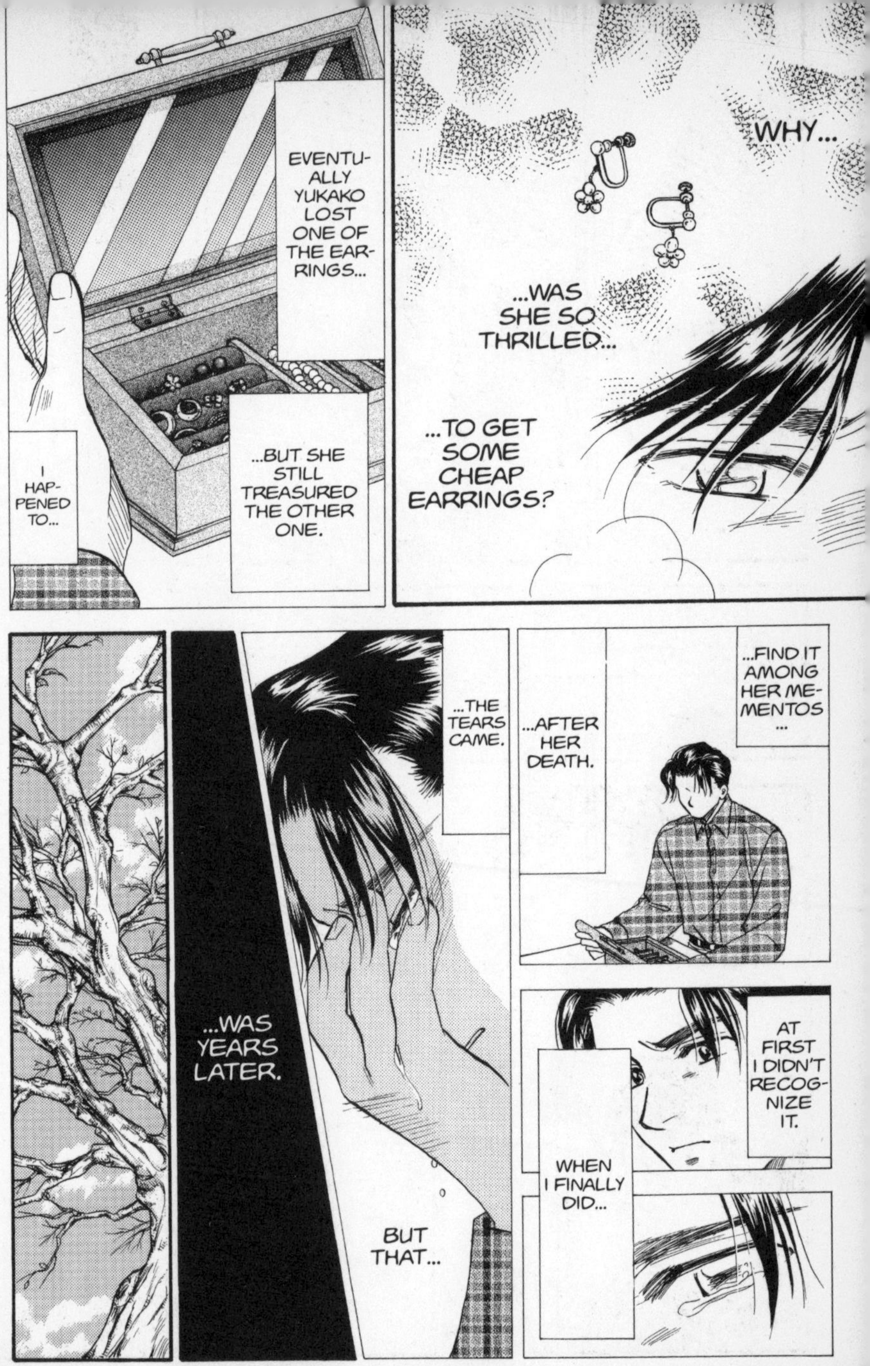
WHY...
...WAS SHE SO THRILLED...
...TO GET SOME CHEAP EARRINGS?
EVENTU-ALLY YUKAKO LOST ONE OF THE EAR-RINGS...
...BUT SHE STILL TREASURED THE OTHER ONE.
I HAP-PENED TO...
...FIND IT AMONG HER ME-MENTOS...
...AFTER HER DEATH.
AT FIRST I DIDN'T RECOG-NIZE IT.
WHEN I FINALLY DID...
...THE TEARS CAME.
BUT THAT...
...WAS YEARS LATER.

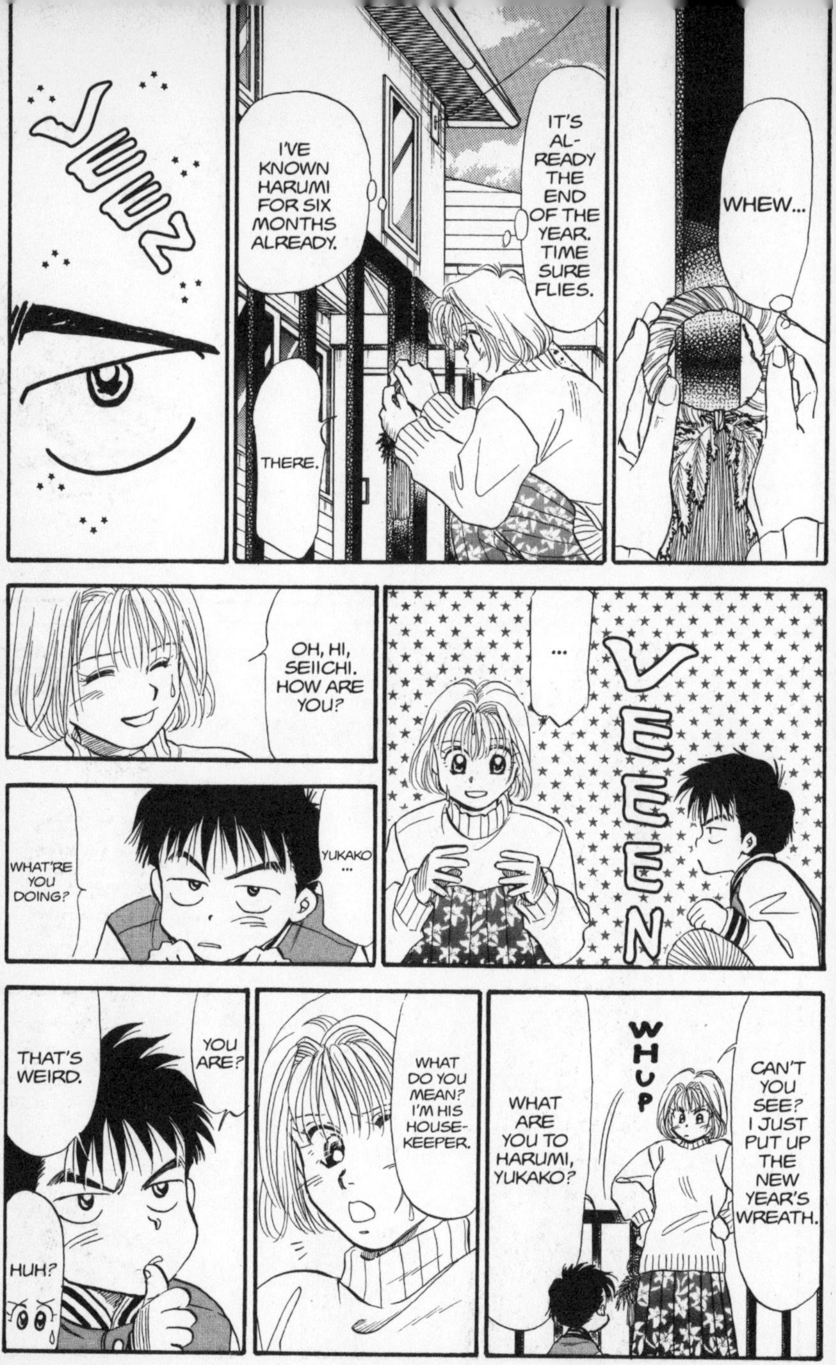
WHEW...
IT'S ALREADY THE END OF THE YEAR. TIME SURE FLIES.
I'VE KNOWN HARUMI FOR SIX MONTHS ALREADY.
THERE.
VEEN
...
VEEEN
OH, HI, SEIICHI. HOW ARE YOU?
YUKAKO...
WHAT'RE YOU DOING?
CAN'T YOU SEE? I JUST PUT UP THE NEW YEAR'S WREATH.
WHUP
WHAT ARE YOU TO HARUMI, YUKAKO?
WHAT DO YOU MEAN? I'M HIS HOUSE-KEEPER.
YOU ARE?
THAT'S WEIRD.
HUH?

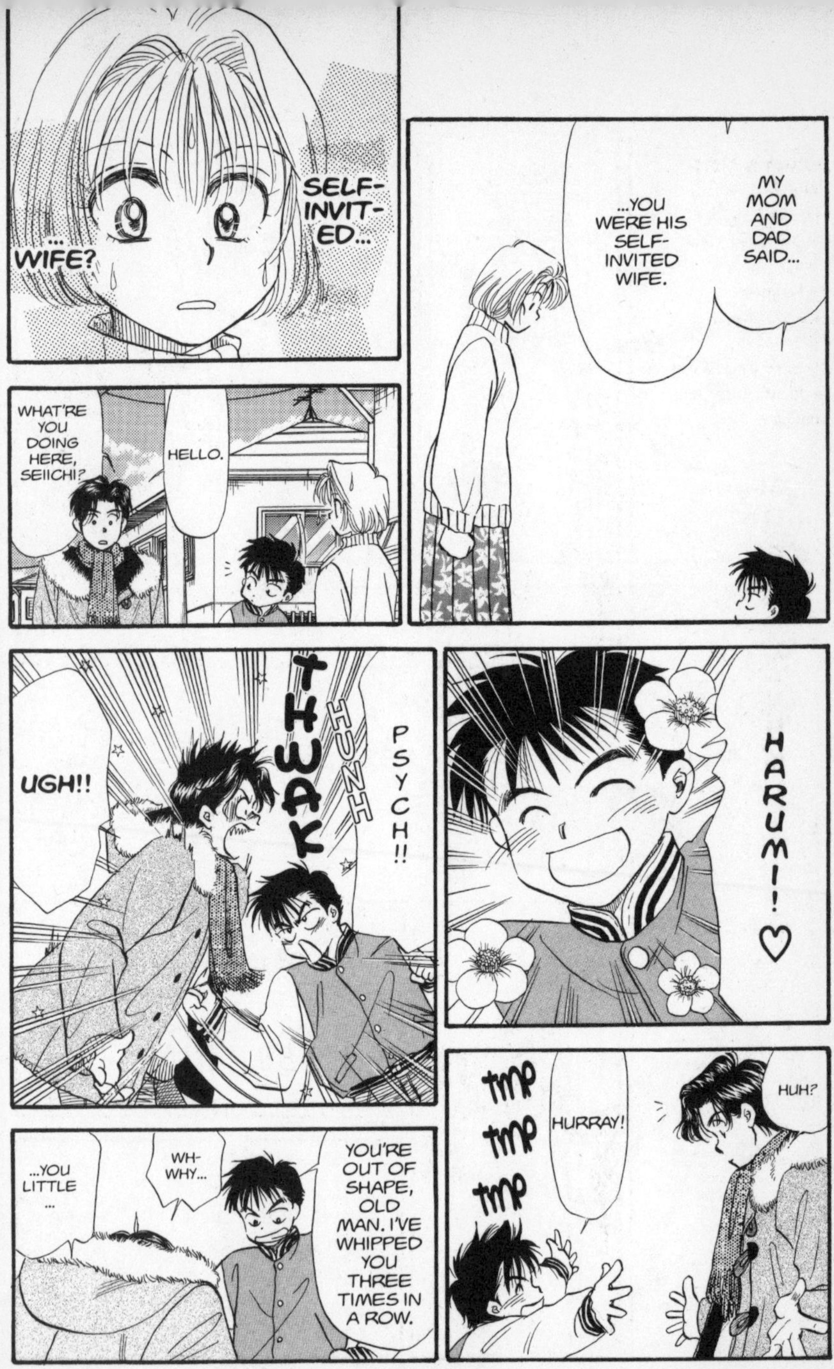
MY MOM AND DAD SAID...
...YOU WERE HIS SELF-INVITED WIFE.
SELF-INVITED...
...WIFE?
HELLO.
WHAT'RE YOU DOING HERE, SEIICHI?
HARUMI! ♡
PSYCH!!
HUNH
THWAK
UGH!!
HUH?
HURRAY!
tmp tmp tmp
YOU'RE OUT OF SHAPE, OLD MAN. I'VE WHIPPED YOU THREE TIMES IN A ROW.
WH-WHY...
...YOU LITTLE ...

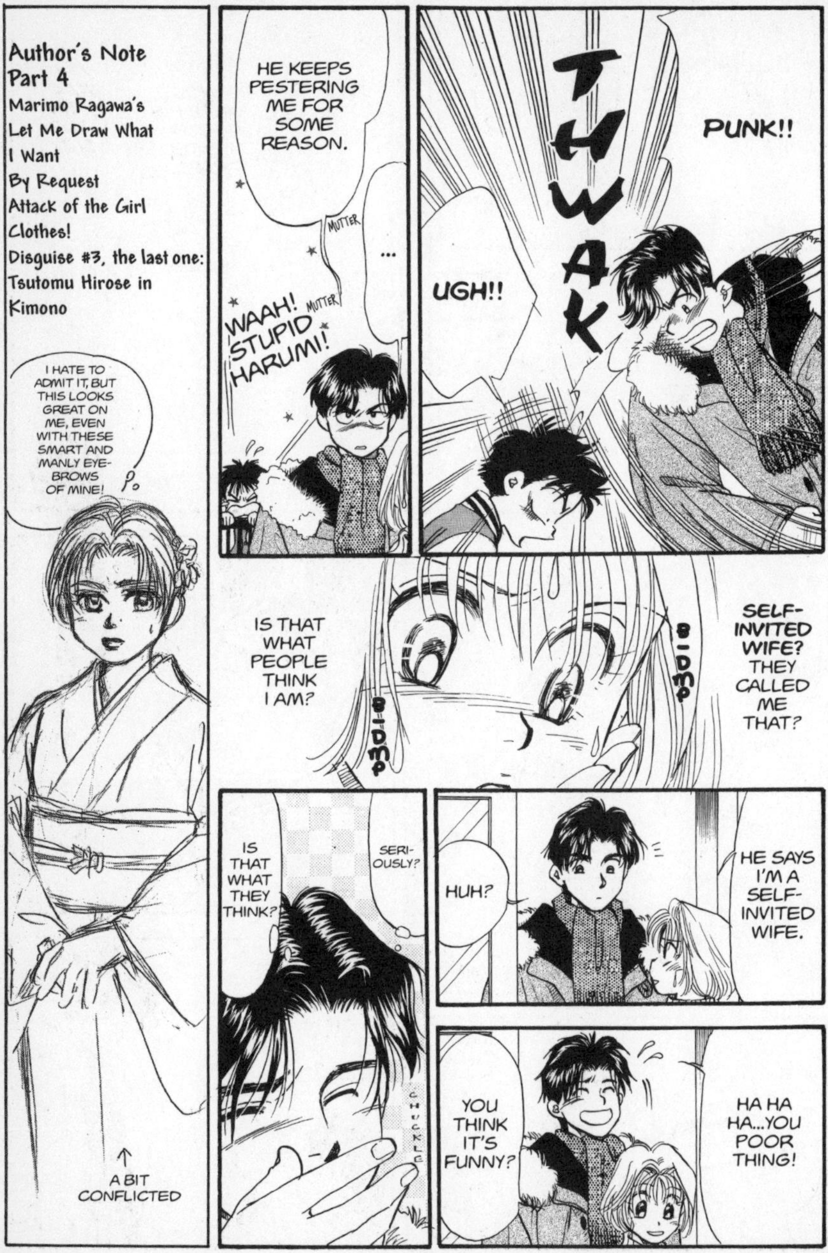
PUNK!!
THWAK
UGH!!
HE KEEPS PESTERING ME FOR SOME REASON.
MUTTER
...
MUTTER
WAAH! STUPID HARUMI!
SELF-INVITED WIFE? THEY CALLED ME THAT?
BIDMP
BIDMP
IS THAT WHAT PEOPLE THINK I AM?
HE SAYS I'M A SELF-INVITED WIFE.
HUH?
HA HA HA...YOU POOR THING!
YOU THINK IT'S FUNNY?
SERI-OUSLY?
IS THAT WHAT THEY THINK?
CHUCKLE
Author's Note Part 4
Marimo Ragawa's Let Me Draw What I Want By Request
Attack of the Girl Clothes!
Disguise #3, the last one: Tsutomu Hirose in Kimono
I HATE TO ADMIT IT, BUT THIS LOOKS GREAT ON ME, EVEN WITH THESE SMART AND MANLY EYE-BROWS OF MINE!
A BIT CONFLICTED

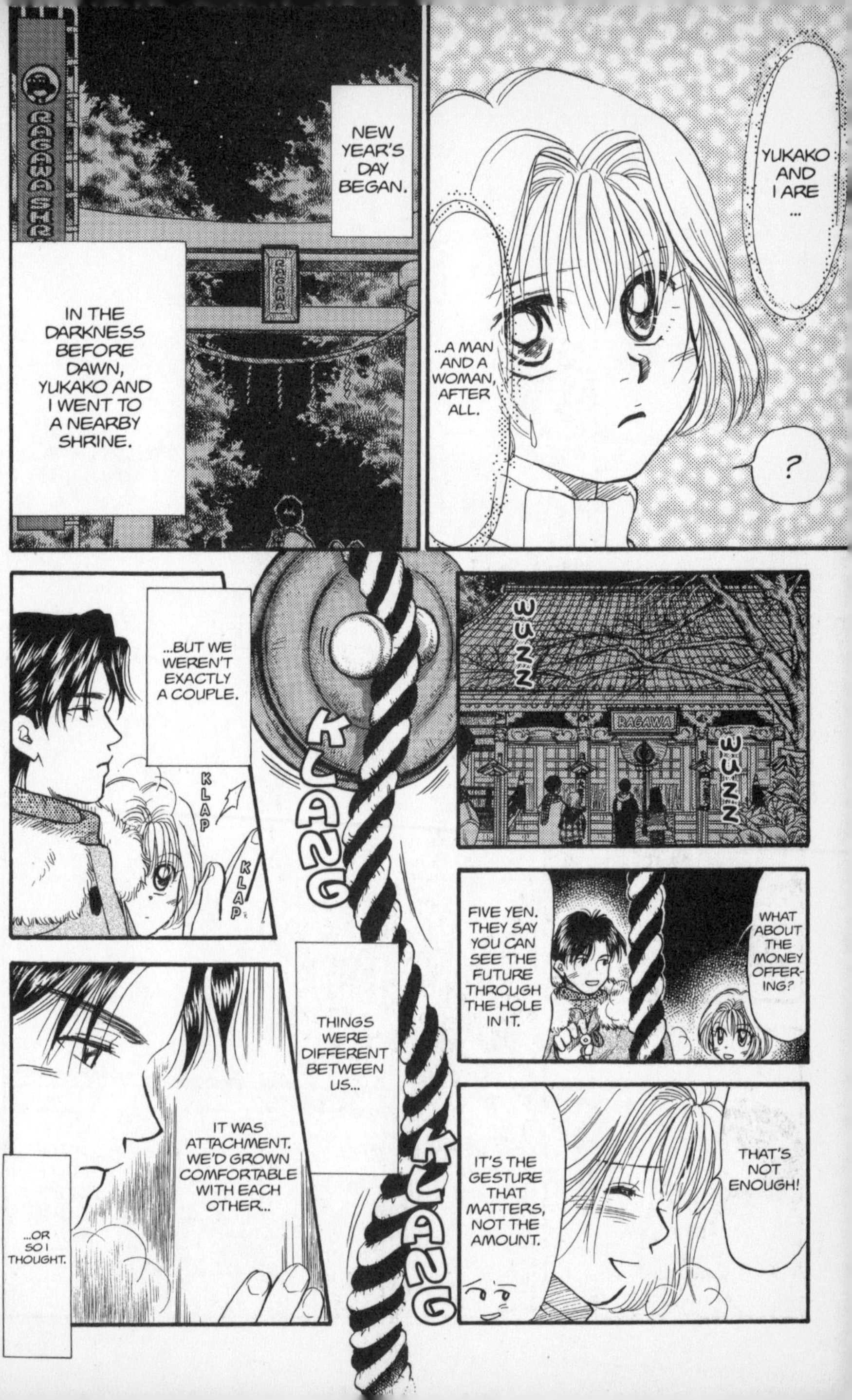
YUKAKO AND I ARE ...
...A MAN AND A WOMAN, AFTER ALL.
?
RAGAWA SHR
NEW YEAR'S DAY BEGAN.
RAGAWA
IN THE DARKNESS BEFORE DAWN, YUKAKO AND I WENT TO A NEARBY SHRINE.
WUNN
RAGAWA
WUNN
WHAT ABOUT THE MONEY OFFERING?
FIVE YEN. THEY SAY YOU CAN SEE THE FUTURE THROUGH THE HOLE IN IT.
THAT'S NOT ENOUGH!
IT'S THE GESTURE THAT MATTERS, NOT THE AMOUNT.
KLANG
...BUT WE WEREN'T EXACTLY A COUPLE.
KLAP
KLAP
THINGS WERE DIFFERENT BETWEEN US...
KLANG
IT WAS ATTACHMENT. WE'D GROWN COMFORTABLE WITH EACH OTHER...
...OR SO I THOUGHT.

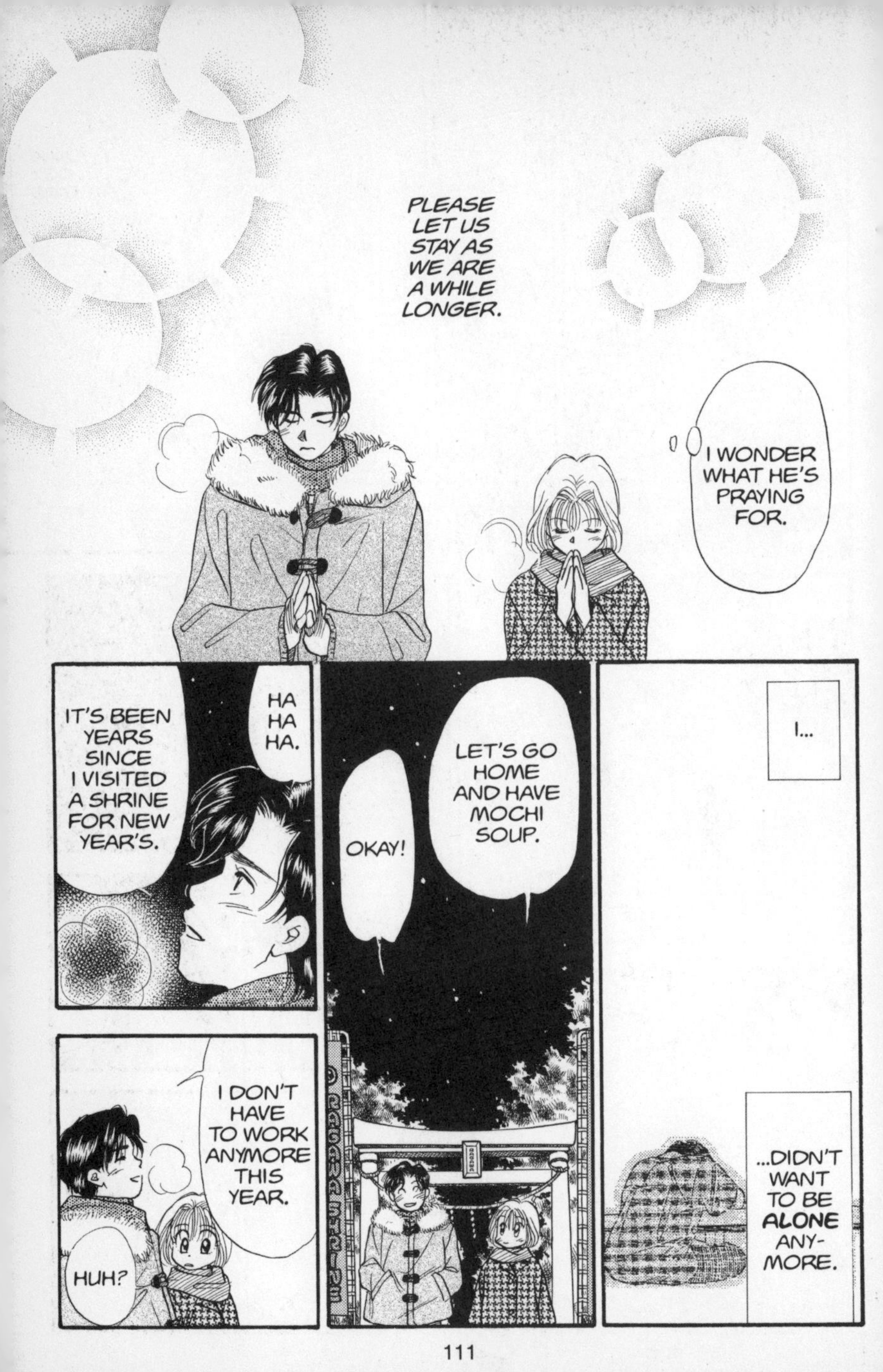
PLEASE LET US STAY AS WE ARE A WHILE LONGER.
I WONDER WHAT HE'S PRAYING FOR.
I...
...DIDN'T WANT TO BE **ALONE** ANY-MORE.
LET'S GO HOME AND HAVE MOCHI SOUP.
OKAY!
HA HA HA.
IT'S BEEN YEARS SINCE I VISITED A SHRINE FOR NEW YEAR'S.
I DON'T HAVE TO WORK ANYMORE THIS YEAR.
HUH?

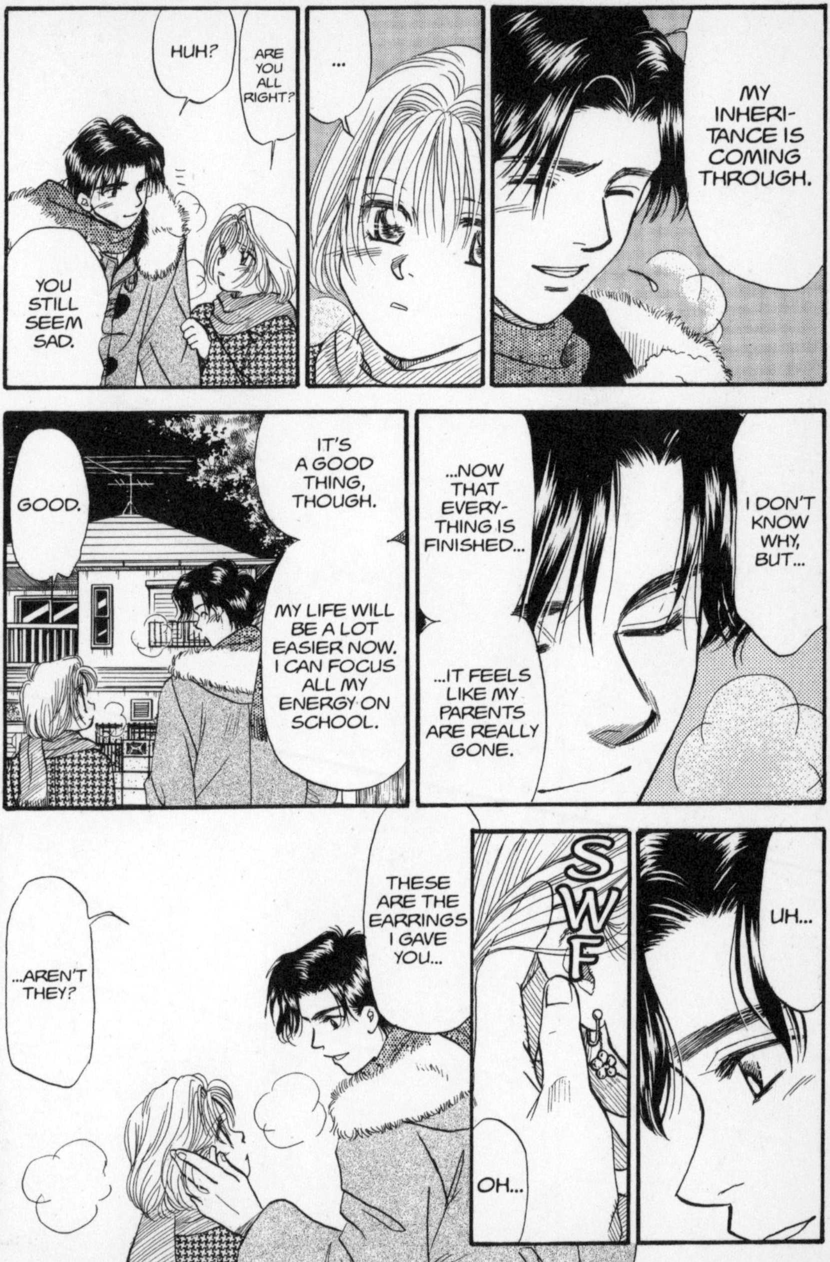

MY INHERITANCE IS COMING THROUGH.
...
ARE YOU ALL RIGHT?
HUH?
YOU STILL SEEM SAD.
I DON'T KNOW WHY, BUT...
...NOW THAT EVERYTHING IS FINISHED...
...IT FEELS LIKE MY PARENTS ARE REALLY GONE.
IT'S A GOOD THING, THOUGH.
MY LIFE WILL BE A LOT EASIER NOW. I CAN FOCUS ALL MY ENERGY ON SCHOOL.
GOOD.
UH...
SWF
OH...
THESE ARE THE EARRINGS I GAVE YOU...
...AREN'T THEY?

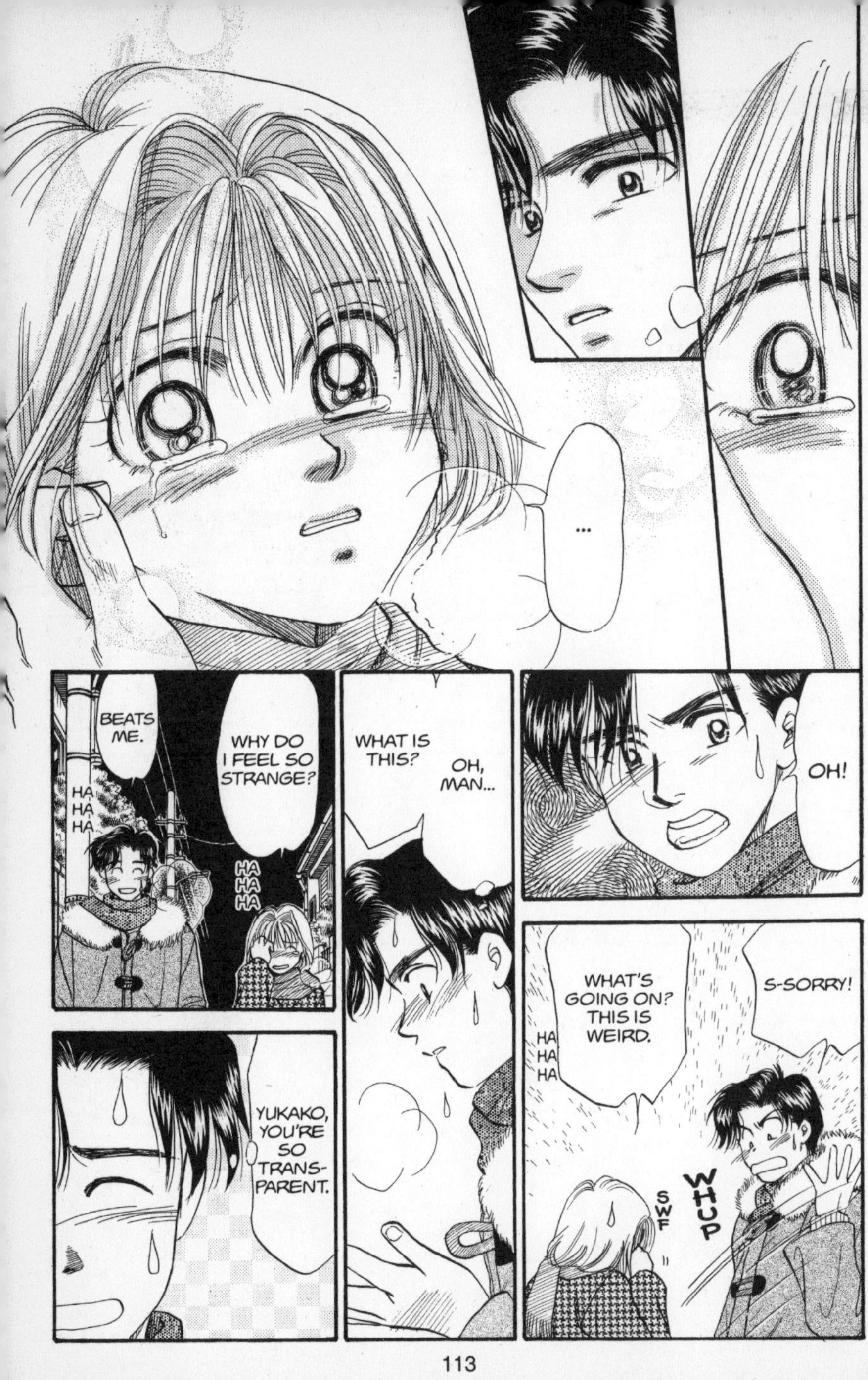
...
OH!
S-SORRY!
WHAT'S GOING ON? THIS IS WEIRD.
HA HA HA
WHUP
SWF
WHAT IS THIS?
OH, MAN...
WHY DO I FEEL SO STRANGE?
HA HA HA
BEATS ME.
HA HA HA
YUKAKO, YOU'RE SO TRANS-PARENT.

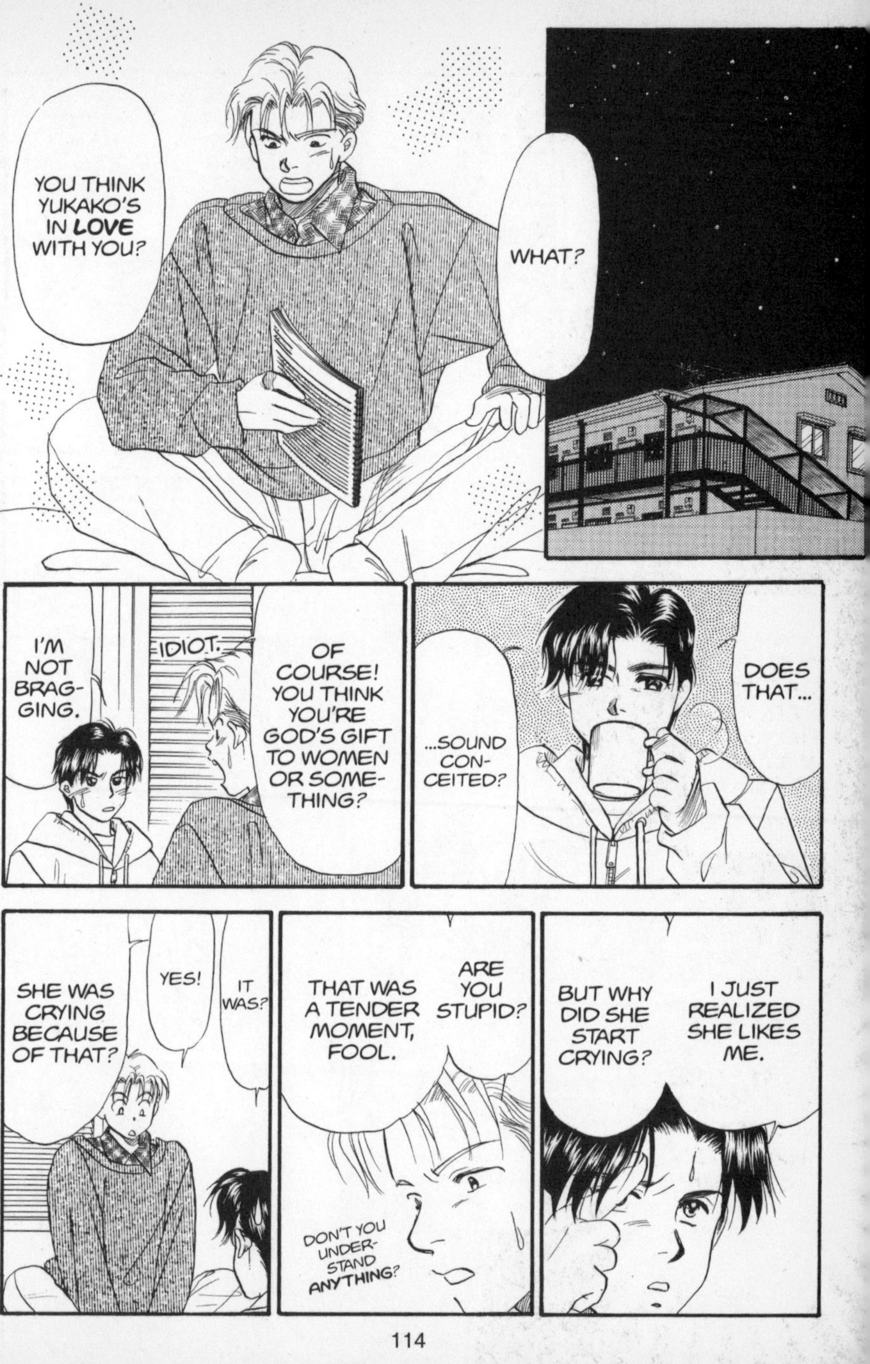
WHAT?
YOU THINK YUKAKO'S IN **LOVE** WITH YOU?
DOES THAT...
...SOUND CONCEITED?
OF COURSE! YOU THINK YOU'RE GOD'S GIFT TO WOMEN OR SOMETHING?
IDIOT.
I'M NOT BRAGGING.
I JUST REALIZED SHE LIKES ME.
BUT WHY DID SHE START CRYING?
ARE YOU STUPID?
THAT WAS A TENDER MOMENT, FOOL.
DON'T YOU UNDERSTAND **ANYTHING**?
IT WAS?
YES!
SHE WAS CRYING BECAUSE OF THAT?

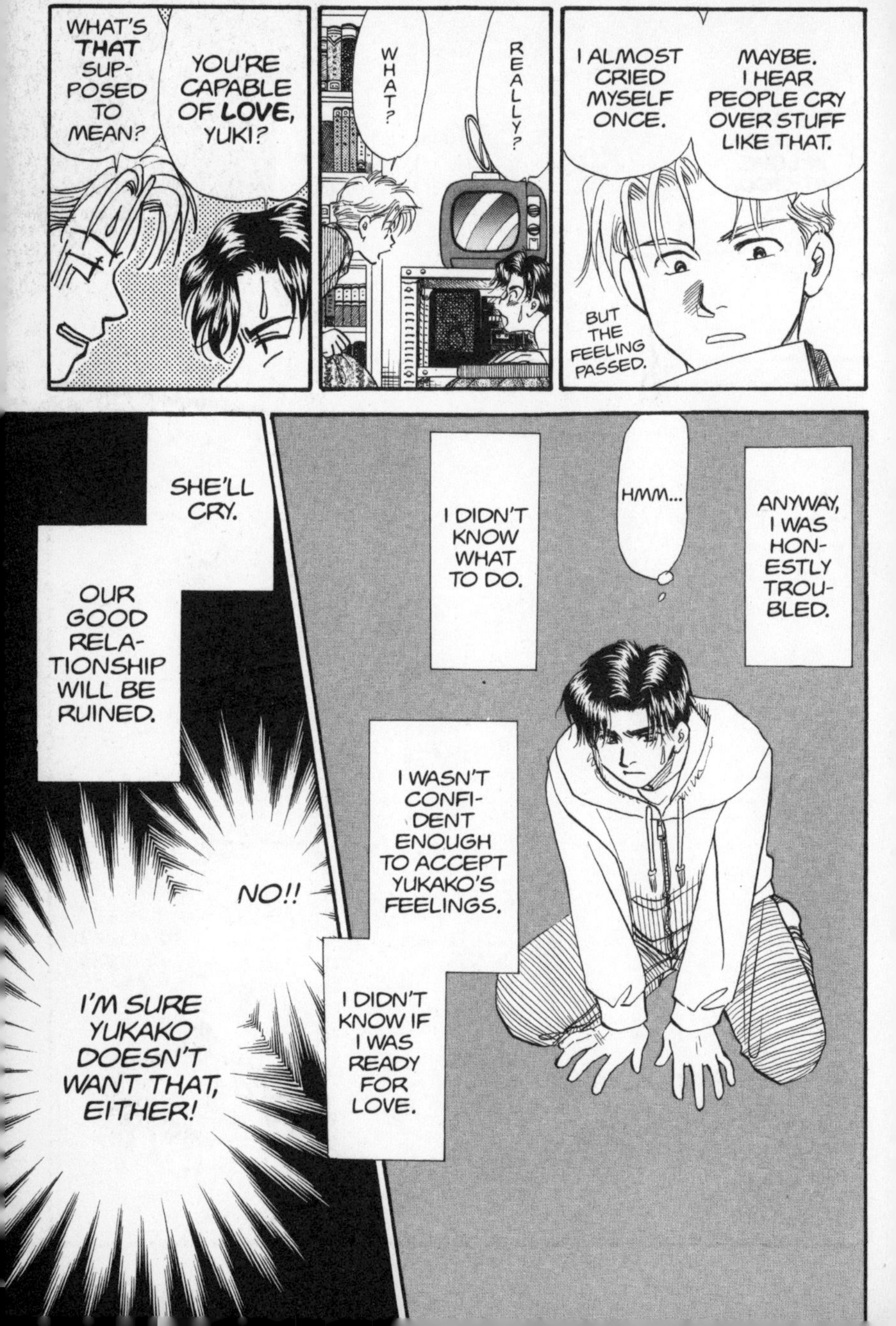
MAYBE. I HEAR PEOPLE CRY OVER STUFF LIKE THAT.
I ALMOST CRIED MYSELF ONCE.
BUT THE FEELING PASSED.
REALLY?
WHAT?
YOU'RE CAPABLE OF **LOVE**, YUKI?
WHAT'S **THAT** SUP-POSED TO MEAN?
ANYWAY, I WAS HON-ESTLY TROU-BLED.
HMM...
I DIDN'T KNOW WHAT TO DO.
I WASN'T CONFI-DENT ENOUGH TO ACCEPT YUKAKO'S FEELINGS.
I DIDN'T KNOW IF I WAS READY FOR LOVE.
SHE'LL CRY.
OUR GOOD RELA-TIONSHIP WILL BE RUINED.
NO!!
I'M SURE YUKAKO DOESN'T WANT THAT, EITHER!

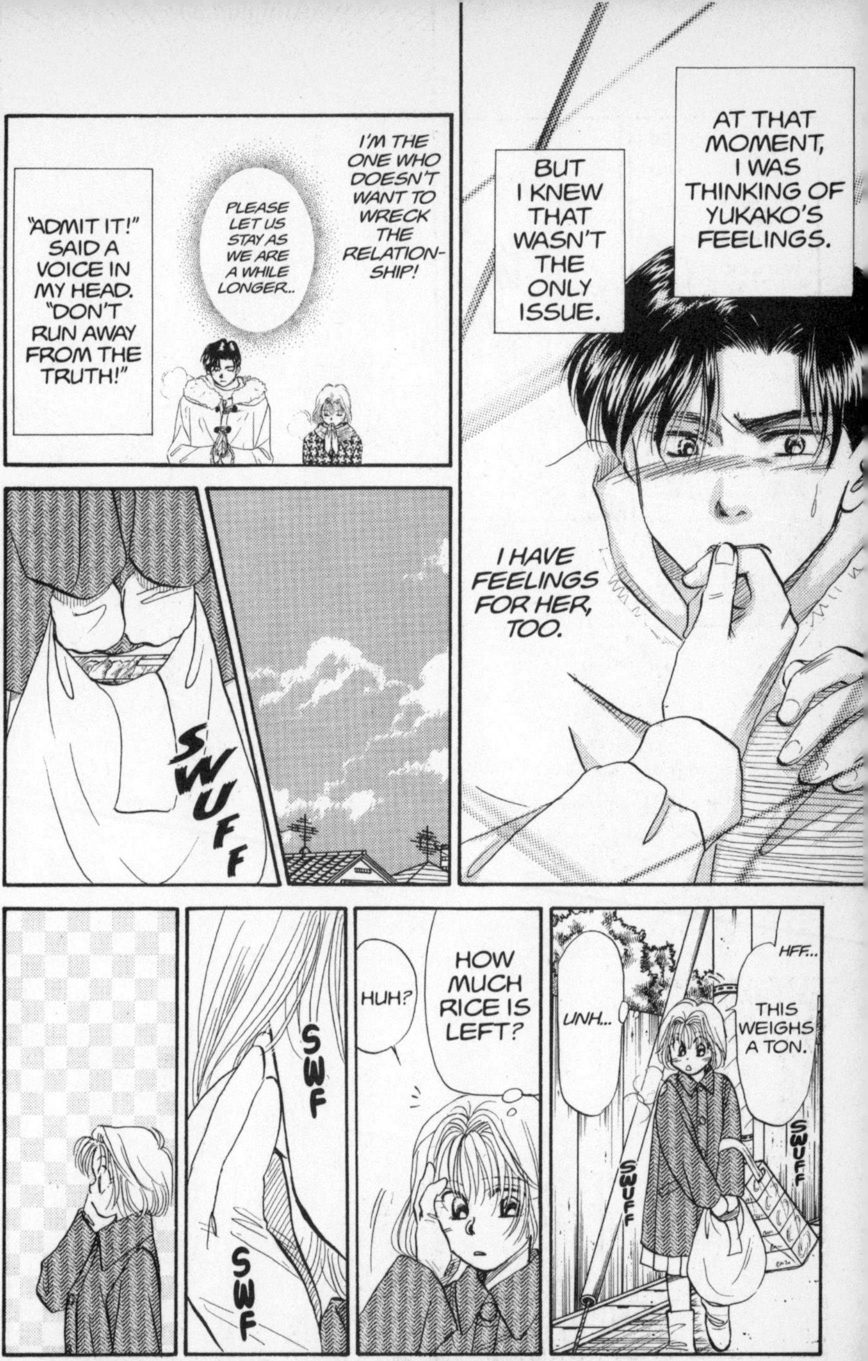
AT THAT MOMENT, I WAS THINKING OF YUKAKO'S FEELINGS.
BUT I KNEW THAT WASN'T THE ONLY ISSUE.
I HAVE FEELINGS FOR HER, TOO.
I'M THE ONE WHO DOESN'T WANT TO WRECK THE RELATIONSHIP!
PLEASE LET US STAY AS WE ARE A WHILE LONGER...
"ADMIT IT!" SAID A VOICE IN MY HEAD. "DON'T RUN AWAY FROM THE TRUTH!"
SWUFF
HFF...
THIS WEIGHS A TON.
SWUFF
SWUFF
UNH...
HOW MUCH RICE IS LEFT?
HUH?
SWF
SWF

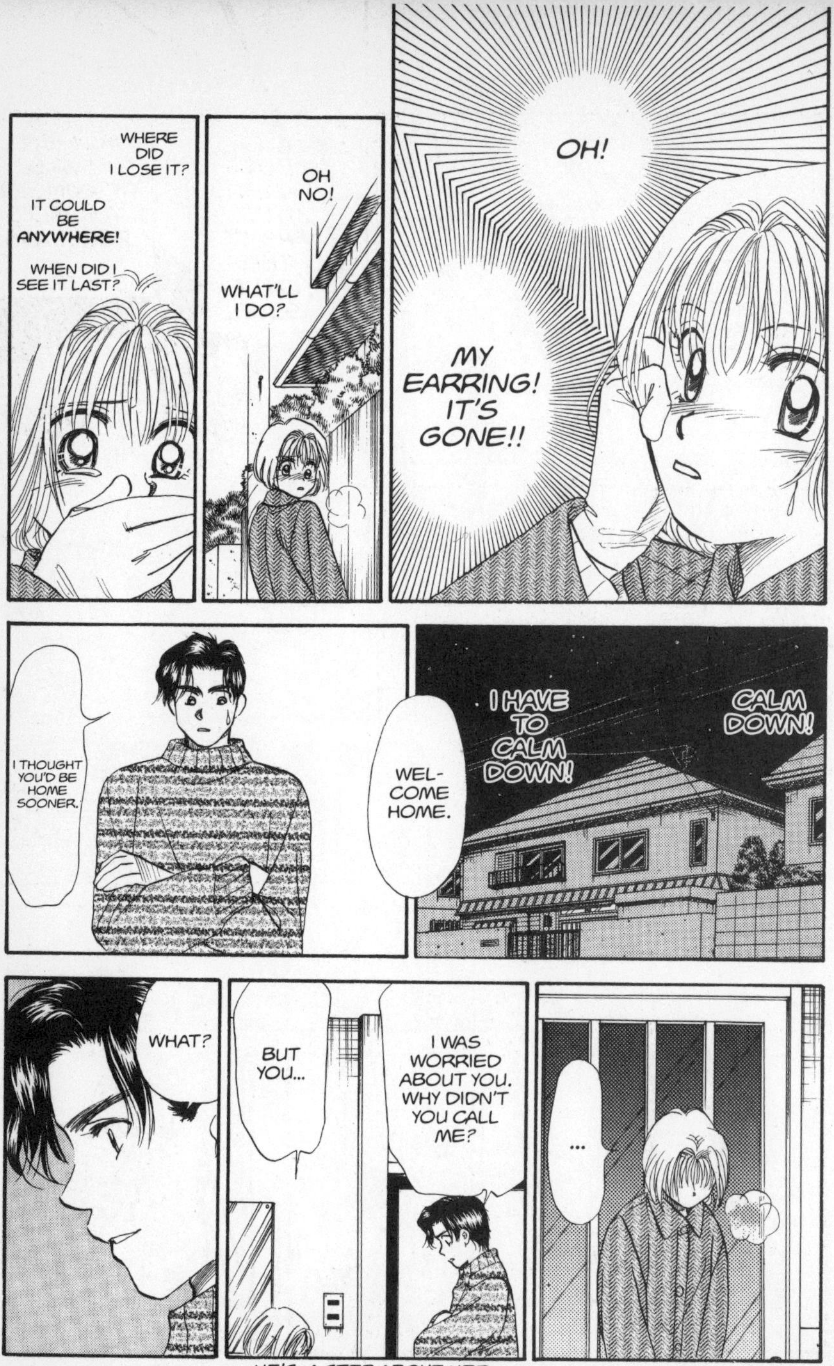
OH!
MY EARRING! IT'S GONE!!
OH NO!
WHAT'LL I DO?
WHERE DID I LOSE IT?
IT COULD BE **ANYWHERE!**
WHEN DID I SEE IT LAST?
CALM DOWN!
I HAVE TO CALM DOWN!
WEL-COME HOME.
I THOUGHT YOU'D BE HOME SOONER.
...
I WAS WORRIED ABOUT YOU. WHY DIDN'T YOU CALL ME?
BUT YOU...
WHAT?

HE'S A STEP ABOVE HER.

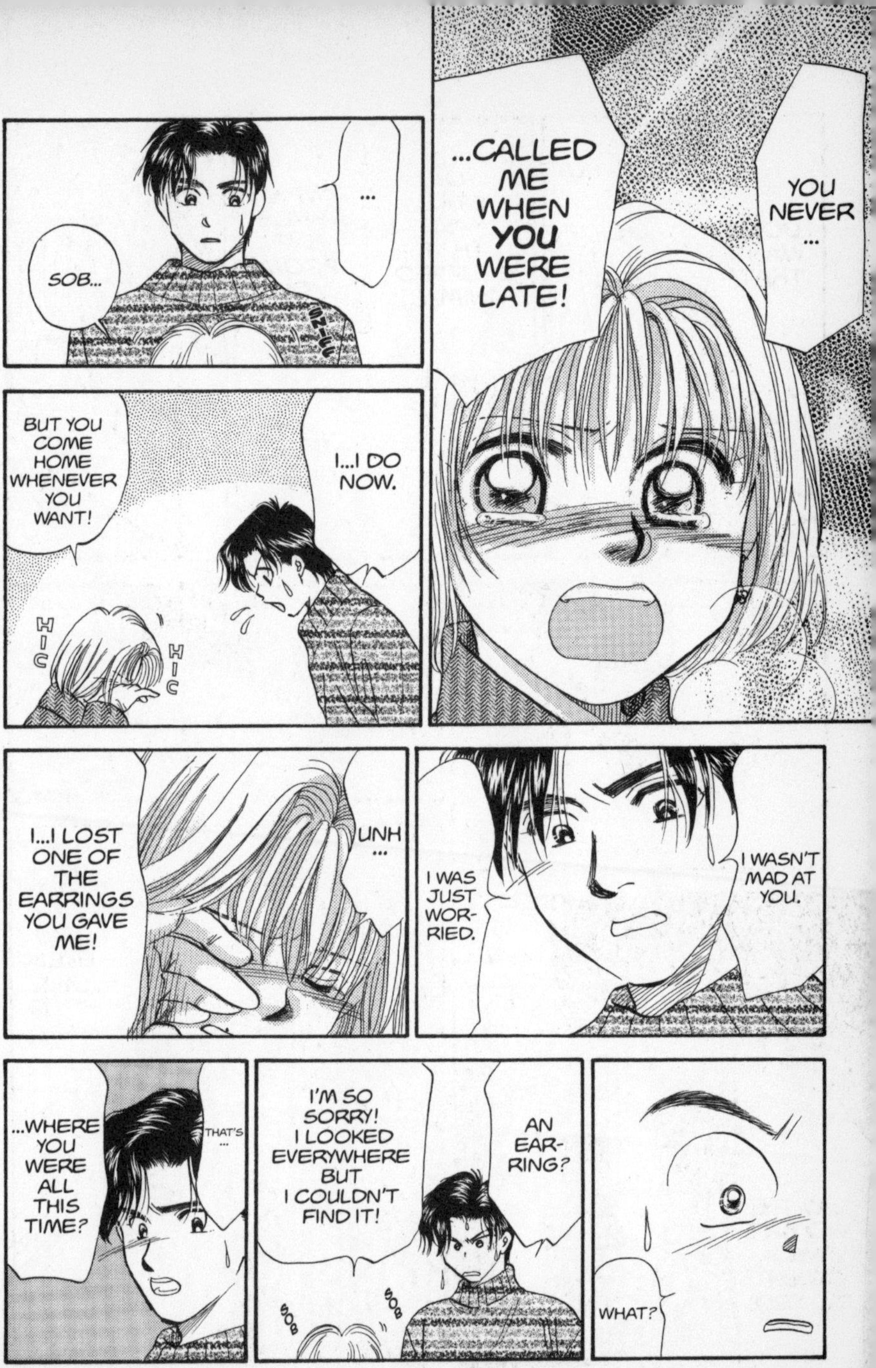
YOU NEVER ...
...CALLED ME WHEN YOU WERE LATE!
...
SOB...
SNIFF
I...I DO NOW.
BUT YOU COME HOME WHENEVER YOU WANT!
HIC
HIC
I WASN'T MAD AT YOU.
I WAS JUST WORRIED.
UNH ...
I...I LOST ONE OF THE EARRINGS YOU GAVE ME!
WHAT?
AN EAR-RING?
I'M SO SORRY! I LOOKED EVERYWHERE BUT I COULDN'T FIND IT!
SOB
SOB
THAT'S ...
...WHERE YOU WERE ALL THIS TIME?

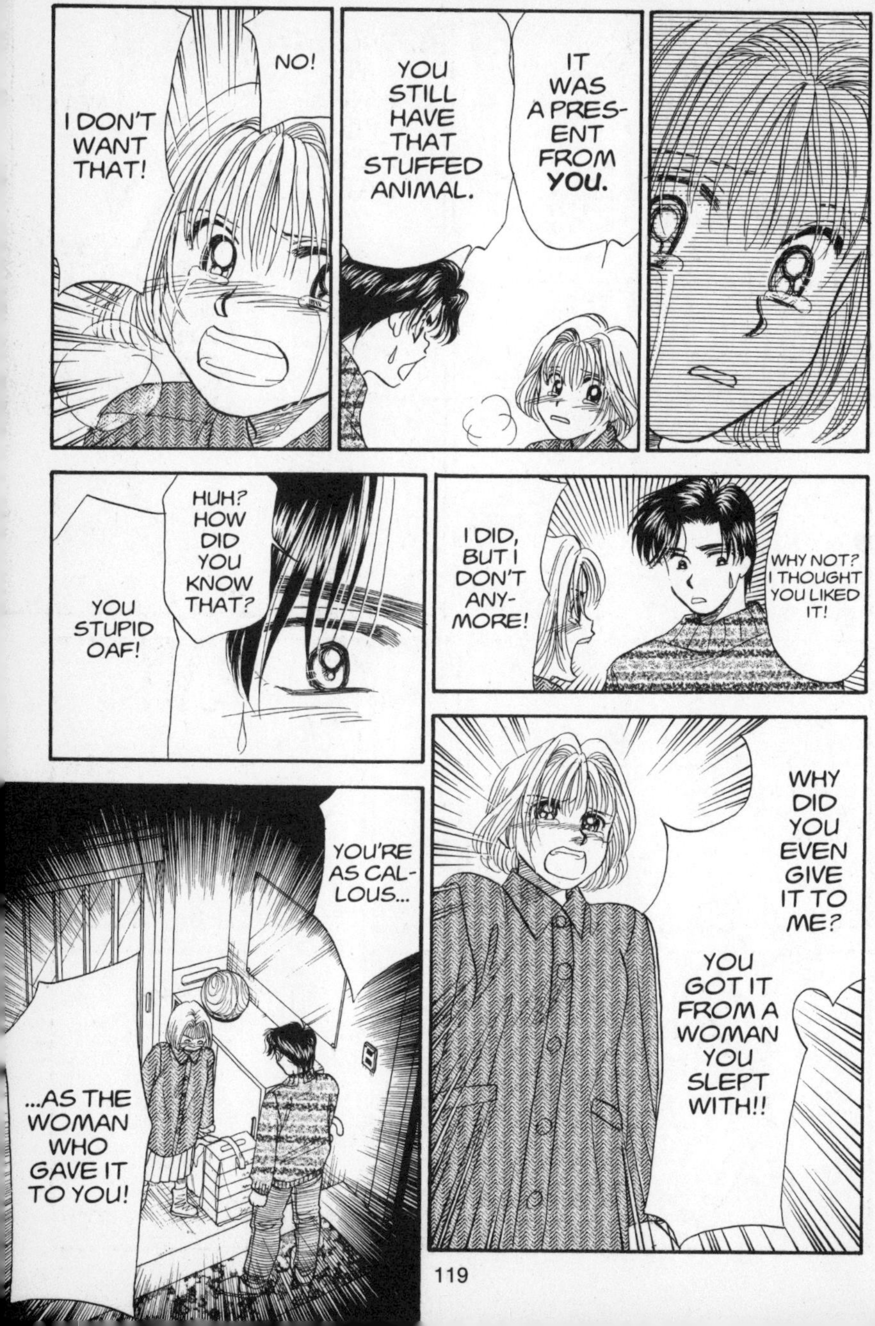
IT WAS A PRESENT FROM **YOU.**
YOU STILL HAVE THAT STUFFED ANIMAL.
NO!
I DON'T WANT THAT!
WHY NOT? I THOUGHT YOU LIKED IT!
I DID, BUT I DON'T ANYMORE!
HUH? HOW DID YOU KNOW THAT?
YOU STUPID OAF!
WHY DID YOU EVEN GIVE IT TO ME?
YOU GOT IT FROM A WOMAN YOU SLEPT WITH!!
YOU'RE AS CALLOUS...
...AS THE WOMAN WHO GAVE IT TO YOU!

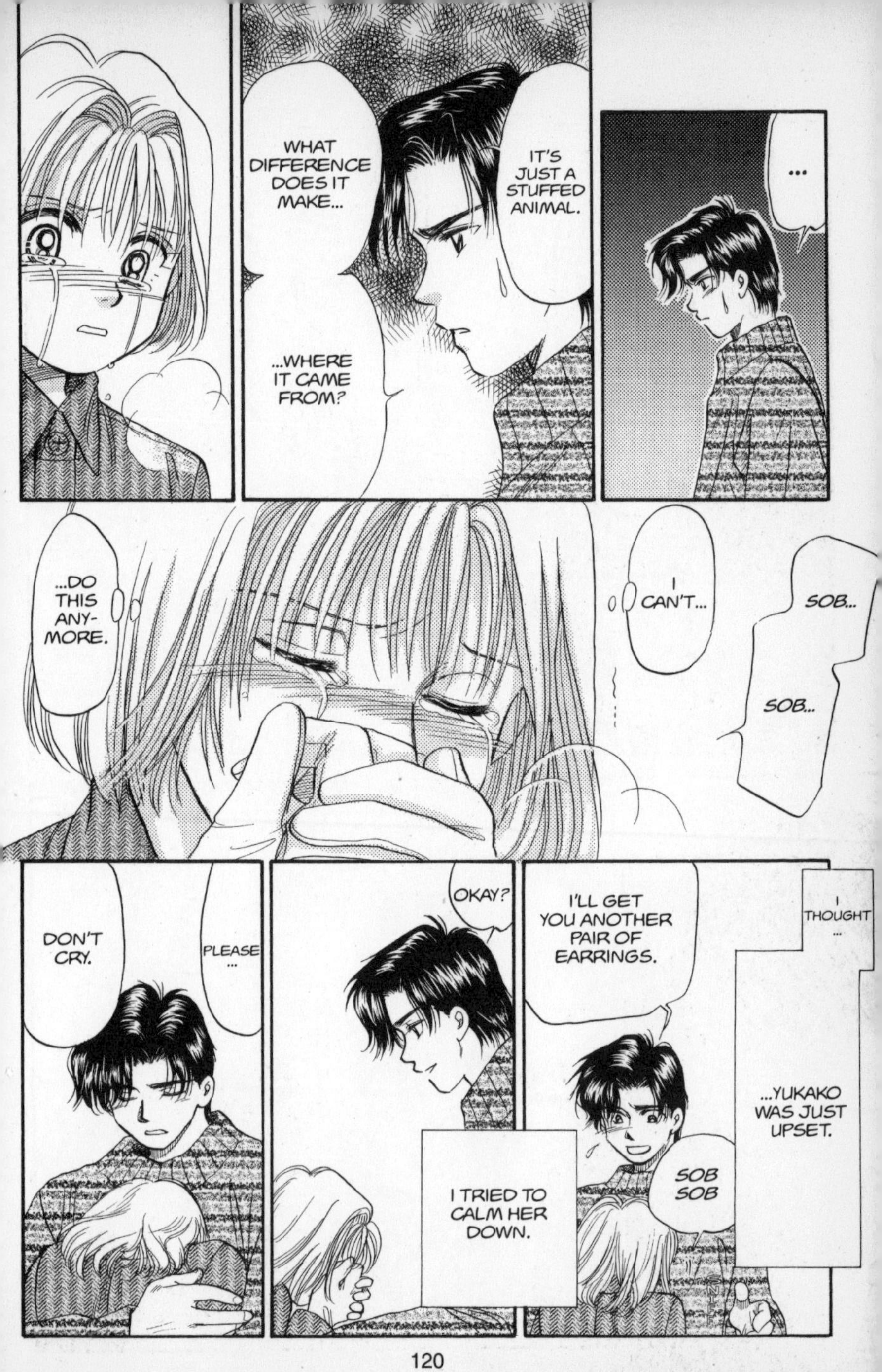
...
IT'S JUST A STUFFED ANIMAL.
WHAT DIFFERENCE DOES IT MAKE...
...WHERE IT CAME FROM?
SOB...
SOB...
I CAN'T...
...DO THIS ANY-MORE.
I THOUGHT...
...YUKAKO WAS JUST UPSET.
I'LL GET YOU ANOTHER PAIR OF EARRINGS.
SOB SOB
OKAY?
I TRIED TO CALM HER DOWN.
PLEASE...
DON'T CRY.

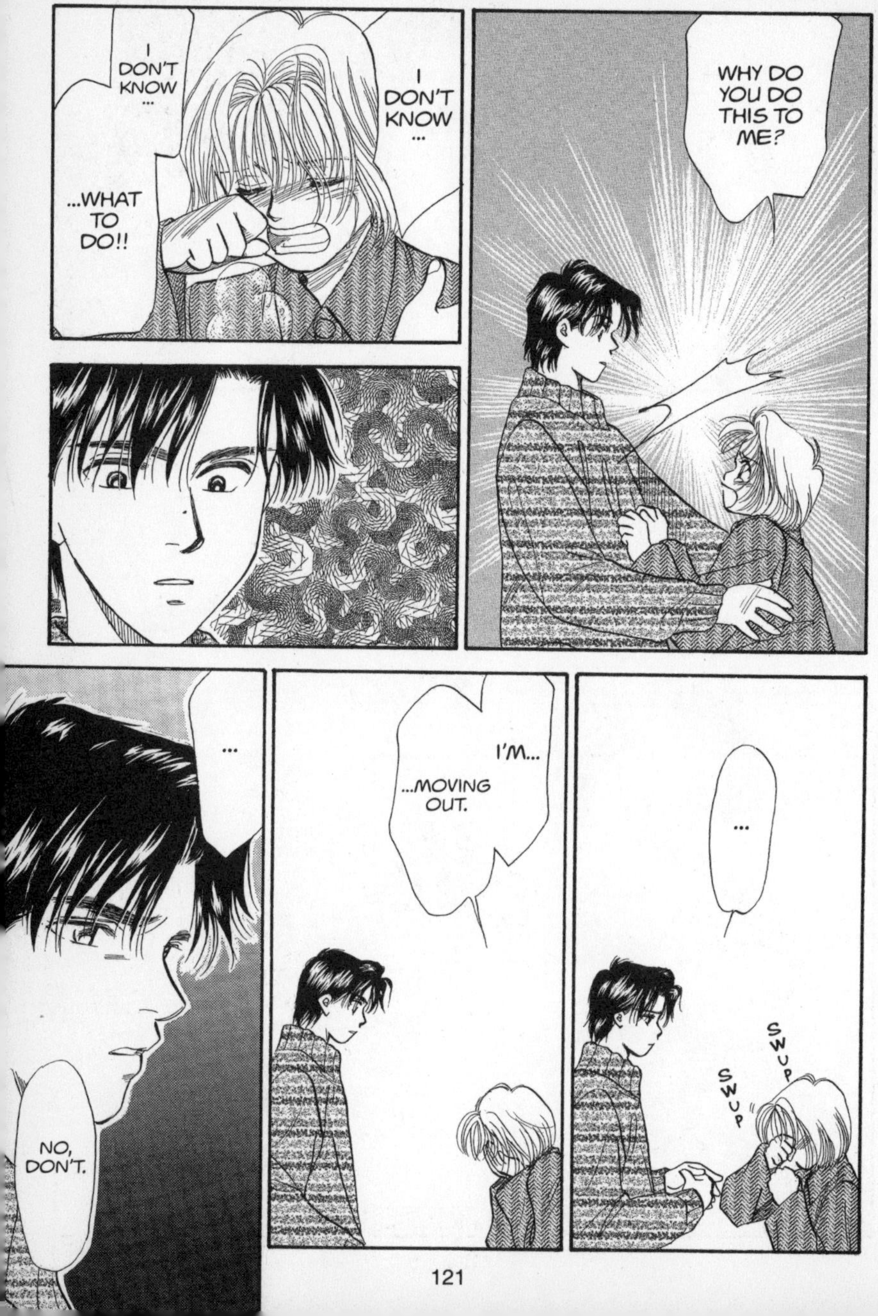
WHY DO YOU DO THIS TO ME?
I DON'T KNOW ...
I DON'T KNOW ...
...WHAT TO DO!!
...
SWUP
SWUP
I'M...
...MOVING OUT.
...
NO, DON'T.

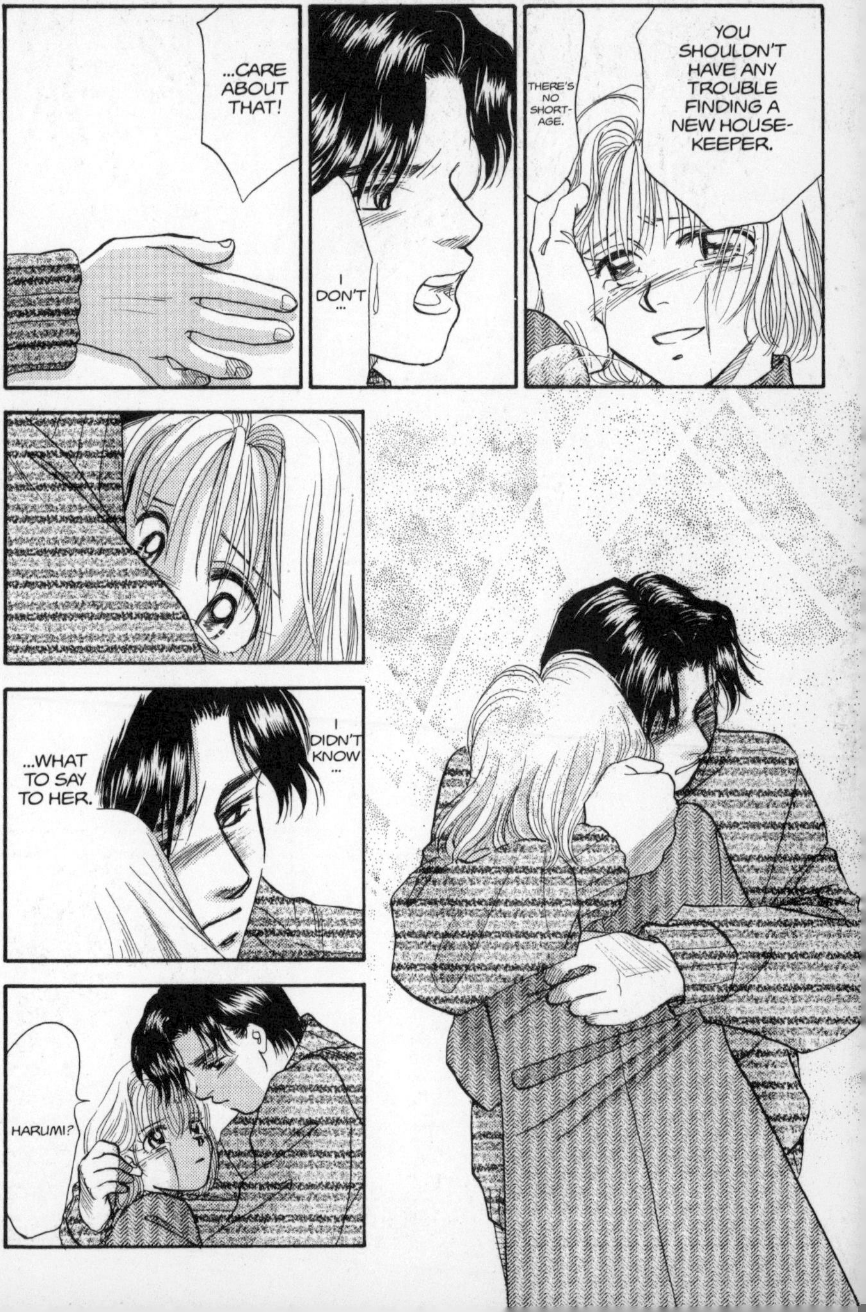
YOU SHOULDN'T HAVE ANY TROUBLE FINDING A NEW HOUSE-KEEPER.
THERE'S NO SHORT-AGE.
I DON'T ...
...CARE ABOUT THAT!
I DIDN'T KNOW ...
...WHAT TO SAY TO HER.
HARUMI?

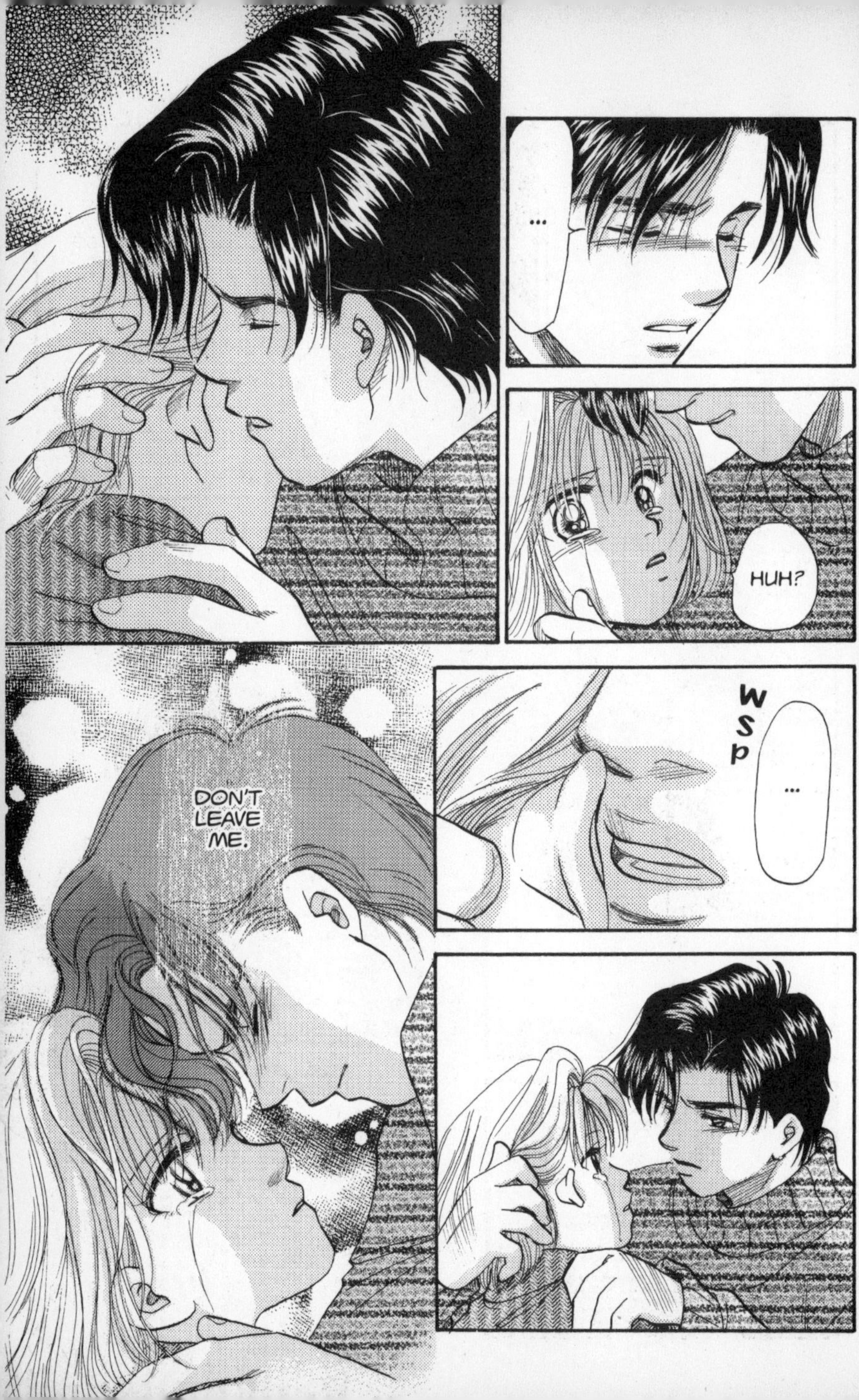
...
HUH?
WSP
...
DON'T LEAVE ME.

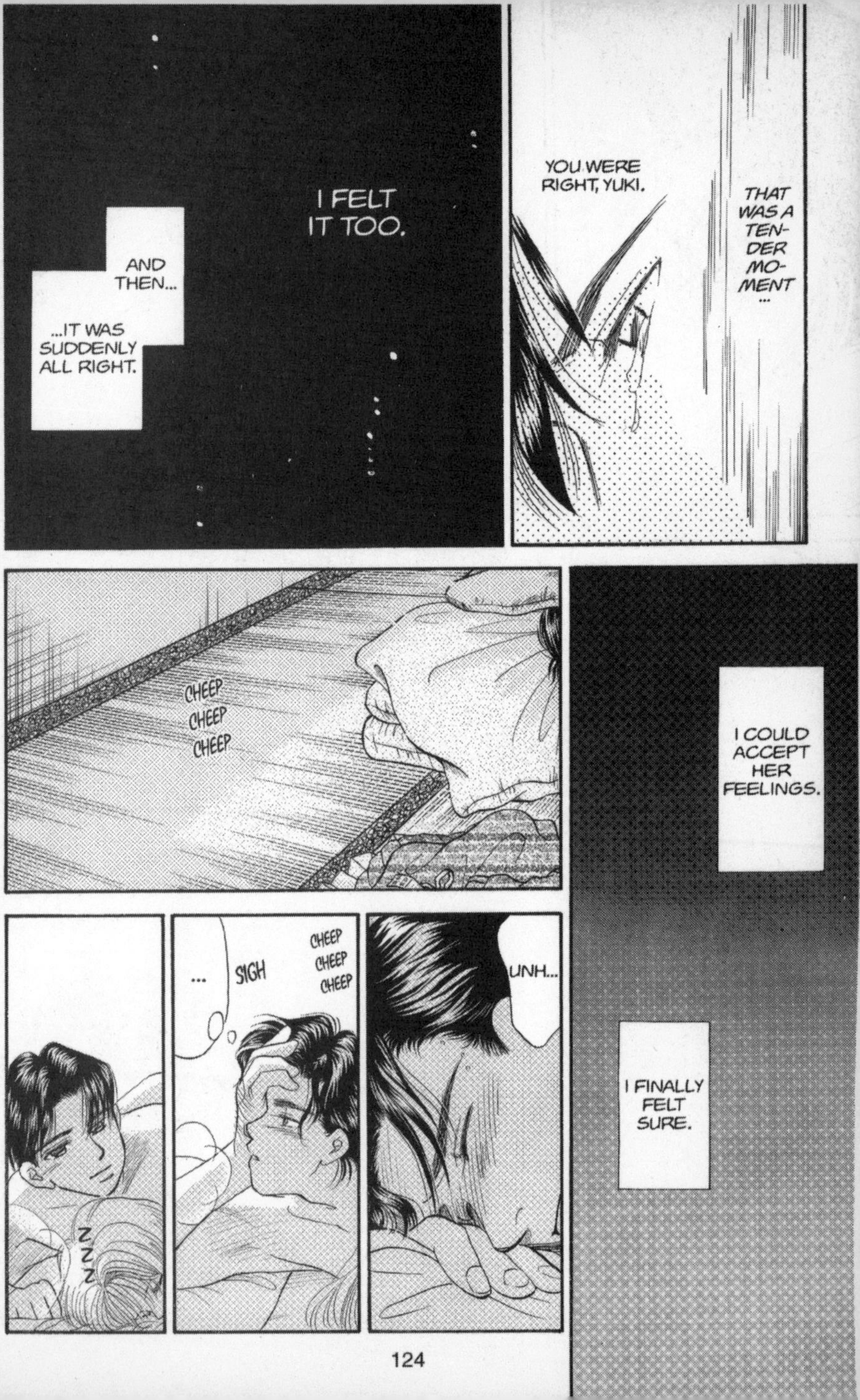
YOU WERE RIGHT, YUKI.
THAT WAS A TEN-DER MO-MENT...
I FELT IT TOO.
AND THEN...
...IT WAS SUDDENLY ALL RIGHT.
I COULD ACCEPT HER FEELINGS.
I FINALLY FELT SURE.
CHEEP CHEEP CHEEP
UNH...
CHEEP CHEEP CHEEP
SIGH
...
Z Z Z

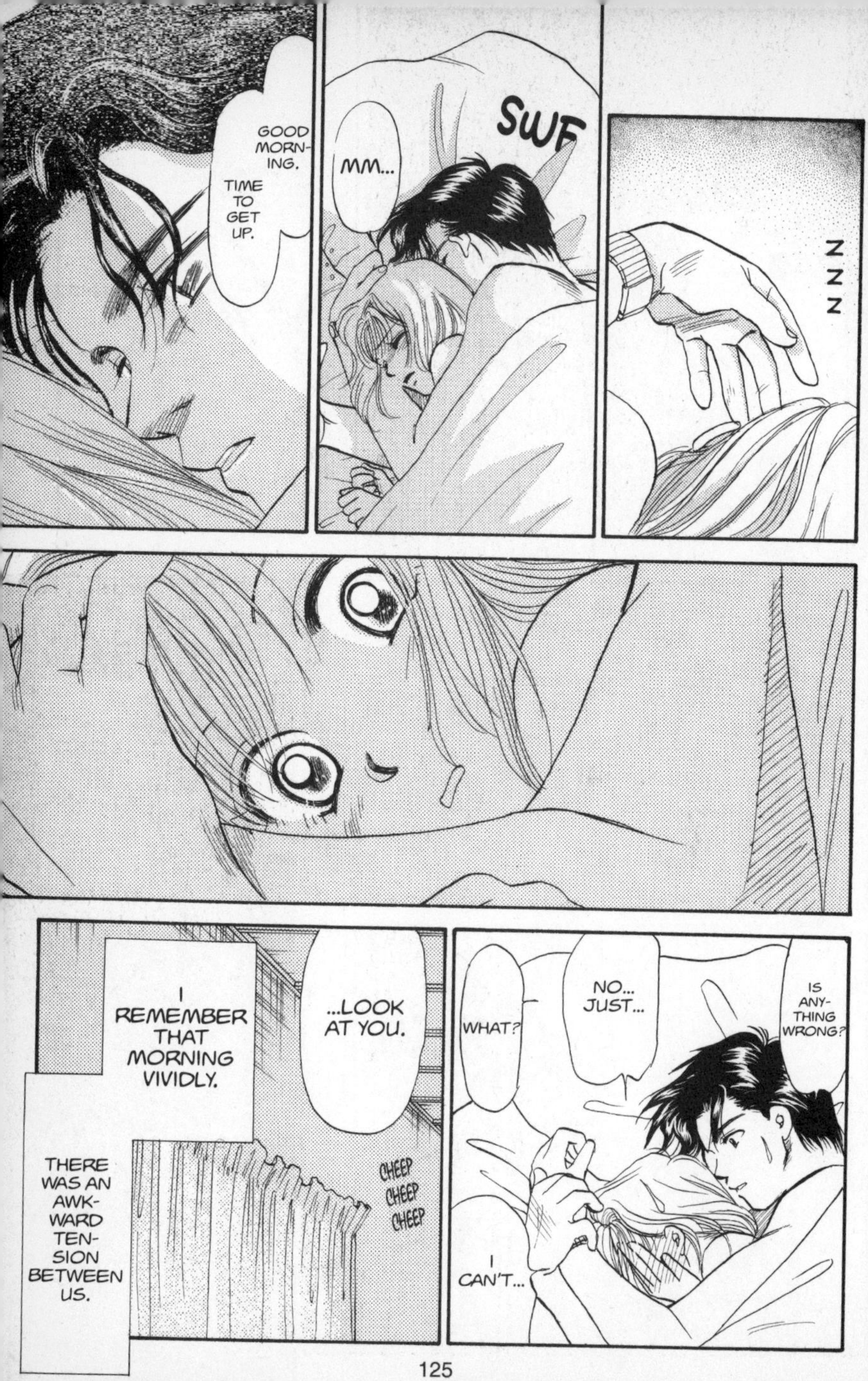
Z Z Z
SWF
MM...
GOOD MORNING.
TIME TO GET UP.
IS ANYTHING WRONG?
NO... JUST...
WHAT?
I CAN'T...
...LOOK AT YOU.
I REMEMBER THAT MORNING VIVIDLY.
THERE WAS AN AWKWARD TENSION BETWEEN US.
CHEEP CHEEP CHEEP

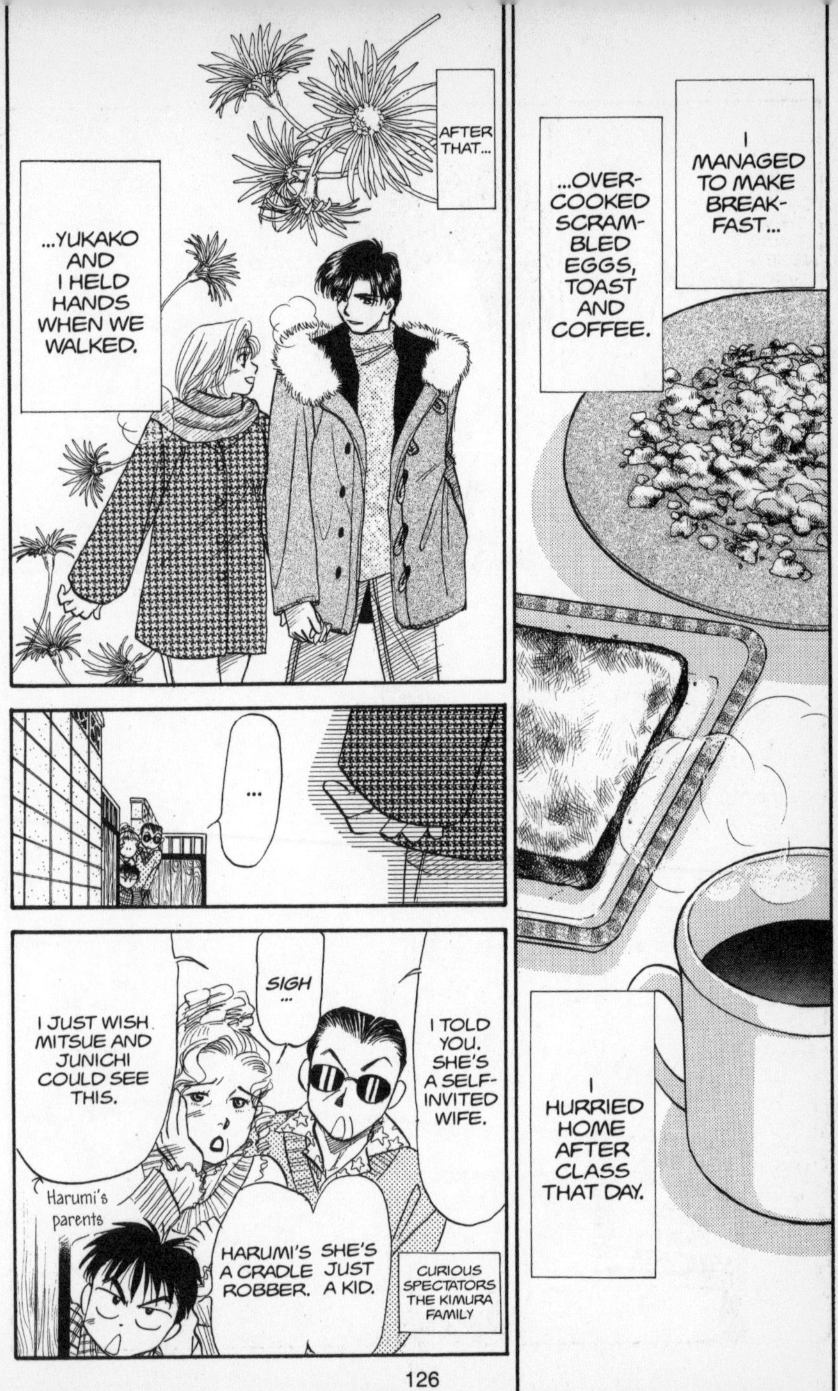
I MANAGED TO MAKE BREAK-FAST...
...OVER-COOKED SCRAM-BLED EGGS, TOAST AND COFFEE.
I HURRIED HOME AFTER CLASS THAT DAY.
AFTER THAT...
...YUKAKO AND I HELD HANDS WHEN WE WALKED.
...
I TOLD YOU. SHE'S A SELF-INVITED WIFE.
SIGH...
I JUST WISH MITSUE AND JUNICHI COULD SEE THIS.
Harumi's parents
CURIOUS SPECTATORS THE KIMURA FAMILY
SHE'S JUST A KID.
HARUMI'S A CRADLE ROBBER.

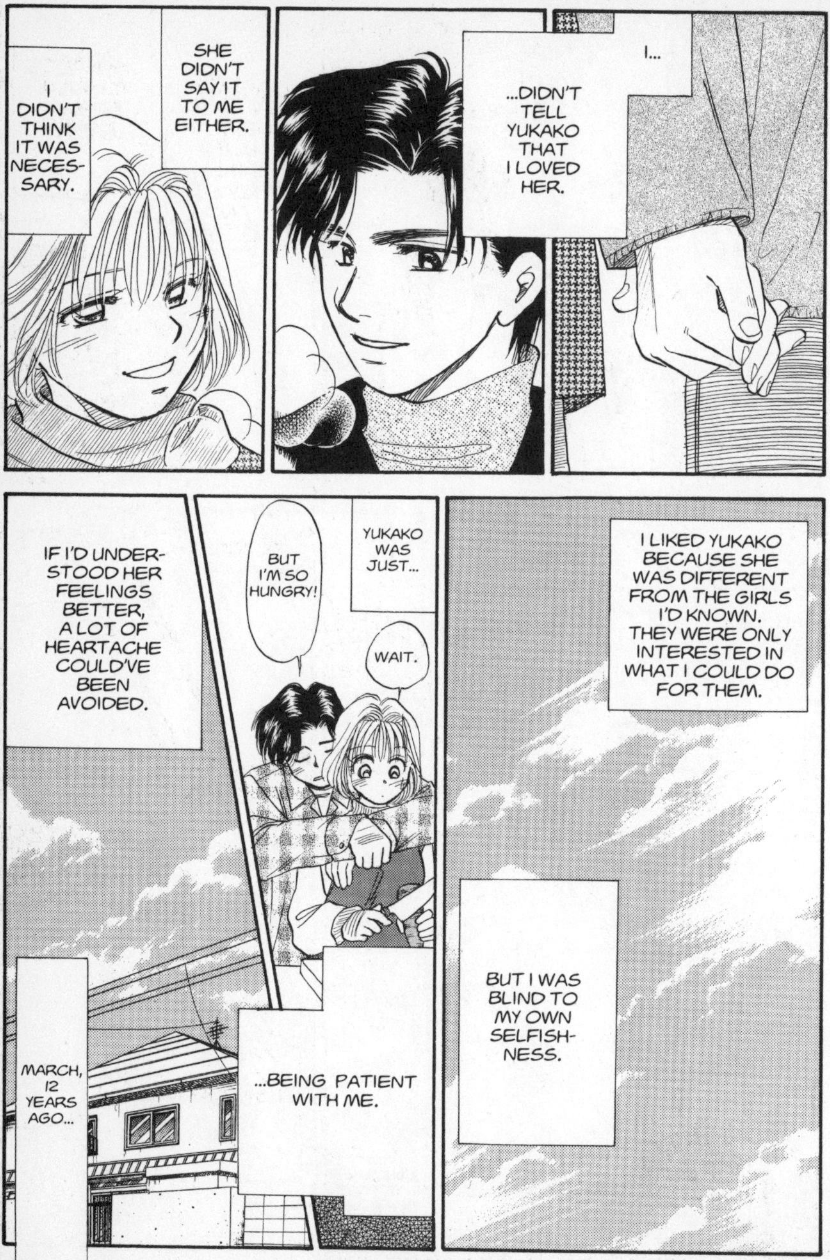
I...
...DIDN'T TELL YUKAKO THAT I LOVED HER.
SHE DIDN'T SAY IT TO ME EITHER.
I DIDN'T THINK IT WAS NECES-SARY.
I LIKED YUKAKO BECAUSE SHE WAS DIFFERENT FROM THE GIRLS I'D KNOWN. THEY WERE ONLY INTERESTED IN WHAT I COULD DO FOR THEM.
BUT I WAS BLIND TO MY OWN SELFISH-NESS.
YUKAKO WAS JUST...
BUT I'M SO HUNGRY!
WAIT.
...BEING PATIENT WITH ME.
IF I'D UNDER-STOOD HER FEELINGS BETTER, A LOT OF HEARTACHE COULD'VE BEEN AVOIDED.
MARCH, 12 YEARS AGO...

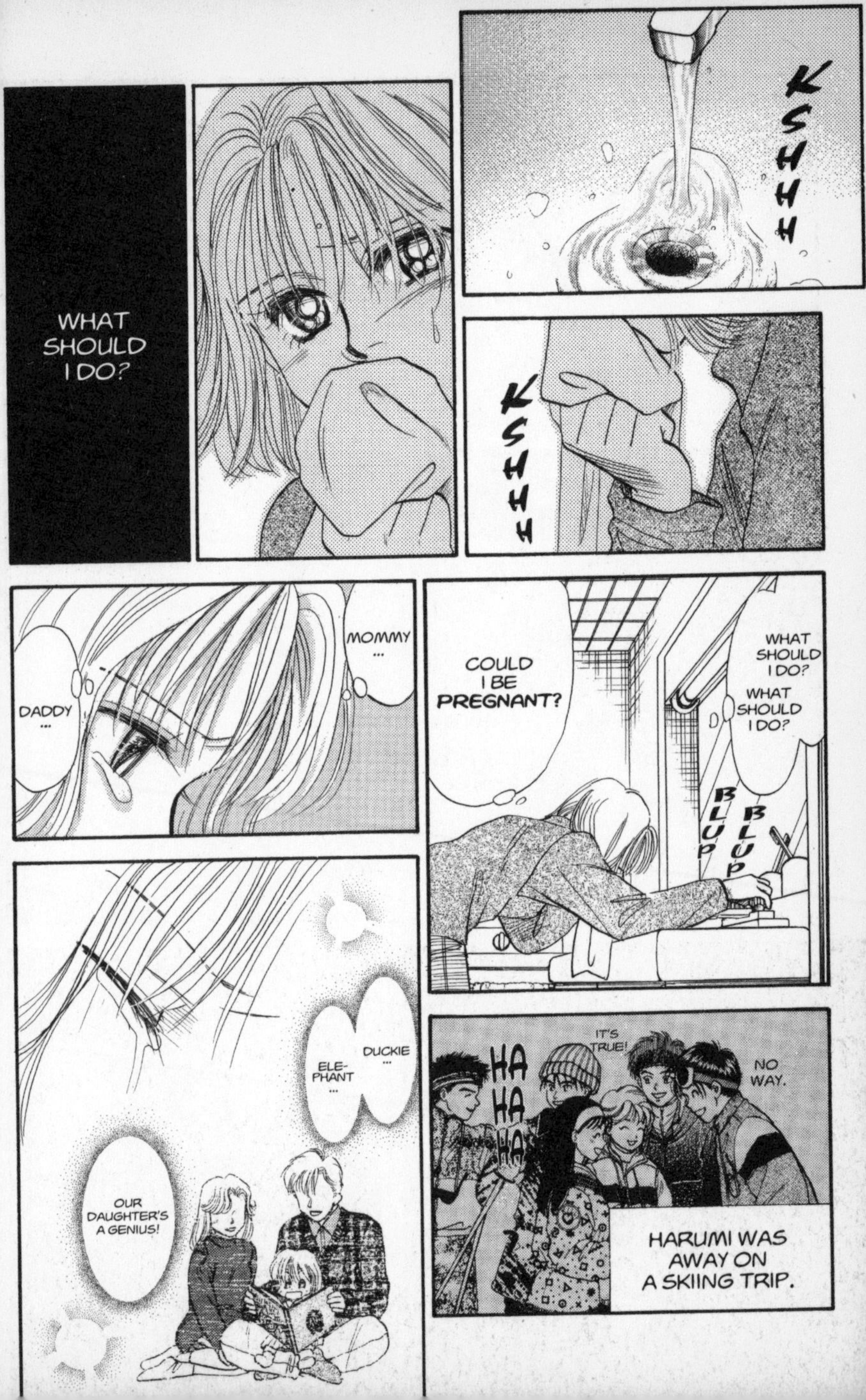
KSHHH
KSHHH
WHAT SHOULD I DO?
WHAT SHOULD I DO?
WHAT SHOULD I DO?
COULD I BE PREGNANT?
BLUP BLUP
MOMMY ...
DADDY ...
DUCKIE ...
ELE-PHANT ...
OUR DAUGHTER'S A GENIUS!
NO WAY.
IT'S TRUE!
HA HA HA
HARUMI WAS AWAY ON A SKIING TRIP.

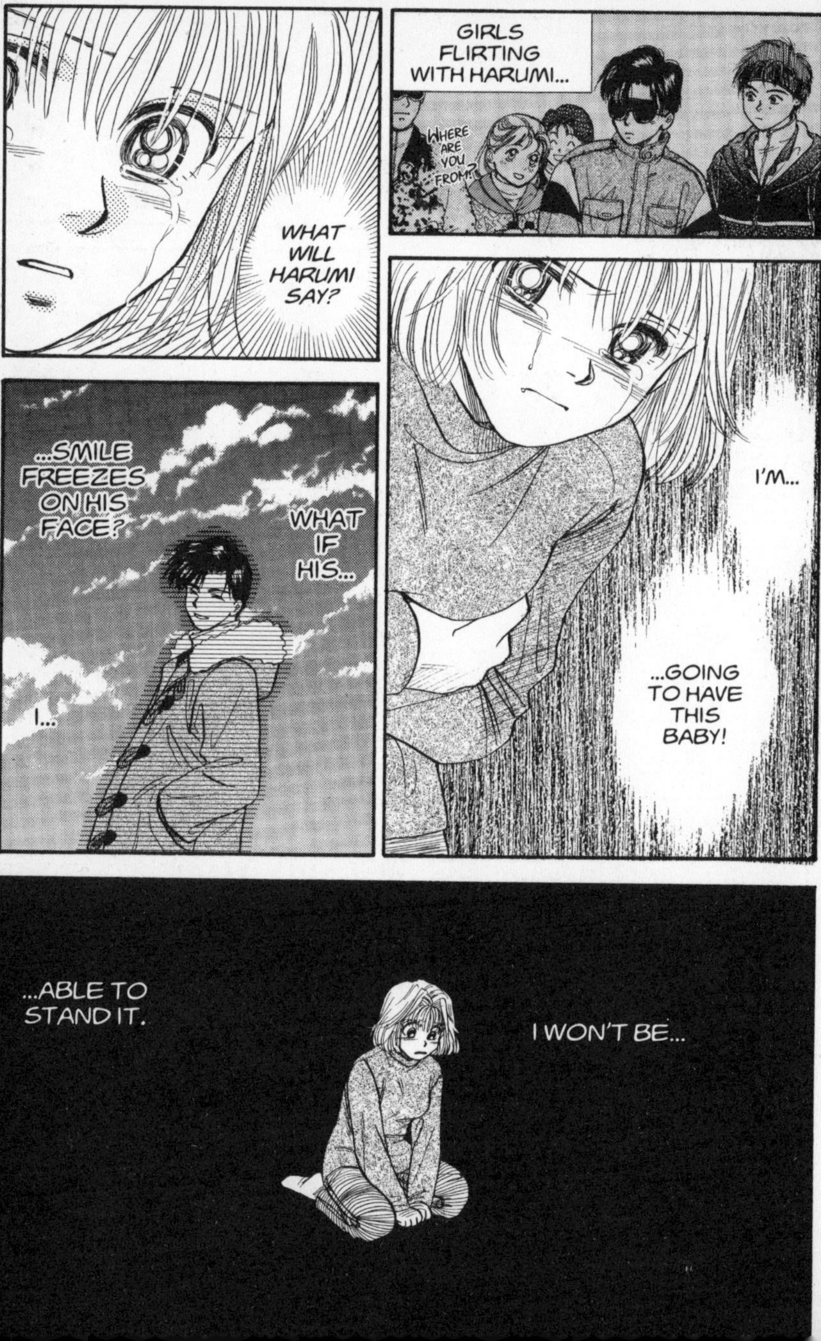
GIRLS FLIRTING WITH HARUMI...
WHERE ARE YOU FROM?
WHAT WILL HARUMI SAY?
I'M...
...GOING TO HAVE THIS BABY!
WHAT IF HIS...
...SMILE FREEZES ON HIS FACE?
I...
I WON'T BE...
...ABLE TO STAND IT.

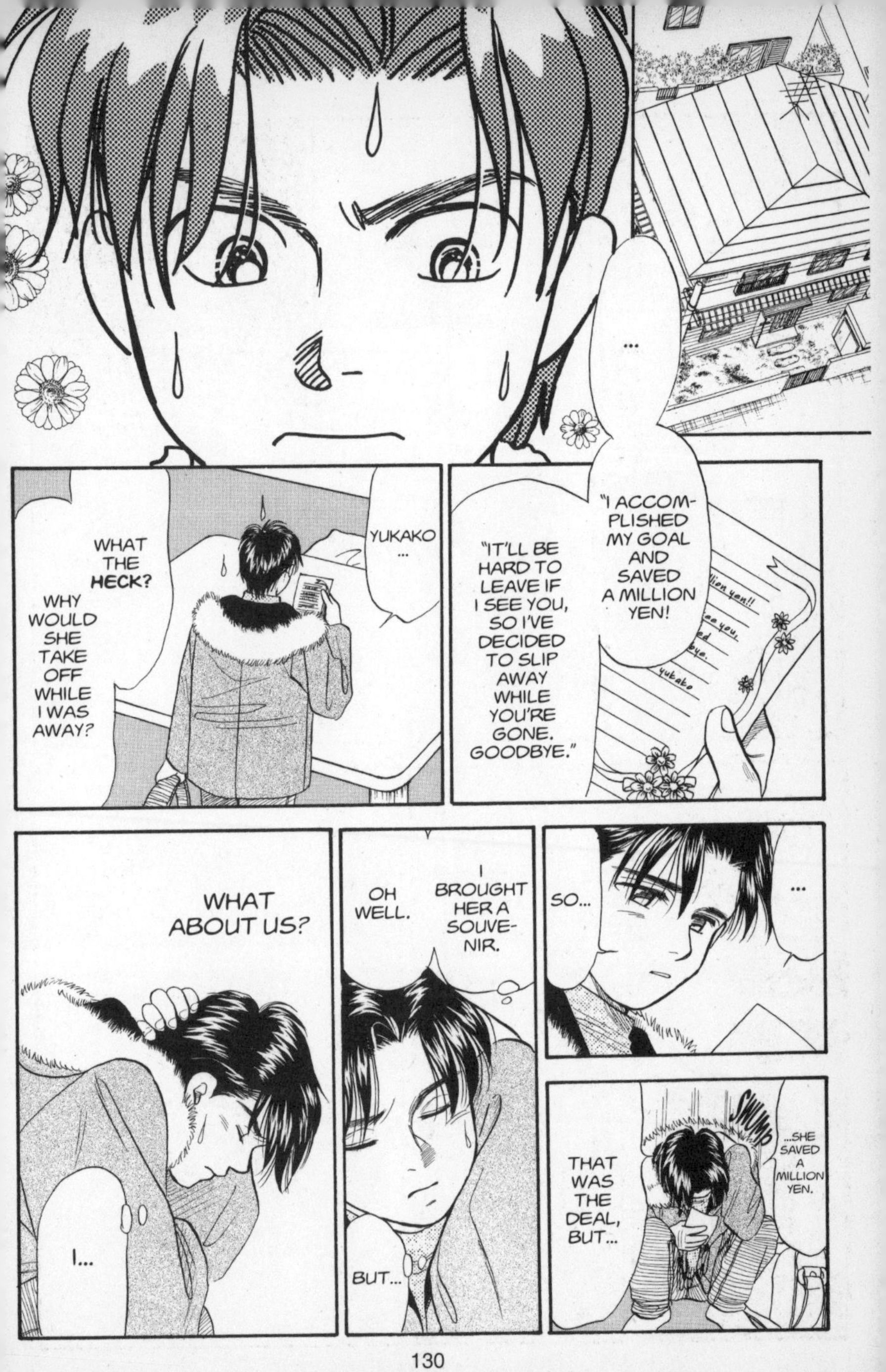

...
"I ACCOMPLISHED MY GOAL AND SAVED A MILLION YEN!
"IT'LL BE HARD TO LEAVE IF I SEE YOU, SO I'VE DECIDED TO SLIP AWAY WHILE YOU'RE GONE. GOODBYE."
YUKAKO ...
WHAT THE **HECK?**
WHY WOULD SHE TAKE OFF WHILE I WAS AWAY?
...
SO...
...SHE SAVED A MILLION YEN.
SWUMP
THAT WAS THE DEAL, BUT...
I BROUGHT HER A SOUVENIR.
OH WELL.
BUT...
WHAT ABOUT US?
I...

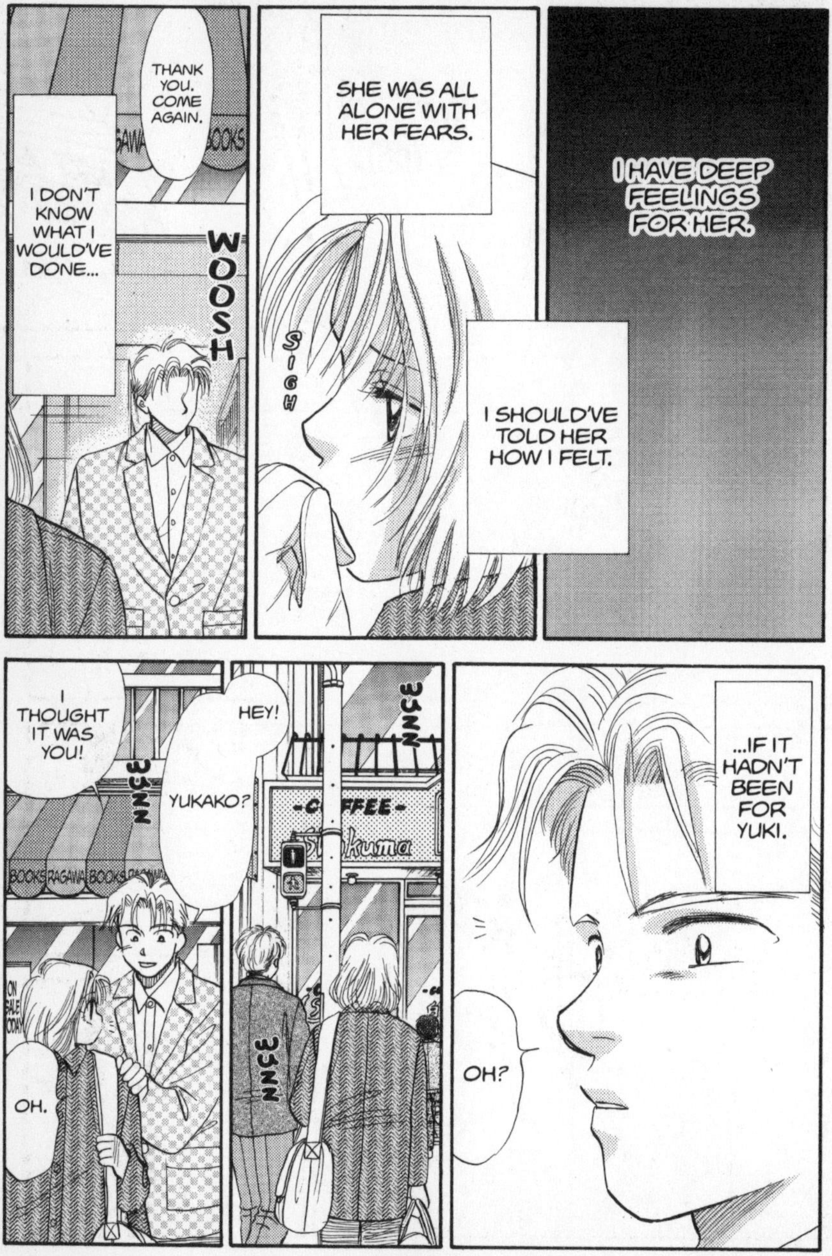
I HAVE DEEP FEELINGS FOR HER.
I SHOULD'VE TOLD HER HOW I FELT.
SHE WAS ALL ALONE WITH HER FEARS.
SIGH
THANK YOU. COME AGAIN.
I DON'T KNOW WHAT I WOULD'VE DONE...
WOOSH
...IF IT HADN'T BEEN FOR YUKI.
OH?
HEY!
YUKAKO?
-COFFEE-
I THOUGHT IT WAS YOU!
OH.

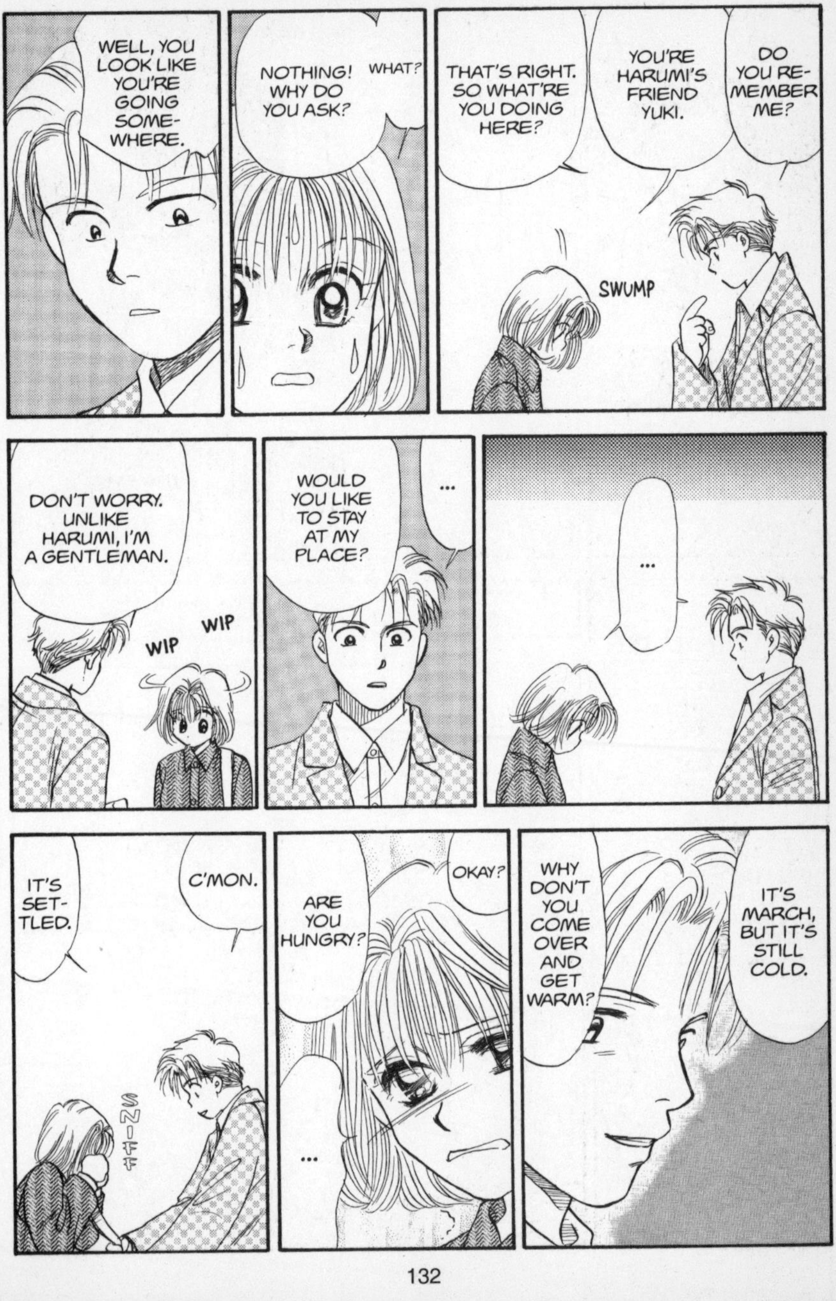
DO YOU RE-MEMBER ME?
YOU'RE HARUMI'S FRIEND YUKI.
THAT'S RIGHT. SO WHAT'RE YOU DOING HERE?
SWUMP
WHAT?
NOTHING! WHY DO YOU ASK?
WELL, YOU LOOK LIKE YOU'RE GOING SOME-WHERE.
...
...
WOULD YOU LIKE TO STAY AT MY PLACE?
DON'T WORRY. UNLIKE HARUMI, I'M A GENTLEMAN.
WIP
WIP
IT'S MARCH, BUT IT'S STILL COLD.
WHY DON'T YOU COME OVER AND GET WARM?
OKAY?
ARE YOU HUNGRY?
...
C'MON.
IT'S SET-TLED.
SNIFF

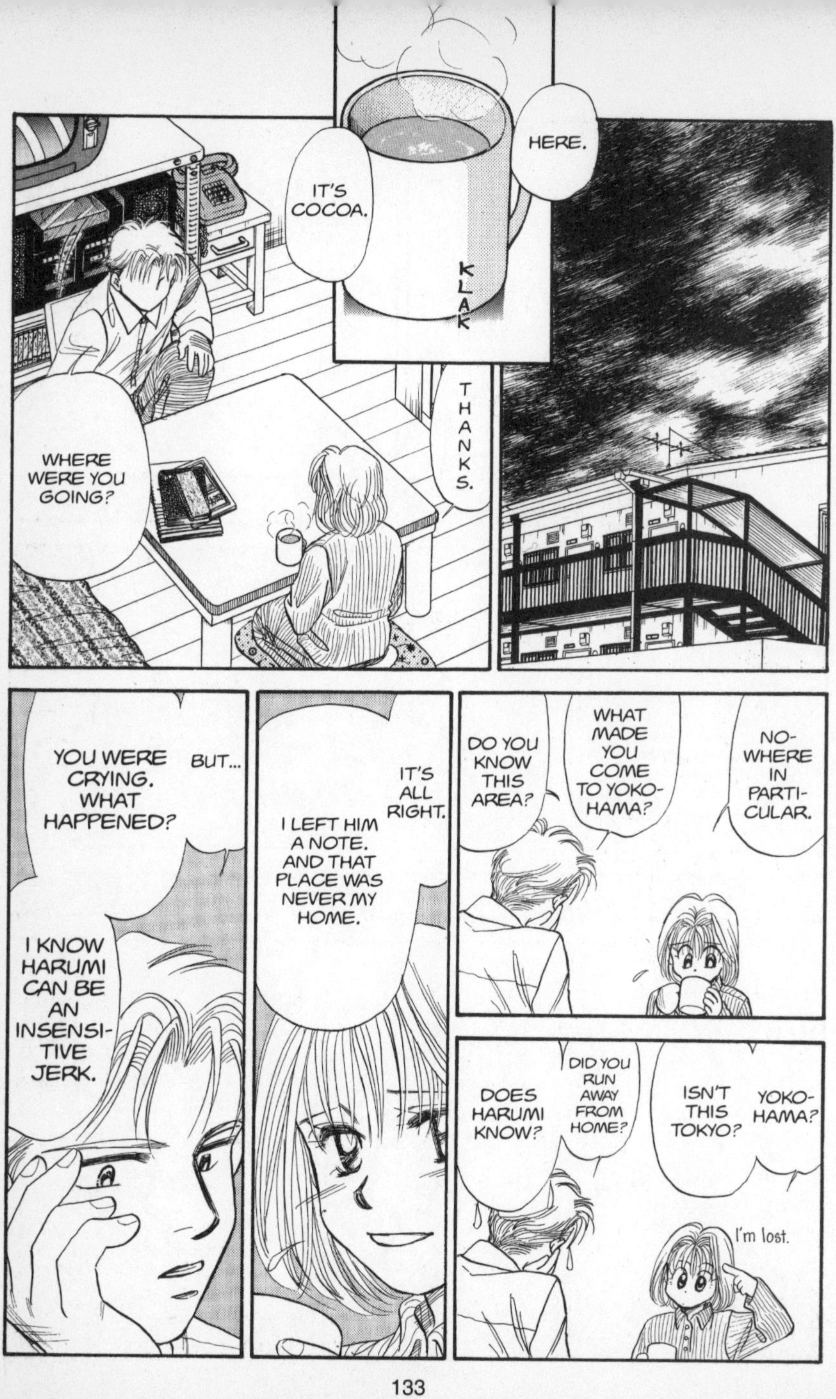
HERE.
IT'S COCOA.
KLAK
THANKS.
WHERE WERE YOU GOING?
NO-WHERE IN PARTICULAR.
WHAT MADE YOU COME TO YOKO-HAMA?
DO YOU KNOW THIS AREA?
YOKO-HAMA?
ISN'T THIS TOKYO?
I'm lost.
DID YOU RUN AWAY FROM HOME?
DOES HARUMI KNOW?
IT'S ALL RIGHT.
I LEFT HIM A NOTE. AND THAT PLACE WAS NEVER MY HOME.
BUT...
YOU WERE CRYING. WHAT HAPPENED?
I KNOW HARUMI CAN BE AN INSENSI-TIVE JERK.

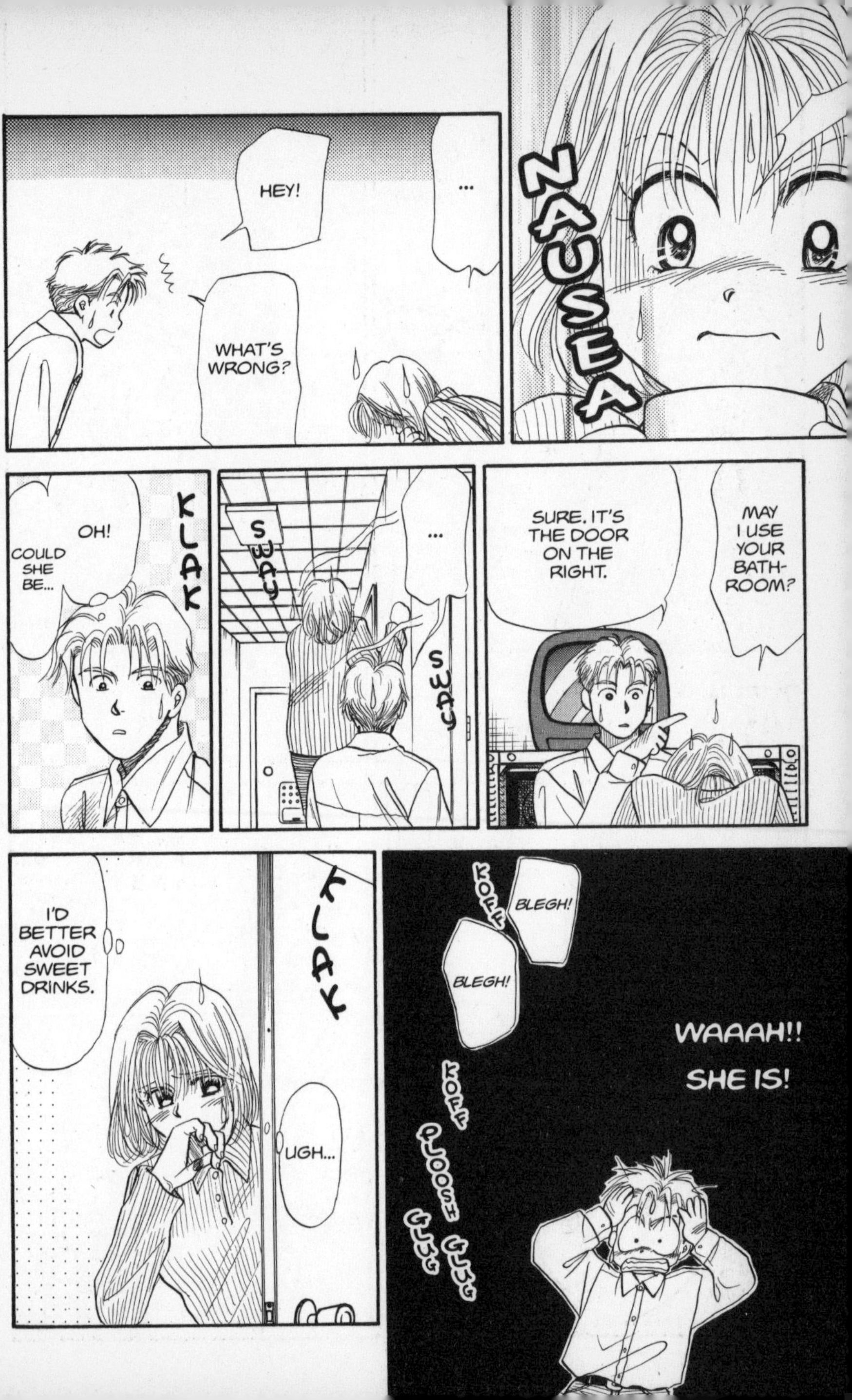
NAUSEA
...
HEY!
WHAT'S WRONG?
MAY I USE YOUR BATH-ROOM?
SURE. IT'S THE DOOR ON THE RIGHT.
...
SWAY
SWAY
KLAK
OH!
COULD SHE BE...
BLEGH!
KOFF
BLEGH!
WAAAH!! SHE IS!
KOFF
PLOOSH
GLUG
GLUG
KLAK
I'D BETTER AVOID SWEET DRINKS.
UGH...

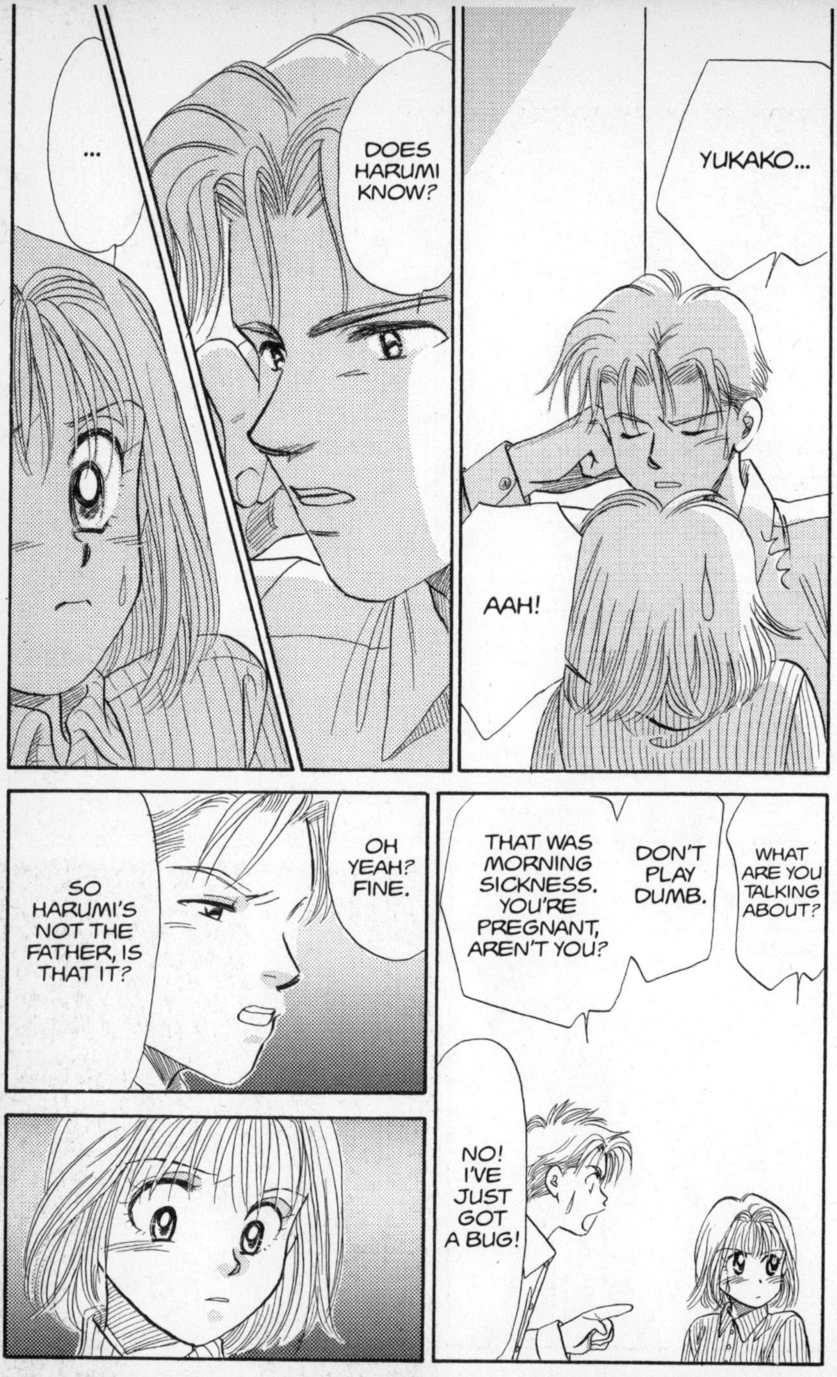
YUKAKO...
AAH!
DOES HARUMI KNOW?
...
WHAT ARE YOU TALKING ABOUT?
DON'T PLAY DUMB.
THAT WAS MORNING SICKNESS. YOU'RE PREGNANT, AREN'T YOU?
NO! I'VE JUST GOT A BUG!
OH YEAH? FINE.
SO HARUMI'S NOT THE FATHER, IS THAT IT?

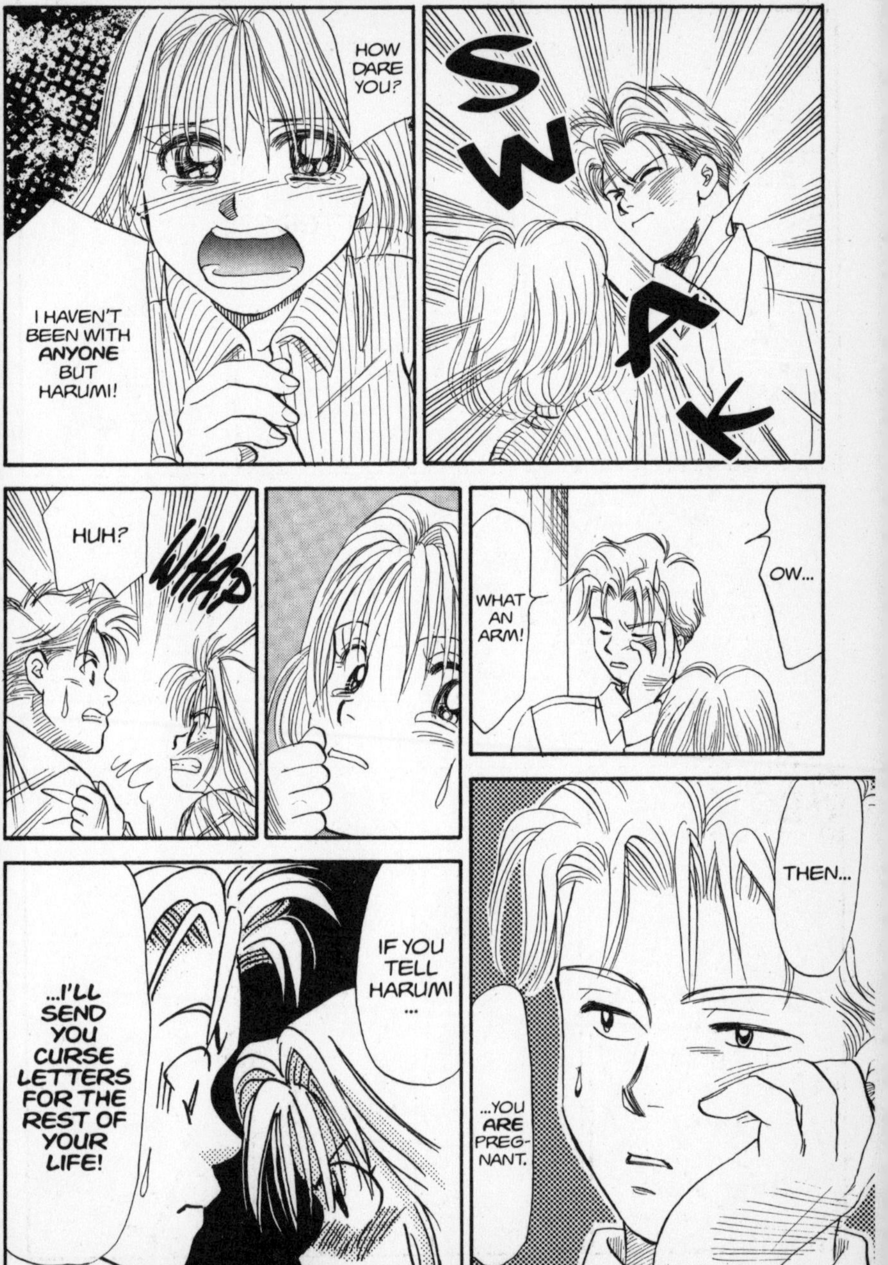
SWAK
HOW DARE YOU?
I HAVEN'T BEEN WITH ANYONE BUT HARUMI!
OW...
WHAT AN ARM!
WHAP
HUH?
THEN...
...YOU ARE PREGNANT.
IF YOU TELL HARUMI...
...I'LL SEND YOU CURSE LETTERS FOR THE REST OF YOUR LIFE!

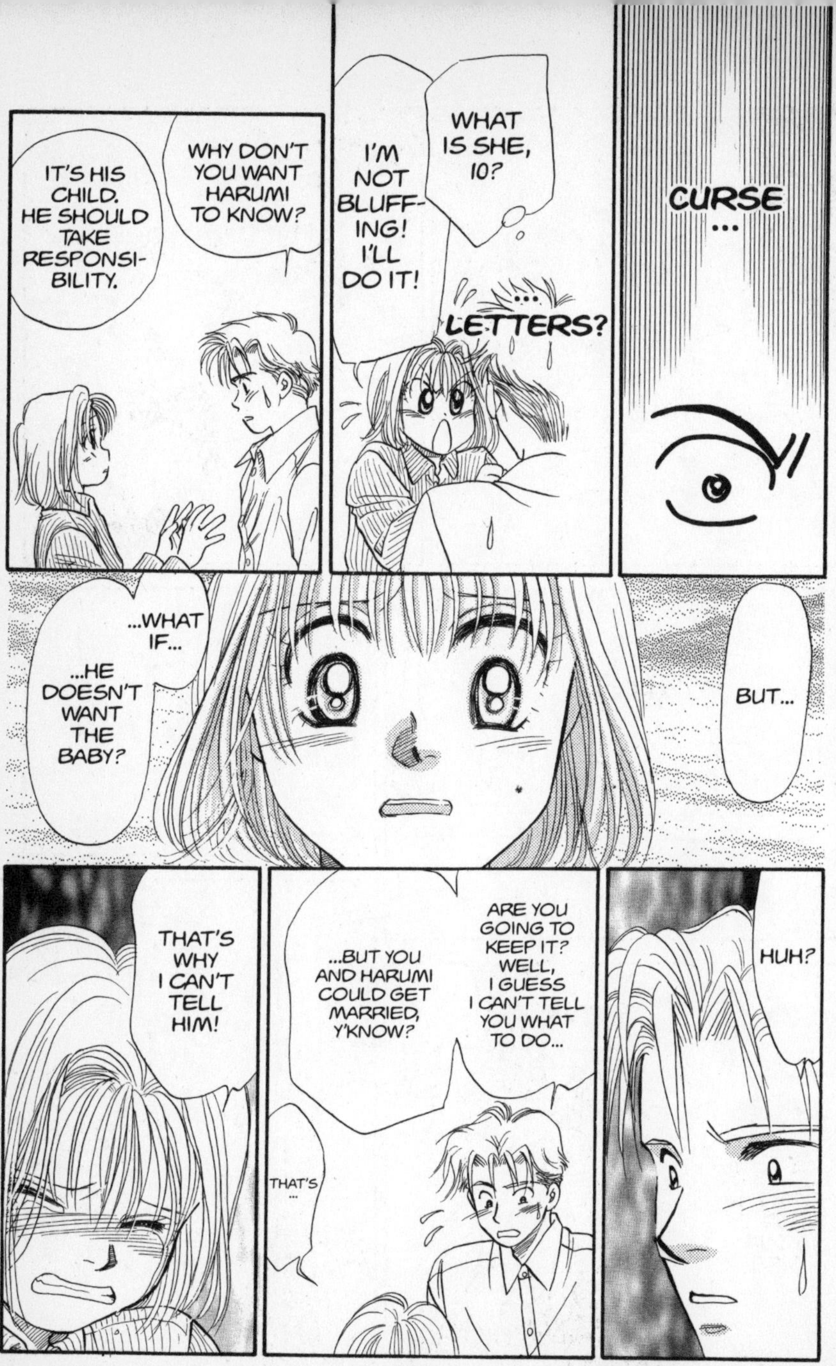
CURSE ...
WHAT IS SHE, 10?
I'M NOT BLUFF-ING! I'LL DO IT!
... LETTERS?
WHY DON'T YOU WANT HARUMI TO KNOW?
IT'S HIS CHILD. HE SHOULD TAKE RESPONSI-BILITY.
BUT...
...WHAT IF...
...HE DOESN'T WANT THE BABY?
HUH?
ARE YOU GOING TO KEEP IT? WELL, I GUESS I CAN'T TELL YOU WHAT TO DO...
...BUT YOU AND HARUMI COULD GET MARRIED, Y'KNOW?
THAT'S ...
THAT'S WHY I CAN'T TELL HIM!

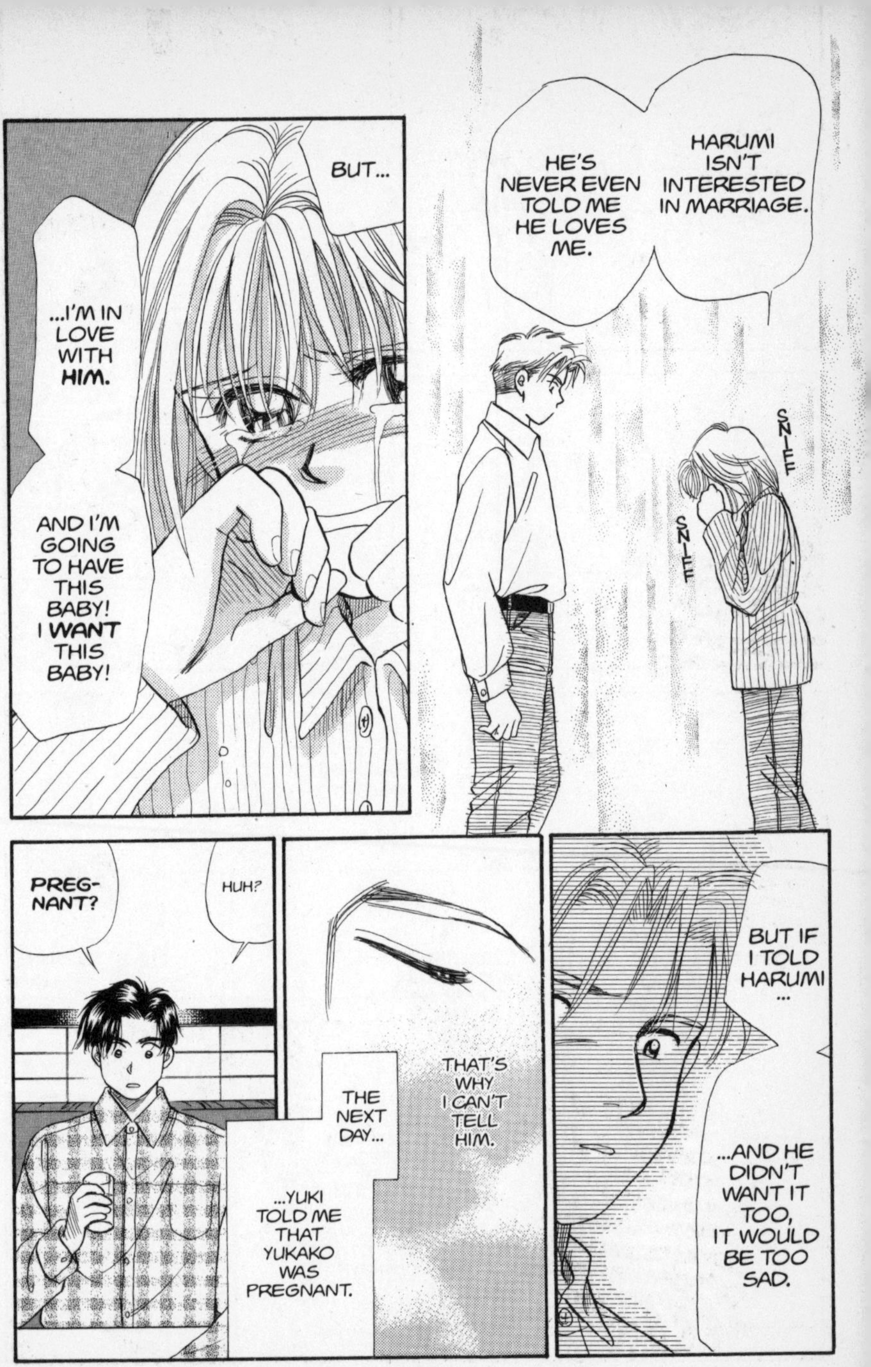
HARUMI ISN'T INTERESTED IN MARRIAGE.
HE'S NEVER EVEN TOLD ME HE LOVES ME.
SNIFF
SNIFF
BUT...
...I'M IN LOVE WITH **HIM.**
AND I'M GOING TO HAVE THIS BABY! I **WANT** THIS BABY!
BUT IF I TOLD HARUMI ...
...AND HE DIDN'T WANT IT TOO, IT WOULD BE TOO SAD.
THAT'S WHY I CAN'T TELL HIM.
THE NEXT DAY...
...YUKI TOLD ME THAT YUKAKO WAS PREGNANT.
HUH?
PREG-NANT?

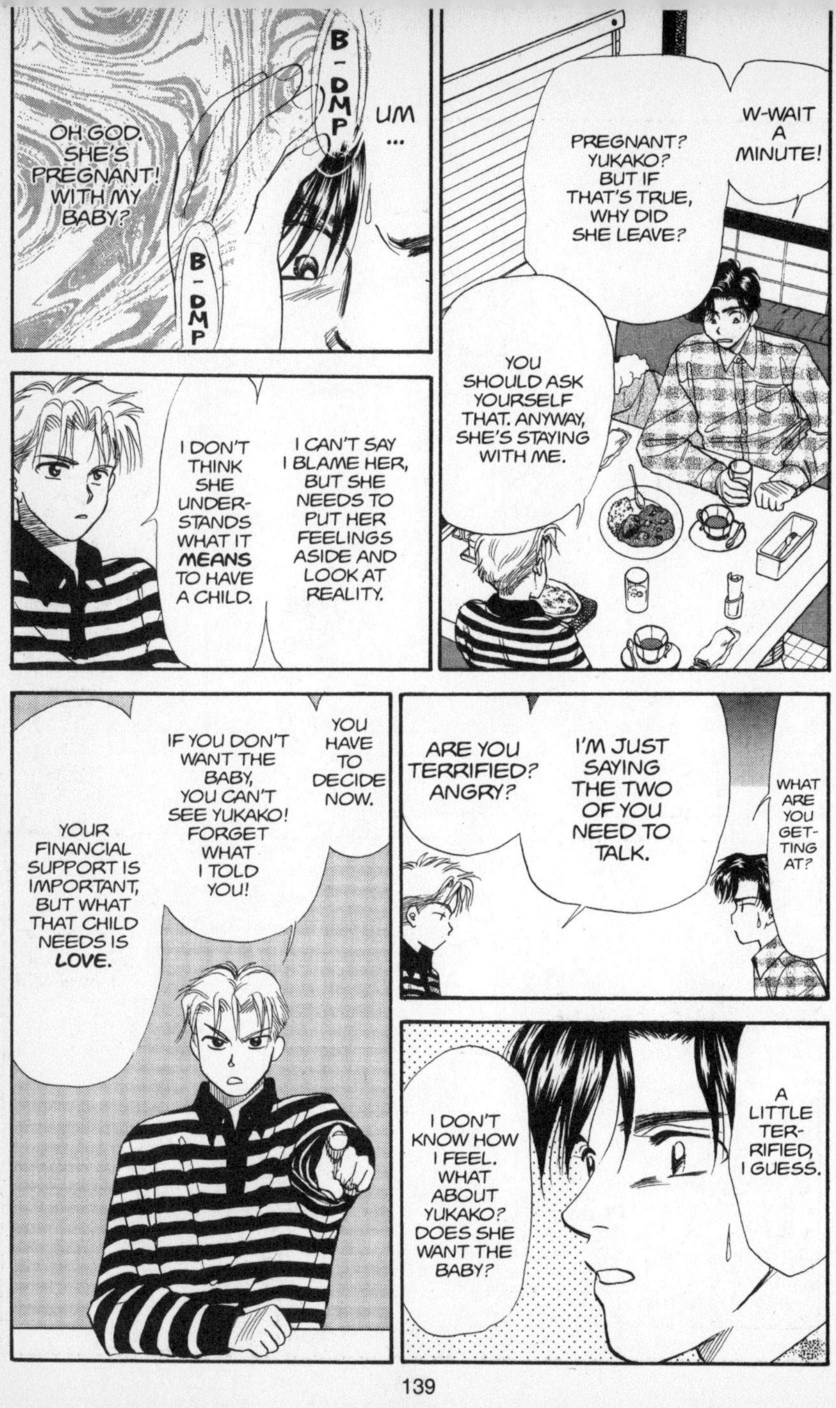
W-WAIT A MINUTE!
PREGNANT? YUKAKO? BUT IF THAT'S TRUE, WHY DID SHE LEAVE?
YOU SHOULD ASK YOURSELF THAT. ANYWAY, SHE'S STAYING WITH ME.
UM ...
B-DMP
OH GOD. SHE'S PREGNANT! WITH MY BABY?
B-DMP
I CAN'T SAY I BLAME HER, BUT SHE NEEDS TO PUT HER FEELINGS ASIDE AND LOOK AT REALITY.
I DON'T THINK SHE UNDERSTANDS WHAT IT **MEANS** TO HAVE A CHILD.
WHAT ARE YOU GETTING AT?
I'M JUST SAYING THE TWO OF YOU NEED TO TALK.
ARE YOU TERRIFIED? ANGRY?
A LITTLE TERRIFIED, I GUESS.
I DON'T KNOW HOW I FEEL. WHAT ABOUT YUKAKO? DOES SHE WANT THE BABY?
YOU HAVE TO DECIDE NOW.
IF YOU DON'T WANT THE BABY, YOU CAN'T SEE YUKAKO! FORGET WHAT I TOLD YOU!
YOUR FINANCIAL SUPPORT IS IMPORTANT, BUT WHAT THAT CHILD NEEDS IS **LOVE**.

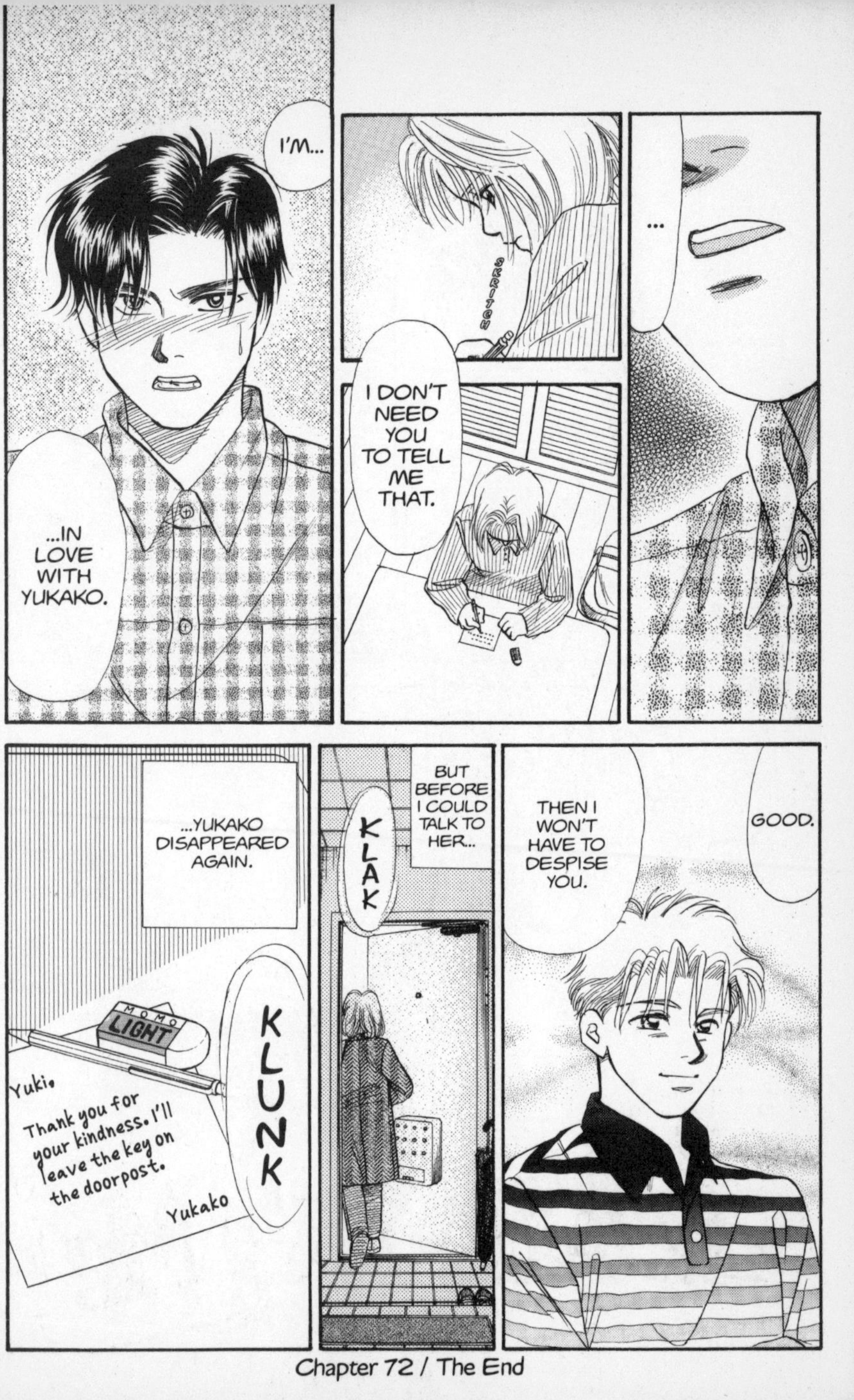
I'M...
...IN LOVE WITH YUKAKO.
SKRITCH
I DON'T NEED YOU TO TELL ME THAT.
...
...YUKAKO DISAPPEARED AGAIN.
MOMO LIGHT
Yuki,
Thank you for your kindness. I'll leave the key on the doorpost.
Yukako
KLUNK
BUT BEFORE I COULD TALK TO HER...
KLAK
THEN I WON'T HAVE TO DESPISE YOU.
GOOD.

Chapter 72 / The End

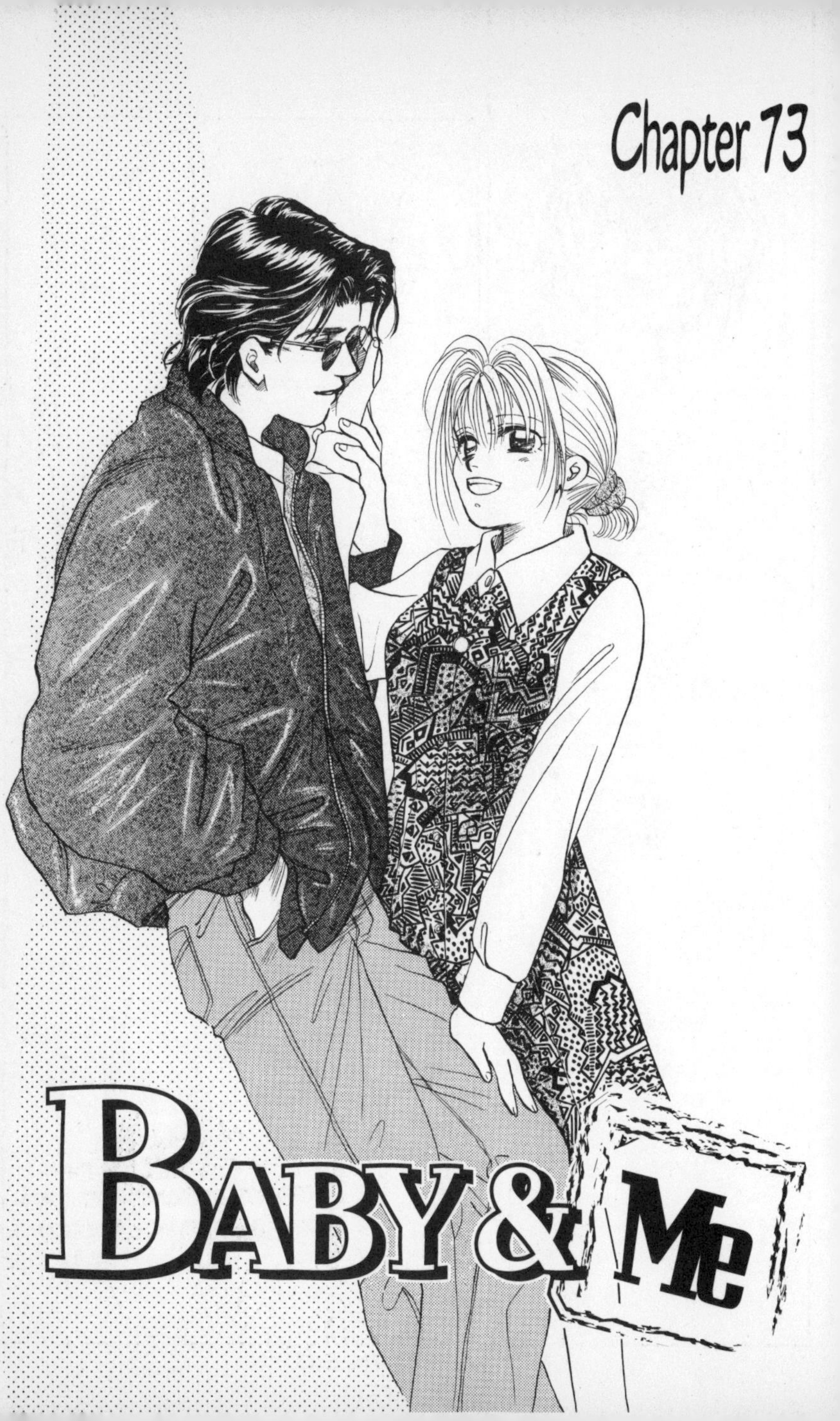
Chapter 73
BABY & Me

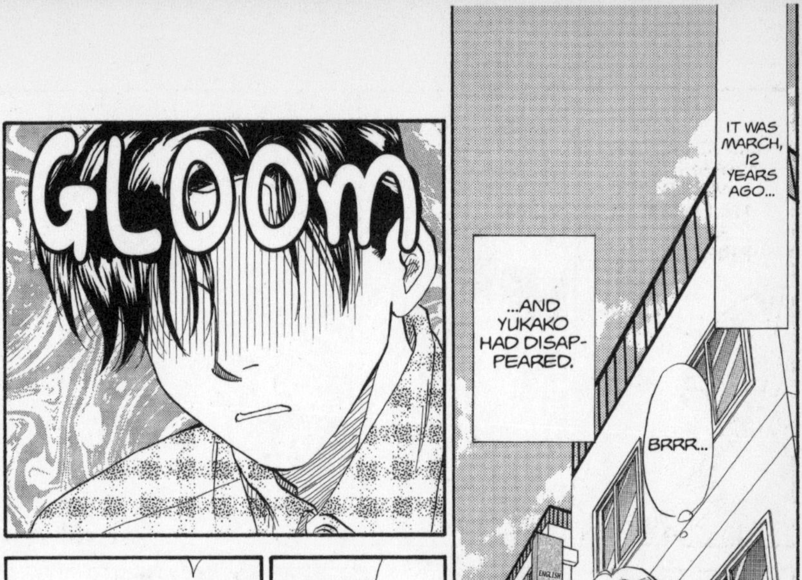
IT WAS MARCH, 12 YEARS AGO...
...AND YUKAKO HAD DISAP-PEARED.
BRRR...
ENGLISH CONVER-SATION SCHOOL ABC CLUB
Kinokuniya
GLOOM
HARUMI! WANT SOME COFFEE?
YOU'RE A LIAR.
YOU TOLD ME YUKAKO WOULD BE HERE!
GRR
GRR
TAKE IT EASY.

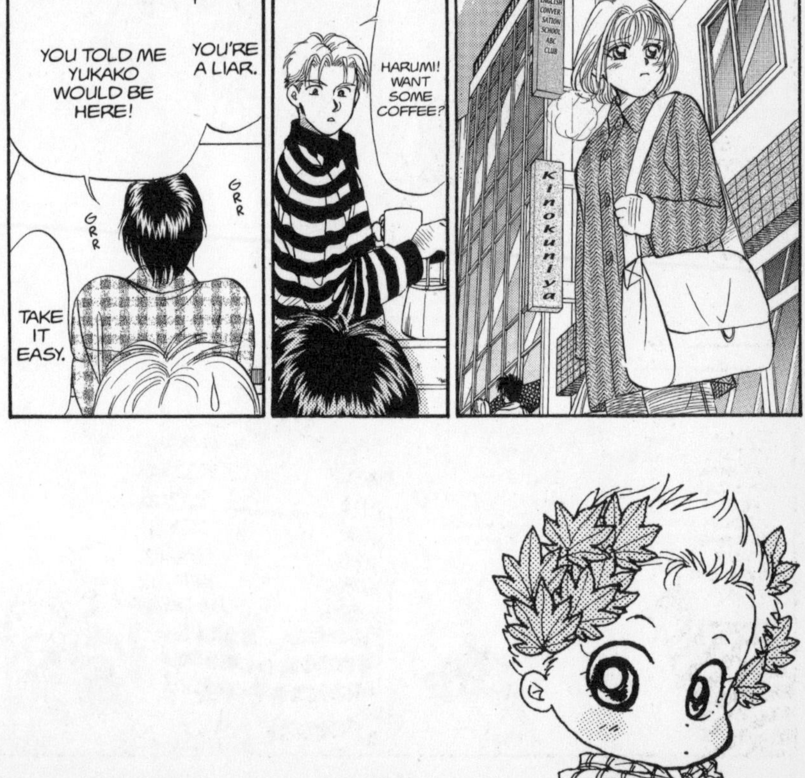

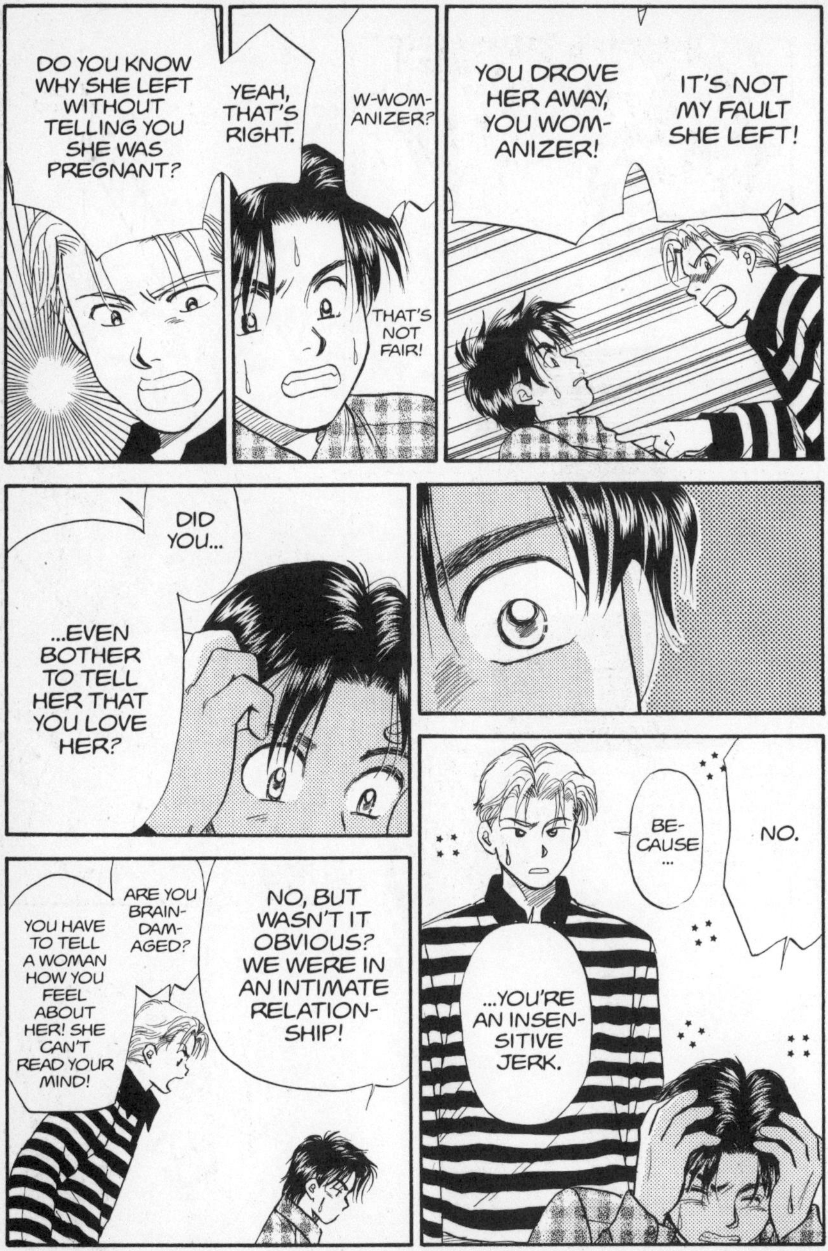
IT'S NOT MY FAULT SHE LEFT!
YOU DROVE HER AWAY, YOU WOM-ANIZER!
W-WOM-ANIZER?
YEAH, THAT'S RIGHT.
THAT'S NOT FAIR!
DO YOU KNOW WHY SHE LEFT WITHOUT TELLING YOU SHE WAS PREGNANT?
DID YOU...
...EVEN BOTHER TO TELL HER THAT YOU LOVE HER?
NO.
BE-CAUSE...
...YOU'RE AN INSEN-SITIVE JERK.
NO, BUT WASN'T IT OBVIOUS? WE WERE IN AN INTIMATE RELATION-SHIP!
ARE YOU BRAIN-DAMAGED?
YOU HAVE TO TELL A WOMAN HOW YOU FEEL ABOUT HER! SHE CAN'T READ YOUR MIND!

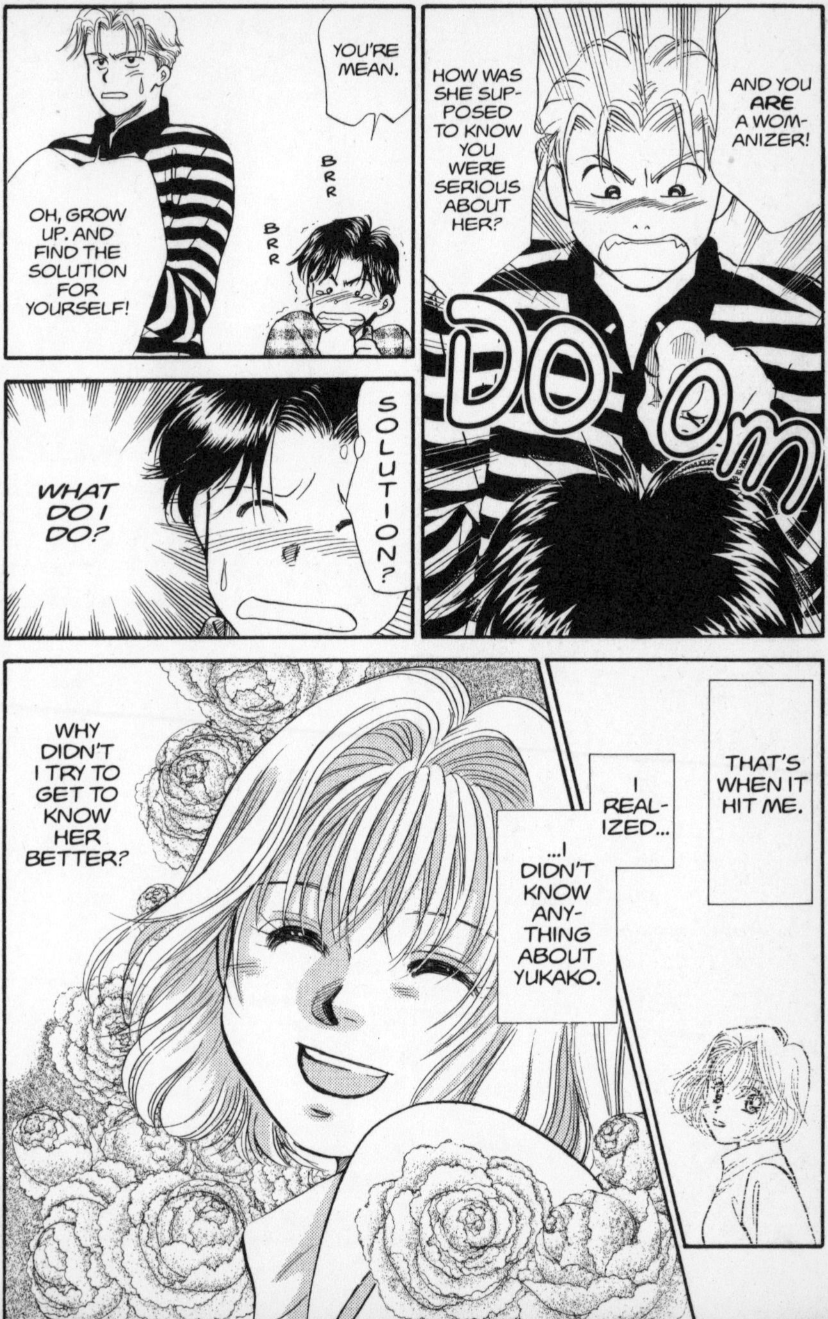
AND YOU ARE A WOMANIZER!
HOW WAS SHE SUPPOSED TO KNOW YOU WERE SERIOUS ABOUT HER?
DOOM
YOU'RE MEAN.
BRR
BRR
OH, GROW UP. AND FIND THE SOLUTION FOR YOURSELF!
SOLUTION?
WHAT DO I DO?
THAT'S WHEN IT HIT ME.
I REALIZED...
...I DIDN'T KNOW ANYTHING ABOUT YUKAKO.
WHY DIDN'T I TRY TO GET TO KNOW HER BETTER?

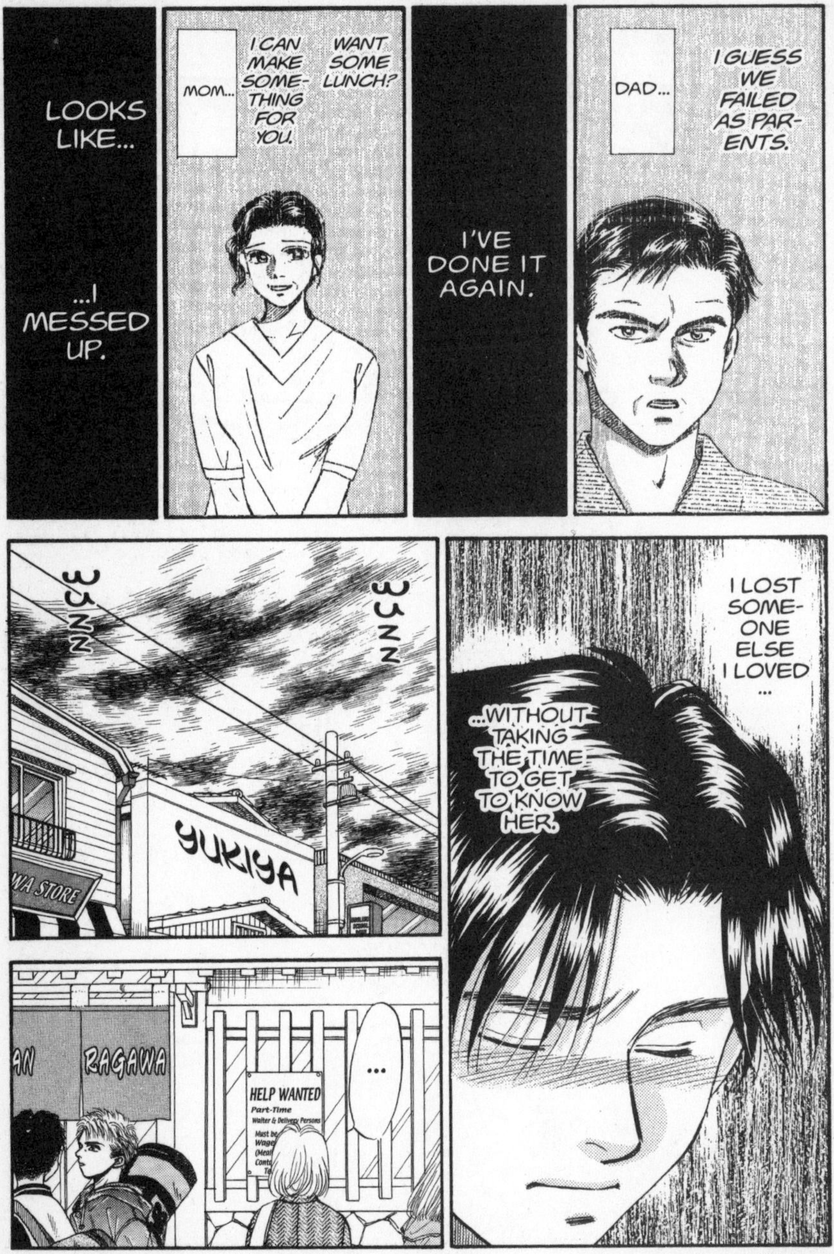
DAD...
I GUESS WE FAILED AS PARENTS.
I'VE DONE IT AGAIN.
MOM...
WANT SOME LUNCH?
I CAN MAKE SOMETHING FOR YOU.
LOOKS LIKE...
...I MESSED UP.
I LOST SOMEONE ELSE I LOVED ...
...WITHOUT TAKING THE TIME TO GET TO KNOW HER.
WUNN
WUNN
YUKIYA
WA STORE
...
HELP WANTED
Part-Time
Waiter & Delivery Persons
RAGAWA
AN

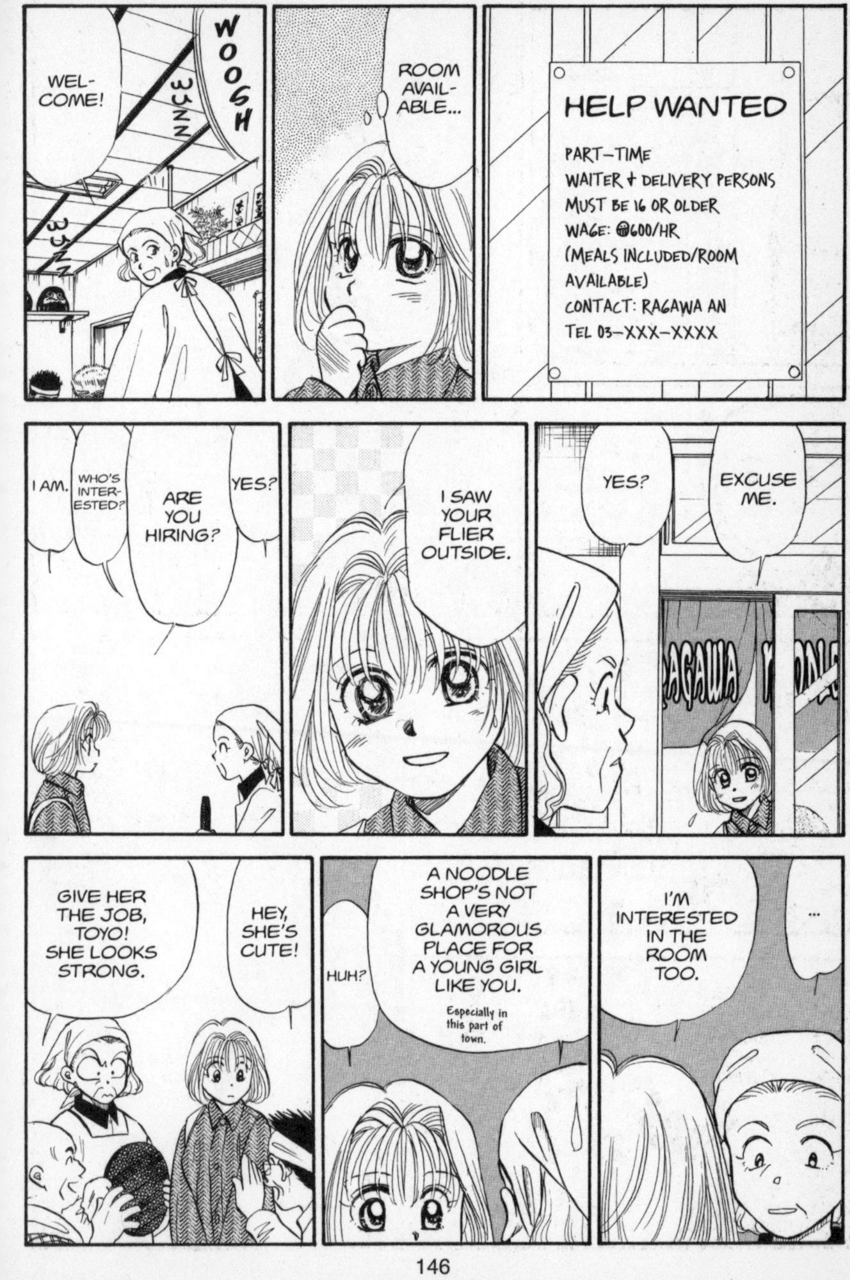

HELP WANTED
PART-TIME
WAITER + DELIVERY PERSONS
MUST BE 16 OR OLDER
WAGE: ¥600/HR
(MEALS INCLUDED/ROOM AVAILABLE)
CONTACT: RAGAWA AN
TEL 03-XXX-XXXX
ROOM AVAILABLE...
WOOSH
WEL-COME!
EXCUSE ME.
YES?
I SAW YOUR FLIER OUTSIDE.
YES?
ARE YOU HIRING?
WHO'S INTERESTED?
I AM.
...
I'M INTERESTED IN THE ROOM TOO.
A NOODLE SHOP'S NOT A VERY GLAMOROUS PLACE FOR A YOUNG GIRL LIKE YOU.
Especially in this part of town.
HUH?
HEY, SHE'S CUTE!
GIVE HER THE JOB, TOYO! SHE LOOKS STRONG.

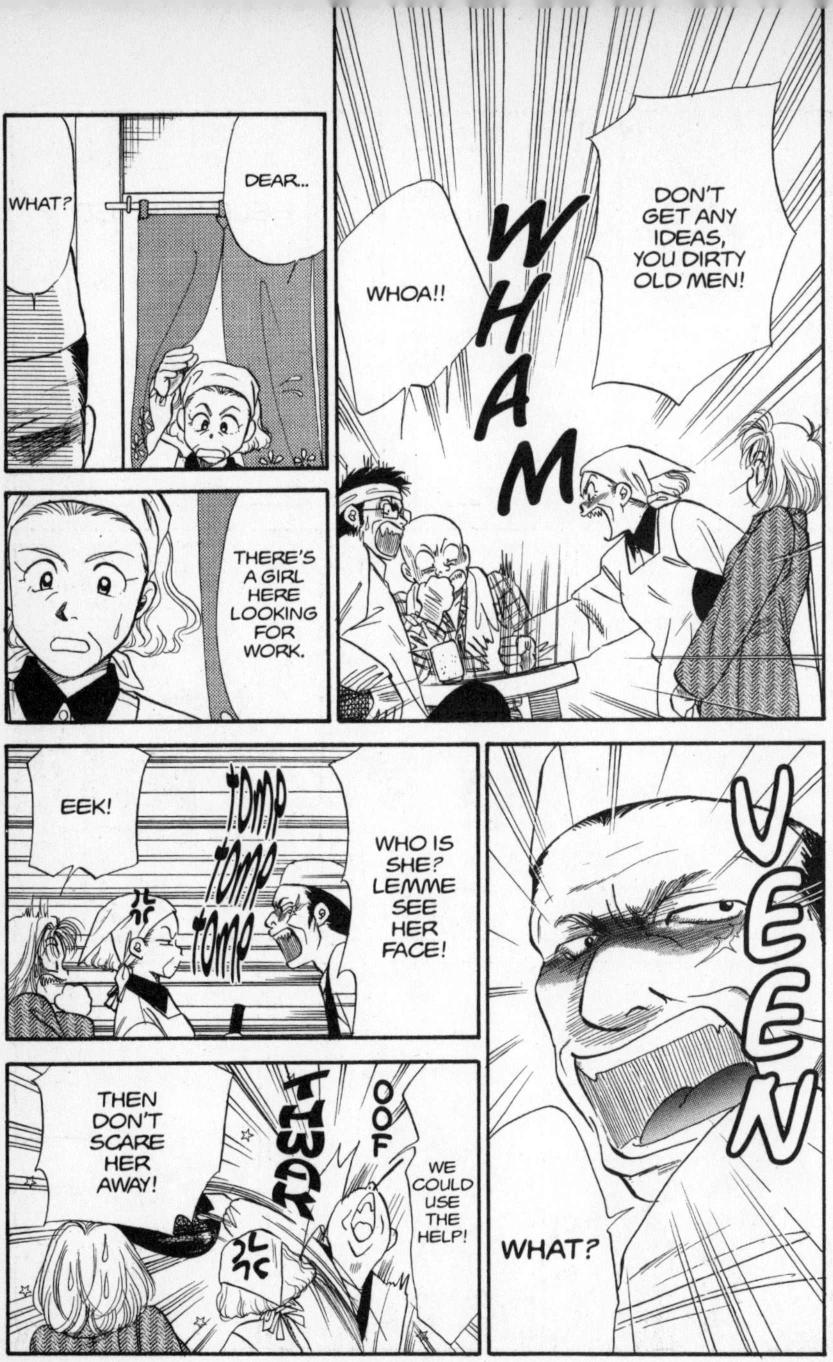
DON'T GET ANY IDEAS, YOU DIRTY OLD MEN!
WHAM
WHOA!!
DEAR...
WHAT?
THERE'S A GIRL HERE LOOKING FOR WORK.
VEEN
WHAT?
WHO IS SHE? LEMME SEE HER FACE!
TOMP TOMP TOMP
EEK!
OOF
WE COULD USE THE HELP!
THUD
THEN DON'T SCARE HER AWAY!

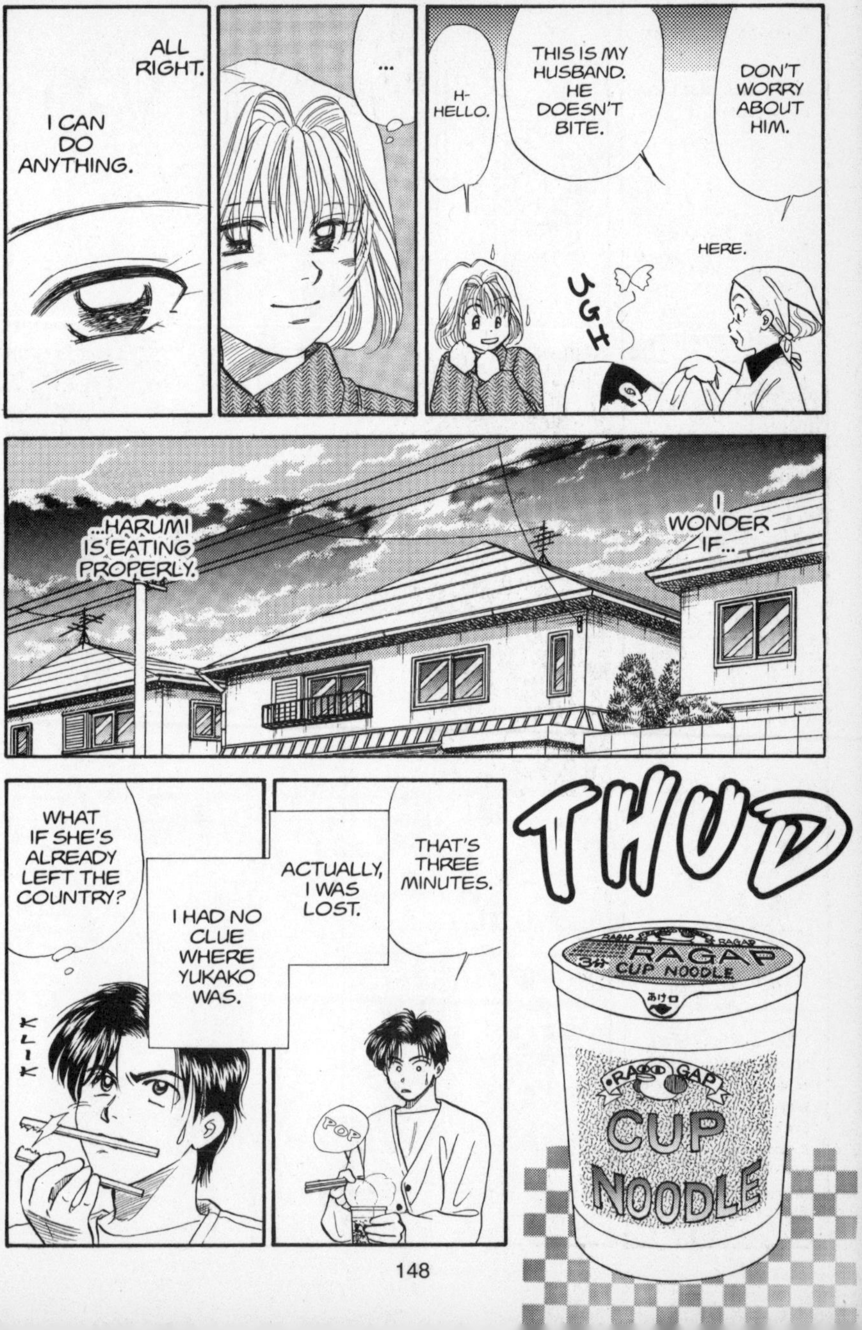
DON'T WORRY ABOUT HIM.
HERE.
THIS IS MY HUSBAND. HE DOESN'T BITE.
H- HELLO.
UGH
...
ALL RIGHT.
I CAN DO ANYTHING.
I WONDER IF...
...HARUMI IS EATING PROPERLY.
THUD
RAGAP CUP NOODLE
CUP NOODLE
THAT'S THREE MINUTES.
ACTUALLY, I WAS LOST.
POP
I HAD NO CLUE WHERE YUKAKO WAS.
WHAT IF SHE'S ALREADY LEFT THE COUNTRY?
KLIK

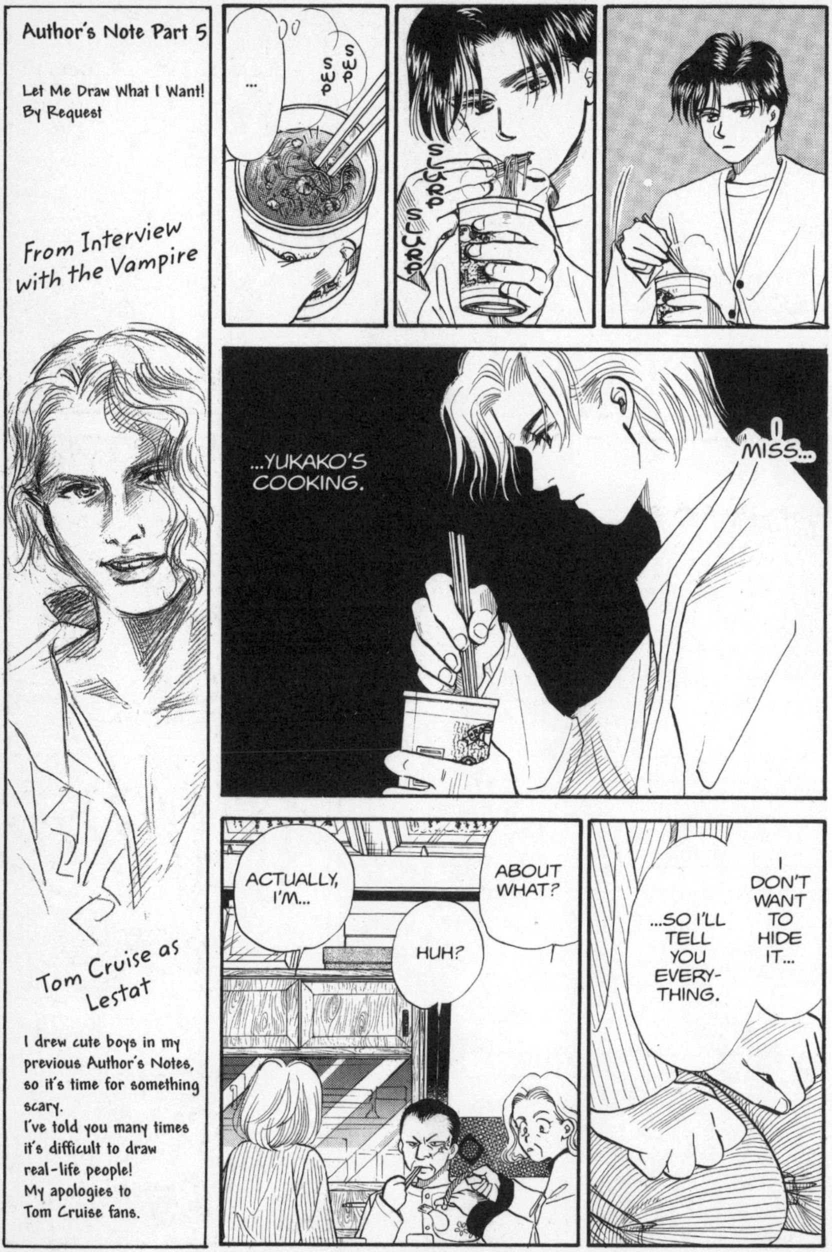
SLURP SLURP
SWP SWP
...
I MISS...
...YUKAKO'S COOKING.
I DON'T WANT TO HIDE IT...
...SO I'LL TELL YOU EVERYTHING.
ABOUT WHAT?
ACTUALLY, I'M...
HUH?
Author's Note Part 5
Let Me Draw What I Want! By Request
From Interview with the Vampire
Tom Cruise as Lestat
I drew cute boys in my previous Author's Notes, so it's time for something scary.
I've told you many times it's difficult to draw real-life people!
My apologies to Tom Cruise fans.

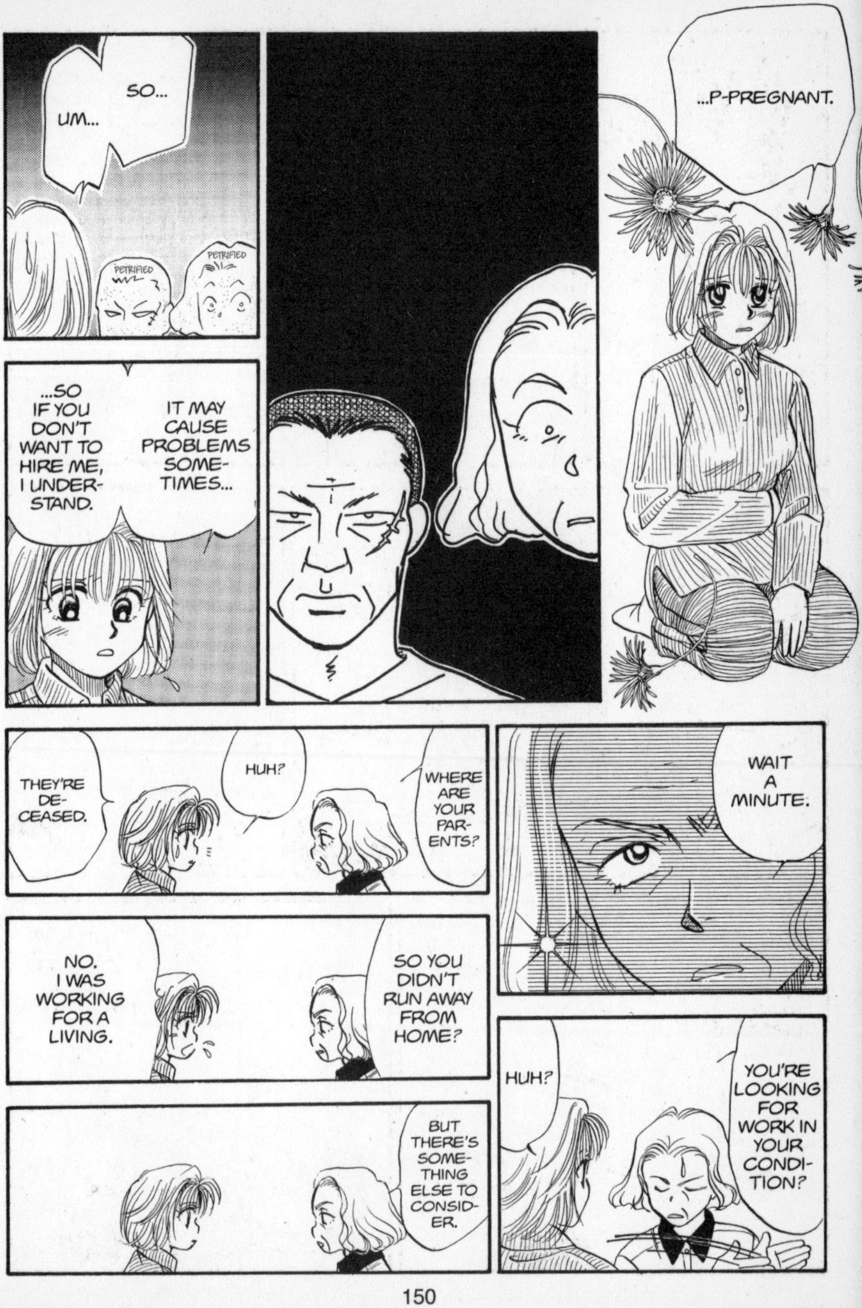

...P-PREGNANT.
UM... SO...
PETRIFIED
PETRIFIED
IT MAY CAUSE PROBLEMS SOMETIMES...
...SO IF YOU DON'T WANT TO HIRE ME, I UNDERSTAND.
WAIT A MINUTE.
YOU'RE LOOKING FOR WORK IN YOUR CONDITION?
HUH?
WHERE ARE YOUR PARENTS?
HUH?
THEY'RE DECEASED.
SO YOU DIDN'T RUN AWAY FROM HOME?
NO. I WAS WORKING FOR A LIVING.
BUT THERE'S SOMETHING ELSE TO CONSIDER.

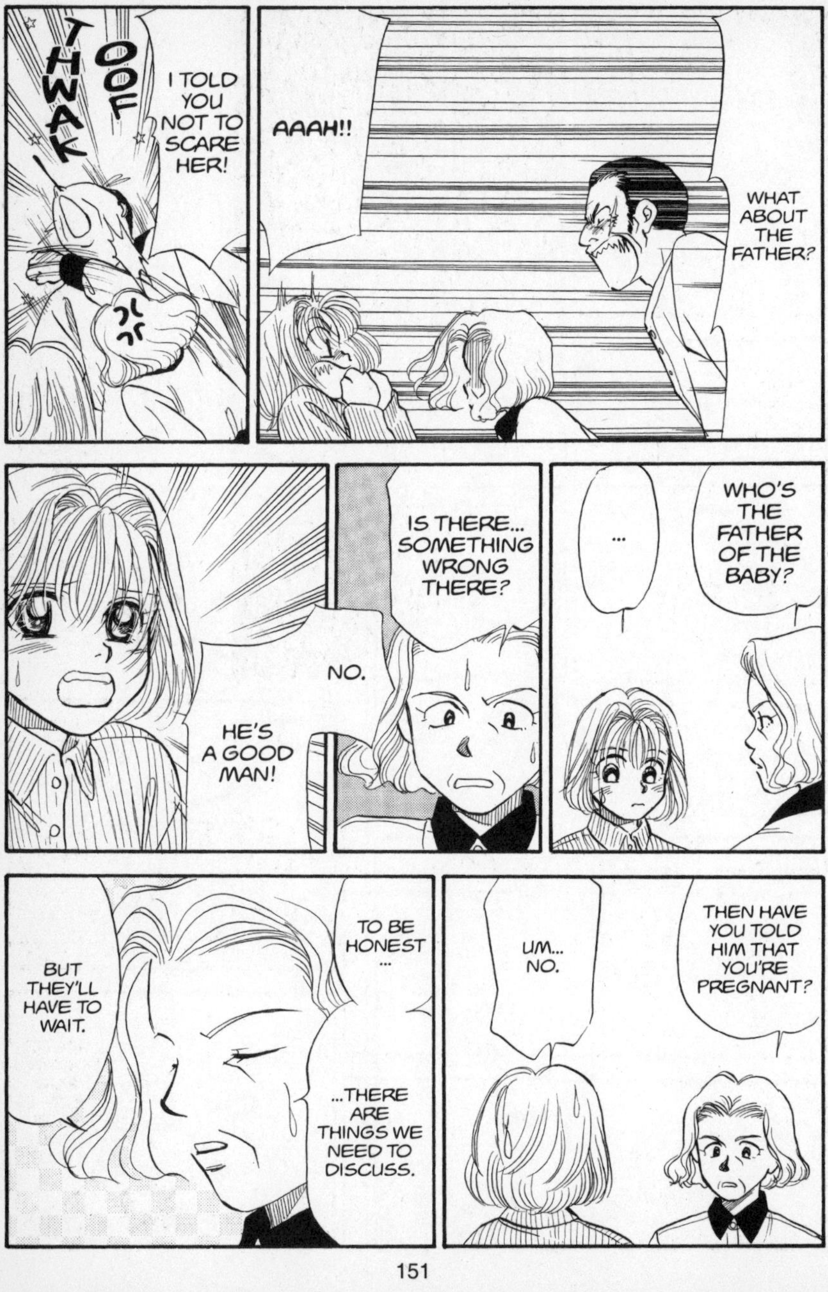
WHAT ABOUT THE FATHER?
AAAH!!
I TOLD YOU NOT TO SCARE HER!
OOF
THWAK
WHO'S THE FATHER OF THE BABY?
...
IS THERE... SOMETHING WRONG THERE?
NO.
HE'S A GOOD MAN!
THEN HAVE YOU TOLD HIM THAT YOU'RE PREGNANT?
UM... NO.
TO BE HONEST...
...THERE ARE THINGS WE NEED TO DISCUSS.
BUT THEY'LL HAVE TO WAIT.

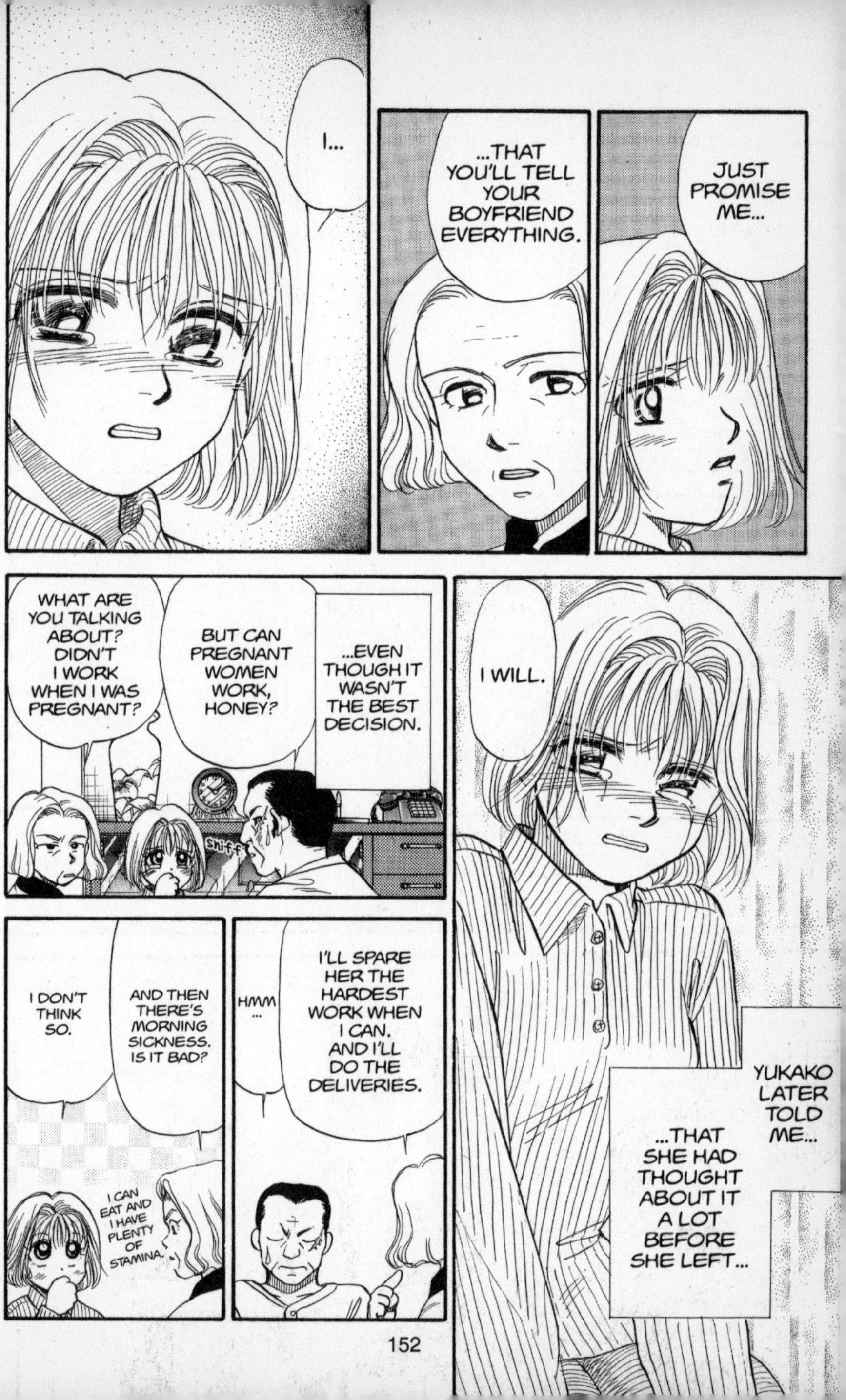
JUST PROMISE ME...
...THAT YOU'LL TELL YOUR BOYFRIEND EVERYTHING.
I...
I WILL.
YUKAKO LATER TOLD ME...
...THAT SHE HAD THOUGHT ABOUT IT A LOT BEFORE SHE LEFT...
...EVEN THOUGH IT WASN'T THE BEST DECISION.
BUT CAN PREGNANT WOMEN WORK, HONEY?
WHAT ARE YOU TALKING ABOUT? DIDN'T I WORK WHEN I WAS PREGNANT?
SNIFF
I'LL SPARE HER THE HARDEST WORK WHEN I CAN. AND I'LL DO THE DELIVERIES.
HMM ...
AND THEN THERE'S MORNING SICKNESS. IS IT BAD?
I DON'T THINK SO.
I CAN EAT AND I HAVE PLENTY OF STAMINA.

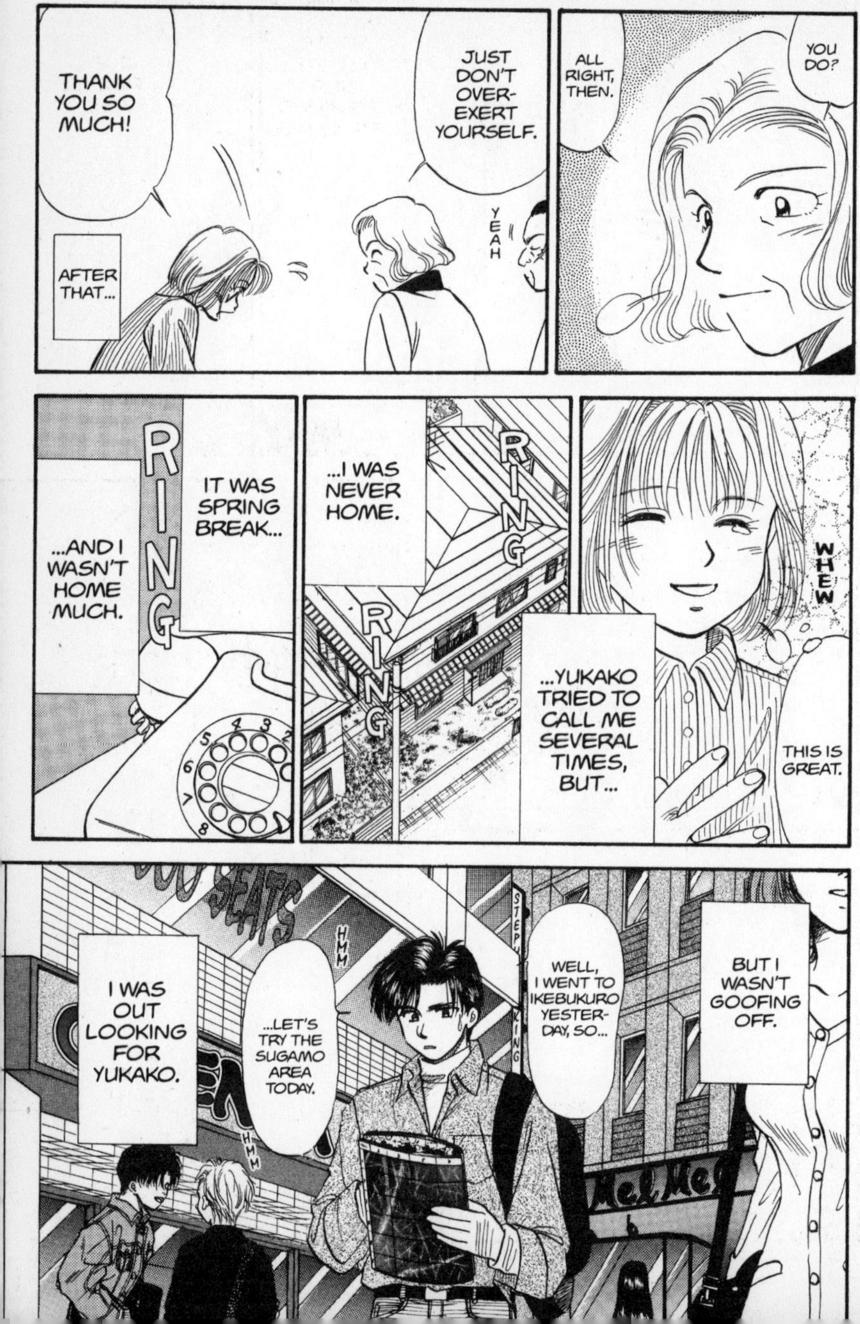
YOU DO?
ALL RIGHT, THEN.
YEAH
JUST DON'T OVER-EXERT YOURSELF.
THANK YOU SO MUCH!
AFTER THAT...
WHEW
THIS IS GREAT.
...YUKAKO TRIED TO CALL ME SEVERAL TIMES, BUT...
RING
...I WAS NEVER HOME.
RING
IT WAS SPRING BREAK...
RING
...AND I WASN'T HOME MUCH.
BUT I WASN'T GOOFING OFF.
WELL, I WENT TO IKEBUKURO YESTER-DAY, SO...
...LET'S TRY THE SUGAMO AREA TODAY.
HMM
HMM
I WAS OUT LOOKING FOR YUKAKO.

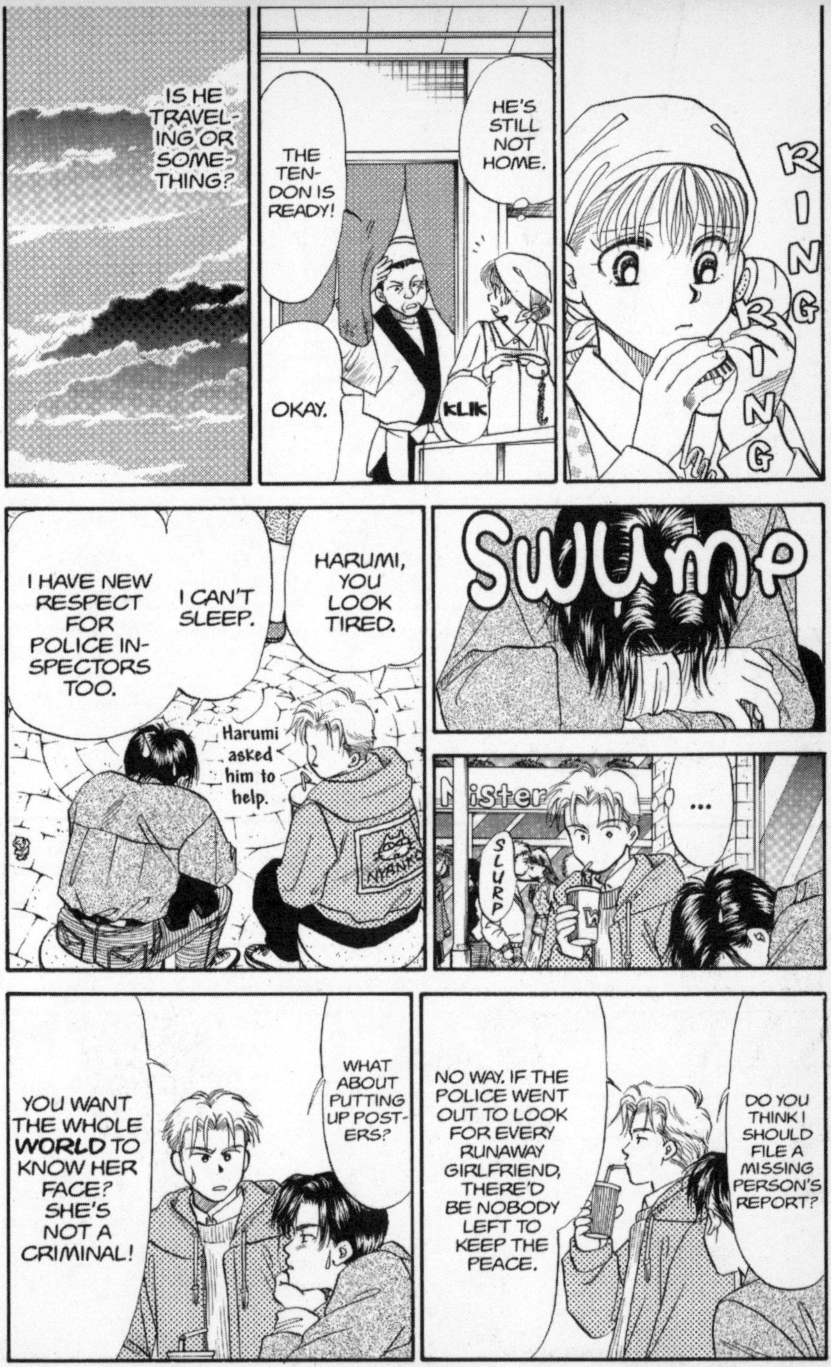
RING RING
RING RING
HE'S STILL NOT HOME.
THE TEN-DON IS READY!
OKAY.
kLIk
IS HE TRAVEL-ING OR SOME-THING?
SWUMP
...
SLURP
HARUMI, YOU LOOK TIRED.
I CAN'T SLEEP.
I HAVE NEW RESPECT FOR POLICE IN-SPECTORS TOO.
Harumi asked him to help.
DO YOU THINK I SHOULD FILE A MISSING PERSON'S REPORT?
NO WAY. IF THE POLICE WENT OUT TO LOOK FOR EVERY RUNAWAY GIRLFRIEND, THERE'D BE NOBODY LEFT TO KEEP THE PEACE.
WHAT ABOUT PUTTING UP POST-ERS?
YOU WANT THE WHOLE **WORLD** TO KNOW HER FACE? SHE'S NOT A CRIMINAL!

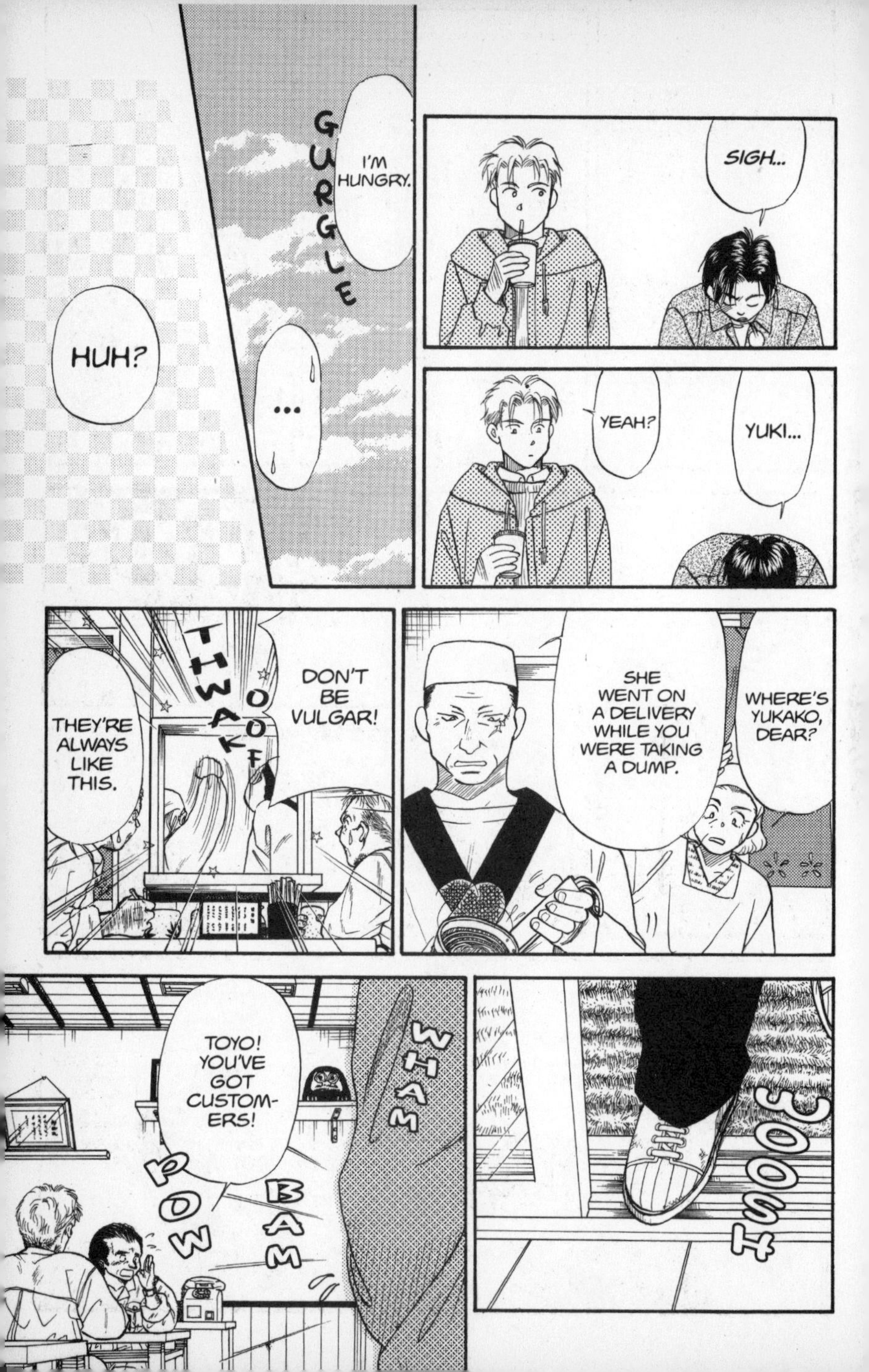
SIGH...
YUKI...
YEAH?
I'M HUNGRY.
GURGLE
...
HUH?
WHERE'S YUKAKO, DEAR?
SHE WENT ON A DELIVERY WHILE YOU WERE TAKING A DUMP.
DON'T BE VULGAR!
THWAK
OOF
THEY'RE ALWAYS LIKE THIS.
WHOOSH
WHAM
TOYO! YOU'VE GOT CUSTOMERS!
BAM
POW

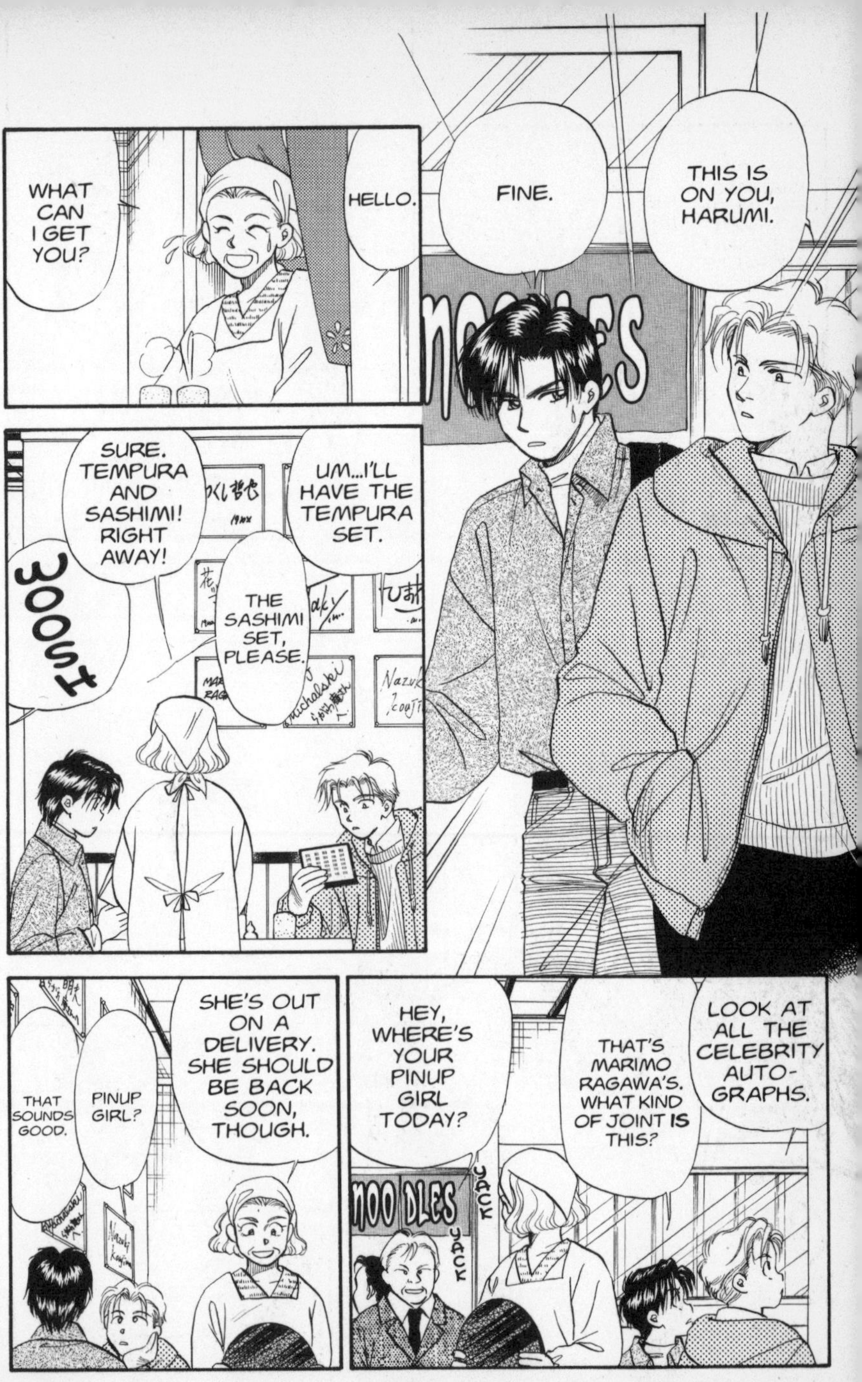
THIS IS ON YOU, HARUMI.
FINE.
HELLO.
WHAT CAN I GET YOU?
UM...I'LL HAVE THE TEMPURA SET.
THE SASHIMI SET, PLEASE.
SURE. TEMPURA AND SASHIMI! RIGHT AWAY!
WOOSH
LOOK AT ALL THE CELEBRITY AUTO-GRAPHS.
THAT'S MARIMO RAGAWA'S. WHAT KIND OF JOINT **IS** THIS?
HEY, WHERE'S YOUR PINUP GIRL TODAY?
NOODLES
YACK
YACK
SHE'S OUT ON A DELIVERY. SHE SHOULD BE BACK SOON, THOUGH.
PINUP GIRL?
THAT SOUNDS GOOD.

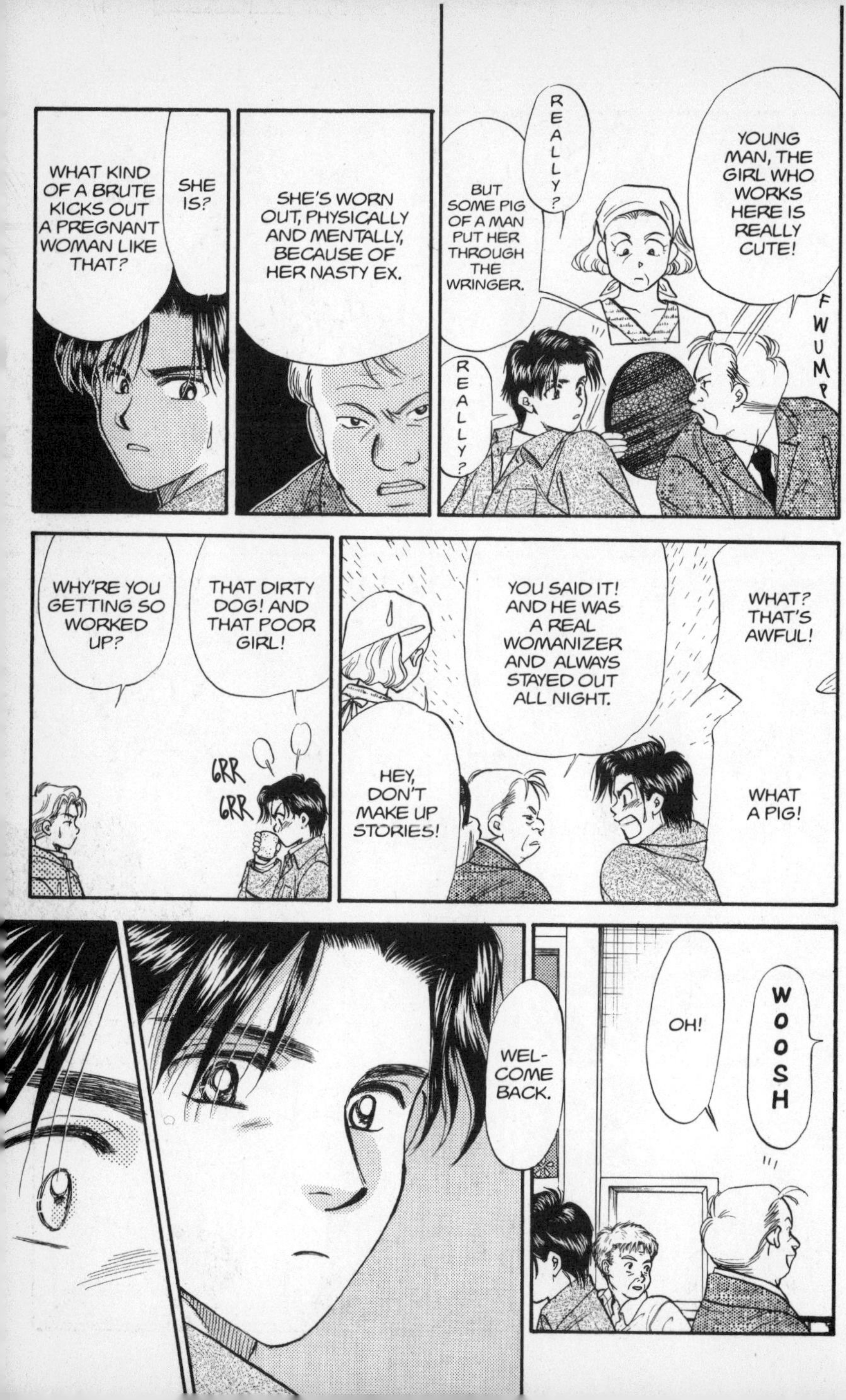
YOUNG MAN, THE GIRL WHO WORKS HERE IS REALLY CUTE!
FWUMP
REALLY?
BUT SOME PIG OF A MAN PUT HER THROUGH THE WRINGER.
REALLY?
SHE'S WORN OUT, PHYSICALLY AND MENTALLY, BECAUSE OF HER NASTY EX.
SHE IS?
WHAT KIND OF A BRUTE KICKS OUT A PREGNANT WOMAN LIKE THAT?
WHAT? THAT'S AWFUL!
YOU SAID IT! AND HE WAS A REAL WOMANIZER AND ALWAYS STAYED OUT ALL NIGHT.
WHAT A PIG!
HEY, DON'T MAKE UP STORIES!
THAT DIRTY DOG! AND THAT POOR GIRL!
WHY'RE YOU GETTING SO WORKED UP?
GRR GRR
WOOSH
OH!
WEL-COME BACK.

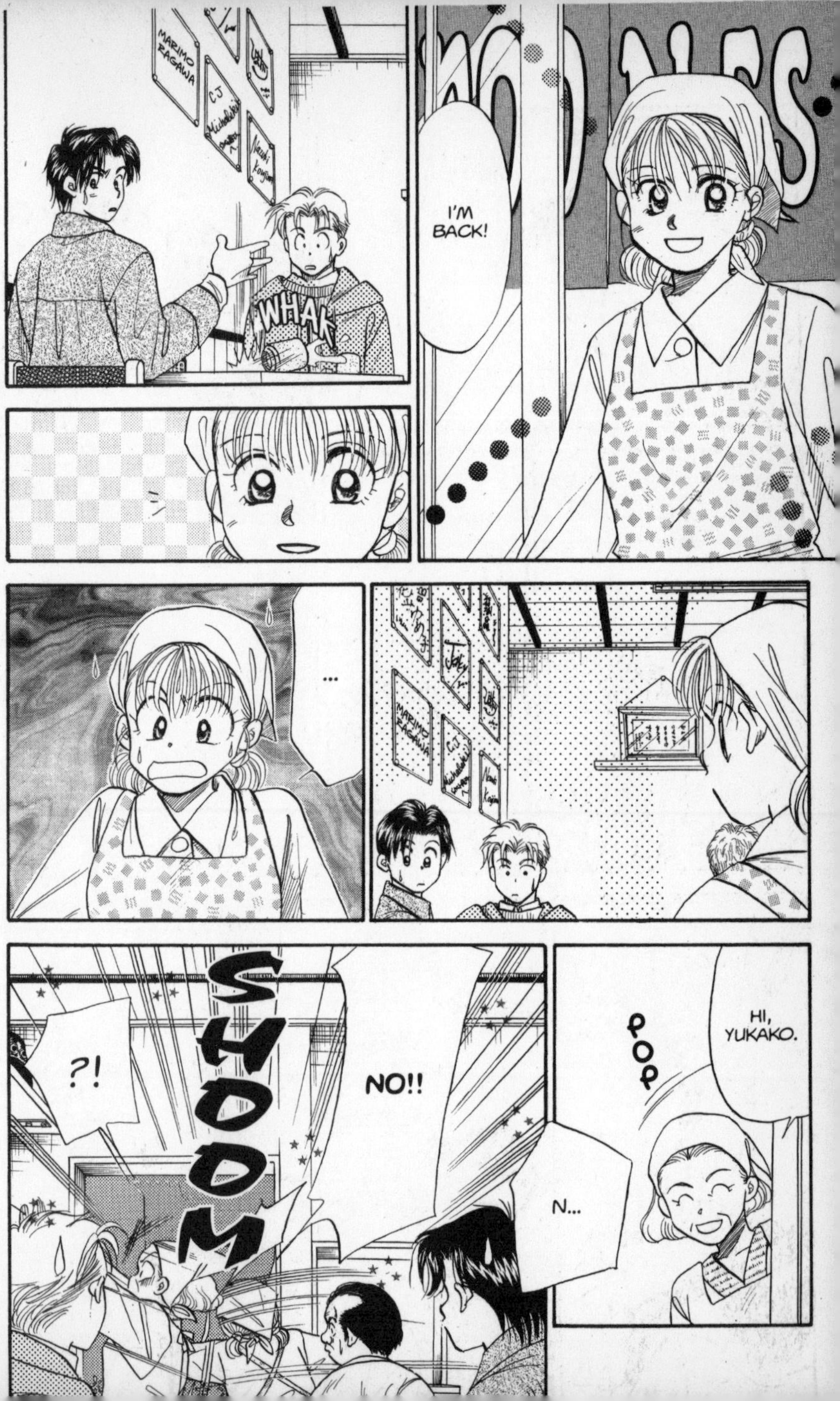
I'M BACK!
MARIMO RAGAWA
WHAK
...
HI, YUKAKO.
POP
N...
NO!!
SHOOM
?!

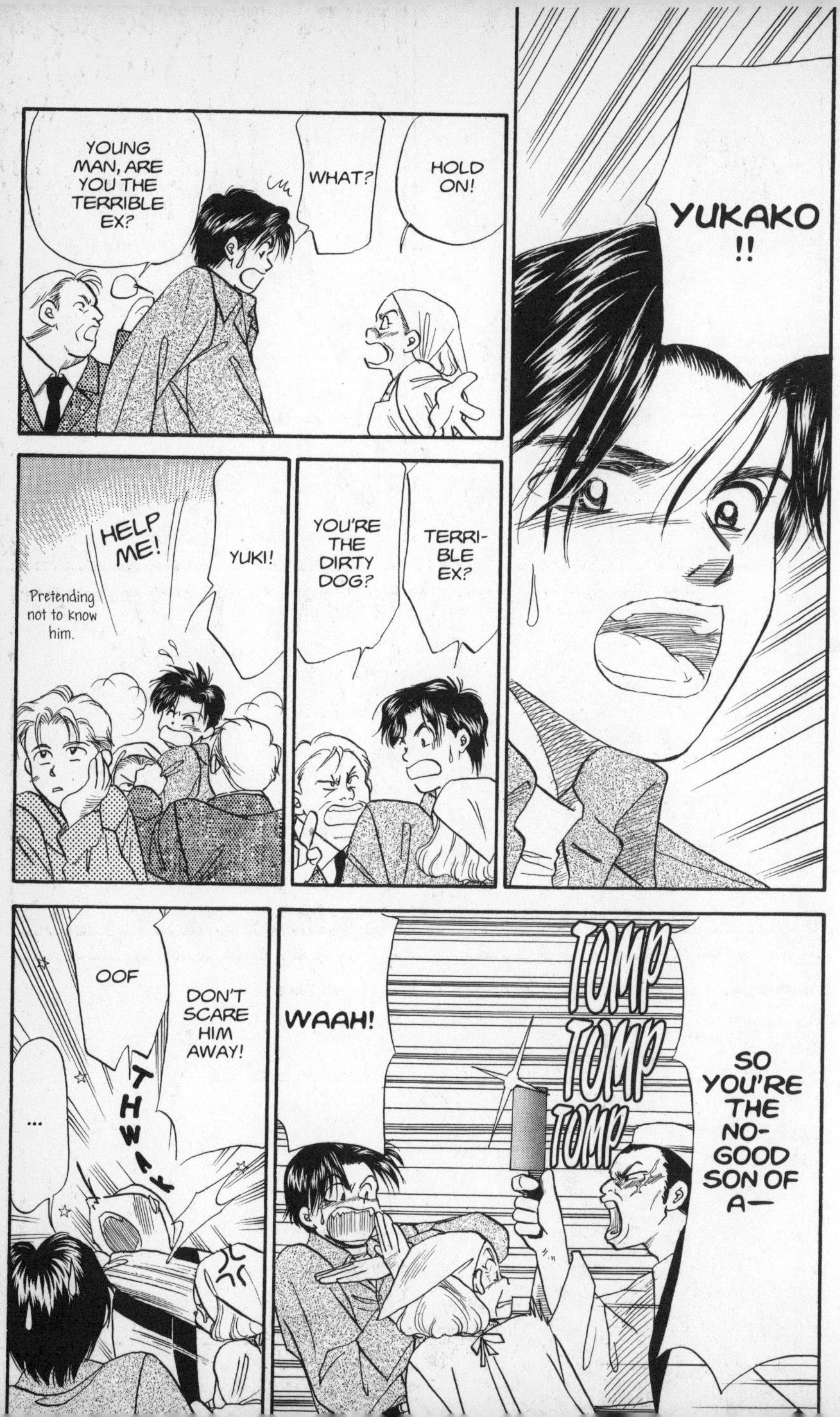
YUKAKO!!
HOLD ON!
WHAT?
YOUNG MAN, ARE YOU THE TERRIBLE EX?
TERRIBLE EX?
YOU'RE THE DIRTY DOG?
YUKI!
HELP ME!
Pretending not to know him.
SO YOU'RE THE NO-GOOD SON OF A—
TOMP TOMP TOMP
WAAH!
DON'T SCARE HIM AWAY!
OOF
THWACK
...

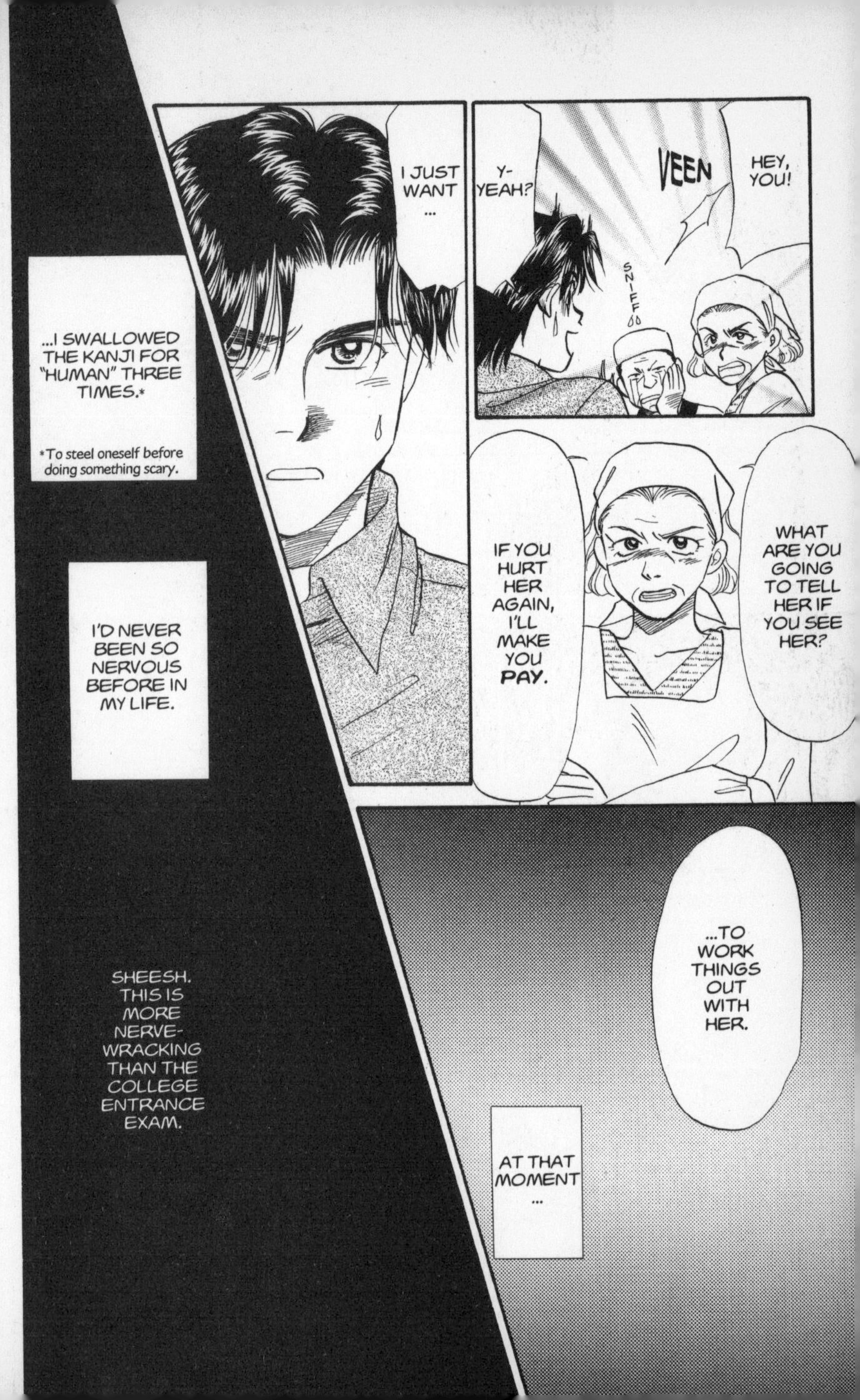
HEY, YOU!
VEEN
SNIFF
Y-YEAH?
WHAT ARE YOU GOING TO TELL HER IF YOU SEE HER?
IF YOU HURT HER AGAIN, I'LL MAKE YOU PAY.
I JUST WANT ...
...I SWALLOWED THE KANJI FOR "HUMAN" THREE TIMES.*
*To steel oneself before doing something scary.
I'D NEVER BEEN SO NERVOUS BEFORE IN MY LIFE.
...TO WORK THINGS OUT WITH HER.
AT THAT MOMENT ...
SHEESH. THIS IS MORE NERVE-WRACKING THAN THE COLLEGE ENTRANCE EXAM.

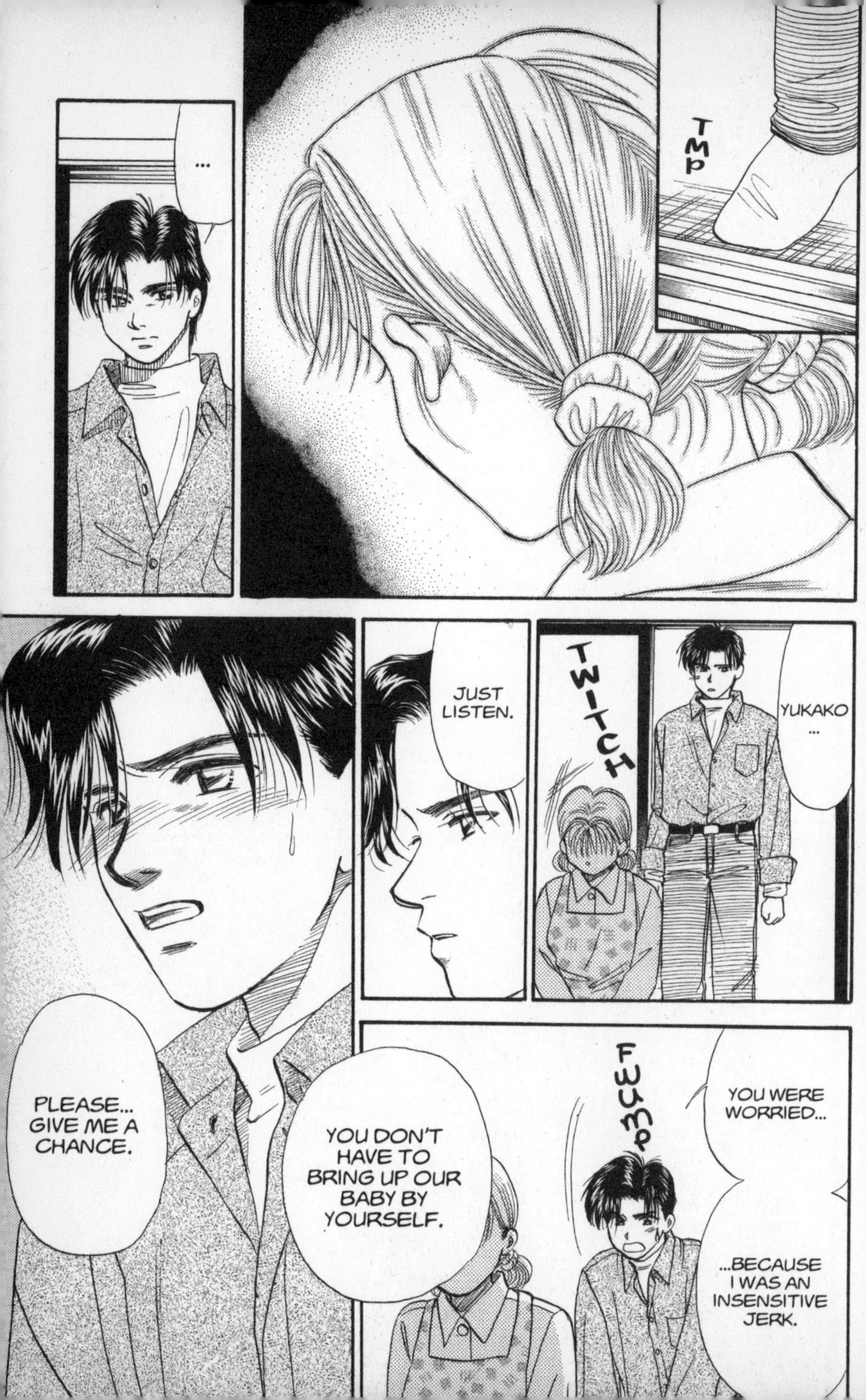
TMP
...
YUKAKO ...
TWITCH
JUST LISTEN.
YOU WERE WORRIED...
FWUMP
...BECAUSE I WAS AN INSENSITIVE JERK.
YOU DON'T HAVE TO BRING UP OUR BABY BY YOURSELF.
PLEASE... GIVE ME A CHANCE.

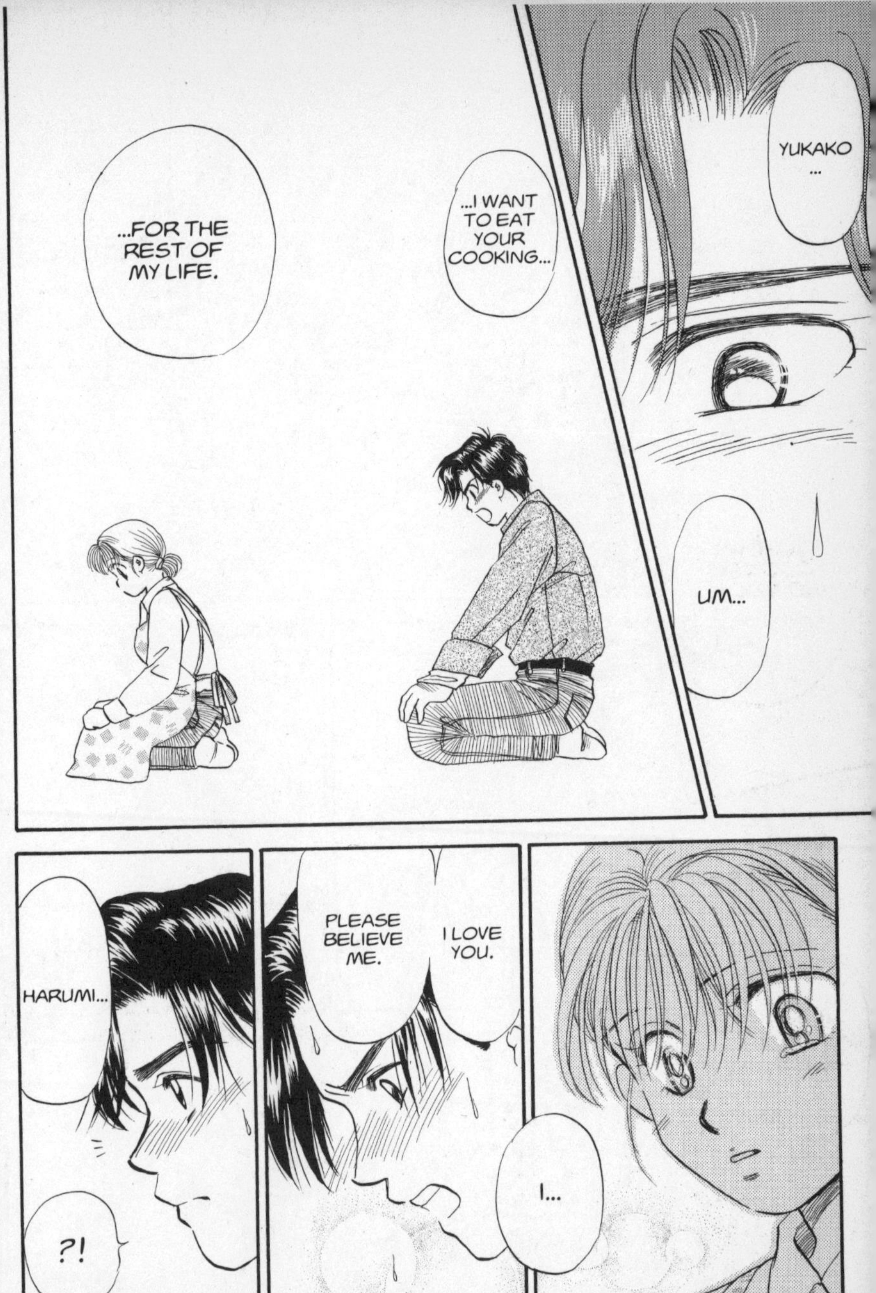
YUKAKO ...
UM...
...I WANT TO EAT YOUR COOKING...
...FOR THE REST OF MY LIFE.
I...
I LOVE YOU.
PLEASE BELIEVE ME.
HARUMI...
?!

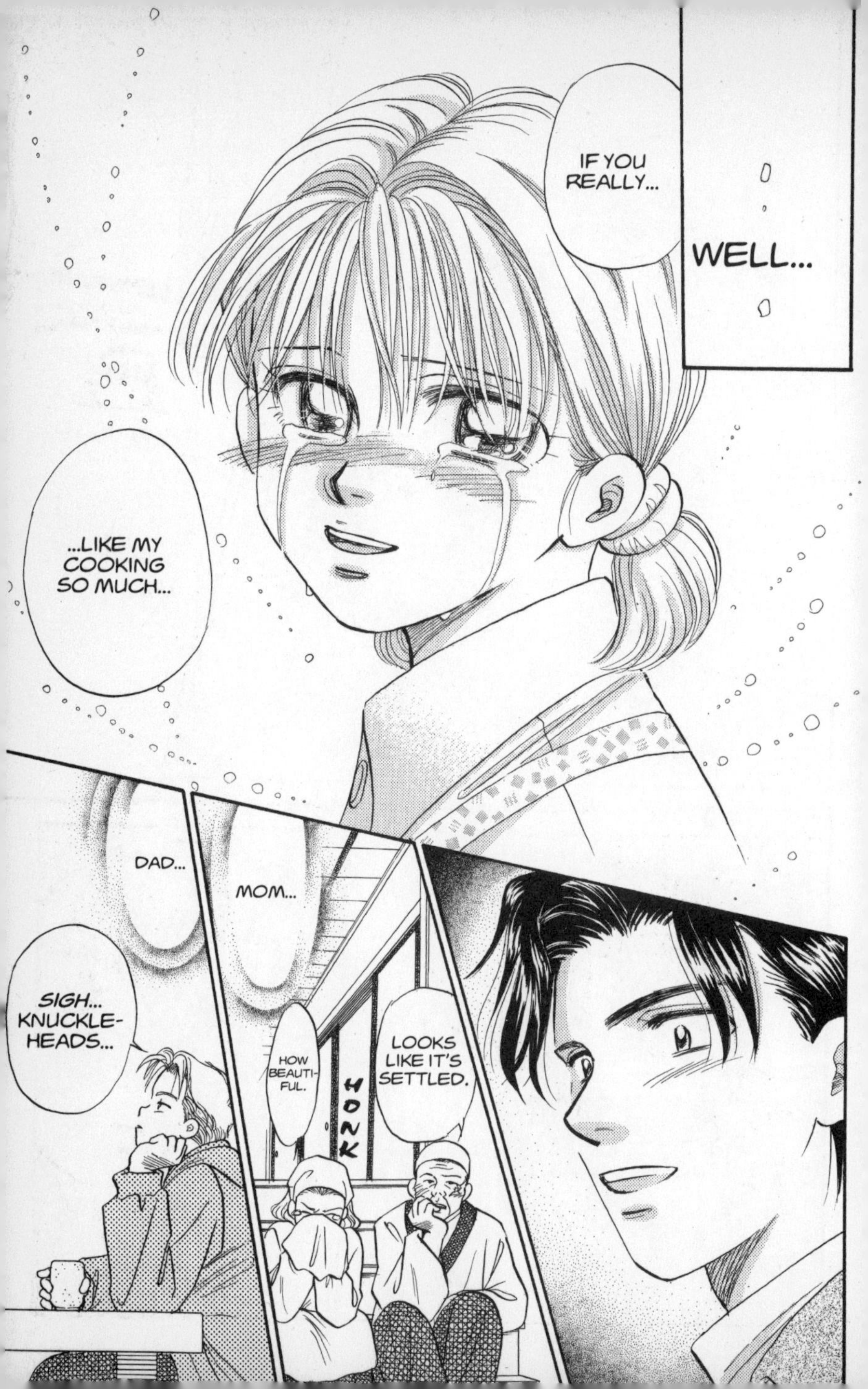
WELL...
IF YOU REALLY...
...LIKE MY COOKING SO MUCH...
MOM...
LOOKS LIKE IT'S SETTLED.
HONK
HOW BEAUTI-FUL.
DAD...
SIGH... KNUCKLE-HEADS...

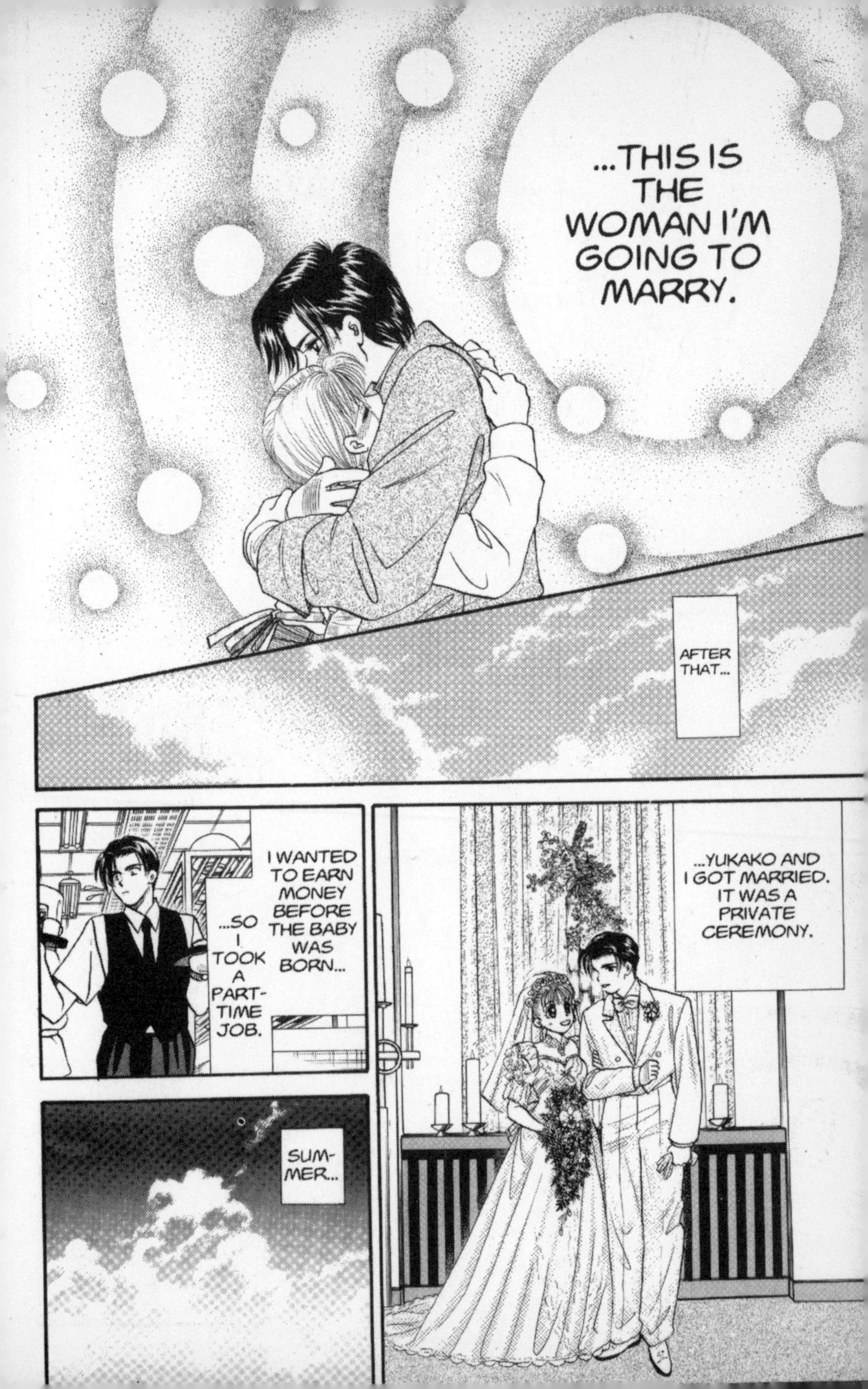
...THIS IS THE WOMAN I'M GOING TO MARRY.
AFTER THAT...
...YUKAKO AND I GOT MARRIED. IT WAS A PRIVATE CEREMONY.
I WANTED TO EARN MONEY BEFORE THE BABY WAS BORN...
...SO I TOOK A PART-TIME JOB.
SUM-MER...

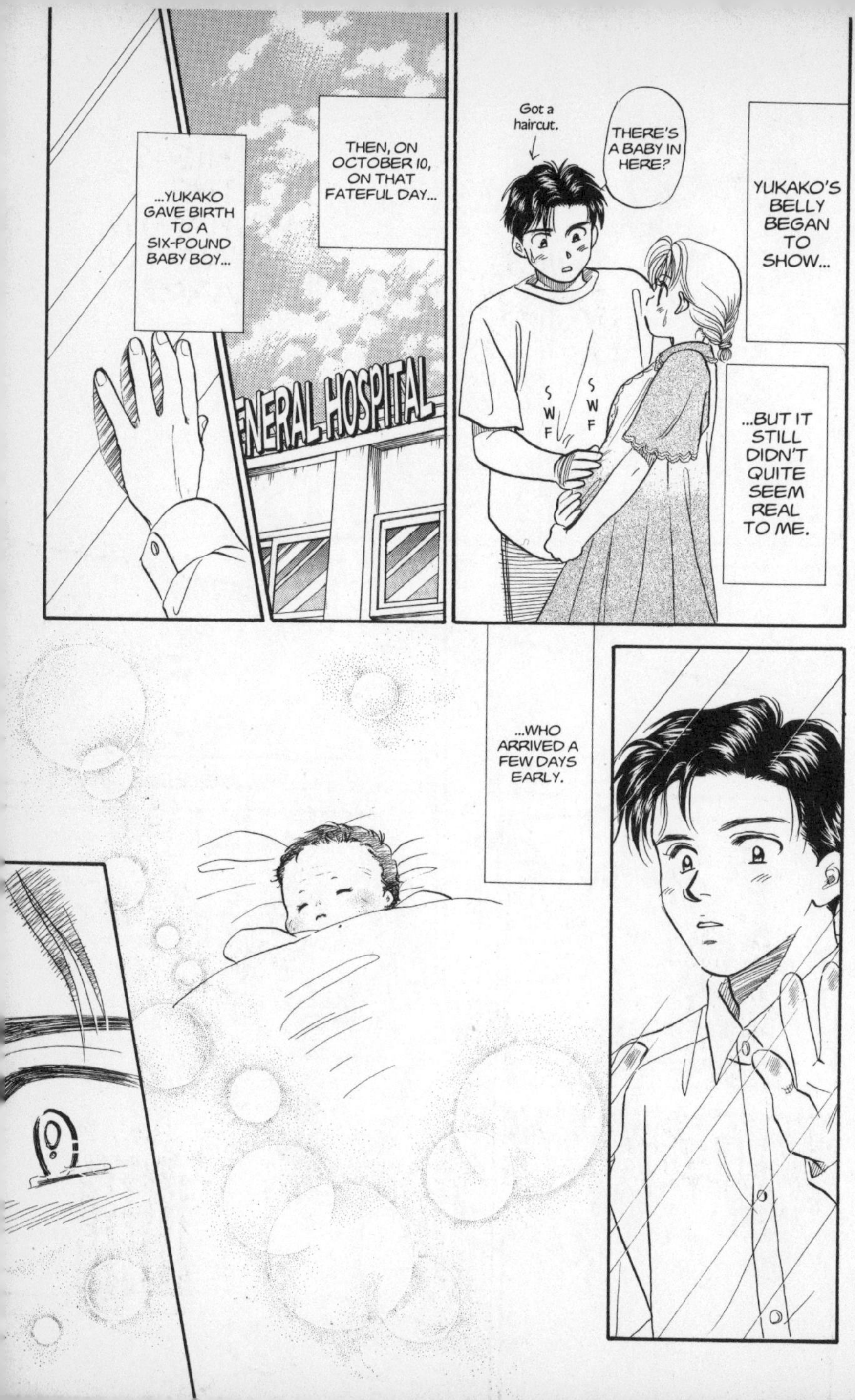
YUKAKO'S BELLY BEGAN TO SHOW...
THERE'S A BABY IN HERE?
Got a haircut.
SWF SWF
...BUT IT STILL DIDN'T QUITE SEEM REAL TO ME.
THEN, ON OCTOBER 10, ON THAT FATEFUL DAY...
GENERAL HOSPITAL
...YUKAKO GAVE BIRTH TO A SIX-POUND BABY BOY...
...WHO ARRIVED A FEW DAYS EARLY.

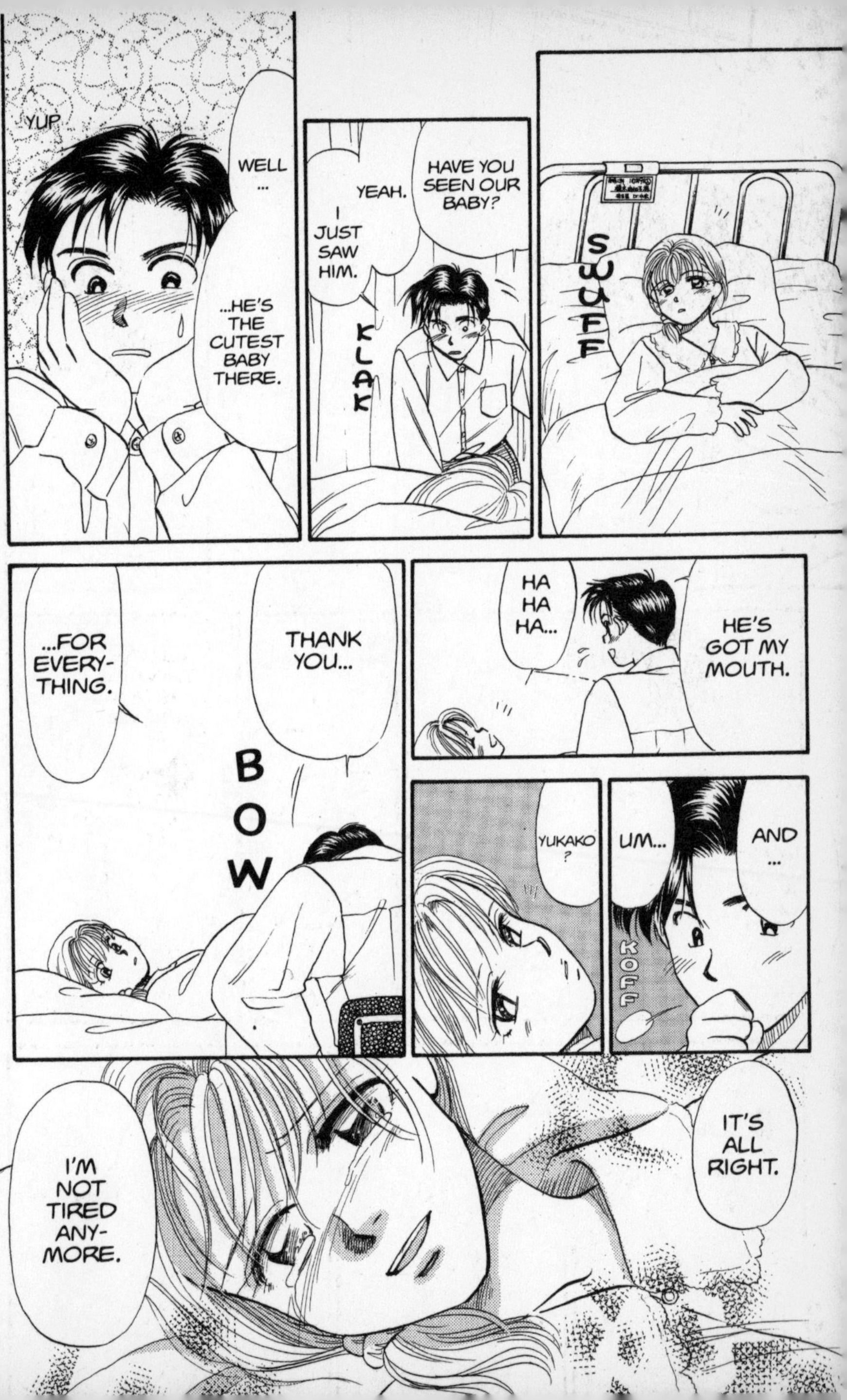
SWUFF
HAVE YOU SEEN OUR BABY?
YEAH.
I JUST SAW HIM.
KLAK
WELL ...
...HE'S THE CUTEST BABY THERE.
YUP
HE'S GOT MY MOUTH.
HA HA HA...
AND ...
UM...
KOFF
YUKAKO?
THANK YOU...
...FOR EVERY-THING.
BOW
IT'S ALL RIGHT.
I'M NOT TIRED ANY-MORE.

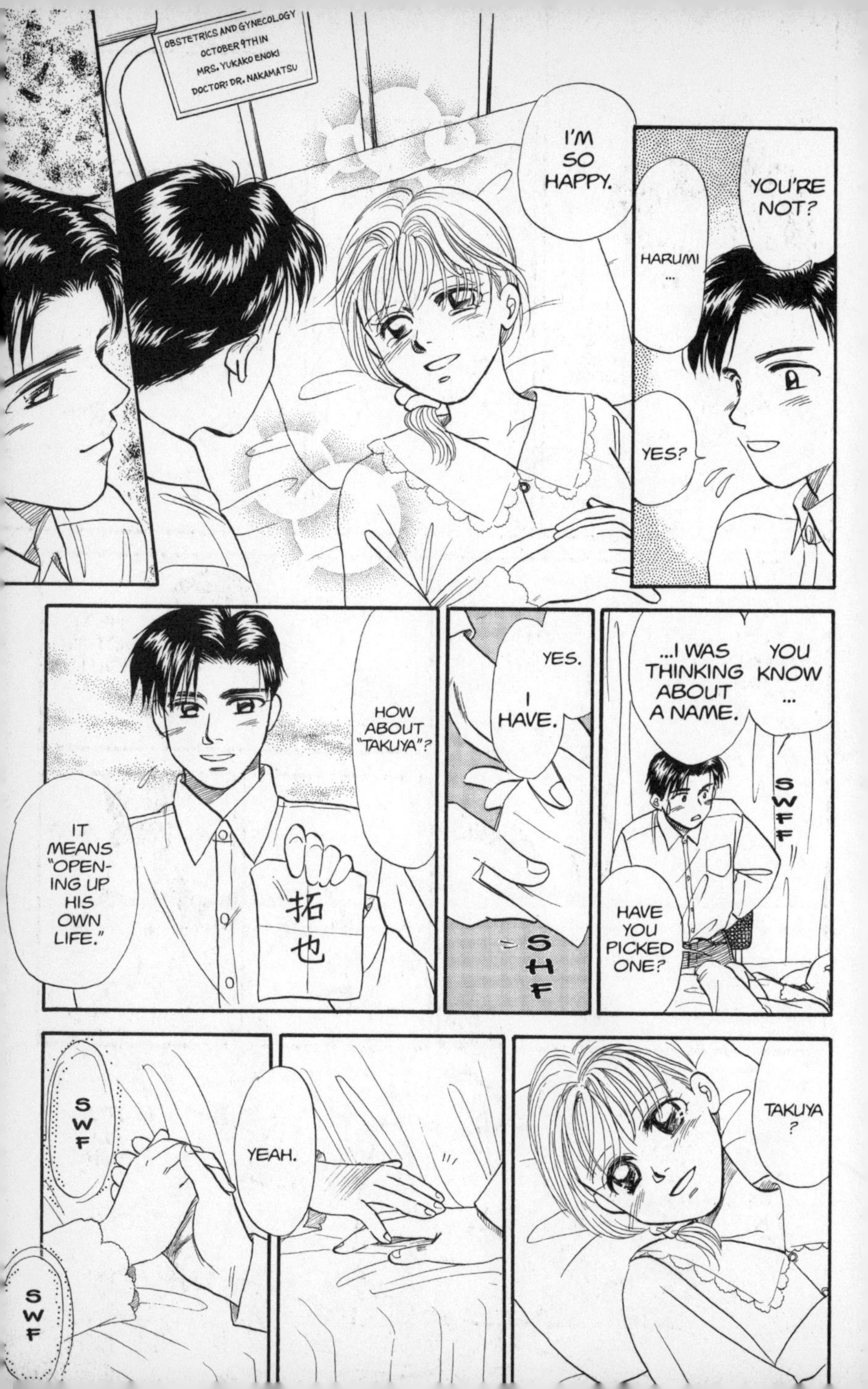
OBSTETRICS AND GYNECOLOGY
OCTOBER 9TH IN
MRS. YUKAKO ENOKI
DOCTOR: DR. NAKAMATSU
I'M SO HAPPY.
YOU'RE NOT?
HARUMI ...
YES?
YOU KNOW ...
...I WAS THINKING ABOUT A NAME.
SWFF
HAVE YOU PICKED ONE?
YES.
I HAVE.
SHF
HOW ABOUT "TAKUYA"?
IT MEANS "OPENING UP HIS OWN LIFE."
拓也
TAKUYA?
YEAH.
SWF
SWF

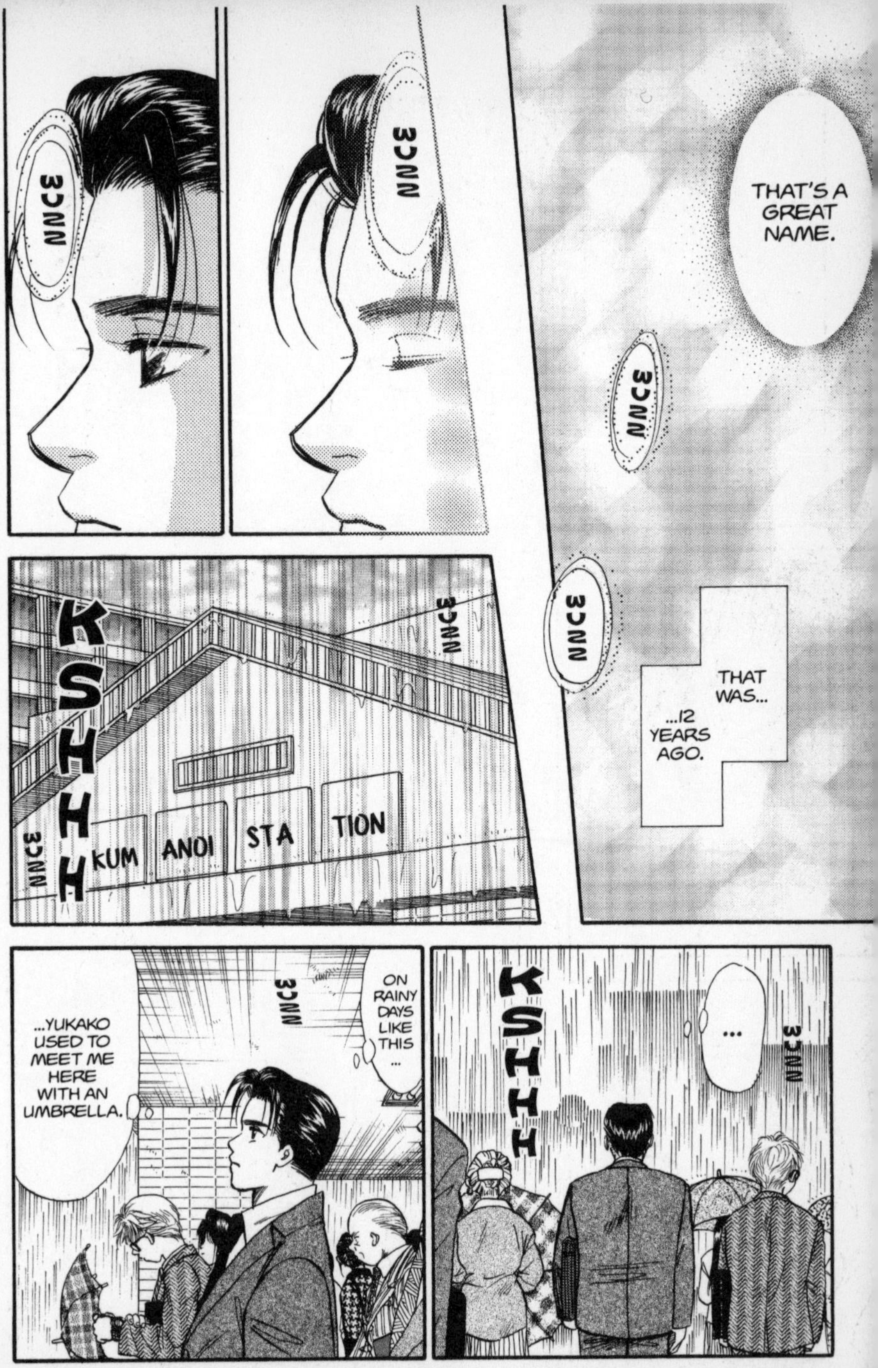
THAT'S A GREAT NAME.
BUZZ
BUZZ
THAT WAS...
...12 YEARS AGO.
BUZZ
BUZZ
BUZZ
KSHHH
BUZZ
KUM ANOI STA TION
KSHHH
...
BUZZ
ON RAINY DAYS LIKE THIS ...
BUZZ
...YUKAKO USED TO MEET ME HERE WITH AN UMBRELLA.

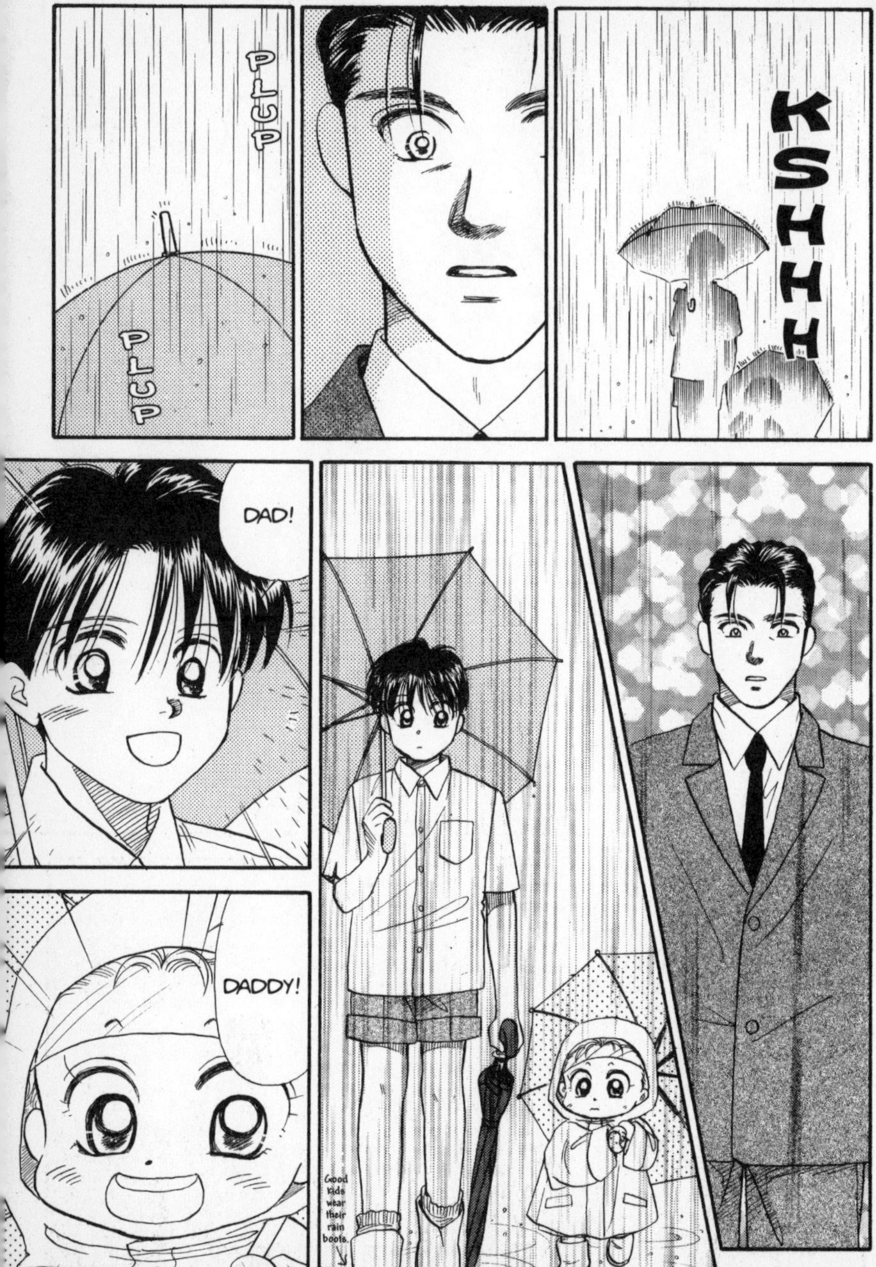
KSHHH
PLUP
PLUP
Good kids wear their rain boots.
DAD!
DADDY!

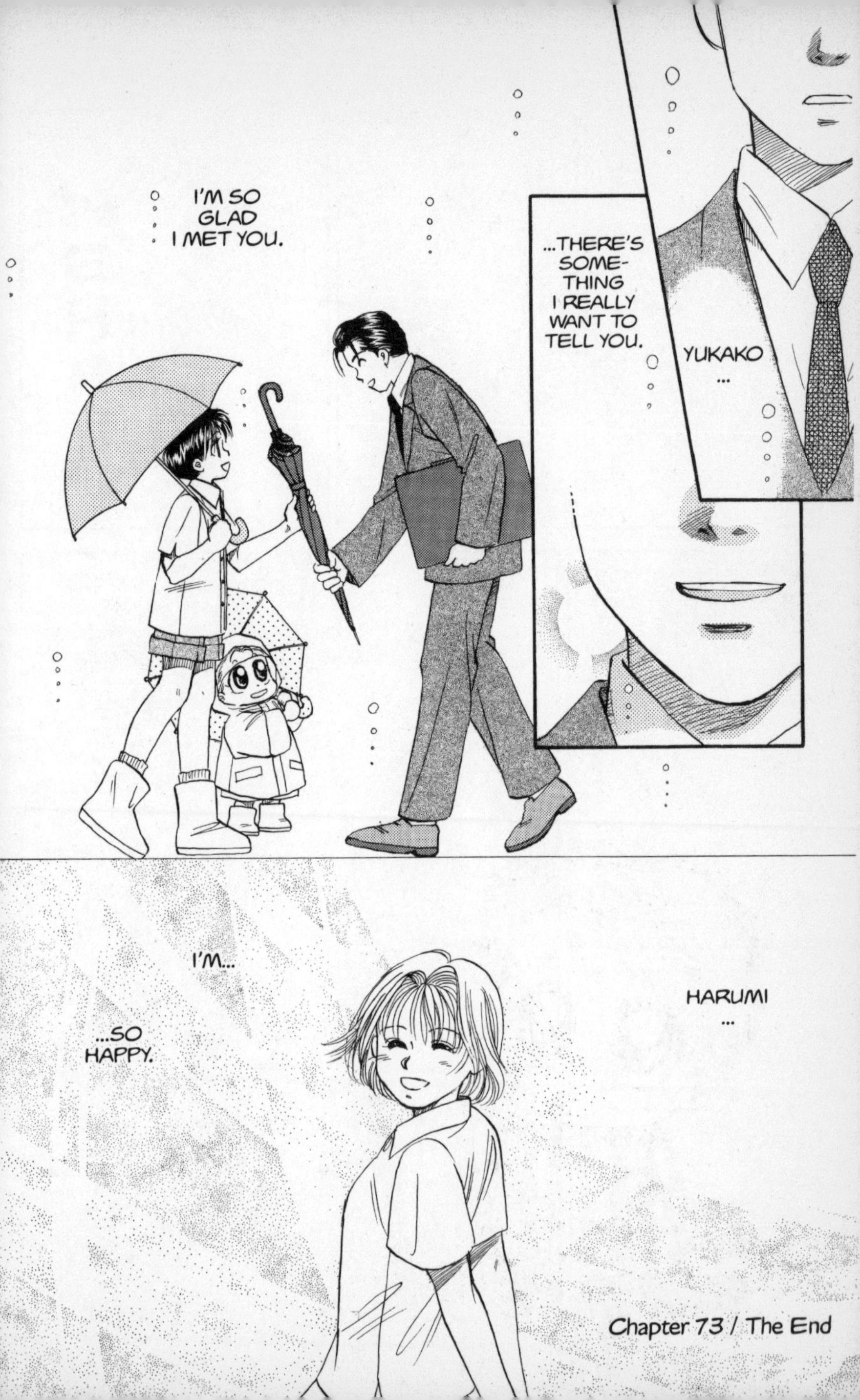
YUKAKO ...
...THERE'S SOME-THING I REALLY WANT TO TELL YOU.
I'M SO GLAD I MET YOU.
HARUMI ...
I'M...
...SO HAPPY.
Chapter 73 / The End

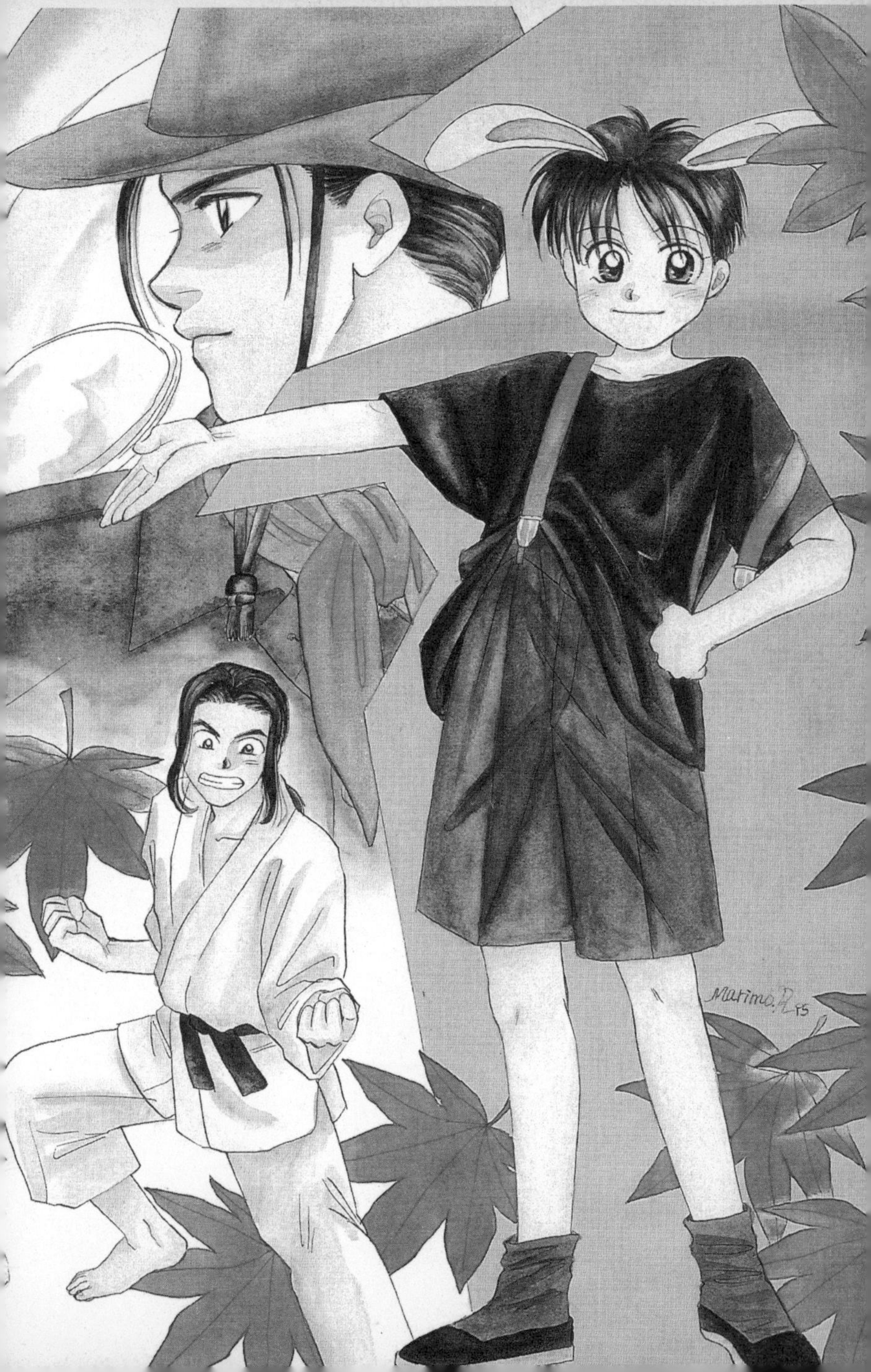

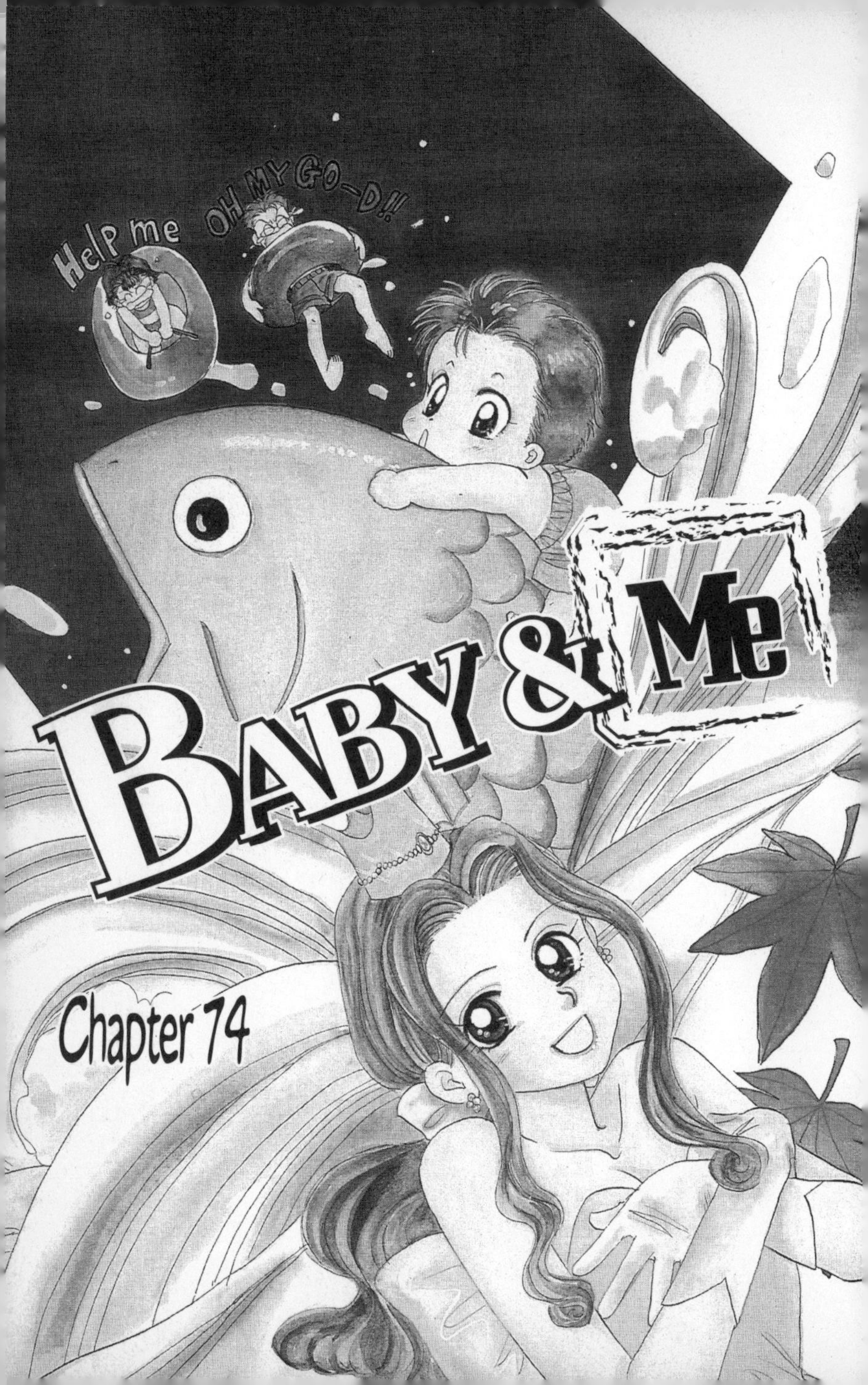
Help me
OH MY GO-D!!
BABY & Me
Chapter 74

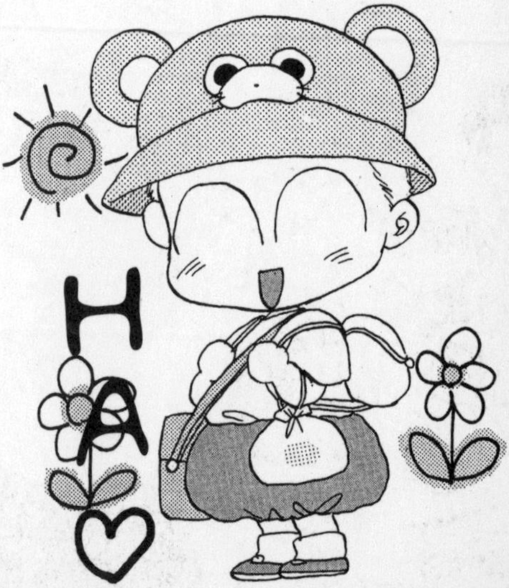
HA♡

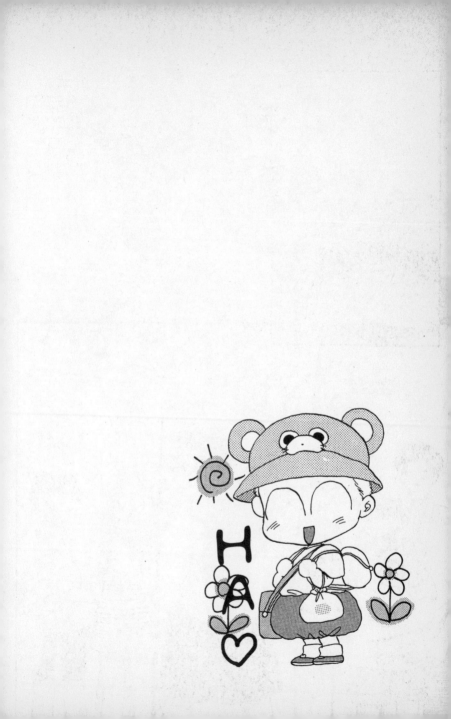

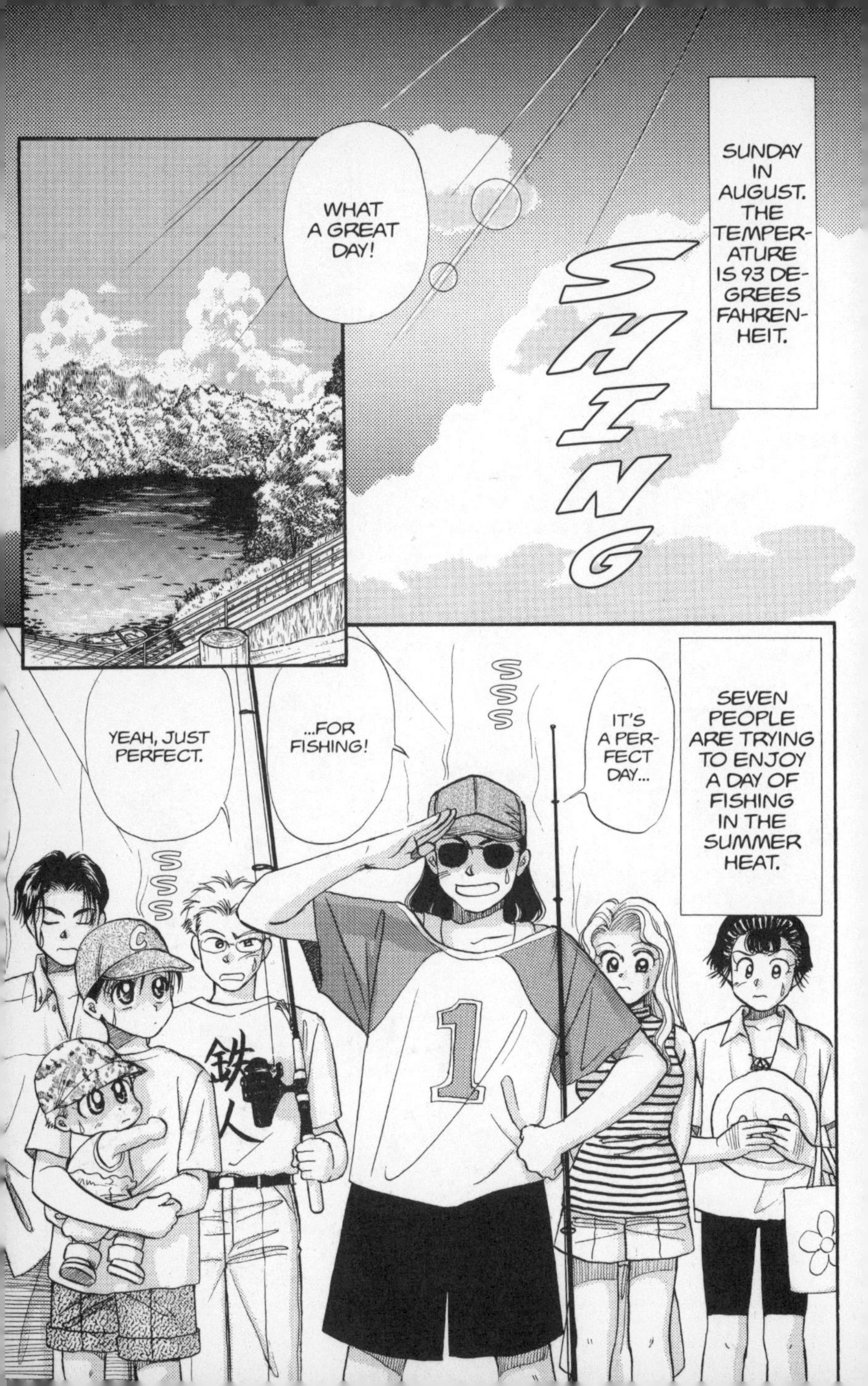
SUNDAY IN AUGUST. THE TEMPERATURE IS 93 DEGREES FAHRENHEIT.
SHING
WHAT A GREAT DAY!
SEVEN PEOPLE ARE TRYING TO ENJOY A DAY OF FISHING IN THE SUMMER HEAT.
IT'S A PERFECT DAY...
SSS
...FOR FISHING!
YEAH, JUST PERFECT.
SSS
鉄人

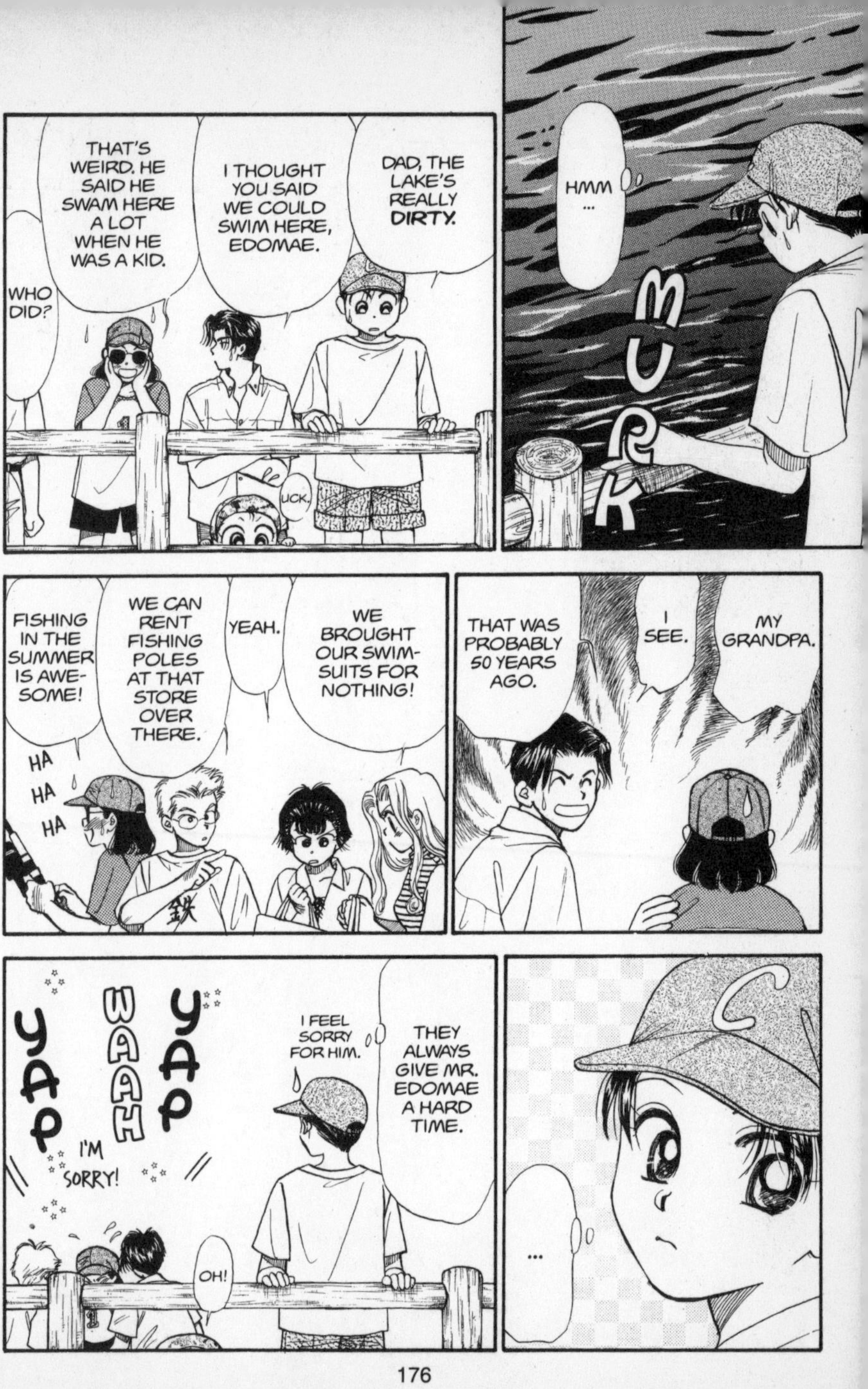
HMM ...
MURK
DAD, THE LAKE'S REALLY **DIRTY.**
I THOUGHT YOU SAID WE COULD SWIM HERE, EDOMAE.
THAT'S WEIRD. HE SAID HE SWAM HERE A LOT WHEN HE WAS A KID.
WHO DID?
UCK.
MY GRANDPA.
I SEE.
THAT WAS PROBABLY 50 YEARS AGO.
WE BROUGHT OUR SWIM-SUITS FOR NOTHING!
YEAH.
WE CAN RENT FISHING POLES AT THAT STORE OVER THERE.
FISHING IN THE SUMMER IS AWE-SOME!
HA HA HA
...
THEY ALWAYS GIVE MR. EDOMAE A HARD TIME.
I FEEL SORRY FOR HIM.
YAP
WAAAH
YAP
I'M SORRY!
OH!

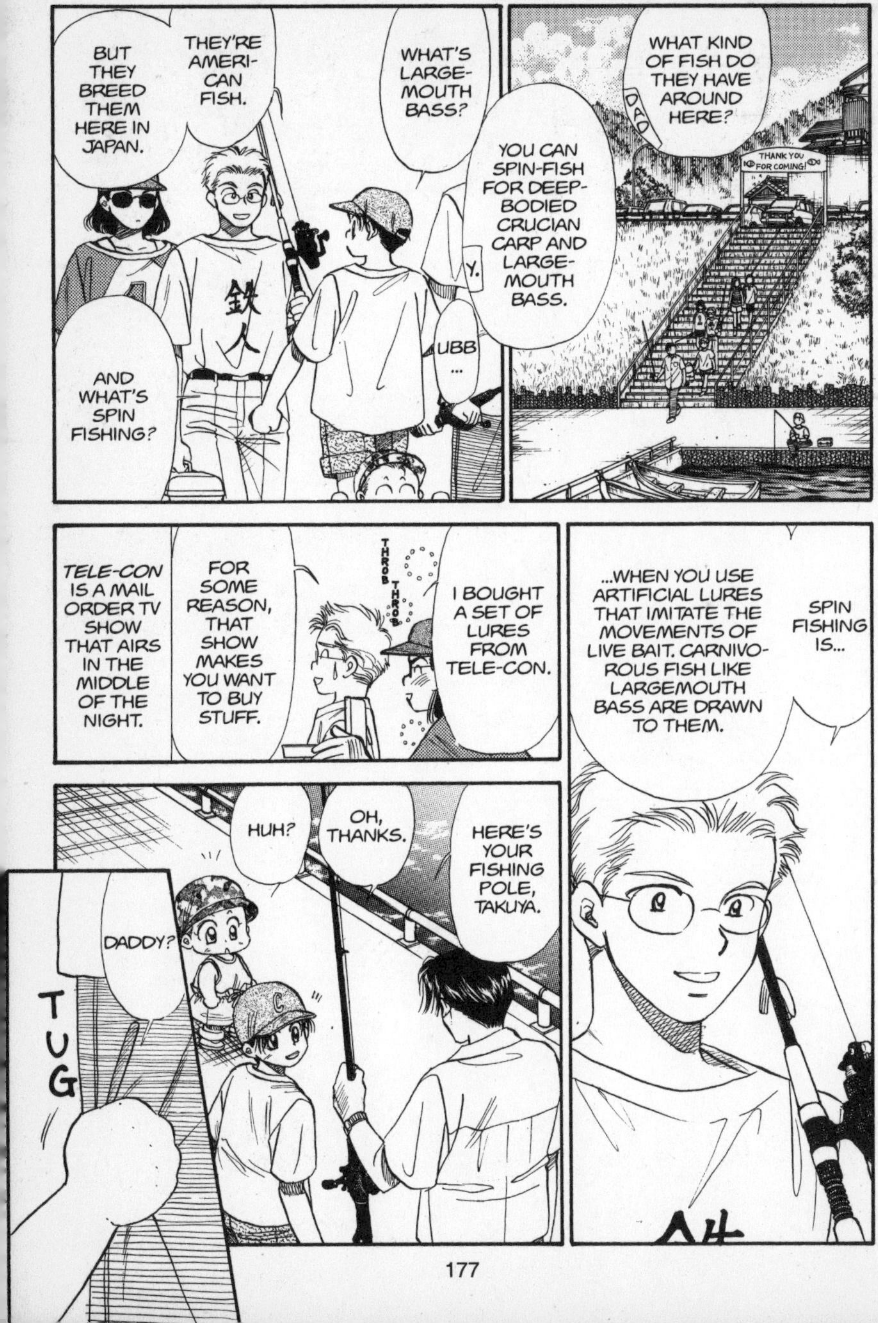
WHAT KIND OF FISH DO THEY HAVE AROUND HERE?
DAD
THANK YOU FOR COMING!
YOU CAN SPIN-FISH FOR DEEP-BODIED CRUCIAN CARP AND LARGE-MOUTH BASS.
WHAT'S LARGE-MOUTH BASS?
Y.
UBB ...
THEY'RE AMERI-CAN FISH.
BUT THEY BREED THEM HERE IN JAPAN.
AND WHAT'S SPIN FISHING?
SPIN FISHING IS...
...WHEN YOU USE ARTIFICIAL LURES THAT IMITATE THE MOVEMENTS OF LIVE BAIT. CARNIVO-ROUS FISH LIKE LARGEMOUTH BASS ARE DRAWN TO THEM.
AH
I BOUGHT A SET OF LURES FROM TELE-CON.
THROB THROB
FOR SOME REASON, THAT SHOW MAKES YOU WANT TO BUY STUFF.
TELE-CON IS A MAIL ORDER TV SHOW THAT AIRS IN THE MIDDLE OF THE NIGHT.
HERE'S YOUR FISHING POLE, TAKUYA.
OH, THANKS.
HUH?
DADDY?
TUG

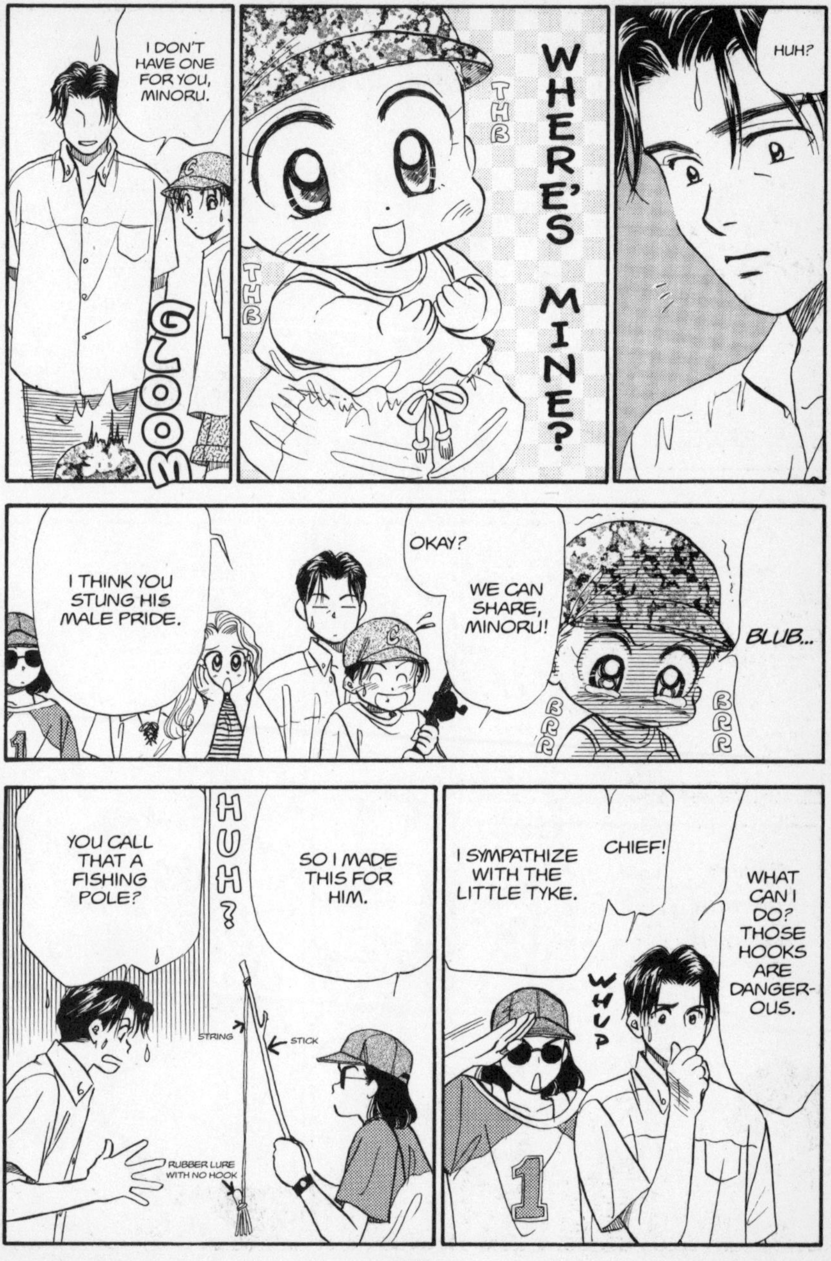
HUH?
WHERE'S MINE?
THB
THB
I DON'T HAVE ONE FOR YOU, MINORU.
GLOOM
BLUB...
BRR
BRR
WE CAN SHARE, MINORU!
OKAY?
I THINK YOU STUNG HIS MALE PRIDE.
WHAT CAN I DO? THOSE HOOKS ARE DANGEROUS.
WHUP
CHIEF!
I SYMPATHIZE WITH THE LITTLE TYKE.
SO I MADE THIS FOR HIM.
STICK
STRING
RUBBER LURE WITH NO HOOK
HUH?
YOU CALL THAT A FISHING POLE?

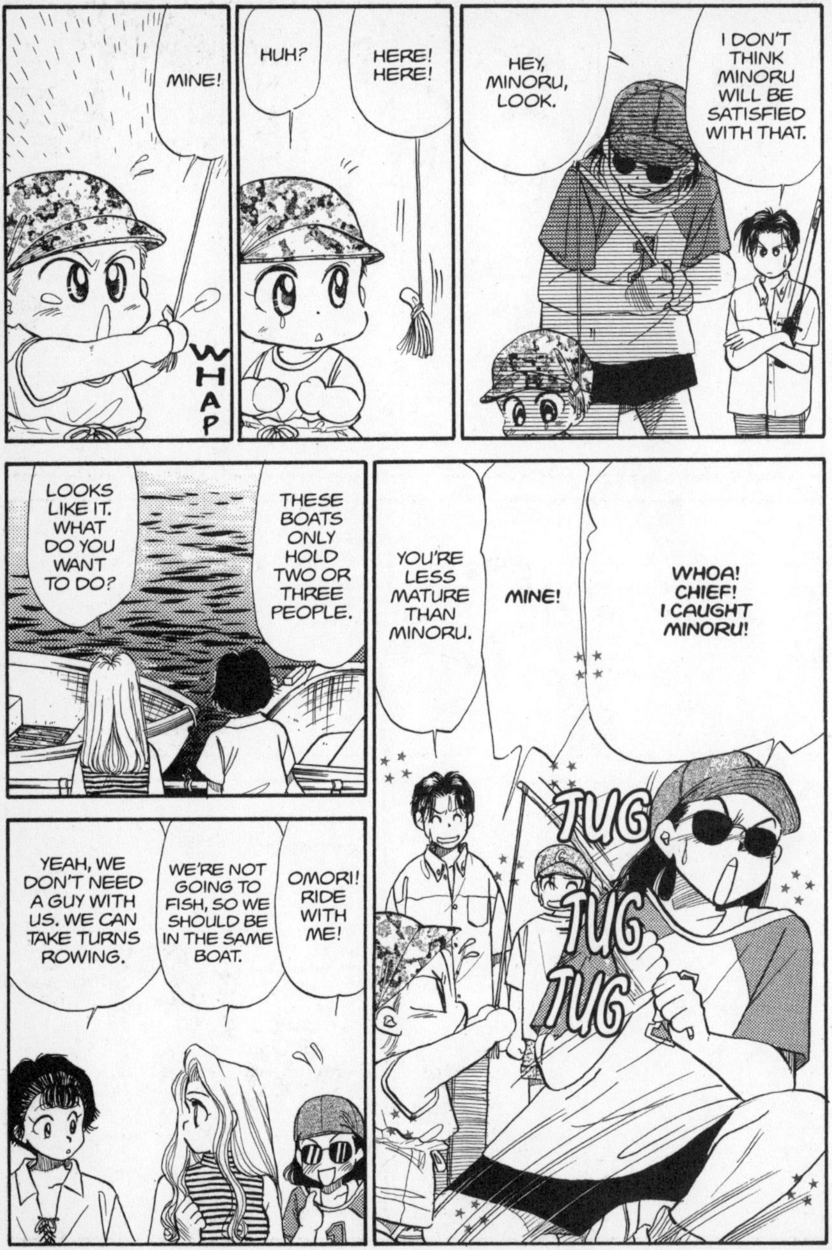
I DON'T THINK MINORU WILL BE SATISFIED WITH THAT.
HEY, MINORU, LOOK.
HERE! HERE!
HUH?
MINE!
WHAP
WHOA! CHIEF! I CAUGHT MINORU!
MINE!
YOU'RE LESS MATURE THAN MINORU.
TUG
TUG
TUG
THESE BOATS ONLY HOLD TWO OR THREE PEOPLE.
LOOKS LIKE IT. WHAT DO YOU WANT TO DO?
OMORI! RIDE WITH ME!
WE'RE NOT GOING TO FISH, SO WE SHOULD BE IN THE SAME BOAT.
YEAH, WE DON'T NEED A GUY WITH US. WE CAN TAKE TURNS ROWING.

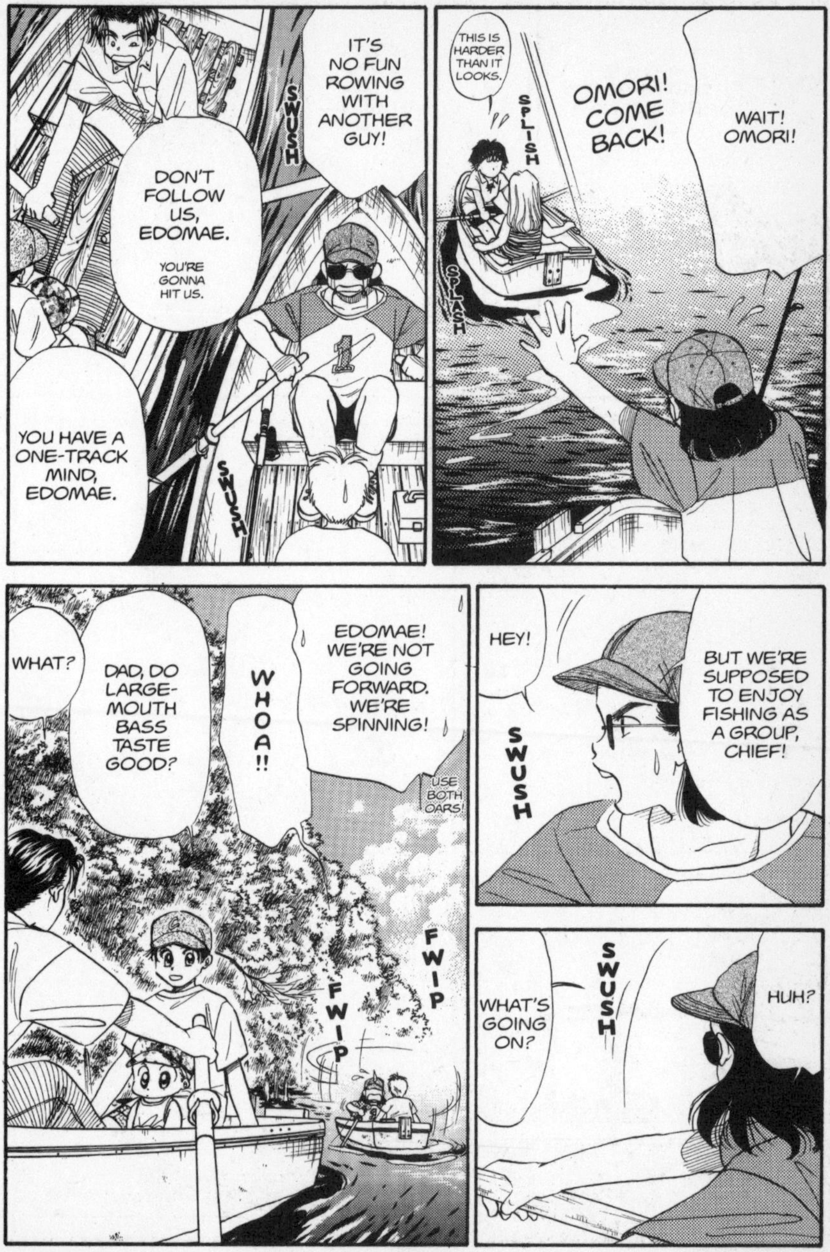
WAIT! OMORI!
OMORI! COME BACK!
SPLISH
THIS IS HARDER THAN IT LOOKS.
SPLASH
IT'S NO FUN ROWING WITH ANOTHER GUY!
SWUSH
DON'T FOLLOW US, EDOMAE.
YOU'RE GONNA HIT US.
YOU HAVE A ONE-TRACK MIND, EDOMAE.
SWUSH
BUT WE'RE SUPPOSED TO ENJOY FISHING AS A GROUP, CHIEF!
HEY!
SWUSH
HUH?
SWUSH
WHAT'S GOING ON?
EDOMAE! WE'RE NOT GOING FORWARD. WE'RE SPINNING!
USE BOTH OARS!
WHOA!!
DAD, DO LARGE-MOUTH BASS TASTE GOOD?
WHAT?
FWIP
FWIP

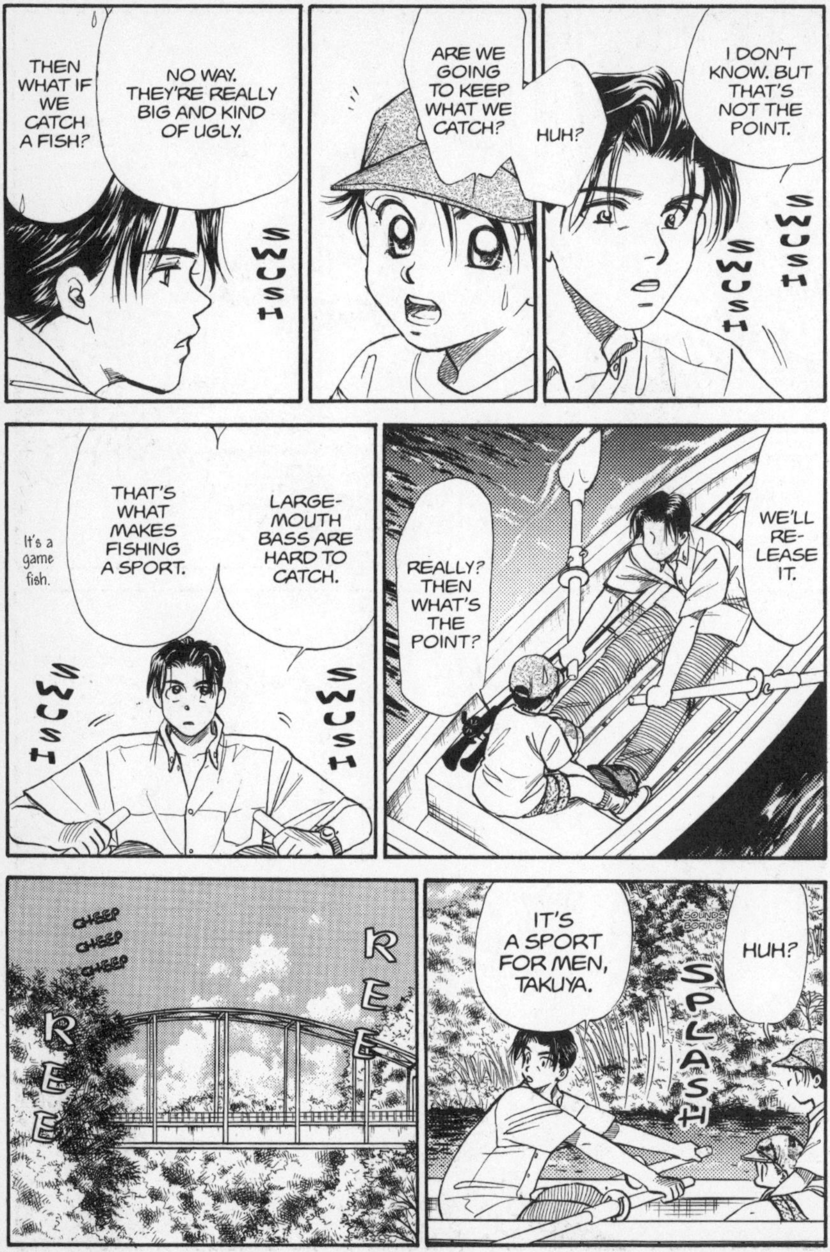
I DON'T KNOW. BUT THAT'S NOT THE POINT.
HUH?
SWUSH
SWUSH
ARE WE GOING TO KEEP WHAT WE CATCH?
NO WAY. THEY'RE REALLY BIG AND KIND OF UGLY.
THEN WHAT IF WE CATCH A FISH?
SWUSH
WE'LL RE-LEASE IT.
REALLY? THEN WHAT'S THE POINT?
LARGE-MOUTH BASS ARE HARD TO CATCH.
SWUSH
THAT'S WHAT MAKES FISHING A SPORT.
It's a game fish.
SWUSH
HUH?
SOUNDS BORING
SPLASH
IT'S A SPORT FOR MEN, TAKUYA.
REE
REE
CHEEP
CHEEP
CHEEP
REE
REE

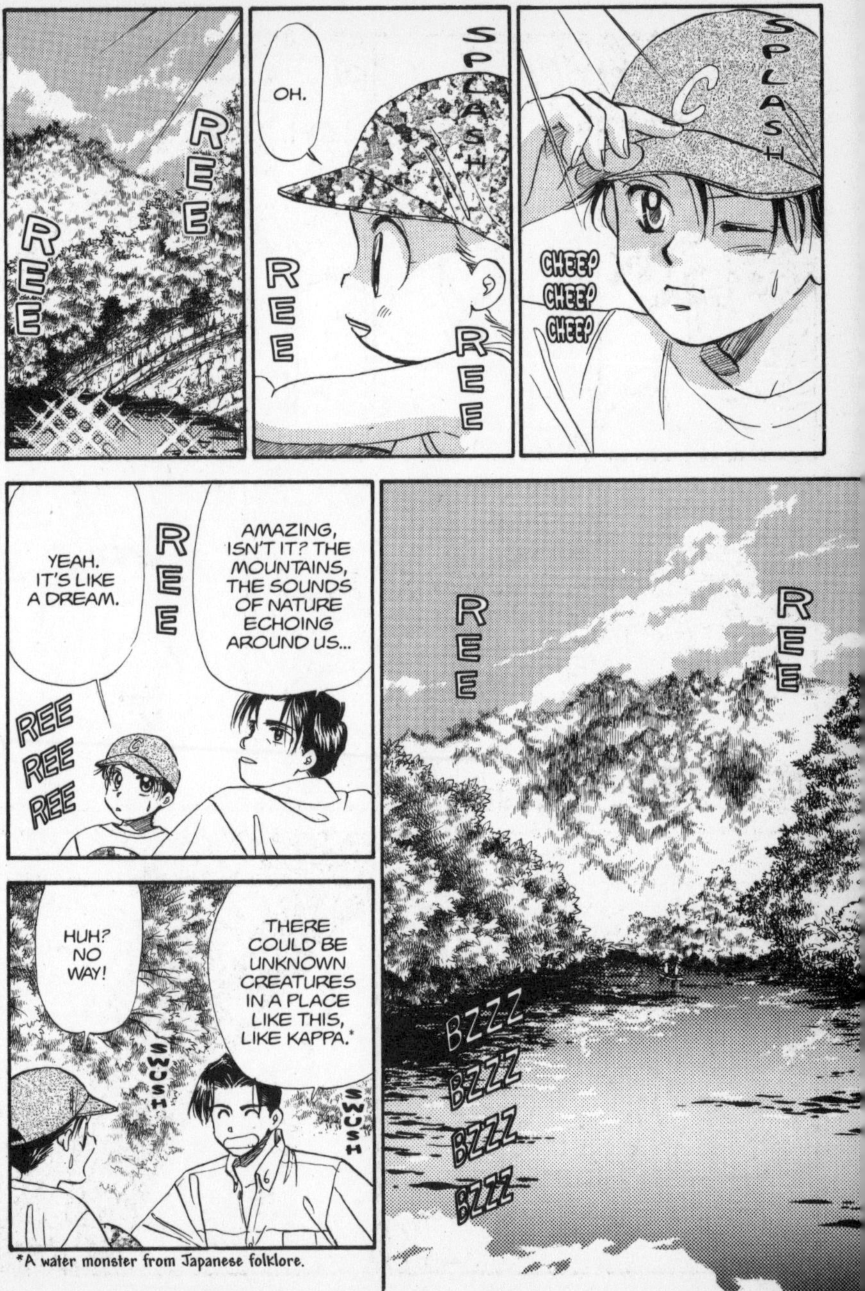
SPLASH
CHEEP CHEEP CHEEP
SPLASH
OH.
REE
REE
REE
REE
REE
REE
REE
BZZZ BZZZ BZZZ BZZZ
AMAZING, ISN'T IT? THE MOUNTAINS, THE SOUNDS OF NATURE ECHOING AROUND US...
REE
YEAH. IT'S LIKE A DREAM.
REE REE REE
THERE COULD BE UNKNOWN CREATURES IN A PLACE LIKE THIS, LIKE KAPPA.*
SWUSH
HUH? NO WAY!
SWUSH

*A water monster from Japanese folklore.

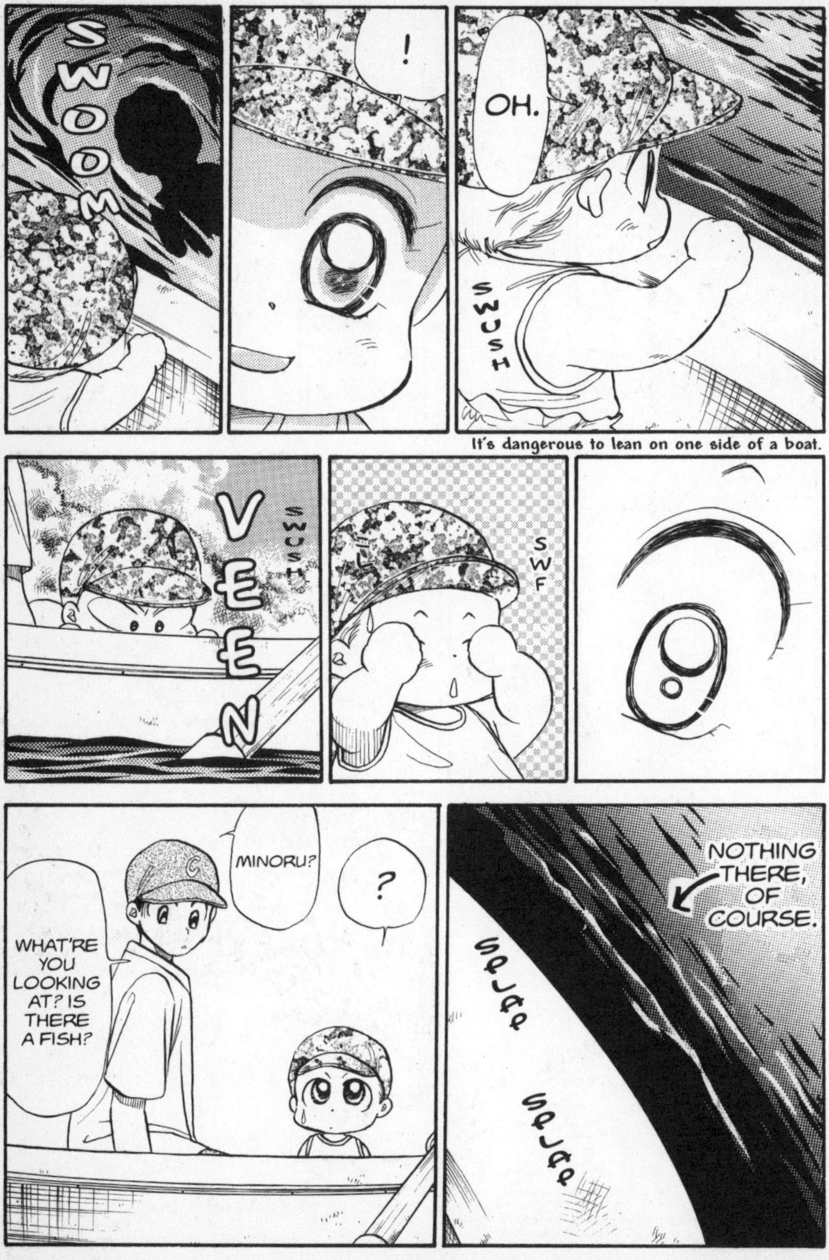
OH.
SWUSH
!
SWOOM
It's dangerous to lean on one side of a boat.
SWF
VEEN
SWUSH
NOTHING THERE, OF COURSE.
SQUEE
SQUEE
MINORU?
?
WHAT'RE YOU LOOKING AT? IS THERE A FISH?

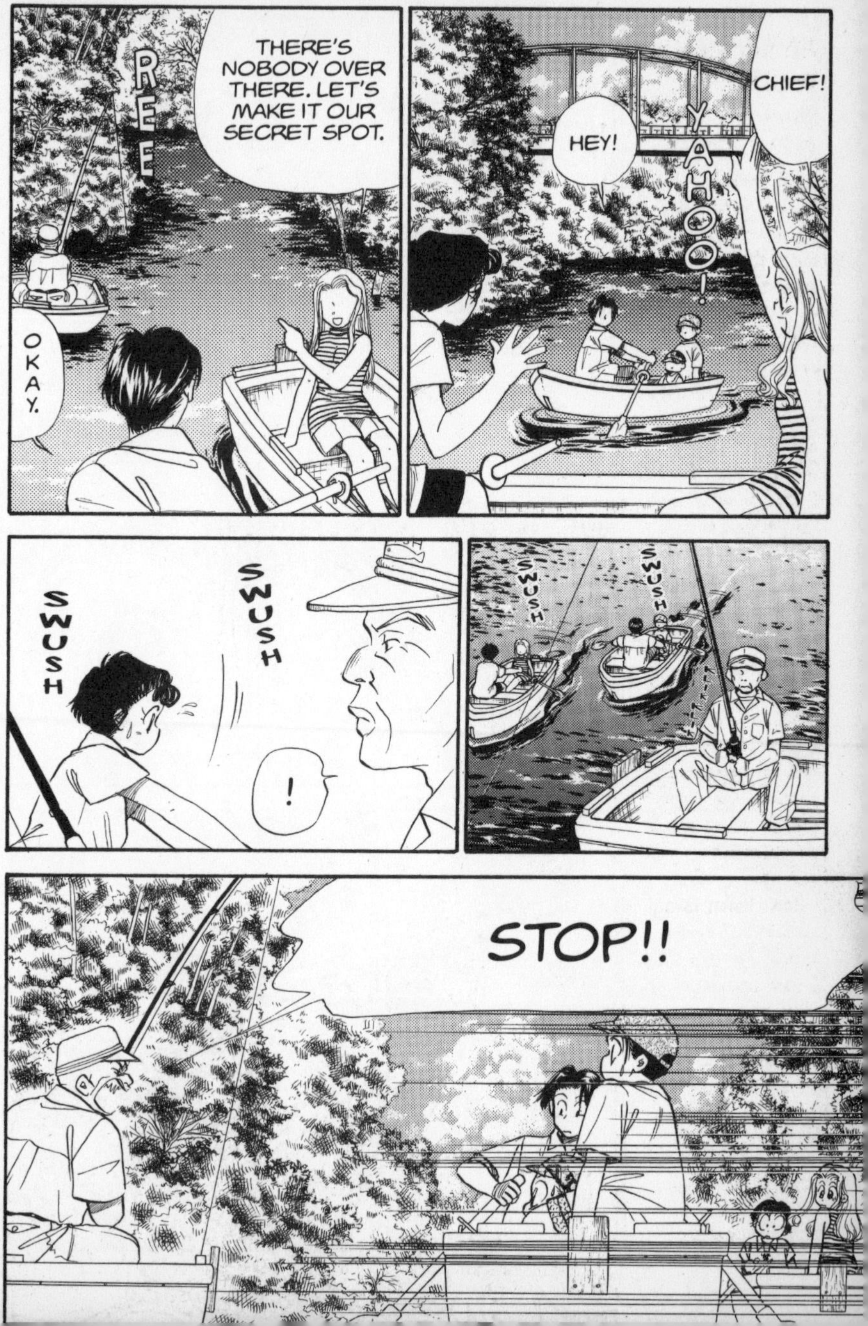
CHIEF!
YAHOO!
HEY!
THERE'S NOBODY OVER THERE. LET'S MAKE IT OUR SECRET SPOT.
REE
OKAY.
SWUSH
SWUSH
SWUSH
SWUSH
!
STOP!!

Author's Note Part 6

Whew. My last Author's Note.

I got cable television, but I'm confused because there are more than 30 channels and there's no guide for all of them. So I usually end up channel surfing and watching whatever catches my eye. But I keep missing the shows I want to watch and forgetting which channels have interesting shows that I've watched before. It's so frustrating.

Still, I really like it. I get to enjoy movies, stand-up comedy, sports and music. But I spend so much time watching TV that I don't listen to my wire radio service. Since I pay for both, I want my money's worth from both!

What should I do? I'm going crazy!

All right, see you again in volume 14! Bye!

Marimo

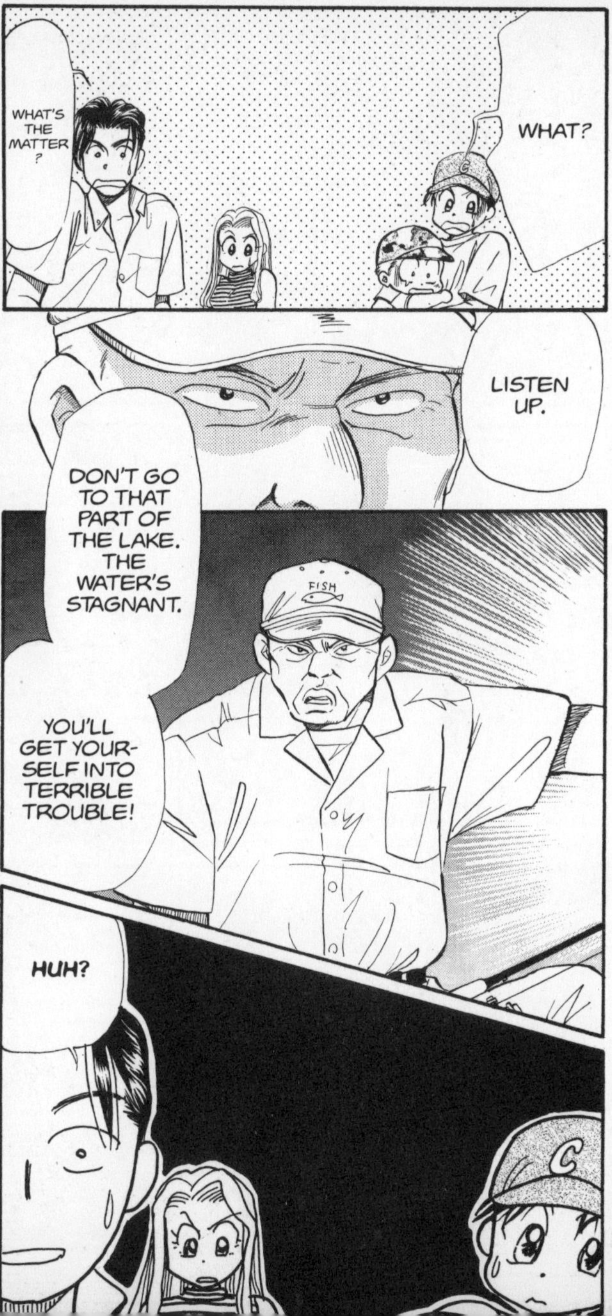
WHAT?
WHAT'S THE MATTER?
LISTEN UP.
DON'T GO TO THAT PART OF THE LAKE. THE WATER'S STAGNANT.
YOU'LL GET YOURSELF INTO TERRIBLE TROUBLE!
HUH?

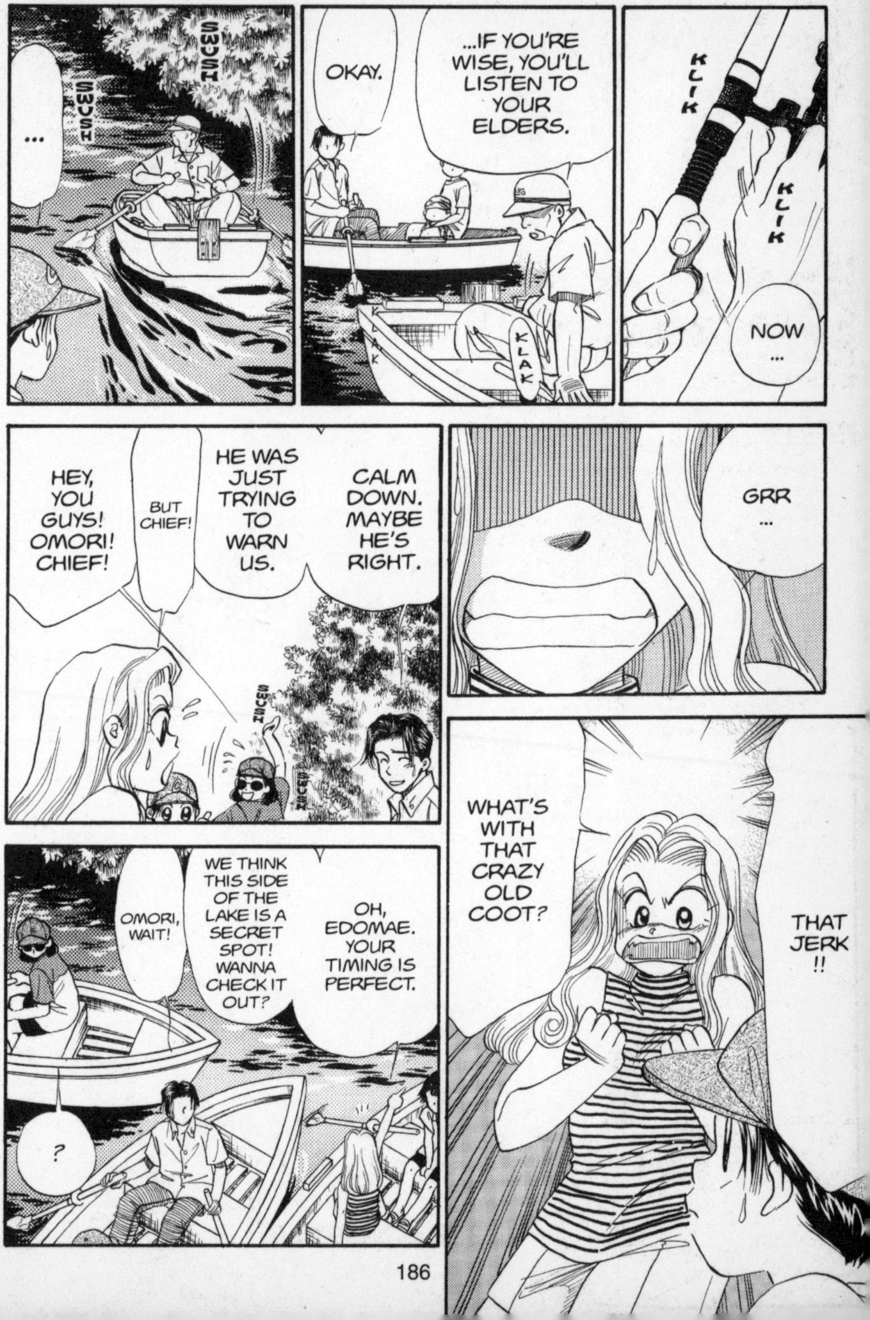
KLIK
KLIK
NOW ...
...IF YOU'RE WISE, YOU'LL LISTEN TO YOUR ELDERS.
OKAY.
KLAK
KLAK
SWUSH
SWUSH
...
GRR ...
THAT JERK !!
WHAT'S WITH THAT CRAZY OLD COOT?
CALM DOWN. MAYBE HE'S RIGHT.
HE WAS JUST TRYING TO WARN US.
BUT CHIEF!
HEY, YOU GUYS! OMORI! CHIEF!
SWUSH
OH, EDOMAE. YOUR TIMING IS PERFECT.
WE THINK THIS SIDE OF THE LAKE IS A SECRET SPOT! WANNA CHECK IT OUT?
OMORI, WAIT!
?

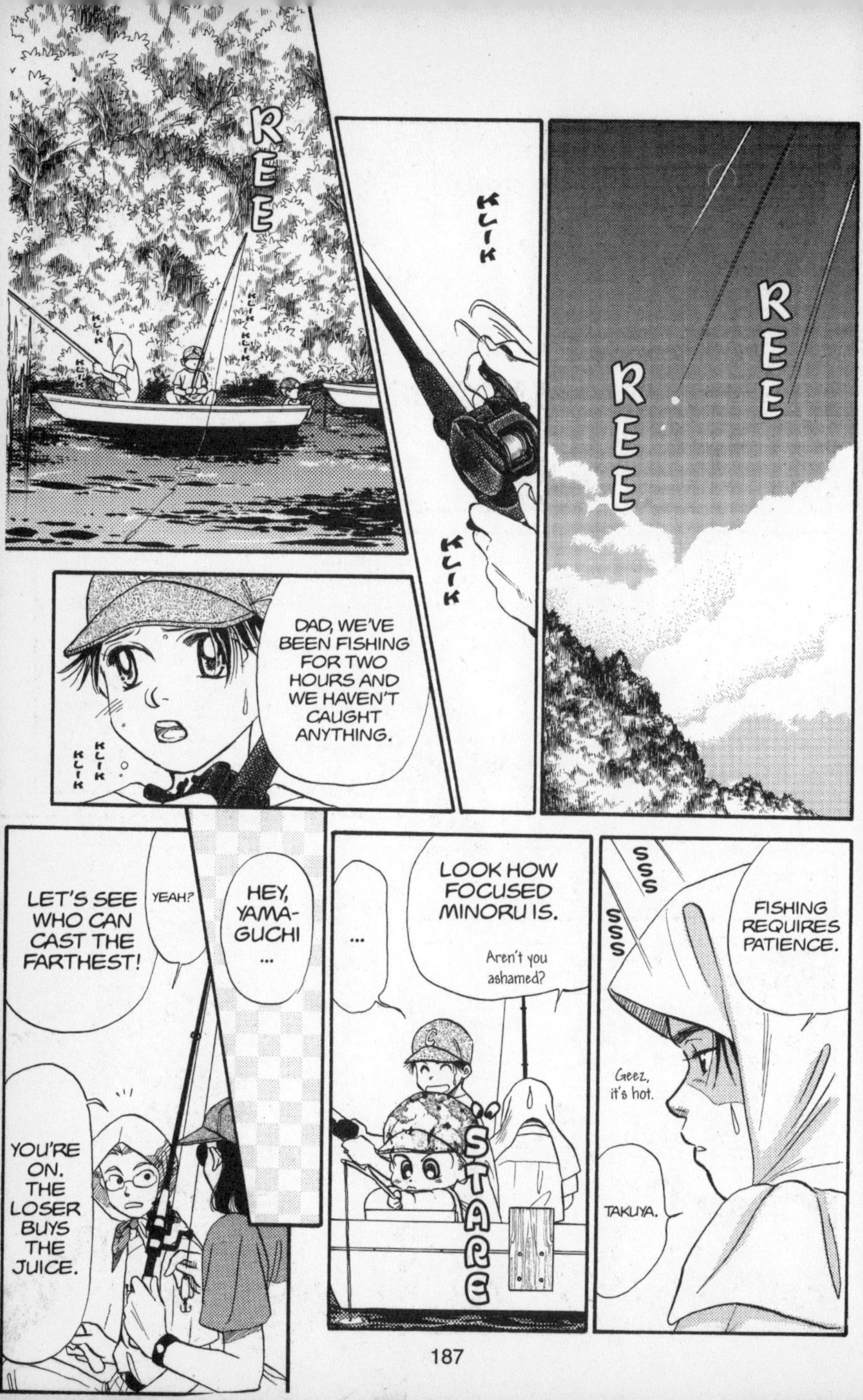

REE REE
REE REE
KLIK KLIK
REE
KLIK KLIK KLIK
KLIK
KLIK
DAD, WE'VE BEEN FISHING FOR TWO HOURS AND WE HAVEN'T CAUGHT ANYTHING.
KLIK KLIK
SSS SSS
FISHING REQUIRES PATIENCE.
Geez, it's hot.
TAKUYA.
LOOK HOW FOCUSED MINORU IS.
Aren't you ashamed?
...
STARE
HEY, YAMA-GUCHI ...
YEAH?
LET'S SEE WHO CAN CAST THE FARTHEST!
YOU'RE ON. THE LOSER BUYS THE JUICE.

No idea what they're saying.

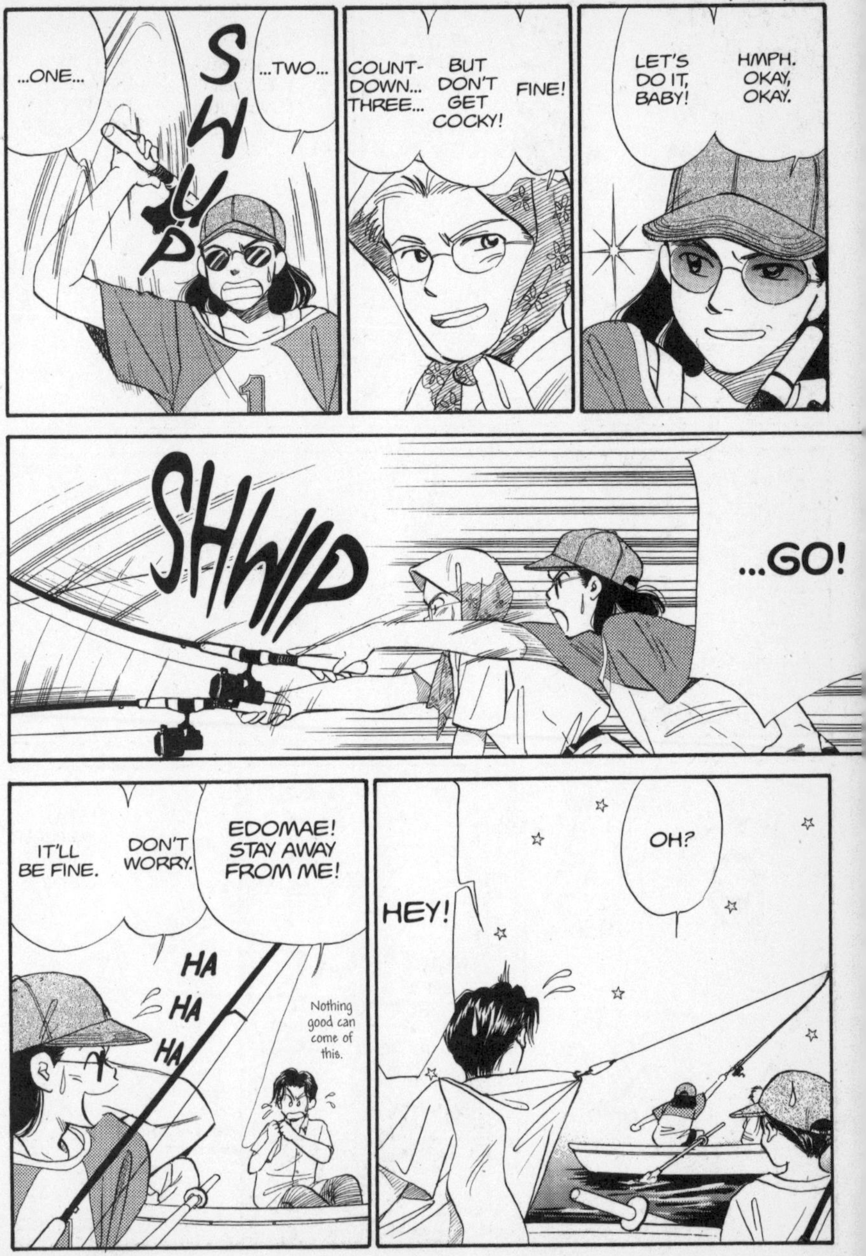
HMPH. OKAY, OKAY.
LET'S DO IT, BABY!
FINE!
BUT DON'T GET COCKY!
COUNT-DOWN... THREE...
...TWO...
SWUP
...ONE...
...GO!
SHWIP
OH?
HEY!
EDOMAE! STAY AWAY FROM ME!
DON'T WORRY.
IT'LL BE FINE.
HA HA HA
Nothing good can come of this.

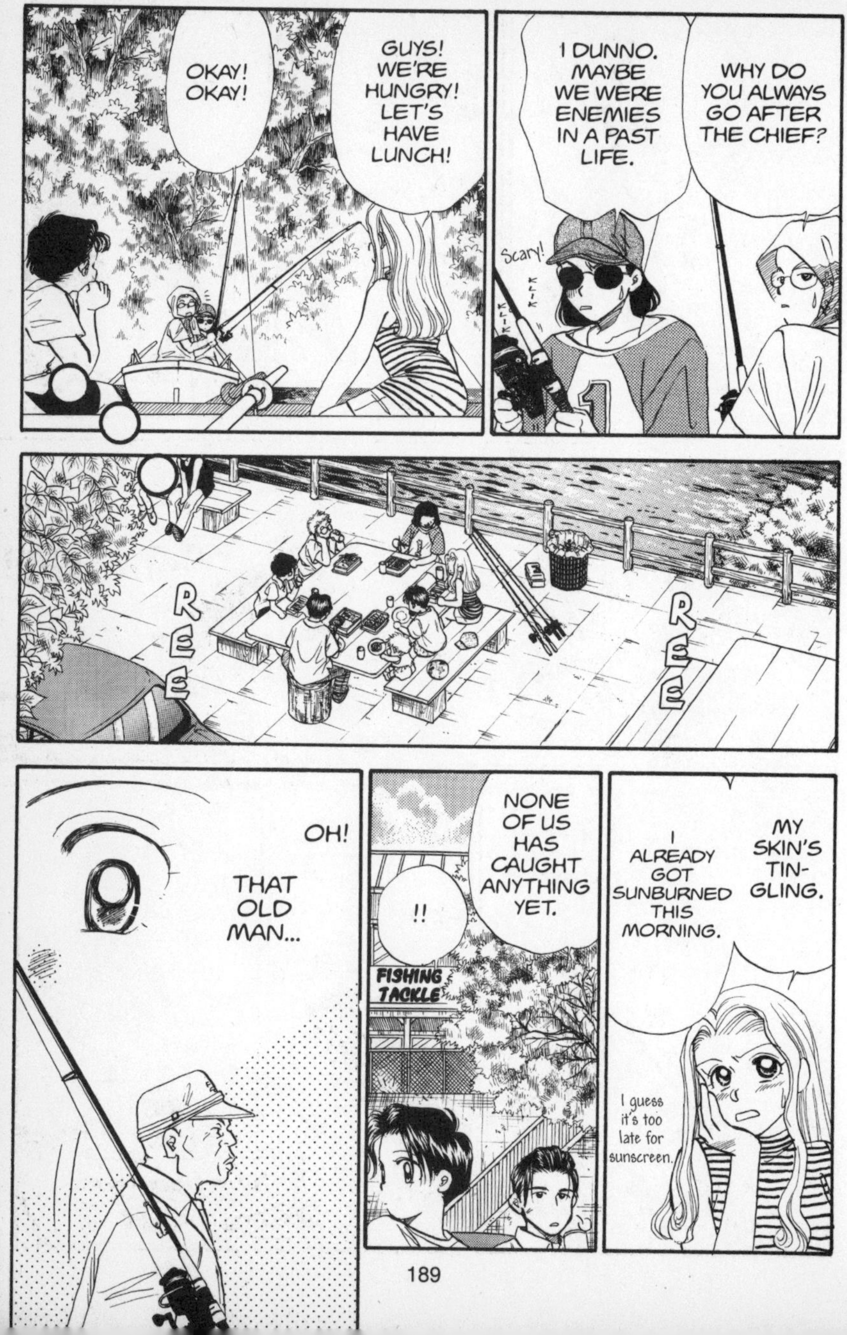
WHY DO YOU ALWAYS GO AFTER THE CHIEF?
I DUNNO. MAYBE WE WERE ENEMIES IN A PAST LIFE.
Scary!
KLIK KLIK
GUYS! WE'RE HUNGRY! LET'S HAVE LUNCH!
OKAY! OKAY!
REE
REE
MY SKIN'S TIN-GLING.
I ALREADY GOT SUNBURNED THIS MORNING.
I guess it's too late for sunscreen.
NONE OF US HAS CAUGHT ANYTHING YET.
!!
FISHING TACKLE
OH!
THAT OLD MAN...

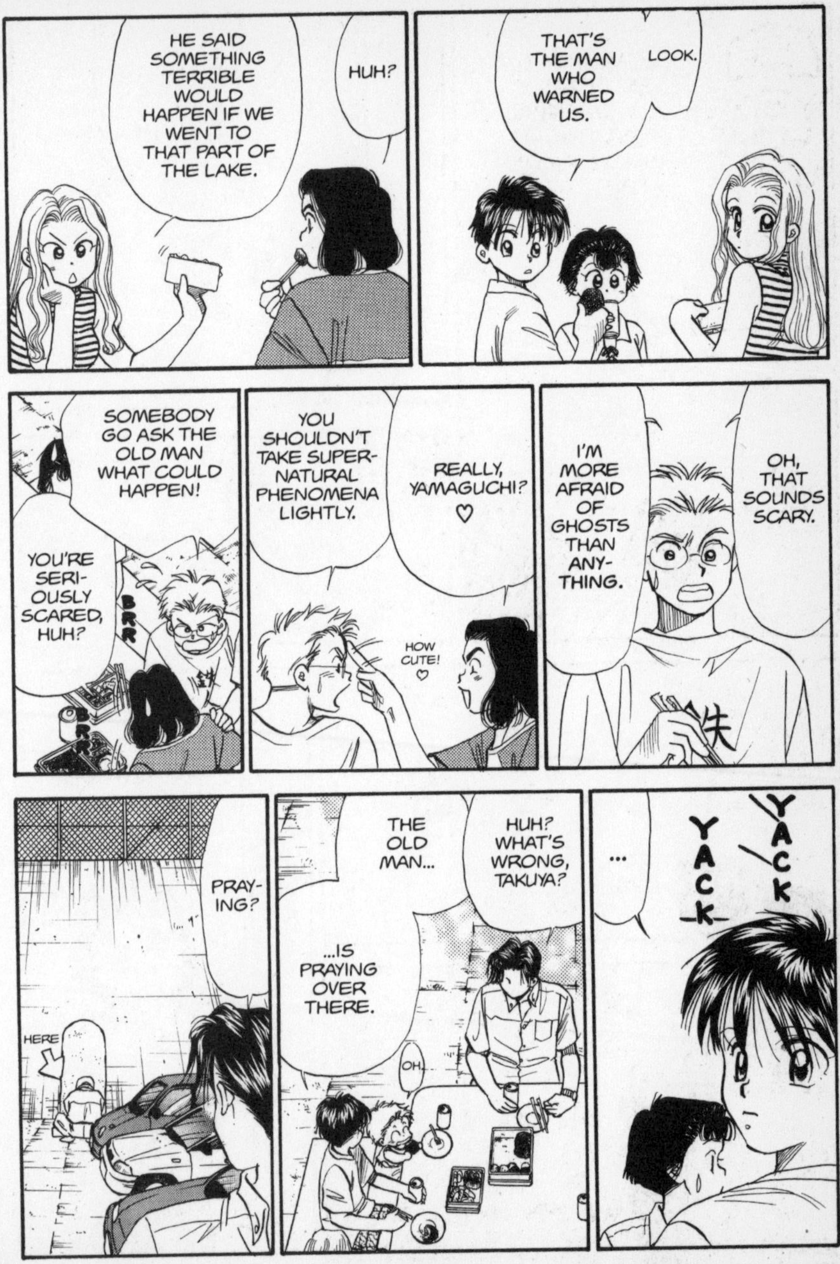

LOOK.
THAT'S THE MAN WHO WARNED US.
HUH?
HE SAID SOMETHING TERRIBLE WOULD HAPPEN IF WE WENT TO THAT PART OF THE LAKE.
OH, THAT SOUNDS SCARY.
I'M MORE AFRAID OF GHOSTS THAN ANY-THING.
REALLY, YAMAGUCHI? ♡
YOU SHOULDN'T TAKE SUPER-NATURAL PHENOMENA LIGHTLY.
HOW CUTE! ♡
SOMEBODY GO ASK THE OLD MAN WHAT COULD HAPPEN!
YOU'RE SERI-OUSLY SCARED, HUH?
BRR
BRR
YACK
YACK
YACK
...
HUH? WHAT'S WRONG, TAKUYA?
THE OLD MAN...
...IS PRAYING OVER THERE.
OH.
PRAYING?
HERE

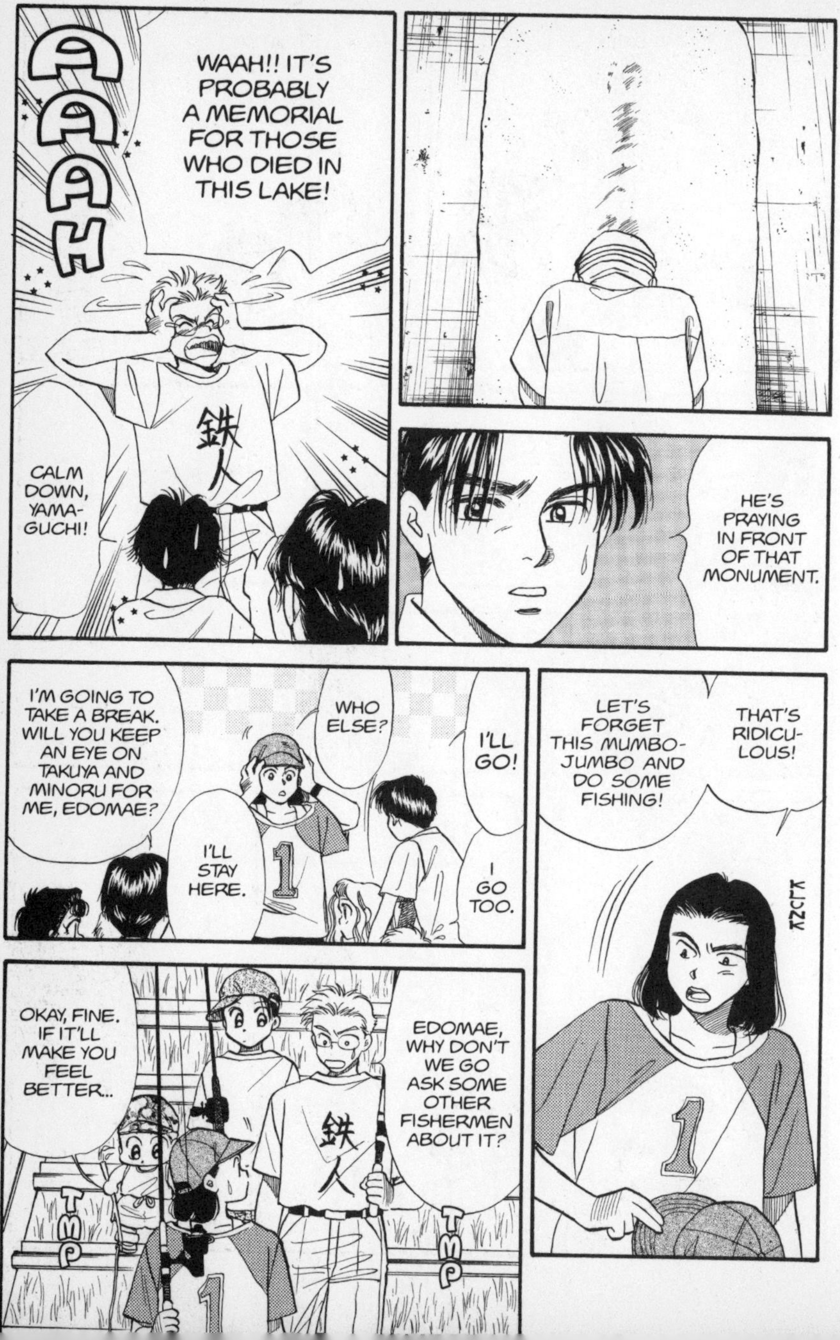
HE'S PRAYING IN FRONT OF THAT MONUMENT.
WAAH!! IT'S PROBABLY A MEMORIAL FOR THOSE WHO DIED IN THIS LAKE!
AAAH
CALM DOWN, YAMA-GUCHI!
THAT'S RIDICU-LOUS!
LET'S FORGET THIS MUMBO-JUMBO AND DO SOME FISHING!
KLUNK
I'LL GO!
WHO ELSE?
I'M GOING TO TAKE A BREAK. WILL YOU KEEP AN EYE ON TAKUYA AND MINORU FOR ME, EDOMAE?
I GO TOO.
I'LL STAY HERE.
EDOMAE, WHY DON'T WE GO ASK SOME OTHER FISHERMEN ABOUT IT?
TMP
OKAY, FINE. IF IT'LL MAKE YOU FEEL BETTER...
TMP

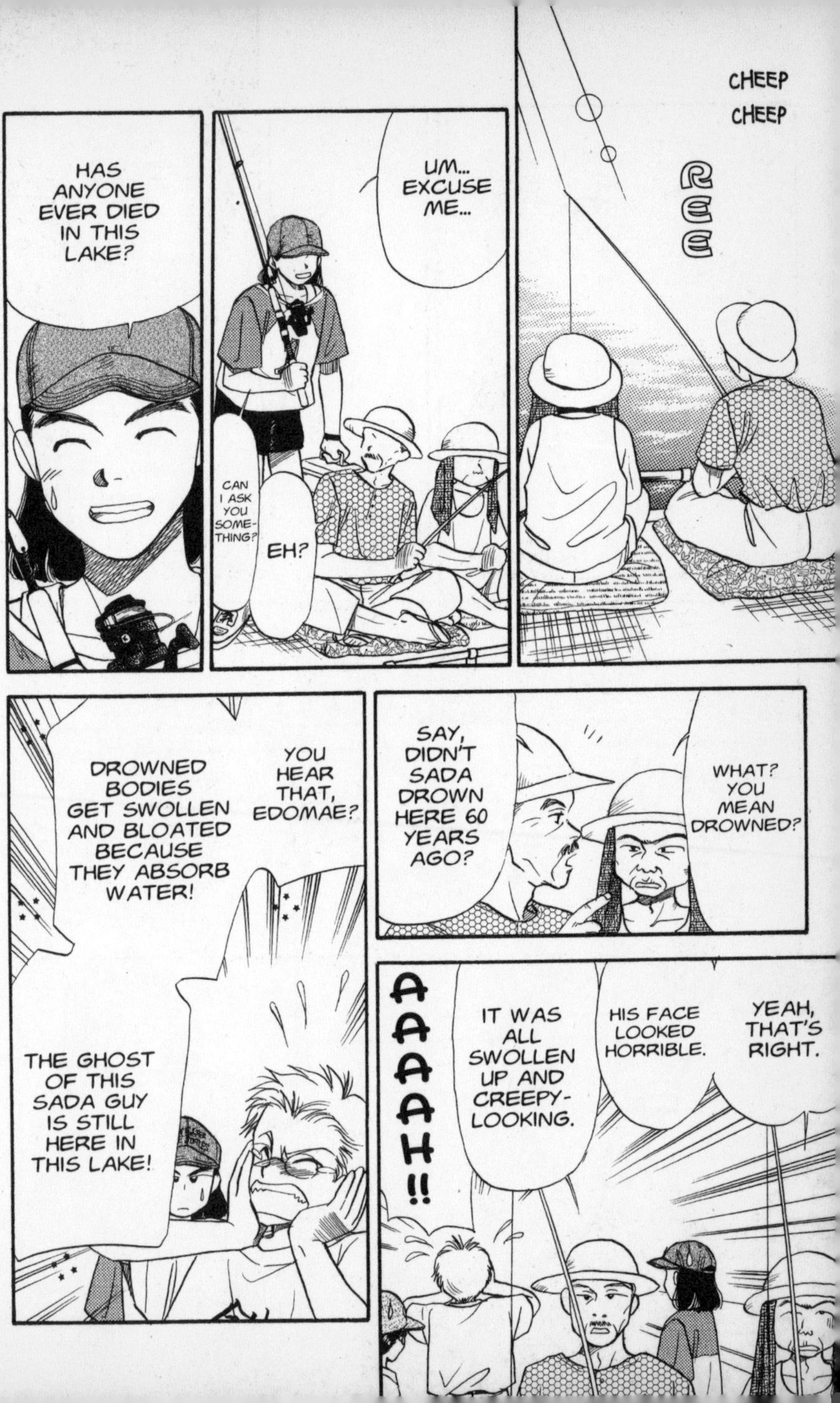
CHEEP
CHEEP
REE
UM... EXCUSE ME...
CAN I ASK YOU SOME-THING?
EH?
HAS ANYONE EVER DIED IN THIS LAKE?
WHAT? YOU MEAN DROWNED?
SAY, DIDN'T SADA DROWN HERE 60 YEARS AGO?
YEAH, THAT'S RIGHT.
HIS FACE LOOKED HORRIBLE.
IT WAS ALL SWOLLEN UP AND CREEPY-LOOKING.
AAAAAH!!
YOU HEAR THAT, EDOMAE?
DROWNED BODIES GET SWOLLEN AND BLOATED BECAUSE THEY ABSORB WATER!
THE GHOST OF THIS SADA GUY IS STILL HERE IN THIS LAKE!

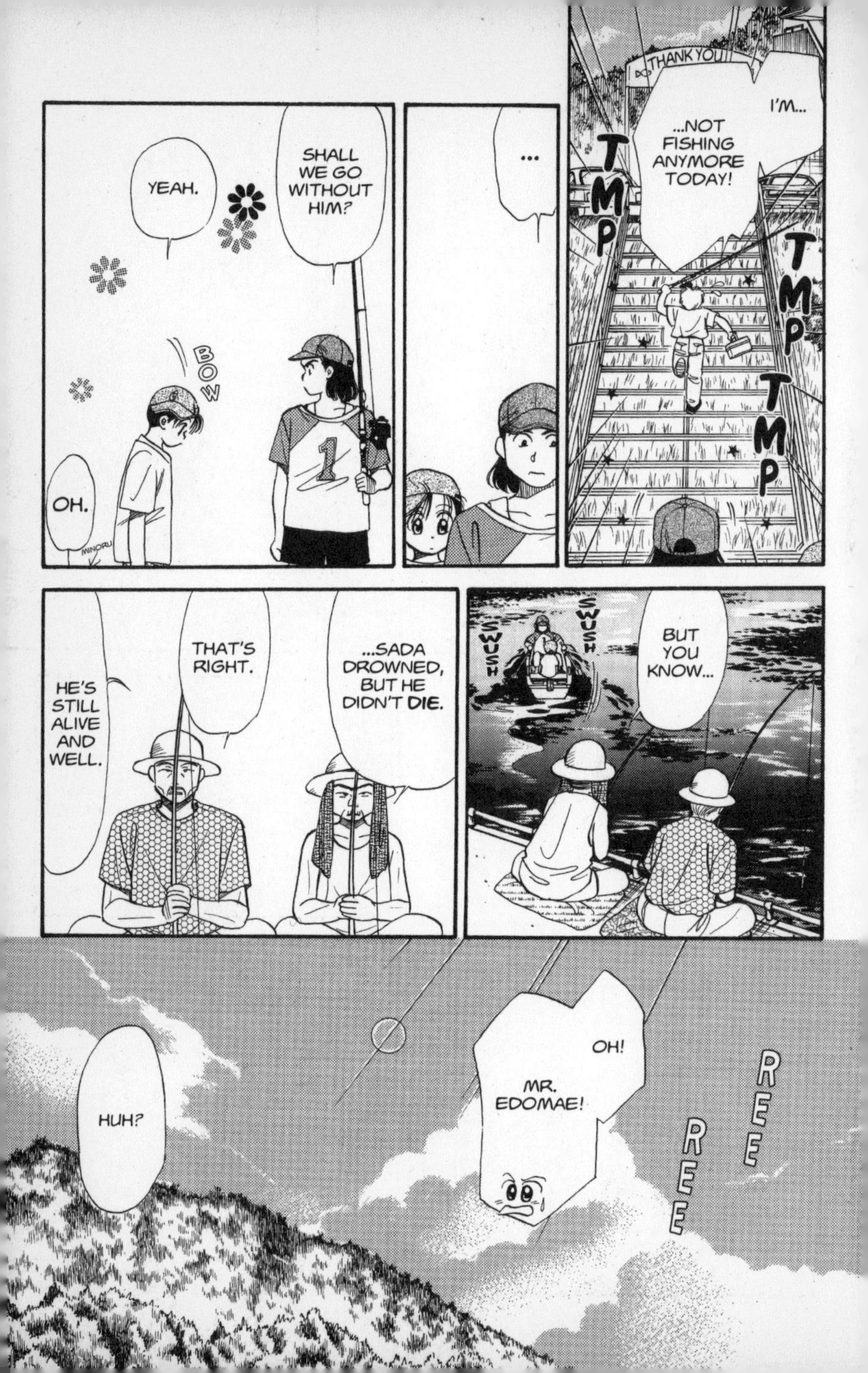
THANK YOU
I'M...
...NOT FISHING ANYMORE TODAY!
TMP
TMP
TMP
TMP
...
SHALL WE GO WITHOUT HIM?
YEAH.
BOW
OH.
MINORU
BUT YOU KNOW...
SWUSH
SWUSH
...SADA DROWNED, BUT HE DIDN'T **DIE**.
THAT'S RIGHT.
HE'S STILL ALIVE AND WELL.
OH!
MR. EDOMAE!
REE
REE
HUH?

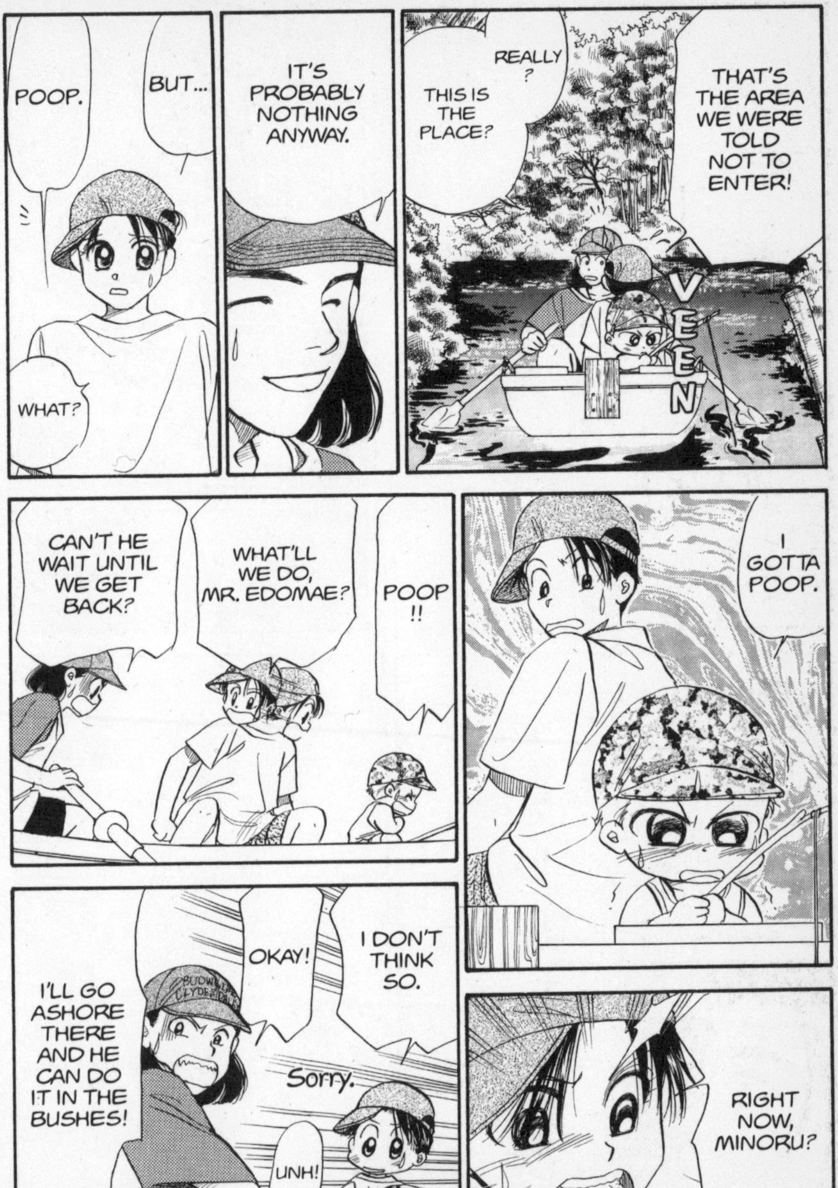
THAT'S THE AREA WE WERE TOLD NOT TO ENTER!
REALLY?
THIS IS THE PLACE?
VEEN
IT'S PROBABLY NOTHING ANYWAY.
BUT...
POOP.
WHAT?
I GOTTA POOP.
POOP!!
WHAT'LL WE DO, MR. EDOMAE?
CAN'T HE WAIT UNTIL WE GET BACK?
RIGHT NOW, MINORU?
I DON'T THINK SO.
OKAY!
I'LL GO ASHORE THERE AND HE CAN DO IT IN THE BUSHES!
Sorry.
UNH!

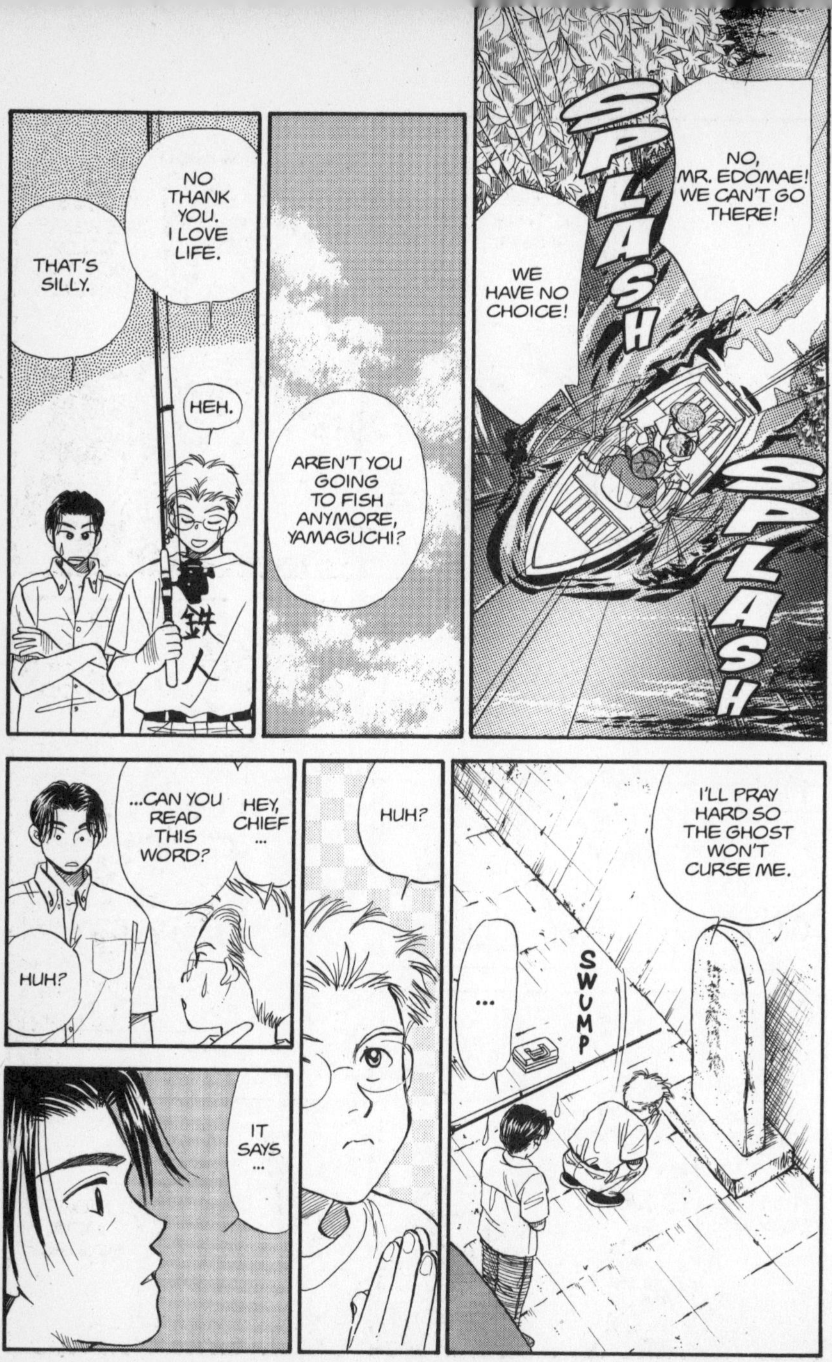
NO, MR. EDOMAE! WE CAN'T GO THERE!
WE HAVE NO CHOICE!
SPLASH
SPLASH
AREN'T YOU GOING TO FISH ANYMORE, YAMAGUCHI?
NO THANK YOU. I LOVE LIFE.
THAT'S SILLY.
HEH.
I'LL PRAY HARD SO THE GHOST WON'T CURSE ME.
SWUMP
...
HUH?
HEY, CHIEF ...
...CAN YOU READ THIS WORD?
HUH?
IT SAYS ...

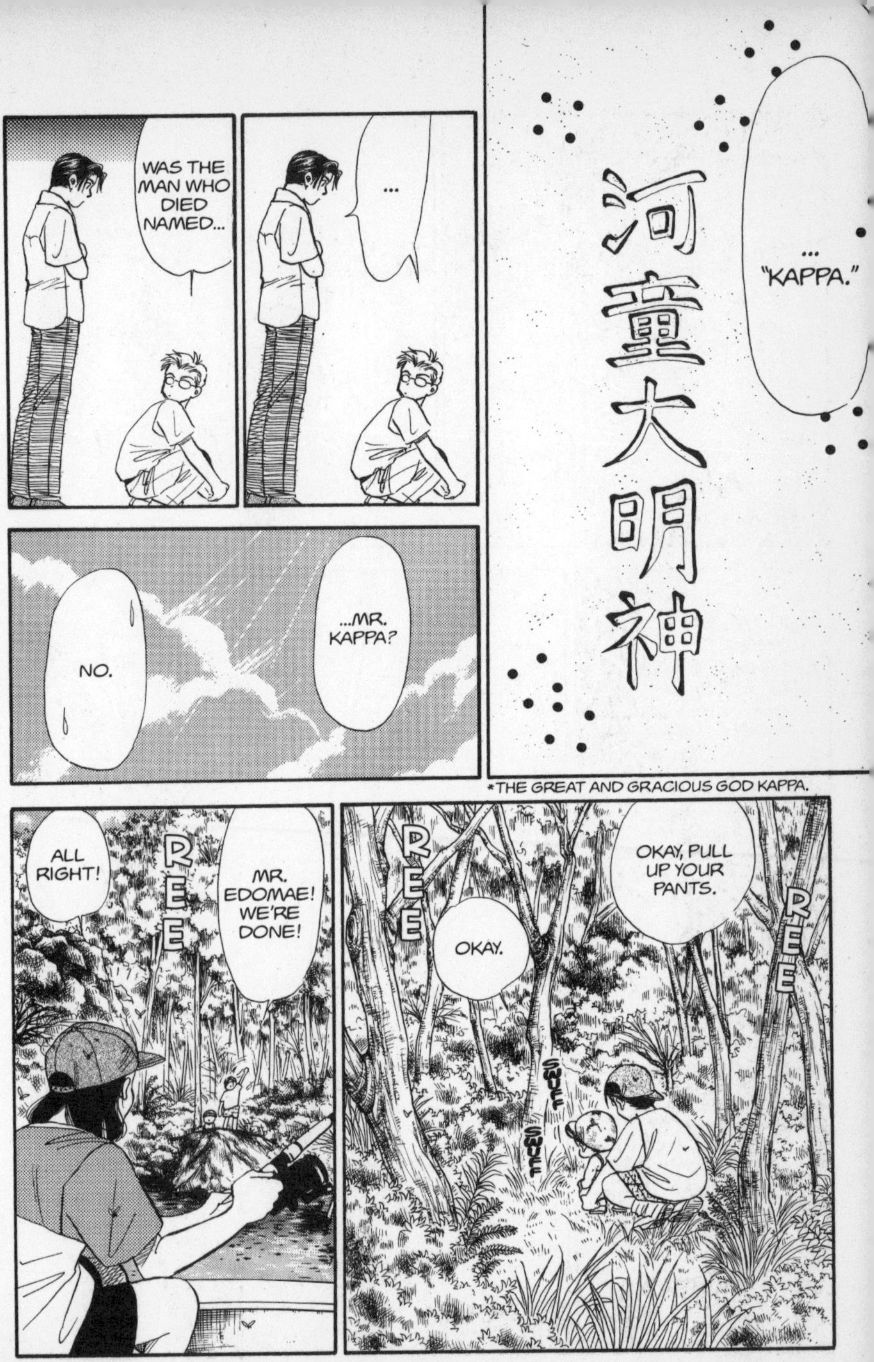

河童大明神
... "KAPPA."
...
WAS THE MAN WHO DIED NAMED...
...MR. KAPPA?
NO.
OKAY, PULL UP YOUR PANTS.
REE REE
OKAY.
SWUFF SWUFF
MR. EDOMAE! WE'RE DONE!
REE
ALL RIGHT!

*THE GREAT AND GRACIOUS GOD KAPPA.

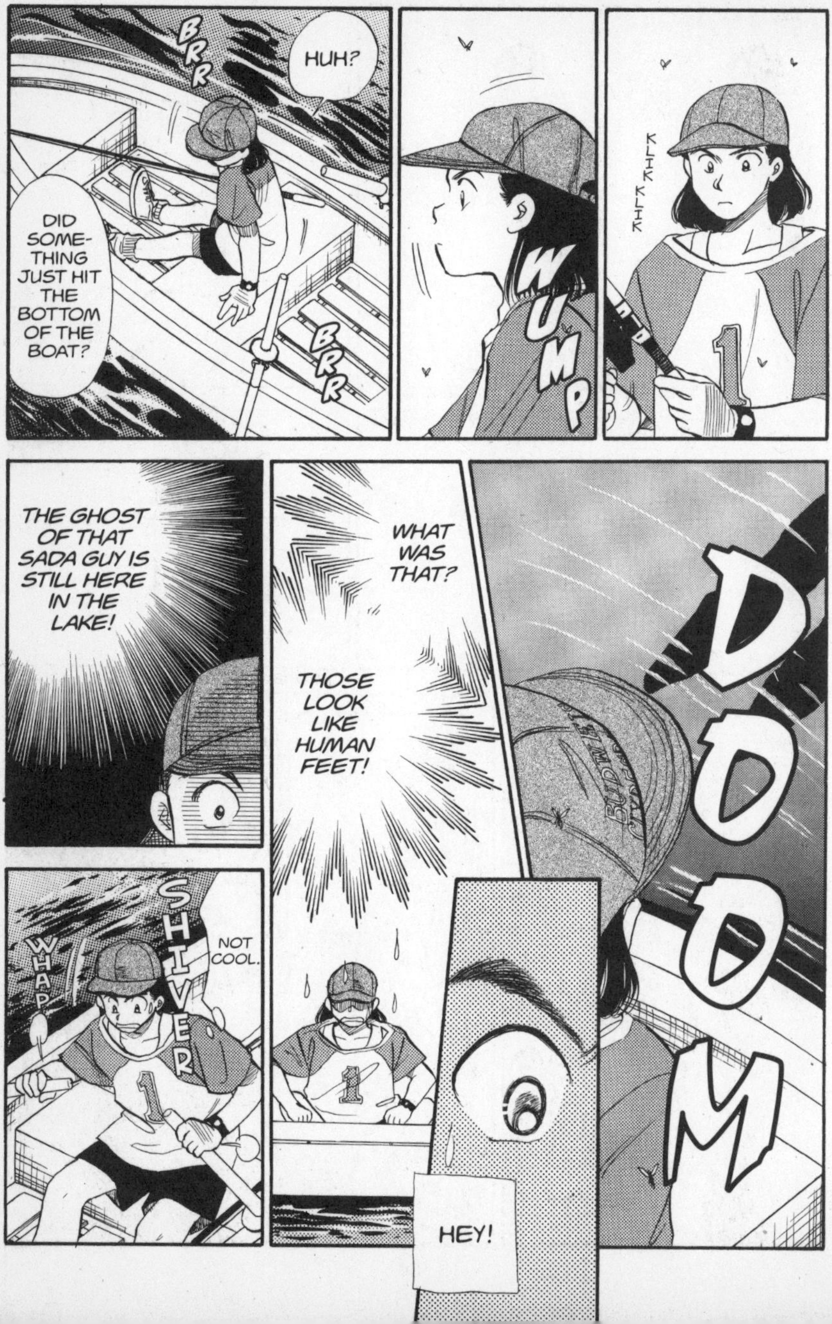
KLIK KLIK
WUMP
BRR
HUH?
DID SOMETHING JUST HIT THE BOTTOM OF THE BOAT?
BRR
DOOM
WHAT WAS THAT?
THOSE LOOK LIKE HUMAN FEET!
THE GHOST OF THAT SADA GUY IS STILL HERE IN THE LAKE!
HEY!
SHIVER
WHAP
NOT COOL.

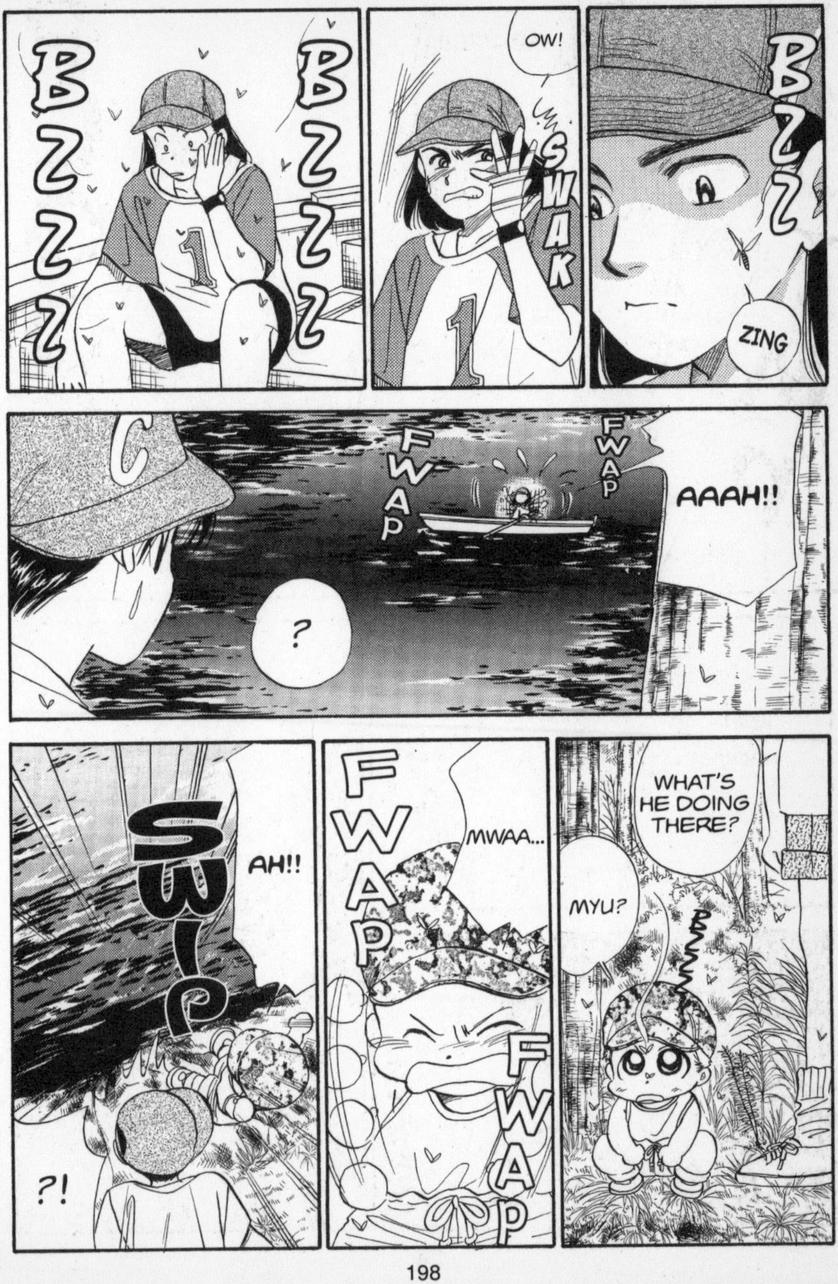
BZZZ
ZING
OW!
SWAK
BZZZZ
BZZZZ
AAAH!!
FWAP
FWAP
?
WHAT'S HE DOING THERE?
MYU?
MWAA...
FWAP
FWAP
AH!!
SWIP
?!

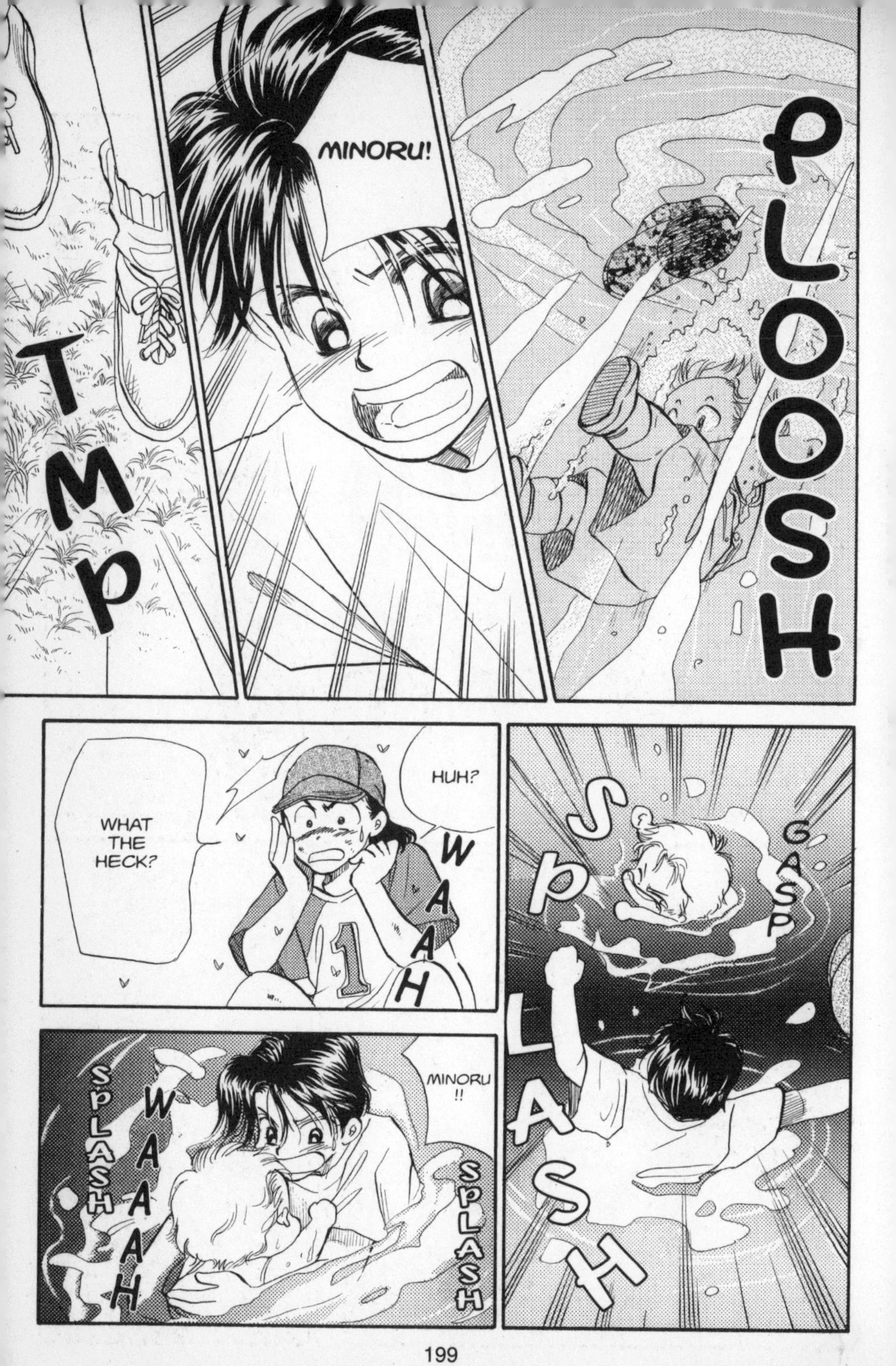
PLOOSH
MINORU!
TMP
SPLASH
GASP
HUH?
WHAT THE HECK?
WAAAH
MINORU !!
SPLASH
WAAAH
SPLASH

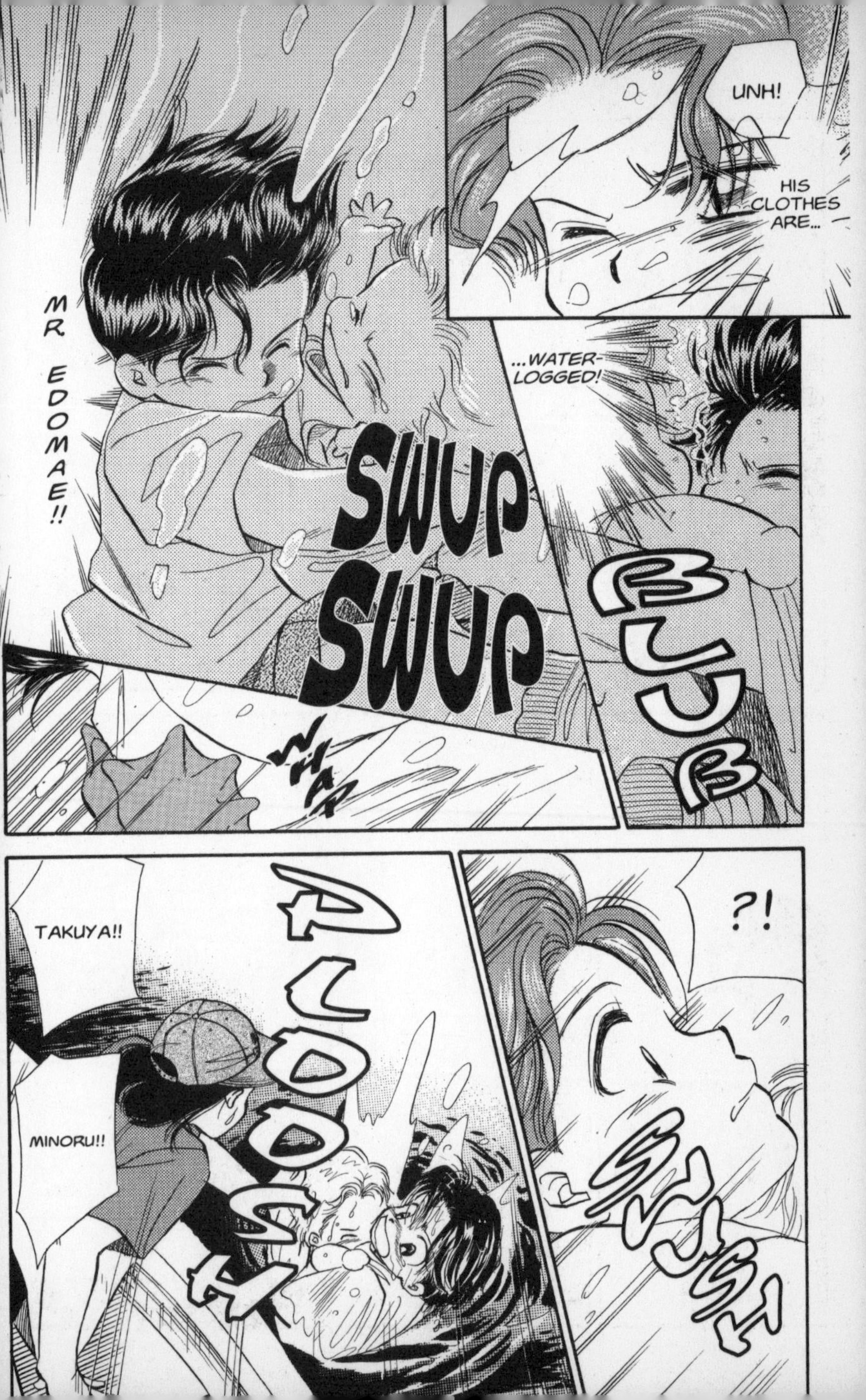
UNH!
HIS CLOTHES ARE...
...WATER-LOGGED!
BLUB
MR. EDOMAE!!
SWUP SWUP
WHAP
?!
SWISH
PLOOSH
TAKUYA!!
MINORU!!

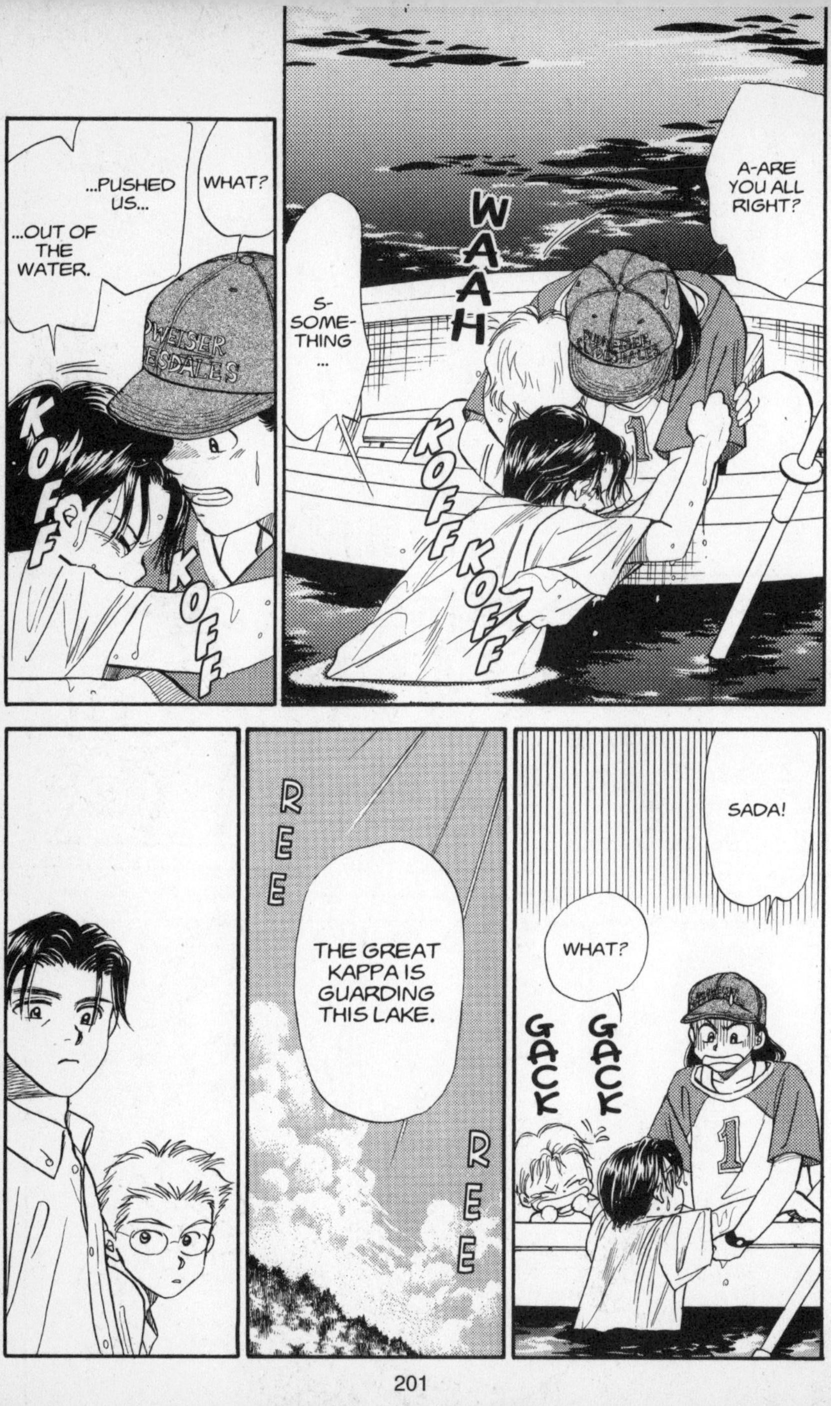
A-ARE YOU ALL RIGHT?
WAAH
S-SOMETHING...
KOFF KOFF
KOFF
WHAT?
...PUSHED US...
...OUT OF THE WATER.
KOFF
KOFF
SADA!
WHAT?
GACK GACK
REE
THE GREAT KAPPA IS GUARDING THIS LAKE.
REE

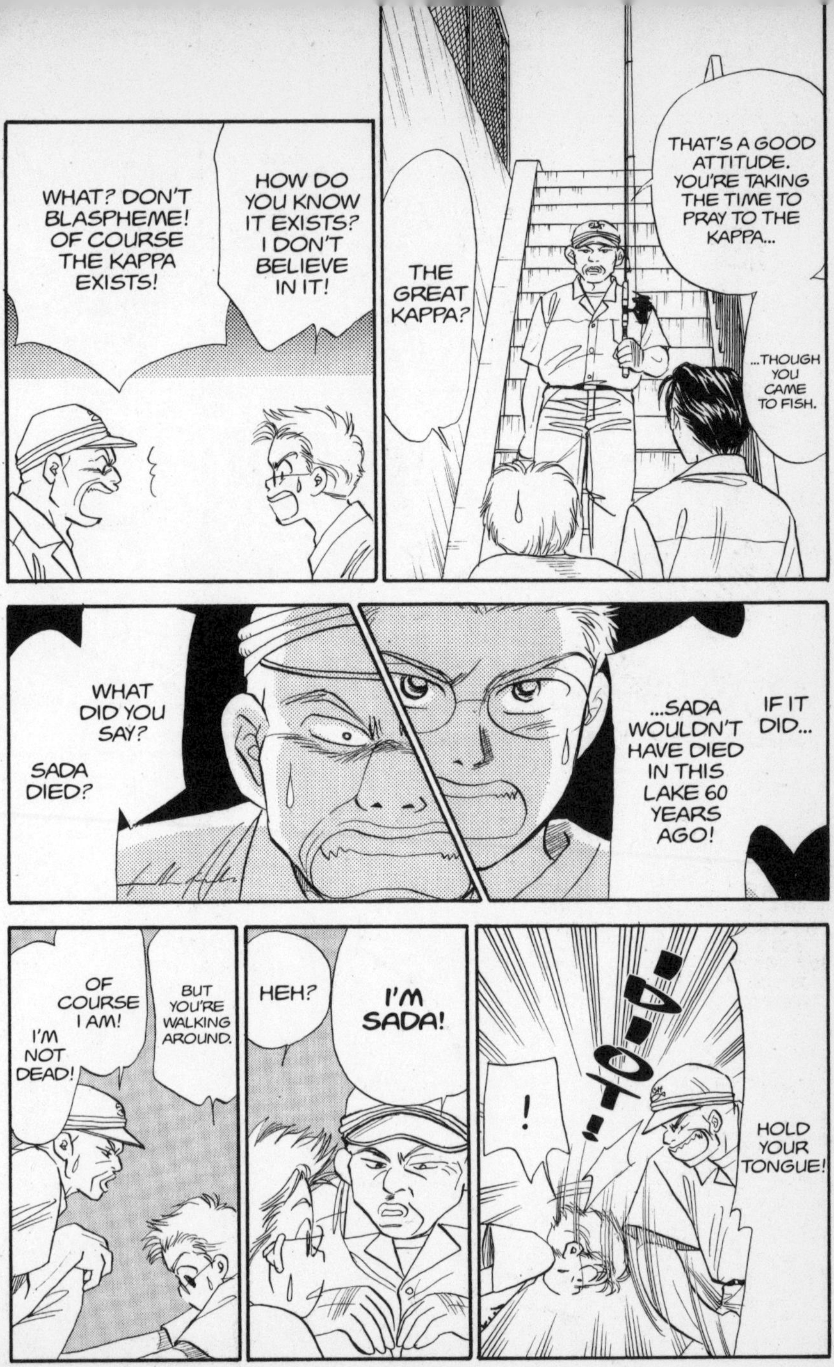

THAT'S A GOOD ATTITUDE. YOU'RE TAKING THE TIME TO PRAY TO THE KAPPA...
...THOUGH YOU CAME TO FISH.
THE GREAT KAPPA?
HOW DO YOU KNOW IT EXISTS? I DON'T BELIEVE IN IT!
WHAT? DON'T BLASPHEME! OF COURSE THE KAPPA EXISTS!
IF IT DID...
...SADA WOULDN'T HAVE DIED IN THIS LAKE 60 YEARS AGO!
WHAT DID YOU SAY?
SADA DIED?
DOT!!
!
HOLD YOUR TONGUE!
I'M SADA!
HEH?
BUT YOU'RE WALKING AROUND.
OF COURSE I AM!
I'M NOT DEAD!

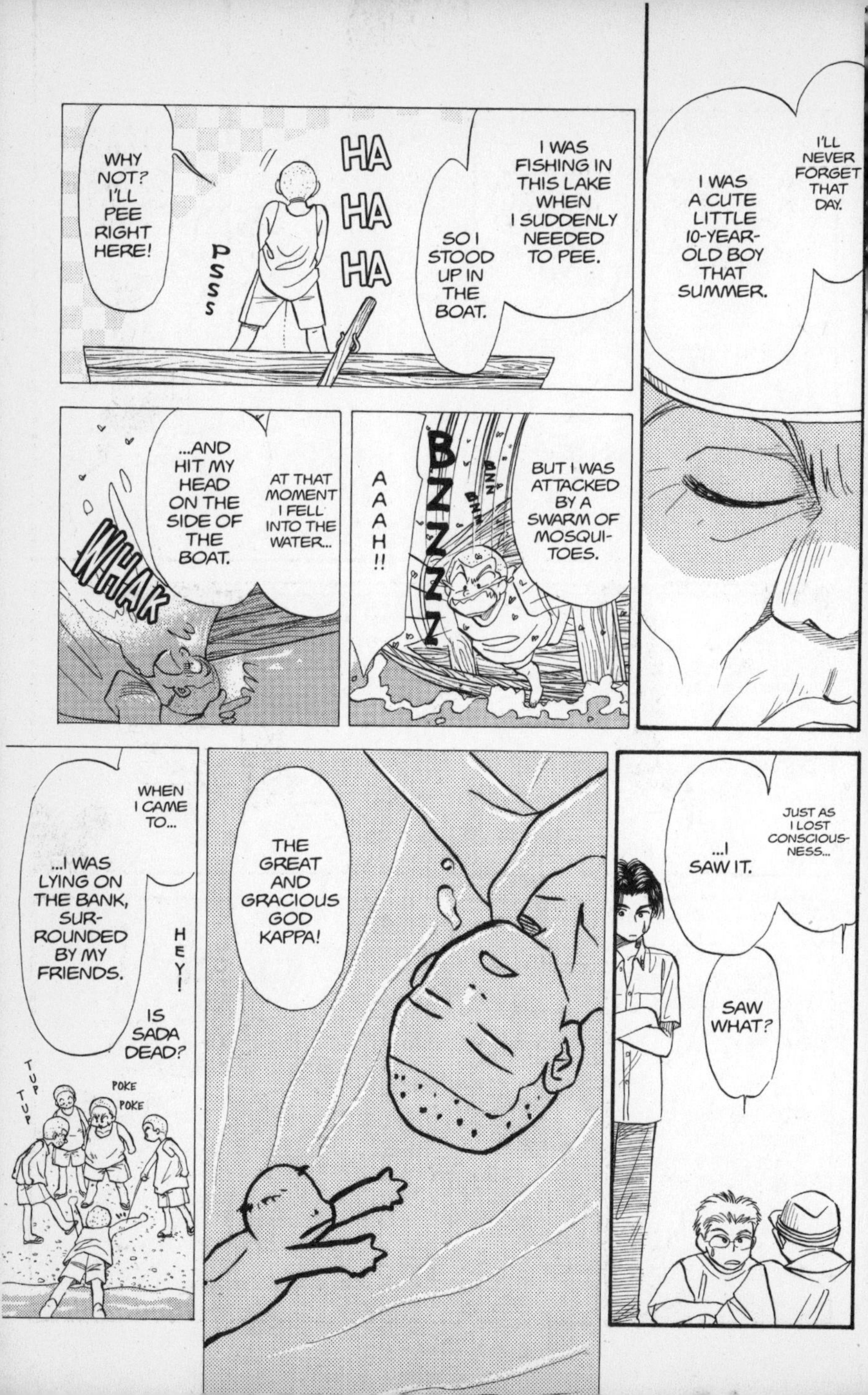
I'LL NEVER FORGET THAT DAY.
I WAS A CUTE LITTLE 10-YEAR-OLD BOY THAT SUMMER.
I WAS FISHING IN THIS LAKE WHEN I SUDDENLY NEEDED TO PEE.
SO I STOOD UP IN THE BOAT.
HA HA HA
WHY NOT? I'LL PEE RIGHT HERE!
PSSS
BUT I WAS ATTACKED BY A SWARM OF MOSQUITOES.
BZZZZ
ZZZ
AAAH!!
AT THAT MOMENT I FELL INTO THE WATER...
...AND HIT MY HEAD ON THE SIDE OF THE BOAT.
WHAK
JUST AS I LOST CONSCIOUSNESS...
...I SAW IT.
SAW WHAT?
THE GREAT AND GRACIOUS GOD KAPPA!
WHEN I CAME TO...
...I WAS LYING ON THE BANK, SURROUNDED BY MY FRIENDS.
HEY!
IS SADA DEAD?
POKE POKE
TUP TUP

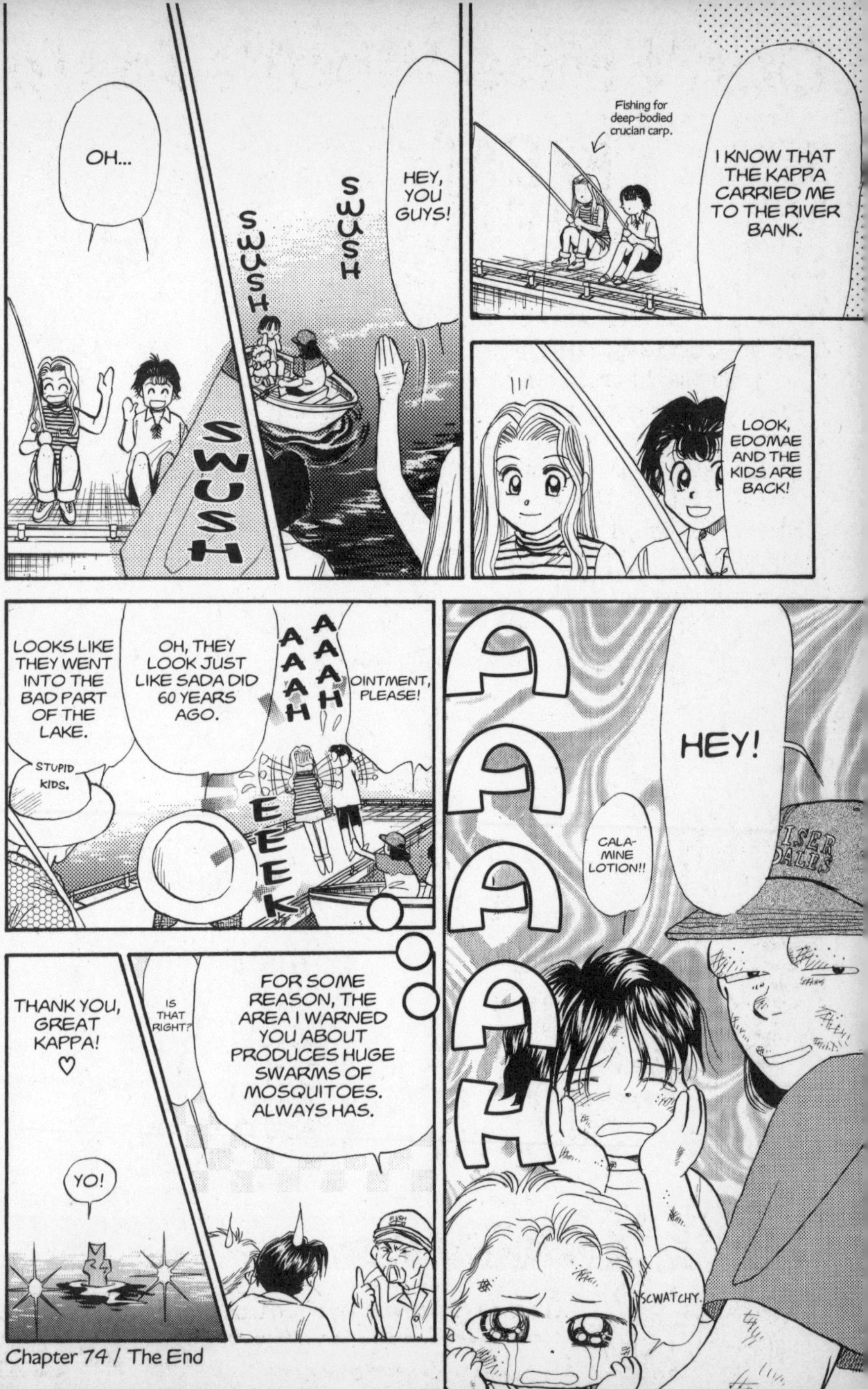
Fishing for deep-bodied crucian carp.
I KNOW THAT THE KAPPA CARRIED ME TO THE RIVER BANK.
LOOK, EDOMAE AND THE KIDS ARE BACK!
HEY, YOU GUYS!
SWUSH
SWUSH
SWUSH
OH...
HEY!
CALAMINE LOTION!!
AAAAH
SCWATCHY.
AAAH
AAAAH
OINTMENT, PLEASE!
OH, THEY LOOK JUST LIKE SADA DID 60 YEARS AGO.
LOOKS LIKE THEY WENT INTO THE BAD PART OF THE LAKE.
STUPID KIDS.
EEEK
FOR SOME REASON, THE AREA I WARNED YOU ABOUT PRODUCES HUGE SWARMS OF MOSQUITOES. ALWAYS HAS.
IS THAT RIGHT?
THANK YOU, GREAT KAPPA! ♡
YO!

Chapter 74 / The End

Tell us what you think about Shojo Beat Manga!

Our survey is now available online. Go to:

shojobeat.com/mangasurvey

Help us make our product offerings better!